THE ART AND RITUAL
OF CHILDBIRTH
IN RENAISSANCE ITALY

THE ART AND RITUAL
OF CHILDBIRTH
IN RENAISSANCE ITALY

Jacqueline Marie Musacchio

YALE UNIVERSITY PRESS
New Haven & London

Published with the assistance of

The Publications Committee,
Department of Art and Archaeology, Princeton University

and

The Getty Grant Program

Designed by Gillian Malpass

Printed in Singapore

Library of Congress Cataloging-in-Publication Data

Musacchio, Jacqueline Marie, 1967–
    The art and ritual of childbirth in Renaissance Italy /
Jacqueline Marie Musacchio.
      p. cm.
    Includes bibliographical references and index.
    ISBN 0-300-07629-0 (cloth : alk. paper)
    1. Birth customs – Italy – History. 2. Childbirth – Italy – History.
 3. Women – History – Middle Ages, 500–1500. 4. Renaissance – Italy.
 5. Italy – Social life and customs. I. Title.
GT2465.I8M87 1999
392.1'2'0945 – dc21
                                          98-33417
                                              CIP

A catalogue record for this book is available from
The British Library

Endpapers: Mariotto di Nardi, detail of the back of a wooden
childbirth tray, c. 1420. Private collection.

Page i: Workshop of the Patanazzi family, back of a maiolica
childbirth *tagliere*, late sixteenth century. Musée des Hospices
Civils de Lyon–Hôtel-Dieu.

Frontispiece: Workshop of Orazio Fontana, interior of a maiolica
childbirth *ongaresca*, late sixteenth century. Civiche Raccolte
d'Arte Applicata, Castello Sforzesco, Milan. (Photo Saporetti)

Contents

Acknowledgements

THIS BOOK HAS INCURRED a great deal of debt, financial, intellectual, and emotional. It began as a paper on Renaissance domestic art for Katharine Park in my senior year at Wellesley College. Although I found the general topic appealing, I had no idea where it would lead. But the notion of working with objects for the home, and combining that with a broader historical treatment of life in the Renaissance, stayed with me as I began graduate school. After my first year at Princeton, I took a work study position at The Art Museum there with Betsy Rosasco, primarily researching the maiolica collection. Princeton's *scodella da parto* fascinated me; I had no idea what it was, or how many similar objects there were, or what it meant. Neither, apparently, did many other people. Suddenly, I found myself with a dissertation topic.

Obviously my topic grew and changed over the years. But one of the most basic questions I wanted to answer was why, exactly, did Renaissance women have so many objects associated with their pregnancies and childbirths? Instead of finding an answer, I found more and more objects to complicate the issue during the course of my research. In addition to the objects, documentary sources revealed even more items that no longer survived. After a year of research in Italy, I had documentary evidence for an enormous number of birth-related accessories, ranging from sheets to towels, hats to cloaks, charms to sweetmeats, and a great deal in between. I had records of successful deliveries, and records of not so successful ones. I could trace some children from birth to marriage to old age and death, while others lived barely long enough to be given a line in their father's memorandum. I had birth records, death records, expense accounts, last testaments, household inventories, diaries, legislation, and letters. Basically, I had more information than I could ever utilize. There remains much more work to be done on the subject.

Financial support for my dissertation research and writing was provided by the Rensaleer W. Lee Fund and the Spears Fund of the Department of Art and Archaeology at Princeton University, and the Committee for Italian Studies, also at Princeton, as well as a Horton-Hallowell Grant from Wellesley College and a dissertation writing fellowship from the Andrew W. Mellon Foundation. My research was conducted at the Archivio di Stato, the Kunsthistorisches Institut, the Biblioteca Nazionale Centrale, and Villa I Tatti, all in Florence, as well as the Archivio di Stato in Prato, and Marquand and Firestone Libraries at Princeton University. I am grateful to the staff at all of these institutions for much guidance and attention. Special mention needs to be made of Gino Corti, who taught me how to read Renaissance hands and whose unsurpassed patience, excitement, and interest made my work much more enjoyable. While I was preparing the manuscript for publication, I received a great deal of much-appreciated support from Princeton Day School, Princeton University, the Walters Art Gallery, and Trinity University.

Many of the illustrations in this book were provided through the generosity of the Publications Committee of the Department of Art and Archaeology at Princeton. In addition, Shreve Simpson and Joaneath Spicer at the Walters Art Gallery helped me purchase photographs and transparencies, and I am extremely grateful for their kindness in this and other matters. Financial support was absolutely critical. Despite the guidelines distributed by the College Art Association in 1997, obtaining illustrations for scholarly publications has continued to be an outrageously expensive venture. In a number of instances, I made substitutions when the cost was simply too prohibitive for a particular object. This book could not have been published without the help of Princeton and the Walters, and without the kindness of numerous institutions and individuals who waived or substantially reduced their fees. I am especially grateful to Erich Schleier at the Gemäldegalerie, Berlin; Susanne Netzer at the Kunstgewerbemuseum, Berlin; Iparmüsvészeti Múzeum, Budapest; Andrew Morris at the Fitzwilliam Museum, Cambridge; Sally Metzler at the Martin D'Arcy Gallery, Loyola University, Chicago; the Detroit Institute of Arts; the Pinacoteca, Faenza; Gian Carlo Bojani at the Museo Internazionale delle Ceramiche, Faenza; Dora Thornton at the British Museum, London; Keith Christiansen at The Metropolitan Museum of Art, New York; Timothy Wilson at the Ashmolean Museum, Oxford; Dean Walker at the Philadelphia Museum of Art; Chiara d'Afflitto at the Museo Civico, Pistoia; Betsy Rosasco at The Art Museum, Princeton University; the North Carolina Museum of Art, Raleigh; the Virginia Museum of Fine Arts, Richmond; Sabine Hesse at the Württembergisches Landesmuseum, Stuttgart; Triple Gallery, Berne; Sotheby's, Christie's, Phillips, and Bonhams, all in London; Altomani & Co., Pesaro; Alberto Bruschi, Florence; Mario Bellucci, Perugia; and several private collectors who chose to remain anonymous. Unfortunately, for all the kindness shown by these people and their institutions, there were many others who could not accommodate my requests.

Numerous friends and colleagues have contributed to this volume during the many years it took to complete. They read chapters and papers, offered insights and information, found photographs, tracked down references, and, in some cases, held my hand when everything seemed impossible. Some probably don't even remember helping. But all of this was important in its own way, and it always meant a great deal to me. For this, I want to thank Diane Cole Ahl, Giovanna Bandini, Krystin Bandola, Cristelle Baskins, Mary Bergstein, Brendan Cassidy, Chad Coerver, Samuel K. Cohn Jr., Victor Coonin, Laura Coyle, Franco Crainz, Jonathan Davies, Barbara Deimling, Blake De Maria, Anne Derbes, Holly Dollinger, Eamon Downey, James Draper, Marvin Eisenberg, Jesús Escobar, Elena Gandini, Amanda Branson Gill, Richard Goldthwaite, Quint Gregory, Sara Matthews Grieco, Jennifer Hardin, Rab Hatfield, Geraldine Johnson, Christiane Klapisch-Zuber, Teresa Knox, Lynn Laufenberg, Lisa Lee, Susan Lehre, Mary Ann Alexandra Loria, Peter Lynch, Barbara Lynn-Davis, Joyce Lyons, John V.G. Mallet, Kristine Mascoli, Scott Montgomery, Sally Metzler, Jennifer Milam, Jerzy Miziolek, Tina Najbjerg, Norman Muller, Ellen Myhill, Amy Ogata, Roberta Olson, Amy and Nassos Papalexandrous, Jennifer Perry, Adrian Randolph, Sheryl Reiss, Patricia Rubin, Clare Sheridan, Patricia Simons, Joaneath Spicer, Franca Camiz Trinchieri, Julia Triolo, Christie Ward, Paul Watson, Wendy Watson, and Debra Woog. I hope that those I have inadvertently omitted from this list will forgive me.

I want to make special mention of my undergraduate training at Wellesley College. My years at Wellesley, and the friends I made there, made an enormous impact on me. I am especially grateful to Katharine Park, now at Harvard, whose intellectual and emotional support has been an absolute lifeline for me; I hope that my final product lives up to the care she put into critiquing my earliest drafts. I was also fortunate to study with Lilian Armstrong and Margaret Carroll while at Wellesley, two women whose dedication to teaching, scholarship, and art has always impressed and inspired me. Their interest in me and their support of my work has continued through the years, and I know that, without this background, I would not have gone on to accomplish what I have.

Finally, this book would never have happened at all were it not for the support and encouragement of my dissertation committee, Ellen Callmann, Katharine Park, and John

Pinto, and my advisor and friend, Patricia Fortini Brown. These four people had the greatest impact on me and on the book, and I shall always be grateful for their care and attention through the years. Pat's guidance, in particular, and her example as a teacher and a scholar, has been inestimable. I also want to thank Gillian Malpass, my editor at Yale University Press, whose faith in the value of my work has meant a great deal to me from the very beginning. I feel very lucky to have worked with her, and I know the book is much better because of her guidance.

My final thanks go to Anthony Ratyna, who has lived with this book as long as I have. His infinite patience and kindness have sustained me through the whole process, making it fun whenever possible and bearable at all other times. There is probably no person who wants this book finished more than he does.

I have dedicated this book to my grandfather, Nicholas Sala, who died while I was preparing it for publication. I desperately wanted him to see it completed; I know he would have enjoyed holding a copy in his hands.

May 1998

Author's Note

Unless otherwise indicated, all manuscript sources are from the Archivio di Stato, Florence, and all transcriptions and translations are my own. The following abbreviations are used throughout the glossary and notes:

ASP   Archivio di Stato, Prato
BNCF   Biblioteca Nazionale Centrale, Florence
CRSGF   *Corporazione religiose soppresse dal governo francese*
MAP   *Mediceo avanti il Principato*
MPAP   *Magistrato dei Pupilli avanti il Principato*
MPP   *Magistrato dei Pupilli del Principato*

For documentary citations, exact transcriptions are provided in the notes only when a literal translation is used in the text; in these cases, I have added only minimal punctuation to give the reader a true sense of the original. For the same reason, transcriptions (including names) have been left in their original spelling, which often differs from modern conventions. For damaged or otherwise illegible documents, I have used brackets ("[ ]") to represent the omission, whereas ellipses denote my deliberate omissions.

The Florentine monetary system is extremely complicated. Generally, it was based on two systems, the gold *fiorino* and the silver *lira*. The *lira* was strictly a money of account. Although the equivalency varied throughout the period under discussion here, a standard is 1 *lira* = 20 *soldi* = 240 *denari*.

Further information on money, weights, and measures can be found in Marco Spallanzani and Giovanna Gaeta Bertelà, ed., *Libro d'inventario dei beni di Lorenzo il Magnifico*, Florence, 1992, xiv–xvii.

Glossary

The activities surrounding Renaissance childbirth were so elaborate that they required their own particular vocabulary. This glossary defines some of the most common objects and phrases, and includes documentary references to demonstrate the ways in which they were utilized by contemporaries. The spelling of each term follows modern conventions; those in the documents vary greatly, with suffixes often denoting relative size. Specific objects went in and out of favor, and certain terms were used with greater frequency than others.

Afogollare: To suffocate; the term generally appears in connection with a wetnurse smothering a child by rolling over on it in bed. An entry in the Florentine *Libro de' morti* for 1424 reads "1ª fancillina di Canti di Marsilio, popolo San Donato Vecchietti, riposto in detta chiesa, afogolla balia" (*Ufficiali della Grascia*, 188, unpaginated).

Arcuccio: A wooden device placed over a child in bed to prevent accidental suffocation by overlaying. The list of items Ser Girolamo da Colle purchased for his new son Giovanni in 1473 included "uno arcuccio per coprire Giovanni" (*CRSGF*, 111 (140), 79v).

Bacino: A basin, usually of metal, for washing hands. These basins were sometimes associated with childbirth: in 1605 Antonio Mannerini's estate contained "un bacino d'ottone liscio da parto" (*MPP*, 2658, 143r).

Balia: A wetnurse; a woman whose newborn child died or is sent out to nurse so that she can nurse another child for a salary. A letter to Margharita Datini in 1389 asked her assistance in finding "una balia col latte frescho" (*ASP*, *Archivio Datini*, 1103, loose folio).

Balio: The husband of the wetnurse, who usually negotiated the terms of the salary. In 1475 Antonio di Marchione di Ser Antonio Maleghonele described a certain Michele as "mio balio" and pays him for his wife's duties as wetnurse to Antonio's son Ghaletto (*CRSGF*, 102 (86), 19r).

Breve: A charm or amulet, whether sacred or secular, used as a preventative device. In 1598 the estate of Messer Raffaello di Messer Giulio contained "un casettino d'avorio con otto brevi da bambini" (*MPP*, 2668, 90v).

Busto (inbusto) da parto: A bodice or vest, or type of sleeveless garment worn by women during pregnancy or confinement. In 1520 Gismondo di Noferi Lenzoni's wife had "1° inbusto di saia biancha da parto con frange bianche" (*MPAP*, 187, 551r).

Camicia (camiciola) da parto: A special shirt or vest worn during pregnancy or confinement. Antonio di Ser Rosso's estate of 1573 contained "3 camicie da donne di parto" (*MPP*, 2653, 780v), while in 1596 Messer Antonio di Niccola Forti's estate included "una camiciuola da donna di parto di ermisino turchino foderato di rovescio rosso" (*MPP*, 2667, 117v).

Casacca da parto: A special cloak to wear during pregnancy or confinement. In 1602 Marina, the wife of Giuseppe di Giovanni Coscietti, had "una casacca di dommasco turchino fornita d'argento da parto" (*MPP*, 2668, 531r).

Cioppa da parto: An overdress worn during pregnancy or confinement. In 1486 Simone di Matteo's estate included "1ª cipietta paghonaza da dona di parto foderata di gialli e bianchi" (*MPAP*, 186, 174v).

Comare: A godmother, or the woman who held a child at the baptismal font. This word was also used to designate the new mother when discussing the relationship made by the godparent bond. In 1473 Ser Girolamo da Colle listed the items "mia conpari di Giovanni mio figliuolo mandorono a presentare la comare, cioè la Chaterina mia donna" (*CRSGF*, 111 (140), 79r).

Confetto: A general term for sweetmeats. A day after his wife gave birth to a son in 1474, Antonio di Marchione di Ser Antonio Maleghonele wrote, "Richordo chome a dì 5 di novebre detti a Morello e chonpagni, ispeziali ala Luna, lire 2 e soldi 9 . . . per libre 3½ di chofetto mescholatto, tregiea e madorle e pinochi, e per oncie 3 di zuchero fine chonperai da lui dachordo" (*CRSGF*, 102 (86), 3r).

Conpare: A godfather or godparent; a man who held a child at the baptismal font. In 1470 Giovanni di Nicholo di Domenicho Boninsegni described the birth of his daughter Glionarda and listed four men and one woman as "chonpari che me la batezano" (*CRSGF*, 102 (356), 24 left).

Credentino da parto: A set of wares for childbirth, probably made of ceramics. A list of Cardinal Ferdinando de' Medici's maiolica purchases in 1573 included "uno credentino da donne di parto, in 9 pezzi, di detta terra [da Urbino], lavorate a grottesca, auto dal detto [Maestro Framinio da Urbino]" (Spallanzani, "Maioliche di Urbino," 119).

Cuchiaiera: A spoon holder, usually made of silver, and often presented as a childbirth gift. In 1474, in the name of his wife Vaggia, Lorenzo di Matteo di Morello Morelli gave the wife of Lorenzo di Bernardetto de' Medici, who had just given birth to a daughter, "una chuchiaiera d'ariento" (*Archivio Gherardi Piccolomini d'Aragona*, 137, 165 right).

Cuffia da parto: A bonnet worn by a woman in bed during her confinement. In 1602 Giuseppe Coscietti's wife Marina had "una chuffio di bisso lavorata d'oro per il parto" (*MPP*, 2668, 531r). The term *cuffia* could also be used to refer to the small cap worn by a baby at baptism; the estate of Giovanni di Francesco da Rosignano included "dua cuffie da battesimo" (*MPP*, 2658, 3v). These caps could be quite elaborate, such as the "grirlanda di fior di seta da battesimo" in the home of Benedetto and Elisabeta Lanfranco (*MPP*, 2651, 168v).

Desco da parto: A wooden tray used in the childbirth ritual, either painted, intarsiated, or unfinished. In 1448 the estate of Giovanni Parenti included "1° descho tondo da parto dipinto bello" (*MPAP*, 68, 81r).

Falda da parto: A special coverlet placed on the bed during a woman's confinement. In 1605 Giuseppe Simone's wife Alessandra had "una falda da letto per donne di parto con quattro reticelle con fodera rossa" (*MPP*, 2658, 528r).

Fascia: A swaddling band used for infants. In 1474 Brano di Nicholo Ghuiciardini's estate included "3 fascie da fanciuli" (*MPAP*, 172, 313v). Special swaddling was used for baptism: in 1564 Andrea di Rafaelo Villani's estate included "1ª fasciolina da battesimo lavorate di bianco" (*MPP*, 2652, 219v).

Federa da parto: A pillowcase for use during the confinement ritual. In 1551 Domenico d'Agniolo's estate included "3 paia di federe sottile da parto di lino con sue reticelle biancha" (*MPP*, 2650, 153v).

Forchettiera: A fork holder, usually made of silver and often presented at childbirth. After she gave birth to a daughter in 1462, Bernardo Rinieri noted that his wife Bartolomea received "1ª forchettiera e 1ª schatola di treggea" from her brother Lorenzo (*CRSGF*, 95 (212), 159 right).

Fornimento da parto: A complete outfit, whether of clothing or linens, for use during confinement. In 1578 Girolamo di Gino Capponi's estate included "1° fonimentto per letto da donne di partto lavoratta di maglia quadra" (*MPP*, 2654, 341r). *Fornimenti* could also be used for baptism: in 1544 the Bini estate included "1° fornimento da bambini da battezare lavorato, coè 1ª fascia, capino, e spallino" (*MPP*, 2647, 136r).

Gamurra da parto: A type of simple dress for a woman to wear during pregnancy or confinement. In 1472, in the room of Madonna Bartolomea, the widow of Franciescho di Bindo, Pupilli officials found "1° ghamurrino bigio biancho da parto foderato di pelle biancha" (*MPAP*, 172, 269r).

Giubbone da parto: A special jacket for use during pregnancy or confinement. In 1573 the estate of Cesari Nocetti included "un giubbone di veluto nero trinciato foderato di raso biancho et tela nera da donna da parto" (*MPP*, 2664, 302r).

Gonella da parto: A type of simple dress worn during pregnancy or confinement. Andrea di Mariano's estate included "1° ghonellino mormorino foderato loghoro da donne di parto" in 1480 (*MPAP*, 176, 82r).

Grossa: Pregnant. Antonio di Marchione di Ser Antonio Maleghonele removed his daughter from her wetnurse because "la balia disse esere grossa" (*CRSGF*, 102 (86), 20r).

Guanciale da parto: A special pillow placed on the bed during the confinement ritual. The Inghirrami family stored many precious items at a local monastery, including "2 ghuancali lavorati con federe a reticelle di baldichino chon nappe di seta e botoni d'oro begli da donne di parto rinvolti in un telo" (*MPAP*, 173, 271v).

Guardacuora da parto: A nightshirt or loose garment worn in bed during pregnancy or confinement. In 1443 Mona Betta, the widow of Niccholo di Filippo, had "1° ghuardaquore da parto puglonazzo foderato di vari vecchi" (*MPAP*, 170, 190v).

Guardadonna: Literally a "woman watcher"; a woman who tends to the new mother for a fee for a specific amount of time. Giovanni d'Antonio Rucellai recorded that, "Monna Maria di Michele di Chianti è mia ghuardadonna. De'avere a dì 18 d'ottobre 1454 lire cinque piccioli sono per suo salaro . . . per ghuardatura di iiii setimane ghuardo la Piera mia donna" (*Archivio Galetti*, 1, 46 right).

Impagliata: A woman who has just given birth. An Italian–English dictionary of 1611 defines *impagliuolata* as "laid in child-bed. Also a woman lying in child-bed" (Florio, *New world of words*, 237). See also **Scodella da impagliata.**

Lenzuolo da parto: A sheet for a bed, often part of a multi-sheet set, used during the confinement ritual. Ser Antonio di Bartolomeo's estate in 1476 included "1° paio di lenzuola sotile da dona di parto lavorate 1° no l'altro" (*MPAP*, 174, 128v).

Mantello da parto: A special cloak or mantle worn by a pregnant woman or new mother. In 1478 Domenicho di Neri Bartolini's wife had "2 mantili sotili da parto ala parigina" (*MPAP*, 175, 233v). Special mantles were also worn by babies during baptism: the estate of Alessandro di Michele Bacanelli included "un mantellino da battesimo di panno di casentino bianco foderato di rovescio rosso fornito di velluto nero" (*MPP*, 2655, 10v).

Mensa da parto: A particular table used during the confinement ritual. In 1558 the estate of Giovanbattista di Michele Pappagalli included "una mensina di noce da donne di parto" (*MPP*, 2651, 319r).

Nappo: A goblet, usually of metal and often exchanged among relatives at childbirth. Antonio Ghondi noted the expense for "uno nappo mandato a donare alla Maria nostra sorella quando fe'la banbina" (*Carte Gondi*, 32, 17 right).

Ongaresca da parto: A bowl on a low foot given to a pregnant woman or new mother. Maiolica *ongaresche* were included in Piccolpasso's *scodella da impagliata*.

Pane di confetto or **pane bianco:** A type of sweet cake. In 1453 Francesco Castellani wrote, "Comperai a dì 22 d'aprile un pane di confetto grande dallo speziale della Palla per mandarlo alla donna d'Andrea di Bocchacino che avea partorito una figlola ch'a nome Isabetta in sino a dì 19 di decto" (*CRSGF*, 90 (84), 52r).

Panno lino: A linen cloth used to make swaddling for babies. In 1363 Messer Lapo da Castegliochio noted his costs "per panno lino per fare fascie per lo mio fanicullo Bernardo" (*Carte strozziane*, II, 3, 36r).

Pezza lina: A swaddling band. Among the many items Tribaldo de' Rossi provided for his daughter to take to the wetnurse were "14 peze line" (BNCF, *Fondo nazionale*, II, II, 357, 111r).

Pinocchiato: A pine nut sweetmeat. After his daughter Marietta gave birth to her first son in 1488, Filippo di Matteo Strozzi sent her a silver goblet "pieno di pinochiati" (*Carte strozziane*, V, 41, 164 left).

Poppa: A breast; often used in the phrase "dare poppa" or "to nurse." In 1433 a certain Madonna Antonia came to the Antinori home, "per dare poppa a Tommaso nostro figliuolo" (*Archivio Gherardi Piccolomini d'Aragona*, 713, 29v).

Predella da parto: A particular chair or stool used by a woman in labor. In 1568 the estate of Noferi di Francesco Dazzi contained "1ª predella di legnio da donne di parto" (*MPP*, 2652, 757r).

Rimboccatura da parto: A type of coverlet to put on the bed of the mother during confinement. In 1623 Francesco Partini's estate included "una rimbocchatura da donne di parto bianca agiglietti" (*MPP*, 2660, 735v).

Saccone da parto: A special mattress used during pregnancy or confinement. In 1595 Bernardo di Curcio Thomassi's estate included "1 saccone uno da parto usato" (*MPP*, 2667, 142r).

Saliera da parto: A particular salt presented to a pregnant woman or new mother. Maiolica *saliere* were part of Piccolpasso's *scodelle da impagliata*. But they could also be independent wares: a shipment of Faentine maiolica in 1640 included "una saliera da donne di parto" (Guasti, *Caffagiolo*, 459).

Scacchiera da parto: A special game board for entertaining a confined woman. Pagholo Bandini's estate in 1425 contained "1 schachiera da parto" (*MPAP*, 159, 55v).

Scanno da parto: A special chair used by a woman during labor. In 1571 the inventory of Francesco and Messer Domenico Bruni's estate included "uno scanno da donna di parto vechia" (*MPP*, 2653, 139v).

Sciugatoio da parto: A towel or cloth used during pregnancy or confinement. In 1591 the estate of Simone d'Antonio Mazetti included "1 sciugatoio grande da donne di parto" (*MPP*, 2656 511r). These were also used at baptism; Domenico di Antonio Berti's estate contained "uno sciugatoio da battezare di velo lavorate con cerri d'oro e un nome di Jesu nel mezzo d'oro" (*MPP*, 2656, 912r).

Scodella da parto: A special bowl on a high foot given to pregnant women or new mothers, usually made of ceramic. In 1547 Teseo di Mariotto's estate included "una schudella da maiolicha da parto coperta" (*MPP*, 2649, 332r).

Scodella da impagliata: The phrase used by Piccolpasso to designate five- or nine-piece sets of interlocking maiolica wares for pregnant women or new mothers. It may be used interchangeably with *scodella da parto*. In 1558 a household inventory in Pesaro included "una scodella da impaiata di quattro pezzi" (Albarelli, *Ceramisti pesaresi*, 406).

Sconciare: To miscarry. Bartolomeo Valori noted in his memorandum that "si schoncio la Caterina di 3 mesi in una fanciulla femmina che non ebbe l'anima" (BNCF, *Panciatichi*, 134, 4r).

Sedia da parto: A special chair used by a woman during childbirth. In 1619 Messer Lorenzo di Messer Francesco Nati's estate included "una sedia da donna di parto di legno" (*MPP*, 2660, 377r).

Seggiola da parto: A special chair used by a woman during childbirth. In 1471 the Inghirrami estate included "1ª seggiola da donna di parto" (*MPAP*, 173, 272r).

Spoppare: To wean. In 1449 Marco Parenti's son Piero was nursed by a certain Monna Mattea who lived in the Parenti home for almost two years, until "partissi la detta Mona Mattea e spoppo il fanciullo" (*Carte strozziane*, II, 17 bis, 18v).

Tafferia da parto: A low bowl for pregnant women and new mothers, usually made of wood. The estate of Chimenti di Davitto in 1545 included "1ª tafferia da parto dipinta" (*MPP*, 2663, 98r).

Tagliere da parto: A round or oval tray given to pregnant women and new mothers, often made of maiolica by the sixteenth century but perhaps of wood before that. The estate of Domenicho d'Antonio Burni in 1473 included "2 taglieri grandi da donna di parto" (*MPAP*, 173, 317r). Piccolpasso includes *taglieri* in his *scodelle da impagliata*.

Tavola da parto: A table or tray for use in the childbirth ritual. In 1468 Stagio d'Antonio Nonni's estate included "1ª tavola dipintta da donne di partto" (*MPAP*, 172, 124v).

Tavoliere da parto: A game board to entertain pregnant women or new mothers. In 1432 the estate of Francesco di Michele Ruote included "1 tavoliere tondo da parto" (*MPAP*, 50, 97v).

Telo da parto: Some sort of cloth used by pregnant women or new mothers. In 1581 the estate of Simone di Amerigo Zati contained "dua teli di rensa sottile da donne di parto" (*MPP*, 2654, 886r).

Tondo da parto: A round tray for use during the child-birth ritual, usually made of wood. In 1516 Barone di Francesco Balduci's estate included "1° tondo da parto al'anticha dipinto" (*MPAP*, 187, 289r).

Tovaglia da parto: A cloth to cover a tray or table during pregnancy or confinement. In 1501, when the inventory of the Cennini estate was made, the widowed Mona Piera was recorded as having "3 tovagliottine di renza da desco da partto" in her possession (*MPAP*, 181, 358v).

Trebbiano: A type of white wine often drunk by pregnant women and new mothers. In 1490, during his wife Nanina's confinement, Tribaldo de' Rossi bought "uno fiascho di trebiano per la Nanina" (*BNCF, Fondo nazionale*, II, II, 357, 59r).

Tunica da parto: A particular tunic worn by pregnant women or new mothers. In 1550 Tomaso Setteciegli's estate included "1ª tunicha di pano paghonazo da parto fornita di velluto nero" (*MPP*, 2649, 656r).

Usciale da parto: A cloth hanging, perhaps to keep drafts out of the room where a woman was confined. The estate of Girolamo di Lionardo Freschobaldi in 1529 included "uno usciale di rovescio n° per la dona del parto" (*MPAP*, 191, 130r).

Voto (boto): An offering made to a particular saint in gratitude for a prayer granted. This term is often used in reference to the many silver and wax offerings presented to the church of Santissima Annunziata in Florence. An inventory of 1496 recorded a silver *voto* in the shape of "una Nostra Donna in parto," weighing over 3 *oncie* (*CRSGF*, 119 (50), 18r), which was probably presented to the church following a successful childbirth.

Introduction

D<small>URING THE</small> I<small>TALIAN</small> R<small>ENAISSANCE</small>, childbirth was encouraged, celebrated, and commemorated with a variety of objects. This book examines not only the appearance and function of these objects, but also the social and cultural context that necessitated them. I have aimed to illustrate how the demographic tensions inherent in post-plague society required this variety of objects to mediate between the real and the ideal worlds. The material culture of Renaissance childbirth was rich and complex, and an examination of it can reveal much about contemporary family life.

Objects

Wooden trays are the best-known objects associated with Renaissance childbirth, and they survive in significant numbers. It is appropriate to begin by examining one of these, a two-sided, painted wooden tray. On the front, in a cut-away structure, a new mother sits up in a great bed that dominates her crowded room (figure 1). The festive bright red coverlet on this bed is complemented by the mother's cloak; although unbuttoned, it is secured at her neck with a jeweled, floral clasp. Three women tend to the mother, bringing food and drink to her bedside. Three more sit on the floor, one playing a harp while the other two bathe and swaddle the newborn. Another woman looks out of an upper-floor window for approaching visitors. Two matrons do, in fact, come through the door on the left, both in somber colors and heavy dress. They are followed by their five gift-bearing male attendants, indicating both their social position and the importance of the occasion. Another woman and a kneeling man appear at the door on the right. They are dressed simply and watch the activity from a respectful distance. The general composition owes much to monumental scenes of *The Birth of the Virgin* or *The Birth of John the Baptist*, and it is based on a drawing by Lorenzo Monaco.[1]

The reverse of this tray is completely different. It features the single, broadly painted, large-scale figure of a naked boy (figure 2). He squats on a rocky outcropping in front of an elliptical frieze of blooming trees and fertile meadows. A coral branch is suspended around his neck, and he holds a pinwheel and a riding toy. Gazing directly at the viewer, he urinates a gold and silver stream across the rock. The inscription around the edge of the tray is an invocation for good health and successful childbirth.

The front and back of this dodecagonal tray are painted in tempera. The tray is 59 centimeters in diameter, and it has a raised gilt-wood molding around the front. This protected the painted surface and provided a ledge to secure the objects that were carried on it. A similar molding once safeguarded the back, but it was removed some time ago to level it with the painted surface. This tray, which was painted by the Florentine artist Bartolomeo di Fruosino in 1428, is an example of the type of object often referred to during the Renaissance as a *desco da parto*, or childbirth tray.[2]

Trays like this one were not unique; childbirth was associated with a variety of objects that became indispensable to the event. In fact, the importance of childbirth in the life of a Renaissance woman and her family is emphasized by the very density of the material

1 Bartolomeo di Fruosino, front of a wooden childbirth tray with a confinement room scene, dated 25 April 1428. Private collection. (Photo © 1979 The Metropolitan Museum of Art, New York)

2 Bartolomeo di Fruosino, reverse of the wooden childbirth tray illustrated in figure 1, with a naked, urinating boy. (Photo © 1979 The Metropolitan Museum of Art, New York)

3 Workshop of the Patanazzi family, concavity of a maiolica childbirth *scodella* with a birth scene, c. 1580. Museo Internazionale delle Ceramiche, Faenza.

culture associated with it. A detailed examination of this material culture, aiming to trace the many reasons for its existence, is a central theme of this book.

A wide range of evidence indicates that these objects were both decorative and utilitarian. Some were permanent household accessories, while others were more ephemeral tokens. Wooden trays and bowls and ceramic wares, painted with birth-related images, were especially popular from the late fourteenth century until the early seventeenth. Several of the ceramic wares actually depict childbirth, with what seems to be a high degree of vivid accuracy. For example, the concavity of a maiolica *scodella*, or bowl, from the Patanazzi workshop, is painted with an image of a woman in labor (figure 3). She is seated in a birthing chair facing left, and her legs are spread wide to allow the midwife access. Other women surround her chair, to encourage and comfort her. Barely visible in the background is a curtained bed, situating the scene and contributing to its intimate feel. The exterior of the bowl is decorated with the fanciful *grotteschi* ornament so popular with maiolica painters in the second half of the sixteenth century (figure 4). These assorted vines, cameos, and fantastic beasts were derived from paintings found during Renaissance excavations of the Golden House of Nero in Rome. Interesting as it is, this decoration gave no indication of the more personal and somewhat indiscreet representation inside the bowl, which was seen only by the woman who owned it.[3]

These wooden and ceramic objects constitute, in large part, what is traditionally

4

4 Workshop of the Patanazzi family, exterior of the maiolica childbirth *scodella* illustrated in figure 3. Museo Internazionale delle Ceramiche, Faenza.

considered the art of childbirth. They represent the surviving evidence for an active and material-oriented childbirth ritual. However, in addition to such trays and bowls, this book explores a combination of additional sources to illuminate the objects that do not survive. These sources include contemporary household inventories, private writings, and painted representations of birthing scenes. The study of surviving objects and written source material serves to round out this reconstruction of the material culture of Renaissance childbirth, and to reveal much about the activities and attitudes that surrounded the event.

Inventories

Household inventories from a range of social classes demonstrate the prevalence and popularity of wooden and ceramic childbirth objects in Tuscany, which are the focus of this study. However, these inventories also indicate a vast array of more ephemeral items, making them an especially unbiased and valuable source of information. Some inventories were included in the account books kept by Renaissance men to record their various expenditures. And inventories of *immobili* – unmovable possessions, like homes, shops, and land – appeared in the periodic tax assessments mandated by many of the Italian city-states. But the most comprehensive source of inventories for the city of Florence and its dominions are the surviving records of the Magistrato dei Pupilli, a communal agency that officially catalogued the estates of rich and poor alike from the late fourteenth century until the end of the eighteenth.[4] The agency drew up inventories following the death of the head of house, who was almost always a man.[5] The Pupilli listed all assets, *mobili* and *immobili*, to determine the complete value of a particular estate. And the definition of *mobili*, or movable goods, was quite often freely interpreted; for example, in 1424, the inventory of the estate of Domenico del Milanese included "a slave called Maddalena."[6]

The Pupilli was authorized to sell parts of an estate to pay debts or to provide money for the care of minor heirs. To ensure absolute fairness, the officials, together with a family representative, made careful and sometimes quite detailed inventories of all of the items in the estate. Such an occasion is shown in a late fifteenth-century fresco by Ghirlandaio's workshop in the oratory of the Buonomini of San Martino del Vescovo in Florence (figure 5).[7] The Buonomini formed a charitable organization, dedicated to relieving the suffering of families reduced to impoverished circumstances. The fresco depicts events after a householder's death: the widow stands in the middle of the room, providing information to the clerk seated at the left, while three men peruse the contents of a chest at the right.

Since these inventories were made for accounting purposes, they went into considerable detail recording the actual objects in the home. And they therefore serve as evidence for an astounding number of objects, most of which no longer survive. Several historians have used the Pupilli inventories to examine different aspects of the material culture of Renaissance Italy. Attilio Schiaparelli and E. Polidori Calamandrei were among the first to exploit the richness of this group of documents, the former in his study of the furnishings of the home and the latter in his book about the clothing of women.[8] Christian Bec has examined them to assess the intellectual pursuits and pretenses of the Florentine elite,[9] while John Kent Lydecker used them to analyze art in the context of its domestic setting.[10] I have used these inventories in a similarly quantitative and descriptive manner, but of course have focused on one particular group of objects among the many cited: those associated with pregnancy and childbirth.

From the fourteenth to the sixteenth centuries, the city-states of Italy witnessed an increase in disposable income, an expansion of artisanal industries, and a demand for both

5 Workshop of Domenico Ghirlandaio, fresco in the oratory of San Martino del Vescovo, Florence, late fifteenth century. After the death of a male head of house, officials examine a chest to make an estate inventory, which is recorded by the seated notary. The widow is in the center of the composition. (Scala/Art Resource, New York)

6 Florentine, marriage chest panel depicting the story of the Roman woman Lucrezia, c. 1420. Marriage chests (or *cassoni*) were often painted with didactic scenes of virtuous women for brides to emulate. Tempera on panel. Ashmolean Museum, Oxford.

domestic and imported goods. Richard Goldthwaite has shown that this was a mobile and wealthy society that placed great importance on possession and appearance.[11] Many citizens were involved in the patronage and acquisition of art and material objects to ornament their homes. There was an obvious preference for functional objects that had been made aesthetically pleasing.

This preference can be seen quite clearly in the contemporary proliferation of figuratively painted *cassoni*, or marriage chests. Inventories indicate that the majority of families in the fifteenth century, even at the lower levels of society, had such chests, when plain ones would have served the same utilitarian function. As several studies have indicated, these marriage chests were painted with subjects that were particularly appealing to Renaissance ideals.[12] Although a significant number of non-figural chests are known through surviving examples and documentary citations, these could not have had the same role in Renaissance marriage as chests with representations of, for example, the Roman heroine Lucrezia (figure 6).[13] Her didactic appeal was obvious: since she killed herself after she was raped, rather than bring shame on her family, Lucrezia represented the virtue of chastity. This was a highly valued quality in a Renaissance wife, and iconography associated with it enjoyed significant popularity on marriage furnishings. It was a recognizable subject; in 1450 the estate of Bartolomeo di Ghabriello from Prato included "a chest painted with the story of Lucrezia."[14] The inventory of this estate was one of the very few to go into detail about the iconography of the chests, and could only have done so if the story was both obvious and important. The representation of stories like this one presented the reality of marital expectations to the new bride more emphatically than a painted decorative pattern ever could.

Painted marriage chests were far from the only items of extravagance in these homes. Inventories reveal that Renaissance interiors had a number of private devotional images, as well as purely secular works of art, shining metalware, and sumptuous linens. A sermon by San Bernardino of Siena implied that most people had what he considered to be too many elaborate household objects. He asked:

> How can one describe the luxuries which one may often find not only in the palaces of the great but in the houses of the common citizens? Consider the size and softness of the beds: there you will find silken and linen sheets, with borders of fine gold embroidery, precious coverlets . . . painted and provocative of lust, and gilded and painted curtains.[15]

Inventories and account books make it clear that many of these luxurious accessories were common to families from a range of social levels. It seems that Bernardino's complaint was well founded in daily practice.

These objects were often placed in equally extravagant interiors, brightly frescoed with verdant trees, shrubs, and animal life.[16] Giorgio Vasari described these elaborate interiors in his often-cited life of the early fifteenth-century painter Dello Delli:

> The citizens of those times used to have in their rooms great wooden chests in the form of a sarcophagus, with the covers shaped in various ways, and there were none that did not have the said chests painted . . . And what is more, it was not only the chests that were painted in such a manner, but also the day beds, the wainscoting, the moldings that went around, and other similar ornaments for rooms which were used magnificently in those times, an infinite number of which may be seen throughout the whole city.[17]

With this passage, Vasari reveals the great variety of painted household decorations that were available and popular during this period of burgeoning economic growth. This description accords well with Richard Goldthwaite's examination of consumer demand in Renaissance Italy and his apt phrase "the empire of things."[18] The connection between the newly prosperous economy and the rise in luxury goods is clearly visible in the many objects made for the Renaissance home, and in the insistent presence of these objects in so many household inventories.

A comprehensive study of the material culture Vasari described has been inhibited by the modern perception of such objects – usually considered the decorative arts – as either insignificant or unworthy of study.[19] Yet in the Renaissance relatively little distinction was made between monumental or domestic art, or even between the various types of domestic art, whether home furnishings, clothing, or personal accessories. Only since the 1970s has the art that filled both plebeian and princely homes during the Renaissance become a subject for serious scholarship on its own. But knowledge and understanding of this art is critical to a clear conception of Renaissance society.

Objects related to childbirth were listed regularly in household inventories, attesting to the rich furnishings of the typical Renaissance birth chamber. They reveal that, in addition to trays and bowls, childbirth also called for embroidered sheets and pillows, painted tables and birthing chairs, and ornate tablecloths. New mothers wore various types of elaborately decorated clothing and head coverings, while special mantles and swaddling clothes were made for babies to wear at baptism. Relics, charms, and amulets were also employed in an effort to gain control of forces that posed a threat to either the mother or the child. In many cases, these objects were elaborately and painstakingly executed, by respected master artisans in a variety of fields. From the surviving evidence, it seems that as much effort was exerted on a painted ceramic birth bowl as it was on one of the embroidered and buttoned cloaks for the confined mother to wear in bed.

All of this, of course, was unnecessary from a practical standpoint. Contemporary high-waisted dresses left ample room for expanding midriffs, yet many expectant mothers had specially designated clothing. Similarly, any nondescript tray or bowl could carry food and gifts to the confinement chamber. But most women were provided with utensils specific to the occasion. In almost all cases, similar items already existed in the homes, without the particular birth designation. Inventories reveal that most households were stocked with clothing, trays, and linens for everyday use. But many women received special objects associated exclusively with childbirth, an association the objects continued to carry for years after the actual event.

★ ★ ★

The evidence for and about the material culture of childbirth from surviving objects and household inventories can be further complemented by assessments of the actual event in private writings. Many Renaissance men carefully recorded the milestones in their lives in their memoranda books or in private letters.[20] The birth of a child or grandchild, the death of a wife in childbed, and the baptism of a friend's infant were all duly noted, along with the more regular records of mercantile transactions or agricultural production.

Men did this in different ways. Often, a special section of the memorandum was reserved to record the births (and the deaths) of offspring. In 1393 the cloth merchant Gregorio Dati headed a page, "In praise, glory, honor and benediction of Almighty God, I shall record the fruits that His grace will grant us, and may He in His mercy vouchsafe that they be such as to console our souls eternally, amen."[21] After this preamble, Dati continued with the names and dates of his many children, each added to the same page in order of birth.

In other cases, a formulaic statement would record the date, time, sex, and name of the new child, and occasionally the godparents and associated costs, as well as an invocation to God or to specific saints, chronologically as each birth occurred within the course of the volume. In the midst of his business accounts, Ser Piero Bonaccorsi described the birth – and death – of his first son as follows:

> On June 6, 1509, at about the fourteenth hour, Bendeta, my wife and the daughter of Barone di Bernardo di Ser Salvestro di Ser Tommaso di Ser Salvestro, bore me a son to whom I put the name Giovanfrancescho, Domenico and Romolo. He was baptized in San Giovanni that day at about the twenty-second hour. Godparents were Ser Nicholaio di Silvestro Salamoni and Nofri di Francesco di Baldo di Nofri. It was Wednesday and the Vigil of the Corpus Domini. On the ninth I placed him with the wetnurse Monna Dianora, the wife of Batista di Domenico Bargiani who lives at Pizzulaticho and works for Ser Bastiano from Sitengnola, for the price each month of four *lire piccioli* . . . He died on 28 August 1509 at half-past the ninth hour and was buried in San Piero Scheraggio.[22]

Descriptions like Ser Piero's can reveal a great deal. His entry is an example of the typical Florentine practice of bestowing several names on the new child, one of them being Romolo (or, for girls, Romola), in honor of the patron saint of the nearby city of Fiesole.[23] Ser Piero's son was baptized only eight hours after birth, a rather unusual occurrence unless the child's life was in danger. Two men honored Ser Piero by holding his son at the font for the ceremony; one of the men, like Ser Piero, was a notary and probably a business colleague. Three days after the birth, the child went out to the countryside to a wetnurse, freeing the mother to recover and continue in her daily routine. Less than three months later, however, Ser Piero's son died and was buried in the nearby church. Ser Piero does not reveal the cause of death; it may well have been unknown to him.

As is evident from the account of Ser Piero, who recorded this tragic event stoically, these descriptions rarely include the more subjective emotions of the writer. The formula, in fact, varied little from writer to writer. In a similar way, the invocation at the start of most volumes of memoranda followed a predetermined model to which all tried to conform, making the average text an example of an unvarying literary type; only the individuals and events changed, while the format remained the same. Nevertheless, by reading between the lines and piecing together otherwise disparate comments, these private texts can reveal a great deal about family life.

★ ★ ★

A further source of information on childbirth objects is provided in contemporary images of birth and the birth ritual. These can be sacred scenes from altarpieces, predella panels, frescoes, illuminated manuscripts, and printed books, usually under the guise of the birth of the Virgin or Saint John. Or they can be secular scenes, from manuscripts or books, or from the actual birth trays and bowls themselves.

Contemporary practices surrounding childbirth and confinement must have determined the details in these scenes. Sacred and secular representations often include the array of special objects associated with the event. An altarpiece depicting the Birth of the Virgin, by the Osservanza Master, contains many such details (figure 7). Saint Anne, the Virgin's mother, reclines on an expansive carved and gilt bed, covered first with bright white sheets and then, over these, a red and gold coverlet woven with intricate designs. She leans back on a large red bolster, and washes her hands in a metal basin set on a tripod. The newborn Virgin is bathed and swaddled by two attendants in the foreground, in front of a warm fire. Another attendant walks through the far doorway, carrying two ceramic bowls, with an embroidered towel draped over her shoulder and arm.

The images on this and other monumental altarpieces show elaborate interiors. Sacred subjects were placed in overwhelmingly patrician surroundings, often indistinguishable from the secular scenes on trays and bowls. The new wealth of the middle class and its ability to purchase both functional and decorative home furnishings is reflected in these increasingly well-furnished representations of interiors. It was important to portray the Virgin and her family as prosperous and therefore respectable, and the easiest way to do this was to situate them in recognizably affluent interiors. The gilt furnishings and elaborate geometric tiles in the Osservanza Master's altarpiece are evidence of this, as are Saint Anne's bedclothes and the fine dresses of her attendants. Specific objects such as the embroidered clothes and the bowl carried by the attendant can be closely linked to objects associated with the birth ritual. But above all the scene is comforting. Even the birth tray by Bartolomeo di Fruosino includes a seated harpist among the group of women working in the secular bedchamber (figure 1). Musical accompaniment of this sort certainly would not be provided in every instance, but it represented an ideal situation as a much desired model.

Women easily understood and related to the portrayal of this particular event in devotional art. When a woman saw childbirth objects in a sacred painting, she could recall her own pregnancies and could therefore anchor her devotion to personal experience. There was a degree of comfort and familiarity in these images that were intended to offer reassurance. The numerous details of housewares and linens cluttering these painted chambers made the connection to the everyday world especially tangible. In fact, it was thought that weaker female minds needed extra visual or physical stimuli to assist in devotional practice.[24] Devotional handbooks for women, like the *Zardino de oration* (1454), advised them to imagine the holy stories in familiar settings inhabited by familiar people.[25] By enhancing the appearance of these images with the details of daily life, the Church accommodated the extra needs of women and the necessity of bringing the sacred to the profane in the most tangible manner. Such images generated a response in their audience that can only be imagined in this modern era of more risk-free childbirth. Although most of these paintings are inherently religious by virtue of their subject matter, their contemporary details allowed a direct identification with Renaissance women, generating a devotional impetus that no other type of image could.

Although traditionally referred to as birth scenes, only a few of these images depict actual childbirth. In most cases, such images should be termed confinement scenes, because they focus on the activities and accessories surrounding the post-partum mother

7 Osservanza Master, *The Birth of the Virgin*, 1440s. This altarpiece places the Virgin's birth in a fashionable fifteenth-century interior. Indicative of the exclusively female nature of the event is the way in which Joachim and his companion sit outside the bedchamber, eager to hear the news but unable to enter the room. Tempera on panel. Museo d'Arte Sacra, Asciano. (Scala/Art Resource, New York)

8 Urbino, interior of a maiolica childbirth *scodella*, mid-sixteenth century. The mother relaxes in a curtained bed as a barefoot attendant helps her wash her hands in a basin. The newborn is absent, and the tidy room is empty except for the bed and a nearby table holding a few necessary items. Location unknown. (Photo courtesy Sotheby's, London)

and child. There is an enormous difference in meaning and impact between the painting by the Osservanza Master (figure 7) and maiolica wares like the *scodella* from the Patanazzi workshop (figure 3). In fact, maiolica is almost alone in representing such explicit scenes.[26] Unfortunately, however, few examples are known; whether this is because few have survived or because not many were produced is uncertain. Most of the maiolica depicts secular confinement scenes, often with many of the same details that appear in monumental sacred paintings (figure 8).

Images, however, must be used judiciously. Several early studies employed them to a fault, attempting to discuss all aspects of childbirth in Western Europe using visual arts from different countries and periods.[27] Artists may have embellished structures, costumes, or objects, or combined various sources to construct one fantastic whole. The more reliable efforts at reconstructing private life are based on close examination of images and surviving objects in conjunction with contemporary documentary and literary sources, as in Dora Thornton's book on the Renaissance study and its objects.[28] The use of verbal sources validate (and, occasionally, invalidate) many of the details in visual representations.

★ ★ ★

Examination of surviving objects, documentary evidence, and visual sources provides a great deal of basic information about Renaissance childbirth. As mentioned above, birth objects were most popular from the late fourteenth century until the early seventeenth, in the more economically solvent and artistically advanced regions of north-central Italy, and Tuscany in particular. This period covers the immediate post-plague years to the beginnings of the Grand Duchy, an era when the form of government in Tuscany changed from ostensible democratic rule to hereditary and aristocratic dominance. Concurrently the population figures shifted from a significant low point to slow but steady growth. And childbirth changed from a female-centered event, conducted by a midwife and her assistants, to a gradually more male-dominated business. It was in this period, and in these circumstances, that attitudes toward childbirth, children, and the family necessitated a variety of objects as mediating devices.

The use of childbirth objects was widespread among most social classes. Confinement rooms could be filled with a wide range of items (figure 9). Naturally, the wealthiest members of society had the most objects, and the most elaborate ones. For example, Francesco Inghirammi, an employee of the Medici bank, was an especially wealthy man at his death in 1470, when he left seven children ranging in age from a few months to twelve years.[29] The estate inventory made at this time included two painted birth trays, a box containing birth charms, a birth mantle, two sets of embroidered birth sheets, two embroidered birth pillows, and a birthing chair.[30] This was an excessive number of objects, demonstrating both the affluence of the Inghirammi and the importance they accorded childbirth. Other families of this stature were similarly well equipped for the occasion. At Lorenzo de' Medici's death in 1492, his estate included four birth trays as well as four vests for a new mother to wear during confinement; the woman who used each item is not specified, so it is not known if the trays and vests were used by Lorenzo's wife Clarice Orsini or perhaps even his mother, Lucrezia Tornabuoni.[31]

Despite these somewhat ostentatious cases, however, it is clear that birth objects were available in a variety of price ranges, to supply most levels of society. Domenico d'Agniolo, a blacksmith in Livorno, counted among his possessions in 1551 three pairs of embroidered pillowcases of soft white linen used in childbirth.[32] In 1476 Bartolomeo Sassetti's servant woman in Florence received special clothing, chickens, and wine when she was pregnant.[33] And the Ceppo, a charitable foundation in Prato, purchased sweetmeats, nuts, and candles for various poor families on the occasions of births and baptisms, stating in their records that it was done "for the love of God."[34]

Further indication of the importance of these objects is the evidence of their demand and use. Indeed, they were sometimes loaned to others. The inventory of Filippo Logi's estate in 1553 included a birth sheet belonging to Francesco d'Amadae.[35] Logi's heirs did not want to be financially responsible for the value of the borrowed sheets; anything they could do to lower the estate estimation, and the taxes that accompanied it, was desirable, so they made the ownership clear. On the other hand, in 1388 Jacopo Bombeni's heirs noted that there was a striped and lined birth mantle with pearl and silver

9   Master of the Apollo and Daphne Legend, *The Birth of John the Baptist*, late fifteenth century. Intimate details include the smoking brazier to warm the newborn, the basin and ewer to bathe him, and an attendant bearing a cloth-covered birth tray laden with refreshments. Tempera on panel. Howard University Art Gallery, Washington, D.C. (Photo Samuel H. Kress Foundation and the Photographic Archives, National Gallery of Art, Washington, D.C.)

buttons at the home of Tommaso Sacchetti, although it was part of Bombeni's estate.[36] Bombeni's heirs wanted to ensure that they received the cloak back from Sacchetti; by alerting Pupilli authorities to the absent cloak, they stood a better chance of its return. Others were more prompt in returning borrowed goods, and did not wait until an estate settlement made it a bureaucratic task. In 1493 Tommaso Guidetti loaned a white door curtain to Giuliano Ricasoli to adorn Ricasoli's sister-in-law's birth chamber. The curtain was described as returned two days later, and Guidetti wrote that it was not a prolonged affair, no doubt mindful that it could very well have been.[37]

For those who wanted to own childbirth objects but had limited resources, there was an active second-hand market in them. The *rigattiere*, or used-goods dealer, was active in all aspects of the resale business and probably made a significant profit from continuously desirable objects like these. For example, in 1471 Nicolo Strozzi recorded the payment of 28 *lire* to a second-hand dealer for a pink nightshirt lined with white fur and decorated with ribbons for his pregnant wife, Francesca. At the same time, though from other dealers, he also bought a wooden birth tray and a small lined mantle for the not-yet-born child. Interestingly, the price of the tray was half that of the child's mantle, which was in turn half that of Francesca's nightshirt.[38] It is clear from cases like this one that garments worn for only a short period could receive a good price second-hand.[39]

Nicolo Strozzi was not alone in recording his purchases. In fact, the Pupilli officials often noted the sale of birth objects from estates under their care. These objects were valuable enough to be useful assets in the selective sales of items that occurred when an estate was in the process of settlement.[40] It is likely that most birth items suffered from little depreciation during their somewhat limited use in the home.

Despite this, many people chose to keep their birth objects, rather than resell them. Evidence implies that they had a certain sentimental and dynastic value that required their presence in the household for an extended period of time. Although they may have been used on other, unrelated occasions, they always retained their birth-time identification. For example, although Antonio Baldinaccio's youngest child was six years old when Antonio died in 1476, there was a white woolen nightshirt specifically related to childbirth included in his estate.[41] In some cases, the age or condition of birth objects listed in the inventories is evident from the adjectives used to describe them: they were regularly characterized as used, old, or even broken. The cloak in Tomaso Braci's estate, described as "a sad little mantle for childbirth," was probably little more than a rag in 1430, but it was still important enough to keep, and to include in the official inventory of his possessions.[42] At times, birth objects were put away in a chest and stored in a monastery, whether for safekeeping or for mere lack of space, along with other items too precious to discard or sell but not necessarily needed for daily life. In 1463 Giovanni Strozzi sent a filled chest to the monastery of San Piero Martero, which included five birth mantles among the fine linens and accessories.[43] Birth objects were valuable enough to cause concern when missing from an estate; the accountant in charge of the sequestered Medici estate was declared responsible for a pink childbirth dress when it could not be found with the other estate items in 1497.[44] Such evidence for quantity, demand, use, resale, and retention indicates a certain sentimentality regarding childbirth items that transcends their original function.

Independently, all of this information is somewhat limited. It is useful as the answer to specific questions, but it does not provide a full picture of childbirth in the Renaissance, and it does not demonstrate why, exactly, this proliferation of objects was necessary. An image like the one of two women swaddling a newborn, painted in the concavity of a bowl from Casteldurante, would not be appropriate in any context other than childbirth, for any audience other than a pregnant woman or a new mother (figure 10). But why

10 Casteldurante, interior of a maiolica childbirth *ongaresca*, mid-sixteenth century. Although the curtained bed in the background may hide the sleeping mother, the focus is on the foreground scene. The seated woman, with her legs straight out in front of her to support the child, is in the typical pose for swaddling. The exterior of this bowl is illustrated in figure 92. Iparmüvészeti Múzeum, Budapest. (Photo © Kolozs)

were these objects, painted with images of this type, deemed appropriate during this period in the history of Italy?

Several factors combined to generate a setting that encouraged the purchase and the use of objects such as this bowl as mediating devices between the real and the ideal worlds. This book explores the important role of these objects in family life before, during, and after childbirth. Chapter 1 examines the social and demographic issues behind the objects, and provides a context for their production, popularity, and use. The next three chapters focus on the objects themselves: chapter 2 discusses a wide range of largely ephemeral birth objects, with the purchases of a late fifteenth-century Florentine notary as a case study; chapters 3 and 4 deal, respectively, with childbirth-related wooden trays and bowls and maiolica ware, the two types of birth object that have survived in considerable numbers. Chapter 5 examines the implications of this incredible range of objects and the responses they generated within their intended, female, audience.

The psychological outlook of the plague-decimated family clearly resulted in a rich and varied material culture to encourage, celebrate, and commemorate childbirth. These objects decorated the mother, the child, and the bedroom in honor of the event. They emphasized the family and procreation, and emphatically encouraged Renaissance women to fulfill their maternal role. The focus on childbearing, and the way that focus was developed through the use of art, is a central theme of this book.

The Social, Physical, and Demographic Context for Renaissance Childbirth

BEFORE EXAMINING THE ENORMOUS RANGE of Renaissance childbirth objects in any detail, it is necessary to consider their context. Why did these objects exist, and what were the impulses behind their creation and use? There seem to be three interrelated reasons, and this chapter examines each one in detail. First, there was a great emphasis placed on marriage and the family. Second, there was enormous risk associated with pregnancy and childbirth. And third, there was a drastic drop in the population due to the catastrophic effects of the recurring plague. The very material nature of childbirth needs to be examined in relation to these three factors. Taken together, their impact resulted in the wide variety of objects that encouraged, celebrated, and commemorated childbirth in Renaissance Italy.

Marriage and the Family

Any attempt to discuss childbirth requires a careful look at Renaissance marriage, a subject that has received considerable attention. Christiane Klapisch-Zuber and Samuel K. Cohn Jr., in particular, have discussed the Italian Renaissance as a society which relegated women to a lesser role by virtue of their sex.[1] Within such a society, a great emphasis was placed on the continuation of the lineage. Politically and economically advantageous marriage alliances were carefully negotiated and extravagantly celebrated. A *spalliera*, or wainscoting panel, made to celebrate a marriage in the Adimari family, depicts such a celebration (figure 12). In the street in front of the baptistery and cathedral in Florence, pairs of elegantly dressed ladies and gentlemen perform an elaborate dance under festive striped tenting. A band plays music and attendants bring out refreshments. Like a contemporary Florentine who was not invited to the celebrations, the viewer is understood to be standing at the front, behind the draped balustrade, watching the activity from a distance. As this panel reveals, marriage was a public event, representing the joining of two families in a civic, economic, and political arena amid great festivities.

This sort of pomp was possible only with lavish spending. A meager wedding celebration reflected poorly on the families involved. As a result, those who could afford it – and sometimes those who could not – paid enormous amounts of money to feed and fête their numerous wedding guests in accordance with contemporary practice. Parsimonious at heart, most men kept careful records of these costs, and their records reveal a great deal about the Renaissance love for marital excess. In 1416 Antonio Castellani made an extensive list, all on one much-folded piece of paper, of the guests he invited to each of the six meals he provided to celebrate his wedding. Indicative of his prominent social standing, his many guests came from some of the most notable Florentine families: among them were members of the Medici, Ridolfi, Guiccardini, Davanzati, and Strozzi families. Antonio also listed the food he provided for his guests, the utensils he rented to serve this food, the candleholders he procured to illuminate the meals, and even the twelve attendants he hired to serve the various dishes.[2]

Contemporary paintings of similarly festive wedding banquets also provide an idea of the great festivities over which Antonio presided. The Adimari *spalliera* is one of these. So is Botticelli's series of *spalliere* panels illustrating the story of Nastagio degli Onesti from Boccaccio's *Decamerone* (v:8), which were made for the marriage of Giannozzo Pucci and Lucrezia Bini in 1483. The last panel in the cycle shows Nastagio's wedding feast, with attendants walking into the banquet area bearing dessert plates for the guests (figure 13). The setting is an antique-inspired portico. Costly ceremonial plate, set on a table covered in a richly embroidered tapestry, is centrally placed to emphasize Nastagio's prosperity.[3] There is probably a great deal of accuracy in Botticelli's depiction of a sumptuous Renaissance wedding banquet. In fact, this painting has long been considered surprisingly true to life.[4] Judging from his long list of expenditures and guests, Antonio Castellani's wedding feasts were evidently similarly extravagant. But it is interesting to note that nowhere in Castellani's careful account does he provide the name of his new wife. She was, of course, the ostensible reason for these celebrations, so her absence from the carefully laid plans is rather ironic.

Despite all this evidence for great marital pomp, there would be no wedding at all if there was no dowry.[5] Dowries were necessary for daughters to wed, but throughout this

13 Sandro Botticelli, *spalliera* panel with the wedding banquet from Boccaccio's story of Nastagio degli Onesti. This panel is one of a series of four made for the marriage of Gianozzo Pucci and Lucrezia Bini in 1483. The coats of arms of the couple are prominently placed on the exterior columns and Lorenzo di Piero de' Medici, who arranged the match, is represented by his family arms in the center and by the symbolic laurel bushes and diamond rings contained within the decorative scheme. Tempera on panel. Private collection. (Photo courtesy Christie's, London)

14 Workshop of Domenico Ghirlandaio, fresco in the oratory of San Martino del Vescovo, Florence, late fifteenth century. This scene commemorates the dowering of orphan girls. The notary at the left records the exchange of rings, since marriage was as much a legal activity as an emotional one. (Scala/Art Resource, New York)

period dramatic inflation made them difficult for the less fortunate to provide. Sometimes, money was set aside in testaments to provide for poor or orphaned girls. In his will of 1435 Giovanni Bellaccio stated, "for the love of God and for the soul of this testator, thirty gold florins are given to poor and needy girls to marry."[6] Such a magnanimous (but ultimately self-serving) gesture helped impoverished girls marry and therefore fulfill the role society demanded of them. Other young women benefited from the assistance of organizations like the Buonomini of San Martino, who provided suitable dowries for deserving Florentine girls who otherwise had none, a duty they commemorated in a fresco in their oratory (figure 14).

There was also a strong civic interest in promoting marriage. In Florence many dowries were financed through the assistance of the Monte della Dote, a dowry fund established in 1425, ostensibly to assist the communal debt. Conveniently, while lowering the debt, it also allowed a significant number of marriages to take place, marriages which may not have happened without such financial assistance. In this manner, Florentines irrevocably linked the welfare of their city to that of its individual families. The Monte encouraged both marriage and procreation by enabling women to marry and by legislating that husbands received their dowry only after the consummation of the marriage.

This focus on marriage was not simply a legislative issue. Its presence was also evident in contemporary writings. San Bernardino of Siena, whose series of sermons in the 1420s concern what he perceived as sins and luxuries in private life, lamented the excessive vanity that led so many people to avoid marriage altogether. And this avoidance, most tragically, resulted in a plummeting birth rate. Bernardino observed, "Oh, how many children used to be born, whose conception and birth are now obstructed by vanity!"[7] His long diatribe on this subject, which touched on related problems ranging from prohibitive dowry expenditures to the activities of lascivious sodomizers, basically concluded that the purpose behind marriage was procreation. Others clearly agreed with Bernardino's assertion. In the preface to his *Della famiglia* (1430s), Leon Battista Alberti bemoaned the ruin into which Fortune had reduced so many ancient families, shrinking their size and in some cases wiping them out altogether.[8] In light of this, Alberti affirmed the same emphasis on childbearing as San Bernardino. Children, of course, furthered the lineage and rejuvenated decimated families.

The fact that procreation was advocated by both Bernardino, a preacher to the masses, as well as by Alberti, illegitimately born but an architect and intellect of great sophistication, indicates that it was not simply a humanist tenet upheld by a small and elite percentage of the population, but a general stance advocated in even the more popular guides to matrimony. One such text was Fra Cherubino of Spoleto's *Regole della vita matrimoniale* (1490).[9] Like Alberti before him, Cherubino emphasized the importance of childbearing as a reason to marry. And his advice was no doubt heeded by many, since his text survives in numerous editions and was a popular gift for young wives. In fact, in 1502 the trousseau of Caterina Bongianni included not only fine linens, clothing, and accessories but also Fra Cherubino's text, indicating its personal relevance to Caterina as a young bride.[10]

Even if brides did not realize it themselves, their elders were very conscious of the importance attached to childbearing and on what was needed to accomplish it successfully. Paolo da Certaldo, in his often pithy *Libro di buoni costumi* (1370), warned men of the need to choose beautiful brides, in the interest of the appearance of their future children.[11] Alberti provided even more explicit guidelines for choosing a wife: his very first recommendation was that she be beautiful, a specific quality he equated with "the strength and shapeliness of a body apt to carry and give birth to many beautiful children."[12] When Alessandra Strozzi sought out suitable wives for her sons in the mid-fifteenth century, she must have been well aware of Alberti's precepts. Her letters to her sons are very matter-of-fact regarding the merits of each young woman under consideration. One of her main considerations was health and good looks, because, according to Alessandra, such qualities would lead to beautiful children.[13] And children were vital to the Strozzi, a family whose patriarch had died in exile and whose sons needed influential and fertile marriages to help them in their efforts to return to and prosper in their native city.

When this society emphasized the need for children, however, sons took priority over daughters. The substantial dowries needed to make a beneficial marriage alliance for daughters, who left the natal family to provide children for another, would seem reason enough for such a bias. In a letter to a friend in 1398, Margherita Datini observed that daughters "do not make families but rather unmake them."[14] This was harsh, but quite true. Through marriage, a daughter was effectively removed from her family at a relatively young age, at a sometimes significant financial cost, to the detriment of the remaining male members.

Of course, the birth of a daughter could be a happy occasion in a family that already had at least one healthy son; if they could afford to raise and dower her, they could look forward to gaining important in-laws when she married.[15] Some families were no doubt content with their daughters. But the weight of evidence suggests a decided preference for sons. Such a preference is evident in the tone of a letter written by Antonio da Bibbiena in 1490. He declared, "my wife Piera . . . tonight at the sixth hour gave birth to a baby girl . . . be certain that I am no less happy than if it had been a boy."[16] Antonio must have felt it necessary to state this, given both his own disappointment and the pressure of societal expectations. The birth of a girl could even generate condolences. In a letter of 1469 Marco Parenti tried to cheer his brother-in-law Filippo Strozzi on the birth of a daughter by observing,

It seems to me that since you have a boy, you should be happy that this one is a girl as much as if it were a boy, because you will begin to get advantage from her sooner than with a boy; that is, you will get a good match earlier.[17]

Parenti spoke from experience, since seven of his eight children were female, requiring great expense on his part to dower them appropriately.[18] Statements like Parenti's were quite common in these instances, especially among the elite for whom lineage held special weight. A letter from Federico da Montefeltro to Lorenzo di Piero de' Medici in 1472 congratulated Lorenzo on his new son, although not without a certain amount of jealousy. Federico wrote, "Tell your wife that she has done much better than my wife, who made eight girls before she made my son."[19] Such pressure could drive some people to extremes. Both Richard Trexler and Christiane Klapisch-Zuber have shown that little girls faced higher abandonment rates than boys and may have died at their wetnurses in greater numbers.[20]

The majority of these sadly maligned daughters were conditioned for motherhood from a very early age. So they certainly knew what to expect within the confines of matrimony.[21] The ability to extend a husband's lineage (with sons) and kinship circle (with daughters) was much envied, a true indication of the value placed on childbearing. In fact, this ability sometimes resulted in boasting. Francesco Datini's brother-in-law, confident of the perpetuation of his family after his wife Francesca had produced their fourth son, wrote the following to the childless Datini: "tell [your wife] Margarita that [my wife] will lend her one or two of her sons, but she will not donate them, because Margarita has not proven that she can make them herself."[22] This rather cruel remark is evidence of one husband's pride in his wife's procreative capacity, and another husband's grave disappointment and desperation.

Clearly, the birth of an heir was critical to establish a woman securely in her husband's family and, in many cases, in his affections. As a result, some women were willing to go to great lengths to produce this heir. A drastic example is seen in the case of Bianca Cappello.[23] She was so desperate to provide a son for her lover, Grand Duke Francesco de' Medici, that she took the advice of a variety of doctors and healers. The mysterious medications she took, combined with her perennial poor health, may have reduced her chances for a successful pregnancy; in any case, court documents from that time make only obscure references to possible miscarriages. According to several later sources, Bianca faked a pregnancy in 1576 and sequestered several unmarried and pregnant girls. When one of them gave birth to a son, Bianca allegedly feigned delivery and convinced Francesco that the boy, Antonio, was his much-desired heir.[24] Although this story seems to have been concocted by Francesco's brother Ferdinando, to prevent Antonio from succeeding his father, it does help to indicate the overall awareness of pregnancy and childbirth in Renaissance society.

With this incredible emphasis on marriage and procreation, there is no wonder that so many objects developed to celebrate weddings and births. As noted in the Introduction, the didactic intent of certain subjects on marriage panels has been recognized for some time. It seems that, within this context, birth objects had a similar role. Whereas marriage objects focused both on marriage and on the future family, birth objects were focused more narrowly on pregnancy and childbirth. But they need to be interpreted using this same contextual basis.

Risks

Little is known about the rituals surrounding the actual birth process in the Renaissance. It is important to remember that, in the absence of reliable information, several aspects of female physiology, pregnancy, and childbirth were misunderstood or enveloped in superstition and folklore. In fact, this was a society where the most obvious and persistent image of the mystery of conception was embodied in the many representations of the Annunciation. In Simone Martini's altarpiece, for instance, Mary is depicted as being impregnated by the words of the Archangel Gabriel, which float across the gold ground toward her recoiling body (figure 15). This was a popular subject for monumental altarpieces and frescoes, as well as for smaller, private devotional paintings. For example, in 1480 the estate of Lorenzo Ubaldini included "a canvas of the Annunciation from Flanders."[25] Such a reference indicates both the popularity of the subject and the practice of importing this sort of painting from the North for domestic consumption. Surrounded both at home and at church by these ideal images, and often bombarded with misinformation, many people in the Renaissance would not have understood the complexities of pregnancy and childbirth.

It is difficult to find information about childbirth in the Renaissance, primarily because it was a female-centered event conducted by midwives and female attendants, and these women left few records. Male doctors played only minimal roles in the field of women's health at this time. A few men did specialize in obstetrical care; in 1391 Maestro Naddino d'Aldobrandino identified himself as a *medico da parto* for the communal tax registry.[26] But the numbers of male practitioners were probably quite small.

There were occasions when male doctors attended a birth along with midwives. However, because of their lack of experience with the workings of female bodies, these male doctors may have known even less than their midwife counterparts. In 1476 Filippo Strozzi wrote: "On the twenty-third of that month it pleased God to call to himself the blessed soul of my wife Fiammetta . . . Her illness was that she was not completely purged after childbirth. Although she had a little fever and some pains in the birth, she had been well for four days and was up and around the house. And in the 21st hour a great pain began around her heart. She threw herself on the couch, and from there was carried to the bed, complaining greatly the whole time about her heart. The women and the doctors could do nothing. Around the 23rd hour she died."[27] This description of Fiametta's death is revealing. Her husband distinguished between the (normally attendant) female midwives and the male doctors (whose presence was comparatively rare). But men did come to dire cases, if only to officially pronounce a death. A birthing tragedy was often so evident that it required no practical experience with female bodies. Instead, it required the peace of mind that these university-trained men could provide for the woman's family. In other cases, male doctors were summoned to conduct autopsies.[28] And male doctors assisted with general maladies after the event had taken place; in 1471 Giovanni Buoninsegni recorded the expense of a certain Maestro Lorenzo, who

15 Simone Martini, *The Annunciation*, 1333. The central scene of this altarpiece graphically represents the words of the Archangel Gabriel floating directly into the Virgin's ear, impregnating her with the Holy Spirit. Tempera on panel. Uffizi, Florence. (Alinari/Art Resource, New York)

16 Urbino, interior of a maiolica childbirth *ongaresca*, c. 1570. A laboring woman, still wearing her high-waisted dress, sits back on a low chair, supported by three companions and a midwife. The interior is carefully painted: the walls are brick, the windows leaded, and the fireplace has an imposing classical mantle. Location unknown. (Photo courtesy Phillips, London)

prescribed medicine for Giovanni's wife Lena about a month after she gave birth.[29] Both Strozzi and Buoninsegni were relatively prosperous men, who could afford to pay for this extra care when it was deemed necessary.

But in the majority of cases, when all went as expected, the actual childbirth was managed by a midwife, assisted by female attendants and friends of the expectant mother.[30] Given the gendered nature of the Italian language, this is often obvious in the accounts. Not only images but also documents indicate that it was common for a number of additional women to assist at childbirth. A lack of female attendants was considered exceptional, as a letter regarding a tragedy in the small town of Valdarno Superiore in 1475 demonstrates. This letter described a married woman who gave birth to twins after an illicit affair with her son-in-law. After the delivery, she killed the infants and buried them near her house. The crime was discovered when a dog unearthed one of the children's legs. Amidst the description of the appalling crime, the writer made special note of the fact that this woman gave birth to the twins entirely on her own, an odd enough occurrence that he felt it worthy of note.[31]

The interior of a maiolica bowl from Urbino shows the more typical occurrence, with the pregnant woman surrounded by a midwife and four other women (figure 16). Perhaps she is between contractions; all but one of the women are seated, and the scene is calm, as if they are waiting for something to happen. Another woman warms linens by the fireplace, preparing a place for the child to rest. As such images reveal, childbirth was clearly an activity that called for a certain amount of patience, kindness, and teamwork.

The training of these female practitioners was largely a matter of experience and common sense.[32] Some had the help of illustrated vernacular texts. The most popular texts on female anatomy and obstetrics during the thirteenth to fifteenth centuries were the three treatises attributed to Trotula, the female physician associated with the medical school in Salerno during the eleventh century.[33] The Trotula texts became the basis for a large group of popular, illustrated, vernacular treatises written for women to provide them with guidelines for childbirth procedure. Other Latin texts on gynecology and obstetrics, often transmitted from antiquity, reveal little about obstetrical procedure; instead, they reveal the literary tastes of educated humanists. Few of these tracts dealt with female anatomy and the care of the newborn, and little of the information came from experience with female patients.[34] As a result, these texts were relatively useless in a real birthing situation. The mystery of childbirth was therefore quite compelling to outside observers, and especially to men, who had little opportunity to view the event first-hand. Something of that mystery is evident in a story from Boccaccio's *Decameron* (IX:3), where the jokers Bruno and Buffalmacco convince their gullible acquaintance Calandrino that he is pregnant. Calandrino blames his condition, with great irritation, on his wife's insistence on lying on top during sexual intercourse. As Calandrino stated, "When women are about to give birth I hear them raising such a din, and what they have gives them plenty of space for it; so if I felt that sort of pain, I'm sure I'd be dead before I delivered."[35] There was a certain mystified appreciation evident in Calandrino's statement, despite his fairly negative critique of the activities surrounding this female ritual.

Although it was situated firmly in the women's world, there was an awareness of the dangers and the burden of childbirth and childbearing among much of the general population. In a sermon of 1427 emphasizing the need for husbands to help their wives, San Bernardino stated:

> When she is pregnant, she has toil in her pregnancy; she has toil in giving birth to the children; she has toil in governing them, in rearing them, and also she has toil in governing the husband, when he is in need and ill: she endures toil in governing all the house. And therefore, as you see that in every way she endures toil, so you, husband . . . make sure that you help her bear her toil. When she is pregnant or in childbirth, help her in whatever you can, since that is your child . . . All this toil you see is only the woman's, and the man goes about singing.[36]

Bernardino's surprisingly modern exhortation demonstrates the contemporary perception of women's roles in a vivid manner. Despite this, however, it is unlikely that many men took an active part in pregnancy or childbirth. When all went well, there was little mention in memoranda or letters, beyond a record of basic facts and expenditures. Only the occasional private text describes pregnancy or childbirth in any detail, leading the twentieth-century reader to surmise that few men had first-hand knowledge of the event, and even fewer women left any records at all.

But birthing tragedies were better documented than straightforward births. They represented a deviation from daily events, and they were described in that manner. This event touched a significant segment of the population, rich and poor alike. Although childbirth was much desired as security for the continuation of the family, it was also very difficult and often dangerous. This was no doubt a primary reason for the proliferation of objects surrounding it. Large families were critical to financial and dynastic security, but poor health and unsanitary conditions increased the risks pregnant women had to face. Since they married early, many women spent a significant portion of their childbearing years pregnant. Both the lack of reliable contraceptives and the use of wetnurses decreased the time between pregnancies and took a heavy physical toll on most women during their childbearing years.

From their examination of Florentine death registers David Herlihy and Christiane Klapisch-Zuber concluded that close to a fifth of the recorded deaths of young, married women in early fifteenth-century Florence were associated in some way with childbearing.[37] Unfortunately, the entries in these death registers are formulaic and reveal very little. The majority of specifically designated childbirth-related deaths are described as *sopra parto*; presumably, this term referred to a death during a full-term delivery, whether successful or not.[38] Others are described as *sconcio*, designating a death due to miscarriage, before the child was carried to term.[39] Taking into account the relatively poor diets, the unsanitary conditions, and the limited obstetrical skills of the time, the real numbers were probably even higher than Herlihy and Klapisch-Zuber estimated, especially among the poor who had limited access to the few potentially life-saving methods and materials available.[40]

There were a few ways to mitigate some of the dangers associated with childbirth. Sometimes, family members bought insurance for pregnant women. The eminently practical Alessandra Strozzi purchased insurance to cover her daughter during the young woman's pregnancy in 1449, fearing the loss of the 500 florins already advanced to her son-in-law but not yet relinquished by the Monte delle Dote.[41] Stanley Chojnacki has shown that women, too, were aware of the difficulties they faced; in his study of Venetian testaments he found evidence that pregnant women wrote their wills before their due dates.[42] And, as described in chapter 5, the purchase and use of certain childbirth objects was believed to aid the pregnant mother even further.

Sacred paintings and scenes on childbirth trays and bowls present images of comfortable, safe births and confinements in well-appointed homes. On a maiolica *tagliere* from Casteldurante, a mother rests in her extravagant canopied bed following birth (figure 17). She sits up in the bed and eats from a tray in her lap, with two women and a young boy waiting on her. Another woman kneels at the fire, and the baby sleeps in a rocking crib near the bed. This exemplary scene provided something to hope for at a time when few births would have approached such ease.

Although evidence of personal reactions to childbirth tragedies is relatively rare, there is no reason to believe that the death of a newborn child or a pregnant mother was accepted with equanimity. In 1468 Giovanni Giraldi detailed the agonizing delivery of his wife Maria and her death only four days later. Following this tragedy, Giovanni described himself as "the most disconsolate man in Florence."[43] As a way to "remake" his wife, he changed the name of their daughter Lisabetta, then sixteen months old, to Maria.[44]

There are unfortunately few records of such a personal nature as Giovanni Giraldi's. Yet it is known that, even in prosperous homes, women died during birth or following it, often after a grueling and painful experience. These families, some of the most influential and important in the Renaissance city-states, placed especial emphasis on lineage. The women in these families underwent pregnancy after pregnancy, in an attempt to bear an heir; neither wealth nor high social standing made them exempt from tragedy. Their names read like a list of the most influential families of Renaissance Italy: Beatrice d'Este,[45] Lucrezia Borgia,[46] Maddalena de la Tour d'Auvergne de' Medici,[47] and Grand Duchess Giovanna de' Medici[48] all died as a result of childbirth. For important cases like these, it was likely that a male practitioner would be called to assist, even if this ended up being detrimental to the woman's health. Yet even female practitioners, with years of experience, could not protect these often weak and generally unhealthy women from their dangerous pregnancies.

A description of one such tragic case will illustrate these points. Grand Duchess Giovanna de' Medici, wife of Francesco I of Florence, endured six difficult pregnancies, all resulting in daughters, before her sickly son Filippo was born in 1577. This proved a severe strain on her health, yet in 1578 she was pregnant again. She was attended first by

17 Casteldurante, top of a maiolica childbirth *tagliere*, c. 1530. The ornate architecture and furnishings of the room painted on this tray provide a grand setting for the new mother. Despite the artist's difficulties with scale and perspective, the scene is full of lively details like the alert cat, the striped linens, and the rocking crib. The exterior of this tray and its matching *scodella* are illustrated in figure 90. Walters Art Gallery, Baltimore.

a midwife, who was brought to Florence from Giovanna's native Austria specifically to tend to the birth. When this midwife failed to deliver her, a group of male doctors took over the case. They left an exhaustive report, full of wrenching detail. After several interventions were attempted, they had to admit that "it was better to leave her to live that little bit of life that remained to her without further torment."[49] She died only a few hours later.

Poorer women were, of course, often in worse situations. A letter to Francesco Datini of 1388 states:

Since Tuesday evening your maid has been in labor and it is the most piteous thing one could ever see. Never has a woman suffered so much and there is no heart so hard that it would not sob to see her. She must be held down or she would kill herself, and there are six women who watch her in turns. This morning they fear that the creature in her has died in her body.[50]

It is clear from these references that midwives were capable enough for normal births. But when faced with serious complications, as in the case of Giovanna de' Medici or Datini's servant, there was little that they could do. Even the male doctors had to opt to let the patient die in peace once they had attempted the few procedures known to them.

Just as much confusion surrounded the death of newborn children.[51] According to the death registers, the majority of infants who died due to birth complications were born prematurely.[52] Others died within just a few days of birth, although in most cases no specific reason was provided to explain their deaths.[53] But the passing of such an infant may not have required further comment; the fact that the child was merely three days old may have been sufficient explanation to contemporaries. Miscarriages were routine enough that many of the extensive lists of children in memoranda include references to them without further comment. For example, in 1447 Mano Petrucci wrote simply, "Sandra [my wife] miscarried a baby boy of five months."[54] The stage of the pregnancy is often included, as well as the gender of the fetus, although this information may not have been accurate all the time. When Francesco Giovanni's wife Mea miscarried in 1447, he wrote that she

> miscarried three children of about two months. You could see that two were boys, but you couldn't make out the third. She began at about the third hour and continued until the ninth. She was in danger of death, but thanks to God remains free of it. But she has been very sick for more than fifteen days.[55]

Francesco may have miscalculated the duration of his wife's pregnancy, since it can be difficult to determine the sex of a fetus at that early date.[56] Multiple births like Mea's often resulted in difficulties. There was a certain mystery about them; they were commonly referred to as "two children in one body."[57] These children were often born premature, and babies who did not remain in the womb full term certainly had the odds against them from the start.

Taken as a whole, this information reveals a high mortality rate among newborns and young children. These statistics have fueled debate on the issue of affective ties between parents and children and the role of children in the early modern family, exemplified on the one hand by Philippe Ariès and on the other by Danièle Alexandre-Bidon and Pierre Riché.[58] The established facts regarding Renaissance family life argue strongly for the position held by Alexandre-Bidon and Riché, that children and childhood were of critical importance at this time. Such strong affection was necessary to develop this material culture of childbirth, with its wide range of attendant objects. To further bolster this tenet, Margaret King and Richard Trexler have analyzed two different cases of a father's grief over the death of a son.[59] This sort of sentiment was no doubt echoed by many, despite the matter-of-fact statements usually found in contemporary accounts. We must assume that, for every stoic, terse statement noting a child's death, a great deal of sorrow was kept at bay.[60] The Pisan physician Bernardo Torni, reflecting on the death of a young boy on whom he had conducted an autopsy, observed that, "to lose one's offspring is hard, harder to lose a son, and hardest [to lose him] to a disease not yet fully understood by doctors."[61] Again, it was both the mystery of the event and the sense of loss that caused grief among the survivors.

These tragedies and others like them no doubt created an acute awareness of the dangers associated with childbirth. Given the high mortality rates, it is likely that every Renaissance person could cite a relative, friend, or colleague who had suffered a tragic loss. Objects were therefore used to help mitigate these disasters, and to make the final outcome seem both safer and more secure, as can be seen in a Florentine tray with a confinement room scene painted on its front (figure 18). The cramped, cut-away room holds no fewer than eight women. The mother sits up in her massive bed to receive her guests, while her newborn is swaddled in the foreground. All of the women are dressed well, the linens are sumptuous, and the furnishings are grand. The celebratory and convivial aspects of childbirth are emphasized by the groups of women and their various

accessories. There is no sign of danger, pain, or suffering. An image such as this could only serve to reassure a woman as her delivery drew near.

What happened, then, when something went wrong, and a pregnancy resulted in tragedy? No matter what the cause of death, grief left few tangible manifestations. Most of the trappings of funerals and burials – the candles, draperies, and religious services – were ephemeral.[62] In response to a need for more permanent commemoration, many funerary monuments were constructed in Italy during the fifteenth century. But most of these honored male merchants, scholars, and politicians; there were very few significant tombs built for Renaissance women. One of the most fascinating examples does not even survive intact. This was the tomb of Francesca Pitti and her stillborn child, erected in the Roman church of Santa Maria sopra Minerva by her husband Giovanni Tornabuoni.[63] The couple lived in Rome, where Giovanni was both papal treasurer and manager of the Medici bank. His sister Lucrezia had married Piero di Cosimo de' Medici in 1443, thus cementing the Tornabuoni ties to the ostensible leaders of the city and, incidentally, guaranteeing Giovanni a promising career within their banking empire. Giovanni and Francesca had a son, Lorenzo, in 1468, and a daughter, Ludovica, in 1476, before Francesca's death in childbirth on September 23, 1477. Following her death, Giovanni wrote a much-quoted letter to his nephew Lorenzo di Piero de' Medici:

> My most dear Lorenzo. I am so oppressed by grief and pain for the most bitter and unforeseen accident of my most sweet wife that I myself do not know where I am. As you will have heard yesterday, as pleased God, at the 22nd hour she passed from this life in childbirth, and the infant, having cut her open, we extracted from the body dead, which to me was a double grief still. I am certain that for your usual mercy you will have compassion on me and excuse me if I do not write to you at length.[64]

The attempted Caesarian section is indicative of the desperate measures taken to save at least the child.

Francesca's death, and its manner, made a significant impact on her extended family. Clarice Orsini, Lorenzo di Piero de' Medici's wife, whose marriage in 1469 was at least partly arranged through the machinations of Lorenzo's mother Lucrezia and her brother Giovanni Tornabuoni, remembered Francesca's traumatic death a year later when she was having her own troublesome pregnancy. Giovanni Tornabuoni visited her during this time, but his presence, which probably served as a reminder of Francesca's death, was of little comfort to Clarice. Agnolo Poliziano, who also stayed with her, wrote to Lorenzo in Florence that "yesterday evening Clarice was not feeling well. She wrote to your mother that she hopes she will not miscarry, or suffer in the same way as Giovanni Tornabuoni's wife did."[65] Fortunately, Clarice's pregnancy ended well.

A long narrative relief by the workshop of Andrea Verrocchio can be securely associated with Francesca's tomb (figure 19).[66] This relief, carved from a single piece of marble, is divided into two distinct scenes. On the left side of the relief, a loosely arranged group of seven men and three women frame a man in physician's garb. An elderly woman on his left presents a tightly swaddled infant on a small pillow to the man on his right. This man, who is sculpted in high relief, clasps his hands together as if in prayer at the sight. His prominence and position imply that he is the patron, Giovanni Tornabuoni. All the figures lean in to watch the drama. This solemnity suggests a tragedy; the swaddled child is surely dead.

20 Detail of figure 19, showing Francesca Tornabuoni on her deathbed surrounded by her midwife and attendants. The artist adapted ancient poses and expressions to emphasize the pathos of the event. Bargello, Florence.

21 (below) Jacopo della Quercia, marble tomb effigy of Ilaria del Carretto, 1405. Unlike the Tornabuoni relief, Ilaria's tomb gives little indication of the cause of her death, emphasizing instead her beauty, fidelity, and social standing. Lucca Cathedral. (Alinari/Art Resource, New York)

On the right-hand side of the relief, eight women surround a freestanding bed, in which another woman is propped up following childbirth (figure 20). An older, veiled woman, probably her midwife, holds her arm. But the woman slumps forward, her clothes disheveled and her hair hanging loosely; she must be Francesca Tornabuoni. A wetnurse sits in the right corner with the swaddled baby. The laces of her bodice remain tied, for there is no need to nurse a dead infant. A mourner sits huddled in front of the bed, her head in her hands. Her robes, as well as those of the wetnurse, spill over the edge of the relief. All around the bed, women pull their hair and wave their arms in grief as witnesses to a death in childbirth.

The subject matter of this relief is unique; there seems to be no other contemporary Western representation of a death in childbed, whether in obstetrical texts, sacred or secular manuscripts, or monumental art.[67] Despite the high mortality rate, only one other significant monument is known to have been made for a woman who died in childbirth in the Italian Renaissance: the tomb of Ilaria del Carretto, the young wife of the wealthy Lucchese merchant Paolo Guinigi (figure 21). Ilaria died in 1405 and her tomb, by Jacopo della Quercia, has been partly dismantled and now lies in the north transept of Lucca Cathedral.[68] There has been no discussion of the monument as one made for a woman who died in childbirth, and what effect that had on the final work. But there is good reason for this, since Ilaria's tomb makes no obvious reference to the cause of her death. The remarkable effigy of the young woman, with her long, sweeping robe, adopts a pose favored by Gothic tomb monuments but also features the more realistic, fully three-dimensional qualities of the Renaissance. Although the placement of her clasped hands over her stomach is typical of earlier tombs, it is possible that Jacopo may have been trying to draw attention to the cause of her death. The artist of the Bargello relief followed a different tradition, however. The continuous frieze of figures across the relief, as well as their gestures and costumes, shows a direct awareness of ancient sarcophagi.[69] This firmly places the relief within the humanist culture that flourished in late fifteenth-century Florence.

When Giovanni's branch of the Tornabuoni family died out in 1588, the chapel changed hands and over the centuries the tomb was dismantled.[70] Its original appearance is largely a mystery. But an important characteristic of tombs during this period was the recumbent effigy on a classically inspired sarcophagus. Francesca's tomb probably had such an effigy, which must be the one depicted by the Dutch artist Martin Heemskerck in his

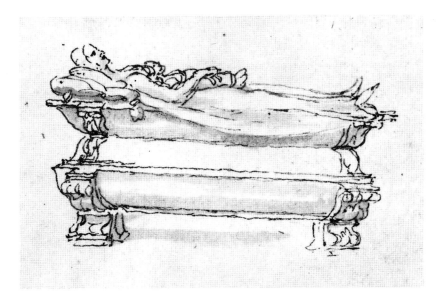

Roman sketchbook of the 1530s (figure 22).[71] Although Heemskerck was most interested in sketching antiquities, he was evidently struck by the pathos of this double effigy, a recumbent woman on a sarcophagus with a small child lying on her chest. This is a clear indication that Giovanni Tornabuoni commemorated both his wife and their stillborn child in the monument. If the child had been baptized while in the womb, a relatively common practice when death was feared, it could have been buried in the sarcophagus with Francesca, thus accounting for the double effigy.[72]

The only other contemporary monument to incorporate a dead child in such a poignant manner is the wall tomb of Beatrice Camponeschi and Maria Pereira in the church of San Bernardino in L'Aquila (figure 23). The Tornabuoni monument was an expression of paternal and husbandly grief, but this tomb exemplifies maternal despair. Maria, a wealthy widowed noblewoman, commissioned the monument herself around 1490, after the death of her fifteen-month-old daughter, Beatrice.[73] Beatrice is shown lying under what was to become the sarcophagus of her mother. The artist, Silvestro dell'Aquila, was familiar with contemporary Florentine and Roman tombs, and he may have known of the earlier monument to Francesca and her child in the Minerva. Although the historical circumstances are different, the representation of both mother and child on one monument is again striking.

Despite the lack of information regarding Francesca Tornabuoni's tomb monument, it surely documents her husband's great devotion and his desire to commemorate her as best as he could afford. His decision to publicly (and expensively) laud his dead wife and child in a major monument with poignant, self-referential iconography is unique for his time. And it indicates how art could be used to commemorate a childbirth catastrophe, just as it could be used to try to deter such a tragedy from occurring in the first place.

★ ★ ★

Plague

Not every man was as lavish in his expenditure as Giovanni Tornabuoni. But many childbirth objects purchased by men were quite costly, and the expenses they incurred were often extensive. Both hopeful and practical, these men lavished childbirth objects on their wives as assurances that all would go well. As discussed above, the material nature of childbirth was interwoven with marital expectations, the desire for children, and an awareness of the attendant mortality that accompanied childbirth. But this should also be seen in relation to mortality in general. In fact, a major underlying cause of the Renaissance emphasis on the family and procreation must have been the recurring outbreaks of the plague and the demographic catastrophes that accompanied them.

After the initial outbreak in 1348, the plague returned more than a dozen times over the next two centuries.[74] Modern demographers estimate the losses at between a third and a half of the entire population of Europe, and there were no significant increases until the late sixteenth century. This situation placed an intense focus on renewing the population in a civic sense and renewing the family in a personal sense. From a pre-plague high in the late 1330s of 120,000, the population of Florence had dropped to 37,000 by 1427.[75] The expansive set of city walls planned and constructed in the prosperous years before 1333 remained largely empty until the nineteenth century, by which time the need for a walled city had become a moot point.[76] Even as late as 1552, the population remained at about half of the pre-plague level.[77]

The emotional effects on those who survived the crisis are incalculable. In 1363 the chronicler Matteo Villani referred to the plague as an extermination,[78] a perception that helped to fuel an incipient interest in the family and a society that strongly advocated reproduction. The continual cycle of pregnancy and childbirth most women underwent during their marriages was the only way to relieve the devastation caused by the plague. Many of the childbirth objects examined in this book can be considered a means through which the cycle was perpetuated and encouraged.

Studies of the plague usually focus on the initial epidemic of 1348, or on the concomitant effects on demography and the environment.[79] Several scholars have also examined the omnipresent specter of death as a phenomenon with strong psychological and social implications for the population.[80] People reacted in various ways. Some followed a new spirituality, others made generous bequests, while still others practiced an unprecedented hedonism, or, at times, discriminated against outsiders due to misguided beliefs regarding transmission of disease and cause of death.

Art historians have also associated the plague with significant changes in monumental sacred art. Millard Meiss was perhaps the first to focus on the stylistic influences of the plague on the monumental art of Florence and Siena.[81] Louise Marshall has discussed certain sacred iconographic motifs as reactions to the effects of the recurring plague,[82] and several earlier scholars focused on the sobering images that the plague inspired.[83] This type of art was seen by everyone in the community, often in an important religious or civic setting. It relied heavily on iconic images and somber subject matter to prove its points.

However, monumental or sacred art was not the only type of art influenced by the plague. In fact, the psychological repercussions of the plague helped generate a wide range of special objects and images. In her examination of death ritual in Renaissance Florence, Sharon T. Strocchia described the proliferation of items that developed around funerary rites at this time as "ceremonial buffers" that offered stability and protection in the plague-ravaged era.[84] These buffers helped many people to adjust to the traumas of this catastrophic period.

Within a domestic setting, the recurring epidemics evidently inspired decorative art with specific, childbirth-related iconography to offset the omnipresent mortality. The

24 Urbino, maiolica childbirth bowl and cover, c. 1580. The exterior of this set is painted with an evocative landscape scene, but the concavity of the bowl has only a standing woman displaying a tightly swaddled child. The charming pair would have been a pleasant surprise to the woman who lifted the cover. © Triple Gallery, Berne, Switzerland.

importance and the uncertainties of childbirth also required what Strocchia aptly called buffers to help establish – however fictitiously – a safe and secure setting. The prospects for the Renaissance mother were precarious, but certain objects could alleviate her difficulties (figure 24). The fact that childbirth objects not only came to prominence at this time but also continued throughout the worst years of the epidemics suggests that they were connected to the overall ideology that childbirth was a vital measure to combat the demographic devastation of the plague.

It is clear that domestic and decorative art, which surrounded women every day in their own homes, was radically affected by the importance attached to childbirth in the context of the plague. Meiss was absolutely correct in his assertion that the plague generated specific works of art, but he did not acknowledge either their variety or the fact that many of them were related to childbirth. In fact, anything that provided a certain amount of protection and mediation – be it clothing, linens, trays, bowls, or a wide assortment of magical aids – was desirable in this context. Renaissance ideals of the family were thus channeled into the production of a rich setting for childbirth. The resulting objects emphasized the family and procreation, both stimulating the imagination of the Renaissance woman and emphatically encouraging her to fulfill her maternal role. And, after the actual birth, many of these objects doubled as utilitarian devices and tangible rewards for the mother. The next three chapters describe these objects in detail, starting with the wide range of childbirth-related ephemera recorded in the accounts of a Florentine notary, Ser Girolamo da Colle.

2   *Caterina di Ser Girolamo da Colle and the Material Culture of Renaissance Childbirth*

25 Masaccio, front of a wooden childbirth tray with a confinement room scene, c. 1427. The back of the tray is illustrated in figure 132. Gemäldegalerie, Staatliche Museen zu Berlin, Preussischer Kulturbesitz. (Photo Jörg P. Anders)

IN 1473 CATERINA, THE WIFE OF Ser Girolamo di Ser Giovanni di Ser Taddeo da Colle, gave birth to their first child, a boy whom they named Giovanni. Both parents were probably delighted; they had been married for several years and Ser Girolamo may have been concerned about the continuation of his lineage. Ser Girolamo was a Florentine notary, as his father and his grandfather were before him; the profession carried with it considerable respect as well as a significant amount of disposable income. Florence had many notaries, indispensable for enacting business and social documents in the litigious city. Ser Girolamo can be considered a relatively ordinary, middle-class citizen. He was not a very important man in the political or economic life of the Renaissance, although he had social ties with more eminent families such as the Niccolini and the Medici.[1] However, he is important here because two of his account books, covering the years 1467–8 and 1472–6, survive in the Archivio di Stato in Florence. In the later volume, together with business dealings and property transactions, Ser Girolamo kept meticulous accounts of the many expenses for his wife's pregnancies, deliveries, and confinements in 1473 and 1475, noting and cross-referencing each individual cost as it was incurred. Combined with examinations of works of art, other account books, inventories, and sumptuary legislation, Ser Girolamo's text helps to illuminate the dense material culture of Renaissance childbirth.

Much can be determined about this material culture from such images as the one on the front of a wooden childbirth tray by Masaccio (figure 25).[2] On the left are trumpeters, blowing horns festively draped with banners bearing the Florentine lily. They herald the arrival of three richly dressed matrons and two heavily swathed nuns. These women enter the confinement room through a door that opens from a classical loggia, the columns connecting via iron tie beams across the passageway. Their hair encased in gold netting or, in one case, an elaborately beaded hat, the three secular women wear long flowing gowns, simply but expensively adorned with gold buttons and trim or magnificent cascading sleeves. Even the somber nuns are enveloped in multiple yards of black fabric; one of them must lift her sweeping skirts as she walks through the portico. These five women are distinguished by such clothing from the four more humbly dressed attendants who have their hair tucked into simple and modestly efficient white veils. A hearty, tightly swaddled baby rests in one woman's lap, and she bends down solicitously to care for it. The new mother is in bed, her hair pulled up into her gold-beaded cap, reclining on sumptuous red sheets and pillows probably too rich for everyday use. Her fashionably decorated room is painted with verdant frescoes and hung with fur pelts.[3] She awaits her guests, who are followed by male attendants carrying a box, perhaps filled with sweetmeats, and a birth tray. The special linens, clothing, and tray that appear in this scene were popular childbirth objects, and they were listed in a variety of contemporary accounts. Veracity was an important feature of these images, as part of their function was encouragement and commemoration. To be convincing, they had to be accurate.

Like the mother on Masaccio's birth tray, most women had special objects to use on the occasion and to keep for extended periods following it. And most women received a number of visitors and gifts following delivery, making childbirth as much of a social event as a physical one.[4] Many new mothers remained confined to bed for a certain period after the birth, whether to follow religious dictates, to appease practical health concerns, or to facilitate visits from female relatives and friends. However, although the mother was in her home and in her bed, she was also on display to her visitors, and the objects that surrounded her were thus indicative of her husband's rank and financial worth. The scene painted on Masaccio's birth tray clearly demonstrates this. The smartly dressed attendants carrying gifts would have walked through the city streets, gathering attention and followers as they went. This chapter aims to reconstruct the mother's chamber in order to examine the objects and the rituals associated with the celebration. Borrowing from the methods of microhistory, I have explored the manner in which one woman, Caterina di Ser Girolamo, was provided for during and directly following her two pregnancies.[5] But this study is not restricted to Caterina alone: other information from this period indicates that her experience was similar to that of many Renaissance women. Caterina's case is unusual only because her husband kept such careful records of the costs, and because those records survive.

The Birth of Giovanni di Ser Girolamo

Ser Girolamo da Colle described his first son's birth with the following entry in his memoranda:

> I record how on the 19th, at about the 23rd hour, by the grace of God and the Blessed Virgin Mary and Saint Niccolò our protector and advocate and all the other male and female saints of God, was born to me of Caterina my wife a baby boy, with all his members and well proportioned, God be praised. And the said Caterina and the little baby are well. The baby was delivered by Monna Mathea, who lives in the house of the barrel maker of San Lorenzo, by the door on the side near the via della Stufa, and Monna Lena, my mother-in-law; and because Mathea stayed about 22 hours and did a lot for us I gave her one large florin . . . And tomorrow at good hour I will baptize him and give him the name of my father, that is Giovanni, and because he was born on Sunday I will give him the name Domenico, and that holy name Romolo. I ask God and his mother Madonna Saint Mary, Saint Niccolò, and all the other saints of Paradise to make him a good boy in the grace of God.[6]

Ser Girolamo's statement is more detailed but nevertheless typical of childbirth descriptions found in the personal records of many of his peers.[7] Most men recorded the day and the hour, invoking the appropriate saints and stating the child's name. But the unique aspect of Ser Girolamo's record is found in the pages leading up to and following this description, where he carefully enumerated all his costs for the event. Few men did this in such detail; it is probable that the customs and expenses surrounding birth were so well established that they required little explanation. For example, in 1462 Bernardo Rinieri stated that his wife received sweetmeats and candles, "as was ordinary."[8] In his accounts, Lorenzo Morelli noted that he paid more than a florin "to provide for the needs of the woman in birth."[9] These men knew what to buy and when to buy it, and no husband wanted his wife to be lacking for this important event. The items were so standard that there was no pressing need to enumerate them in any detail; when looking back over expenditures, the father would have been able to recall exactly what he bought with little difficulty, despite the vague nature of his notation.

26 Fra Angelico, *The Miracle of Saints Cosmos and Damian*, c. 1442. This predella scene depicts the physicians attaching a new leg to a gangrenous patient. In this condition, the patient could not leave his bed, so a urinal was therefore necessary and Fra Angelico's inclusion of it strikes a credible note. As evident in this painting, urinals were often decorously encased with wicker or straw, and had long straps to hang from a bedpost. Tempera on panel. Museo di San Marco, Florence. (Photo Nicolo Orsi Battiglini)

Ser Girolamo, however, was exceptionally careful in his accounts. Whether because he was by nature scrupulous, or impossibly cheap, he began his litany of expenses on January 16 by stating, "I record all the monies spent for my wife Caterina in birth and in her pregnancy."[10] His starting date reveals his optimism: Caterina did not give birth until September 19, nine months and three days later, so any sign of pregnancy by mid-January must have been imagined by the hopeful couple.

A few of his purchases indicate that Caterina's pregnancy progressed with some difficulty. For example, the first thing Ser Girolamo bought that January day was a urinal.[11] This was an accessory for the bed-ridden that often appears in sacred paintings with sickbed iconography (figure 26). The purchase of such an item implies that Caterina was ill enough to be bedridden. On the same day, Ser Girolamo also bought what appears to have been some medicinal items: he described them only as crushed anise seeds and a herbal remedy.[12] The next day, he purchased 3 ounces of dragonwort, a plant often mentioned in Renaissance compendia for its medicinal effects.[13]

Apparently these items were sufficient to soothe Caterina during the early months of her pregnancy. Ser Girolamo recorded no further expenses until late March, when he bought two braziers to heat water for her bath.[14] Interestingly, these were specified as a pregnancy-related expense. Although the home was presumably equipped with several braziers already, and Ser Girolamo himself presumably enjoyed a heated bath on occasion, these two were designated as Caterina's, and associated with her pregnancy. According to Ser Girolamo's records, April, May, and June passed without expenditures for Caterina; warm baths seem to have been sufficient for this period. But then in early July she required an ointment made by a priest at the church of Santa Maria in Campo.[15] The ointment is not described, but it was likely to have been medicinal and intended to relieve a pregnancy-related ache or pain.

During July, August, and September, Ser Girolamo purchased the fabric and notions needed to make birth-related clothing for Caterina: she received three lined and elaborately trimmed cloaks, a nightshirt, and a pair of slippers.[16] Some of these were bought ready-made, while others were sewn from the different lengths of cloth that Ser Girolamo purchased on separate occasions.

Subtle distinctions in splendor that are largely imperceptible today from such descriptions would have been obvious to contemporaries from the fabric or trimmings of Caterina's clothing. Although no contemporary costume has survived in its entirety, a combination of artistic representations, inventories, and a few surviving bits of fabric indicate what typical clothing would have looked like.[17] Italy was a leading textile producer at this time, and a main center for this was Ser Girolamo's town of Florence.[18] The availability of many costly and fashionable fabrics in Florence allowed for great elaboration in what is now generally called maternity clothing. Estate inventories reveal that there were special veils,[19] fur-lined gowns,[20] and embroidered shirts,[21] all of which were used during the birth ritual in various combinations and then retained in the home for an extended period following the event.[22]

From both inventories and accounts like Ser Girolamo's, it is possible to trace how certain clothing went in and out of fashion. In the late fourteenth century, and well through the fifteenth, *mantelli*, or cloaks, were the most popular type of birth clothing. These cloaks are usually visible in birth images: the rich red cloak fastened with a jeweled brooch and wrapped around the shoulders of the new mother on the wooden tray by Bartolomeo di Fruosino is probably a *mantello da parto* (figure 27). Documentary evidence indicates that such cloaks ranged from very basic coverings to the extravagant one worn by Bernardo di Giorgio's wife in 1414, which was pink and lined in gray fur with sixteen small pearl buttons.[23] The three cloaks Ser Girolamo provided for Caterina required five lengths of a fine Flemish gray wool, five and a half further lengths of linen, black fur, and special fringes and silks for lining,[24] suggesting that the finished cloaks were elaborate indeed.

27 Bartolomeo di Fruosino, detail of the wooden childbirth tray illustrated in figure 1. (Photo © 1979 The Metropolitan Museum of Art, New York)

Ornamented nightshirts, or *guardacuore*, were also common from the late fourteenth century until the late sixteenth. They were usually colorful and often ornamented with fancy linings and buttons, such as the red one lined in white fur with twenty-five silver buttons worn by Giuliano di Pierozzo's wife in 1419.[25] Caterina also had a costly nightshirt, for which Ser Girolamo purchased over four lengths of fine fabric.[26] By the late fifteenth century, the *inbusto*, or vest, had become a yet more costly and stylish birth accessory, a distinction it carried for many decades. Such vests were often made of white wool, but sometimes more exotic – and expensive – materials and colors were favored, such as the one of yellow damask made for Cosimo Rucellai's wife in 1549,[27] or the one in red satin with seventy-four gold half-buttons and twenty-eight pairs of enameled gold points listed in Francesco Magniale's estate in 1557.[28] Even Caterina's elaborate *guardacuora* would have looked shabby next to this red satin vest with its complicated closings. Nevertheless, because Ser Girolamo provided his wife with newly made accessories (even if some of them used second-hand fabrics), he paid a significant amount. He could have saved some of the expenses associated with these childbirth objects by borrowing the items, or by purchasing them on the second-hand market.

But clothing was not the only way to prepare a chamber for childbirth. The new mother might be dressed in great finery, but she would make a poor impression on her guests if her bed was not equally well furnished. During the fifteenth century sets of sheets specific to childbirth were found in a variety of styles in many homes. For example, in 1448 Giovanni Parenti's estate included a new set of sheets for childbirth decorated with almond-shaped patterns and worked borders.[29] Such elaborate linens were the rule for the occasion. To add some luster to a sadly worn pair of birth sheets (which had probably seen her through at least one previous confinement in style), one woman had four birth pillows with patterned cases and blue, red, and green tassels.[30] Caterina's bedchamber seems to have been similarly furnished; Ser Girolamo recorded the purchase of materials to make pillows and pillowcases during her pregnancy.[31]

38

Special clothing and linens were also needed to show off the newborn. In 1474 Eleonora of Aragon, the wife of Duke Ercole d'Este of Ferrara, ordered a silk coverlet of white damask and taffeta fringed in gold and silk for her baby's cradle.[32] Clearly the birth of an heir was of utmost importance in a princely home. But ordinary people considered it an equally critical event, although they could not afford to spend on the level of the Este family. For example, in 1550 the estate of Tomaso Setteciegli included an embroidered layette used for the baptism ritual.[33] Such extravagance served the same purpose as clothing for the new mother did: it demonstrated the family's wealth and social status, explicitly connecting their prosperity to the continuation of their lineage. Given the significance attached to childbirth, it is not surprising that Ser Girolamo went on to provide for his future child. He bought a length of cloth from Prato to make a coverlet for the crib, as well as material for a small cloak and swaddling clothes.[34]

As Caterina's due date approached, Ser Girolamo's expenses grew. In September he made preparations for a dowry should the child be a girl. The costs associated with dowering a daughter resulted in a great deal of psychological and financial trauma for many Renaissance fathers. But Ser Girolamo, like a number of other men, anticipated the expense by speculating on his wife's pregnancy. There was an avid interest in the gender of the yet-to-be-born child, and some men were able to take advantage of this interest for their own gain. This is evident in the popular practice of gambling on the outcome of pregnancies, a profitable enterprise for the lucky speculator, involving significant sums of money and, often, professional oddsmakers. The practice was regulated by several different laws, but the restrictions did not deter the gamblers.[35] For example, in 1514 a certain Iacopo and his friend Raffaello made a bet on the outcome of Iacopo's wife's pregnancy. If she had a girl, Iacopo paid Raffaello. On the other hand, if she had a boy, Raffaello owed Iacopo twice as much.[36] This sort of bet was quite common, and could involve more than one woman and more than two gamblers, making it into a sort of lottery with relatively high stakes.[37] The goldsmith Benvenuto Cellini was especially addicted to the game; his estate inventory of 1570 lists several documents concerning wagers in which he was engaged at the time of his death.[38] His great patron, Duchess Eleonora de' Medici, was also fond of gambling. When she was pregnant in 1552, for example, she arranged with a merchant to pay half-price for multiple lengths of costly silver cloth. Should she give birth to a boy, the cloth was hers at this reduced price. Should she give birth to a girl, she was to pay the merchant twice as much. Fortunately for the merchant, she did have a girl, and he was able to turn a profit on the bet.[39]

Although he did not wager the same amount of money as Duchess Eleonora, Ser Girolamo's gamble was high for his economic class. There are no other references to this practice in his accounts; he was evidently not an inveterate gambler, but a rather desperate father-to-be trying to offset his potential costs in an era of escalating dowries. He bet 30 florins as security against an eventual dowry of 400 should Caterina have a girl. But should the child be a boy, he had to forfeit the original investment of 30 florins.[40] As Caterina did produce a son, Ser Girolamo presumably lost his 30 florins. This was a significant sum to risk; a typical skilled laborer of the time would take over half a year to earn that much.[41] Although Ser Girolamo's profit would have been substantial if Caterina had given birth to a girl, his willingness to risk the 30 florins (and to recover from that loss if necessary) indicates the extent of his disposable assets and helps to explain the larger total sum he spent on his wife's pregnancy and confinement.

When Caterina went into labor on 18 September, her mother and the midwife, Mattea, both came to help. So did a certain Domenica, identified as a *guardadonna* (literally a "woman watcher"), whose task it was to care for the new mother during and for some time after the birth. Both the midwife and the *guardadonna* were professionals, hired to

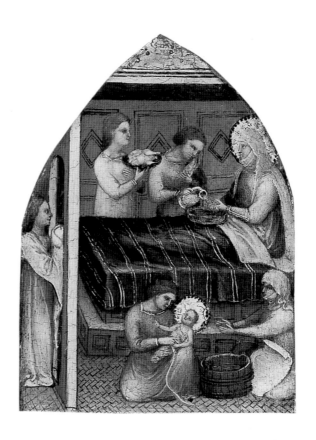

28 Giusto de' Menabuoi, *The Birth of the Virgin*, 1367. This intimate scene was painted on the outer wing of a private altarpiece. The interior has charming details, like the striped linens, coffered chests, herringbone-patterned floor, and roast chicken dinner. Tempera on panel. National Gallery, London.

carry out a specific task. They were paid for their efforts and had a certain degree of empirical knowledge regarding anatomy and nutrition that enabled them to accomplish their jobs successfully.

While these women tended to Caterina, Ser Girolamo spent more money. He had plenty of time to do so, for she was in labor a full twenty-four hours. Nevertheless, he had begun to prepare immediately, noting in his memoranda, "At the 23rd hour Caterina's pains began; and for that reason I bought a fat pigeon, half an ounce of sweetmeats, and three fresh eggs."[42]

Ser Girolamo's references to poultry are particularly interesting. During the previous month, he had paid a considerable amount to stock a pen with poultry and to feed the birds, and he continued to buy assorted fowl during Caterina's pregnancy and confinement.[43] This was an important food in the Renaissance, and many inventories record the number of birds found in the household coop. For example, in 1488 Giovanni di Bernabe's home included a pen of capons on the loggia.[44] But there was also a clear connection to pregnancy and childbirth in the consumption of poultry, and account books often enumerated the costs of birds for these occasions. It was a considerable expense; while his wife, Lucrezia, was pregnant in 1456, Carlo Strozzi bought four pairs of capons and two pairs of fat chickens.[45] The cost of these birds was almost equivalent to the cost of keeping an infant at the wetnurse for over two months.[46] Despite this great expense (or, perhaps, because of it), poultry was recommended by Michele Savonarola, a physician in the Este court of Ferrara, who described it as easy to digest and nutritious for new mothers.[47] Savonarola's recommendations were no doubt taken from his observations of contemporary practice, which may have had a long popular history.

The association between poultry and childbirth was so strong that sacred scenes of confinement even include poultry. On a devotional triptych by Giusto de' Menabuoi, the scene of *The Birth of the Virgin* has an attendant who offers a whole roasted bird to Saint Anne in her bed (figure 28). Such details serve as domestic symbols, to help women relate

to the religious stories on a more personal level. A mother viewing such a painting might remember the poultry she was brought during her own confinement and feel a closer bond with the holy figures because of it.[48] Paintings could thus provide mediation between the real and ideal worlds, a mediation which proved invaluable to many people at this time.

While Caterina was still in labor, Ser Girolamo spent a considerable amount of money on items from the apothecary.[49] Apothecaries were important figures in Renaissance life, since they belonged to one of the most prominent guilds and dispensed not only medicines but also medical advice, spices, and foods.[50] Recipes for many of the apothecary's goods were included in the *Ricettario fiorentino* (1499), the first standardized pharmacopeia for professional use.[51] But some of these items could be made at home, too, and people could exchange recipes for them. Different types of sugar-coated sweetmeats, described as *treggea*[52] or *manuscristi*, as well as, more generally, *confetti*, were especially appropriate for childbirth, and Ser Girolamo bought Caterina several pounds of them during and after her labor.[53]

Boxes of sweetmeats were also given as childbirth gifts, either from relatives and acquaintances if one was reasonably well off, or otherwise from charitable organizations. After she gave birth to a son in 1446, Nanna Arigucci's father sent her a painted box full of sweetmeats, together with twelve silver spoons decorated with gilt Hercules figures.[54] Nanna's experience was that of an affluent woman, whose family could afford to provide her with a number of birth-related items. But

29 Masaccio, detail of figure 25. The attendants carry in a covered box and a birth tray. Gemäldegalerie, Staatliche Museen zu Berlin, Preussischer Kulturbesitz. (Photo Jörg P. Anders)

these things were so important that the less wealthy needed them, too. The Ceppo, a charitable organization in Prato originally founded through the generosity of Francesco Datini, sent the wife of a certain Jacopo di Piero 6 pounds of sweetmeats after she gave birth in 1440; her husband probably could not afford to provide such a gift himself, so the Ceppo stepped in to assist.[55] These items were apparently an essential part of the ritual, so much so that even the poor were entitled to them. The boxes in which they came may have resembled the round, lidded container on Masaccio's birth tray, carried in by one of the male servants (figure 29). On this tray, the box appears to be a gift, probably similar to those received by Nanna Arigucci or the wife of Jacopo di Piero. The tightly stretched seal with decorative fringes kept the items inside fresh. Documents and images reveal that such boxes were purchased from apothecaries: a fresco in Issogne depicts the interior of such a shop, with similar boxes arrayed on the top back shelf (figure 30).

30 Northern Italian, fresco depicting the interior of an apothecary's shop, c. 1500. Note the great variety of objects available for sale in a Renaissance apothecary. On the top shelf, above the maiolica drug jars and the ex-voto offerings, are the same sort of low round boxes, sealed with a tightly stretched skin, as on the birth tray painted by Masaccio. Castello d'Issogne, Valle d'Aosta. (Scala/Art Resource, New York)

Most of these foods were celebratory. They were the usual refreshments for the women who came to visit the new mother, and many men recorded their purchase. A large group of guests, however, could require additional and unexpected expenses. For example, six days after his wife Nannina gave birth to a daughter in 1490, Tribaldo de' Rossi noted that he had to buy more *confetti* for Nannina, since she had received so many guests.[56] Similar to this is the note in Francesco Castellani's account book that he spent 2 florins for sweetmeats and other things for the women who came to visit his confined wife.[57] It seems that it was important to keep such foods on hand. And Ser Girolamo followed this practice, securing additional sweetmeats four days after his son's birth.[58]

In the days following his son's birth, Ser Girolamo also purchased two *pane biancho*, or sweet cakes, as well as liquid refreshments.[59] Both the physician Michele Savonarola and the writer Paolo da Certaldo recommended fragrant and digestible white wines for the occasion.[60] Ser Girolamo recorded the purchase of twenty-eight flasks of wine during the five-week period after his wife gave birth, probably for the enjoyment of Caterina and her guests.[61] This was typical: in 1471 Nicolo Strozzi bought an unspecified quantity of both white and red wine for his wife's delivery.[62] Painted confinement scenes often include similar details: in Ghirlandaio's fresco of *The Birth of John the Baptist* in Florence, an attendant carries two filled carafes to Saint Elizabeth's bedside on a draped tray (figure 31). The fresco is so finely rendered that the upraised bottom of the carafe is visible through the clear liquid. In his description of this fresco, Vasari marveled at the graceful maiden carrying two straw-wrapped bottles and balancing a plate of fruit on her head; he noted that it was a Florentine custom to bring such nourishment from the country home.[63] Custom or not, most new fathers probably did not have to exert much effort in the transport, since many households kept barrels of wine in their ground-floor storage rooms. For example, when Albizo del Toso died in 1424, he had thirty-five barrels of red wine and twelve barrels of white wine in a vault of his Florentine home.[64] Unfortunately Ser Girolamo's household inventory is not known. But the fact that he bought so much wine for Caterina implies that he did not stock much of it in his home.

31 Domenico Ghirlandaio,
The Birth of John the Baptist,
c. 1486–7. Fresco. Santa
Maria Novella, Florence.
(Alinari/Art Resource,
New York)

In most memoranda, the food and drink consumed by the visiting women was well documented, and the expenses they generated were carefully tracked. But little is known about the custom of visiting the new mother, and contemporary references to it are vague. The main memoranda writers of the time were the men, and they did not take part in this activity. This was a woman's ritual, and few women recorded their lives in a manner that has survived.

Among the few contemporary references to the practice is a letter from Contessina de' Medici to her daughter-in-law in 1467: "visits . . . have been paid on your behalf [to the new mother], and everything you requested has been done."[65] This comment explains little, but more information about the visits can be gleaned from paintings of confinement scenes. Ghirlandaio's fresco, for example, includes an ostentatious procession, with a young girl in a pink and gold dress leading two older women, clad more moderately but still expensively, as all come to pay homage to the new mother.

Most confinement visits would not have been as formal as the one in Ghirlandaio's fresco, but they were often as elaborately accessorized. Visitors came bearing gifts, wearing magnificent garments and costly jewels, and the mother ready was to impress them with equally special clothes and a properly outfitted room.

Making an excellent impression, then, was what much of this ritual was arranged to do. Of course, this contradicted the professed beliefs of the parsimonious Florentines, who advocated hiding one's wealth and practicing frugality whenever possible.[66] But such an attitude did not hold true for such important life-cycle rituals as marriage, birth, baptism, or even death. As discussed in the previous chapter in connection with Antonio Castellani's account of his marriage feast, such occasions were opportunities to celebrate and to glorify the family, and to demonstrate its economic and social prowess. This was also the case in other cities on the Italian peninsula. There are several fifteenth- and sixteenth-century accounts of confinement room visits in Venice, considered one of the richest and most extravagant cities of the Renaissance.[67] Appropriately, one visitor to Venice in 1466 observed a sumptuous confinement at the home of a prominent merchant which involved furnishings of alabaster, gold, and silver, at a total cost of 24,000 ducats.[68] Francesco Sansovino's panegyric to his beloved adopted city described the confinement chamber in late sixteenth-century Venice as especially splendid, full of works of art and valuables.[69] And the use of art to help celebrate the occasion is verified by the account of the painter Lorenzo Lotto, who listed the cost of a boat and porters to transport unspecified paintings along the canals of Venice to decorate a cousin's room for childbirth in 1542.[70] Evidently, Venetian birth celebrations involved a huge outlay for durable goods.[71]

The enigmatic painting of *The Birth of Caterina Cornaro* (figure 32) is among the best examples of a spectacular Venetian confinement scene. It is both apocryphal (Caterina

Cornaro was born in Venice in 1454, at least a century before this painting was executed) and mythological (the three Graces dance at the foot of the bed, and putti float above it). But the long lines of well-dressed visitors, most of whom carry gifts for the new mother, the displays of plate on heavy sideboards, and the busy servants preparing foods for the crowd all lend a realistic note to the scene. Such details would have been recognizable as appropriate to both this particular occasion and, in a less fanciful manner, to childbirth in general.

Florence was never known for the same sort of display. Nevertheless, verbal and visual descriptions reveal that Florentine homes were carefully and luxuriously appointed for childbirth. Besides the elaborate clothing and linens used for the occasion, and the more ephemeral objects, such as food and drinks, there could be other items, too. For example, in 1471 Giovanni Buoninsegni bought candles to light before a devotional image of the Virgin when his wife received visitors.[72] This showed respect for the Virgin, and also added a cheerful glow to the room. Inventories indicate that many private chambers had at least one kind of devotional image, whether painted or sculpted, and representations of interiors often include them. In one case, a *sacra conversazione* is hung on the back wall of the confinement room painted on a Florentine birth tray from the early fifteenth century (figure 33).

Confinement visits were evidently highly politicized ritual affairs. Christiane Klapisch-Zuber has shown how gatherings of women, theoretically the most disenfranchised members of the population, were encouraged by men to foster lineal and political ties.[73] The gift exchanges that took place during confinement visits involved silver fork and spoon sets, fabric, sweetmeats, and goblets. These gifts differ considerably from those exchanged at marriage, which were often costlier rings set with various gems. Nevertheless, at both occasions, the roles of objects as obligations and women as passive recipients are suggested by the careful records kept by the participating men. Tommaso Guidetti made a list of what his wife Lisa received at childbirth while he was out of the country, intending to repay his obligations when the opportunity arose.[74] And when Dianora Rucellai gave birth five years later, Guidetti's careful records allowed him to send her the same twelve silver forks she had earlier sent to his wife.[75] In fact, this was common practice; the same or a similar item was often given back when the occasion demanded.[76]

Such an exchange of gifts was a primarily male-orchestrated affair that could endure for many years. Women may have received the gifts, but they were determined by lineal, political, and social ties, and they were paid for by men. The masculine derivation of such gifts was explicitly stated by Lorenzo Morelli in 1478, when he wrote, "I gave in the name of [my wife] Vaggia to Marietta her sister, the wife of Lionardo Ridolfi who gave birth to a boy, golden damask for a tunic with dagged sleeves."[77] While he did, ostensibly, make the gift in the name of his wife, by using her familial relationship as an excuse for bestowing the costly fabric he himself accrued an obligation from the powerful Ridolfi family. Women could be the forces behind these exchanges if they had to be; in a letter to her exiled son Filippo in 1450, Alessandra Strozzi described eight lengths of cloth she sent to a new mother.[78] But Alessandra was a widow, acting as the head of the family in the absence of her sons, and her gift of cloth was intended, like many of the things she did, to further the reputation of the Strozzi family.

The fact that Ser Girolamo followed popular custom and spent quite freely on special clothing, linens, and accessories suggests that he was well aware of the politicized nature of childbirth. But it is difficult to visualize how all of his purchases interacted together in the context of Caterina's actual confinement chamber. We can, however, do the next best thing. In a fortuitous incident, the Pupilli officials evaluating the extensive estate of Girolamo di Lionardo di Stoldo Frescobaldi in 1528 arrived immediately after a birth had taken place; one of the rooms in the house was described as "the room where the woman was confined."[79] Although the unidentified woman may have been Girolamo's wife, the room she lay in was not Girolamo's bedroom, which was listed separately. Such a division was practical; since the new mother remained confined for an extended period, and received visitors on a regular basis, her presence in the main bedchamber would have been disruptive to her husband's normal routine. In fact, in his discussion of the architecture of private buildings, Alberti specifically stated that there should be separate quarters for wives and husbands, "to ensure that the husband be not disturbed by his wife, when she is about to give birth or is ill."[80] In addition, religious law forbade sexual relations between husband and wife for a specified time following birth, so her isolation in a separate bed, in a different room, was especially appropriate.[81] Indeed, the room in the Frescobaldi home had few of the items expected in a master bedroom. There was, for example, no large bed. Instead, there was a day bed, or *lettuccio*, further implying that the room was not used as a main bedchamber.

To enter this room, the Pupilli officials passed through a curtain or hanging specifically designated as a childbirth item. The reason for this designation is not obvious; perhaps it had a special image on it. It does, however, seem clear that such a hanging was used to divide the rest of the household from this special room. Once the officials went past the hanging in to the chamber, they inventoried an impressive number of dresses and cloaks, in a variety of colors, fabrics, and styles, as well as a wide variety of swaddling clothes for the baby. Several sets of sheets, pillows, and crib linens were also listed. In fact, the vast majority of items in this room were clothing and linens. Furniture was minimal; the main items were the walnut day bed with its chests, as well as two small wooden chests and one ivory one, and a crib with a protective ribbing. There were several iron candlesticks for light, carpets to warm the floor, and baskets for storage. In addition, there were a number of anomalous objects, such as a rocking-horse, wolf and goat skins, and even ostrich feathers. Although many of the items listed in this room were part of the daily furnishings, and only the hanging is specifically designated *da parto*, the room contained a large number of ostentatious objects – a round tray with heraldic devices, a borrowed cloak, a painted chest with the arms of the Frescobaldi – that were surely there as part of the celebrations related to the event.

The Frescobaldi inventory helps us fill in the missing information in Ser Girolamo's description, especially if it is combined with the visual evidence discussed so far. In the scene depicted on the front of a Florentine birth tray, for example, the room is virtually empty but for a massive bed and its intarsiated chests (figure 34). The viewer focuses primarily on the bed and its occupant, the woman who has just given birth to the swaddled child cared for by two attendants in the foreground. Her linens are sumptuous and plentiful, and her clothing is equally rich. Even the child's swaddling is elegantly striped in red and white. All of these factors create a setting suitable as a reception room for the mother's visitors.

It can be assumed that this birth tray represents a typical confinement room, similar to the ones in which the wives of Ser Girolamo da Colle and Girolamo Frescobaldi rested following their deliveries. But their husbands' expenses did not end with furnishing these rooms, or with feeding their visitors. The day after Giovanni was born, Ser Girolamo took him to be baptized. Baptism was an important religious event, signifying the child's entry into the Church. It was also an important civic event which welcomed the child into the secular community. At the Florence Baptistery, for example, a black or a white bean (for, respectively, a boy or a girl) was dropped into a till to gauge the official birth rate, irrevocably linking the event to civic ideology.[82]

According to most private accounts, the baptism of the newborn usually occurred only a few days after the birth.[83] Occasionally, if the child was in danger, it was baptized immediately by the midwife. Luca da Panzano described the death of his wife in childbirth, and noted the child's baptism in the house during the delivery.[84] There was fear that, if the child died without the sacred rite, its soul was doomed to limbo. However, when a medical emergency did not take precedence, the children were brought to the local baptismal font as soon as the godparents were selected and gathered. Baptism was an important social event, second perhaps only to marriage for the way that it linked families in the tightly woven network of obligation, represented by the practice of naming godparents.[85] Godparents were called *compari*, implying that their social obligation as coparents was stronger than their religious obligation to care for the infant's soul.

In his account of his son's baptism, Ser Girolamo listed the three men, one of whom was a notary like himself, who held the boy at the font. He also listed the cost of a candle to light for the occasion.[86] The use of such a candle was common; when his son Simone was baptized in 1472, Nicolo Strozzi bought a taper.[87] In some cases, coins were placed in the swaddling clothes of the child at baptism. In 1491, when Tommaso Guidetti and three other men baptized a boy, each put four coins in the child's swaddling.[88] Ser Girolamo makes no mention of such a practice, so it was presumably not a requirement.

Baptism was largely a masculine affair, meant to link the father and his lineage in a spiritual and political manner to the chosen godparents. Since it took place so soon following the birth, the mother was left at home during the ceremony, after which

she could be visited in her confinement chamber. In 1534 Girolamo Cardano noted that, following a baptism, the party went to the mother's bedroom, "according to the customs."[89]

A godmother stood in for the mother at the baptismal ceremony. The midwives or attendants at the birth often became godmothers, thus showing their continuing concern for the child's welfare. But these women were only rarely listed in the father's written account of the ceremony. Although the identity of the godfathers was always recorded, the godmother was of considerably less political importance to the implications of the ritual, and she was therefore often left out of the account.[90] So the baptism functioned largely as the antithesis of the confinement room visits; whereas those were private, female-centered rituals, baptism was public and male-centered.

Ser Girolamo does not describe his exact relationship with his son's godparents, but there is evidence of the bonds other men shared with their *conpari*, some of which extended beyond baptismal duties. Antonio Rustichi chose Alessandro Barbiere as a godfather for two of his sons, in 1422 and 1431, and then in 1426 he loaned a primer to Alessandro for three weeks, for the use of Alessandro's son. This indicates that their relationship was not simply formal and that it lasted for some time.[91] Other fathers secured the patronage of a whole roster of assorted patricians, many of whom may have had strong social or political connections. Mano Petrucci's list was exceptionally long; for his son Chanbio's baptism in 1445 Mano arranged for the participation of five counsels of the Silk Guild, the guild's notary, seven men from especially illustrious Florentine families, two priests, seven country dwellers, and three women.[92] Mano was trying to cover every possibility; he made relationships with merchants, politicians, religious figures, and the poor, and he even kept track of the three godmothers, in case they should come in handy some day. Most men kept a record of their godchildren and, with even more detail, the gifts they gave these newborns. Filippo Strozzi's careful accounts reveal that between 1468 and 1477 he stood at the font with six different infants from some of the most important Florentine families.[93] For his own son Alfonso, Filippo named the child's namesake, the Duke of Calabria, as a godfather, although the duke did not attend the baptism. His proxy at the ceremony was Lorenzo di Piero de' Medici; this was an honor in itself, as Filippo and his brothers had been exiled for many years by Lorenzo's grandfather, Cosimo de' Medici.[94]

Seeking spiritual kinships rather than outright political ones, other fathers named one or two poor people as godparents. This practice was not for the sake of establishing a connection with the paupers, but rather in the hope of becoming closer to God, as recommended by the Dominican friar Giovanni Dominici. Dominici condemned ostentatious baptismal rituals and accessories in his treatise *Regola del governo di cura familiare* (c. 1403), stressing instead the importance of the religious reasons behind the event. He advocated avoiding crowds of unpious participants and expensive and showy clothing and accessories in favor of humble trappings and a few devout godparents.[95] Here he echoed canon law, which insisted on no more than three participants.[96] Among the men to follow Dominici's advice was Francesco Giovanni, who asked an Augustinian monk, along with his wife's midwife and *guardadonna*, to be godparents to his son in 1435.[97] But such restraint was rare.

Many household inventories list magnificent layettes for infants to wear at baptism; these would have made a significant impression in the city streets, as the child was carried to the font. There were baptismal mantles made in gold velvet with silver and red braids.[98] There were also special veils embroidered with the name of Jesus in gold, and fine linen swaddling bands ornamented with lilies, a type of decorated swaddling depicted in Pintoricchio's fresco of *The Birth of John the Baptist* (figure 35).[99] These elaborate items attested to the high status of John the Baptist's family while making recognizable links with current practice.

Most contemporaries considered baptism a way to create and cement ties. But the nature of the godparent relationship was complicated. It was so sacred and so intimate that intermarriage between people linked through this rite had been forbidden by the Church since the early Middle Ages.[100] It really functioned as a unifying ceremony, creating relatives where there were none before. This was symbolized by the presentation of gifts from the godparents to the new mother and her child. The relationship could be interpreted as analogous to that of the Magi, who brought extravagant gifts to the Christ Child (figure 36). Scenes of the Adoration of the Magi depict the first presentation of the Christ Child; likewise, baptism was the first time a new child was shown to those outside

35 Bernardino Pintoricchio, *The Birth of John the Baptist*, c. 1506. Fresco. Baptistery, Siena Cathedral. (Alinari/Art Resource, New York)

36 (*facing page top*) Gentile da Fabriano, *Adoration of the Magi*, 1427. This main panel of the Strozzi Altarpiece was painted for the church of Santa Trinita in Florence. The richly dressed Magi present gifts to the Christ Child in much the same manner that godparents gave special items to their godchildren at baptism during the Renaissance. Tempera on panel. Uffizi, Florence. (Alinari/Art Resource, New York)

37 (*facing page bottom*) Giovanni da Milano and the Rinuccini Master, *The Birth of the Virgin*, c. 1365. The large-scale figures crowd the scene and obscure much of the detail. Note, however, that one of the women carries in a covered object, perhaps meant to be a chicken or a cake. Fresco. Santa Croce, Florence. (Alinari/Art Resource, New York)

the home. Like the Magi, the godparents came to pay their respects and to vow their fidelity to the new child and the child's family, bestowing gifts indicative of their beneficence and respect. In terms of Renaissance society, this drew attention to an individual's ability to give such objects, and the inherent worth of the child and its family to receive them. The recipient became obligated to the donor, and the more obligated one felt, the tighter the societal relationships became.

Baptismal gifts could take a certain amount of time to procure and were not necessarily presented at the ceremony itself. It was not until six days after the ceremony, on September 26, that Ser Girolamo noted the receipt of the godparents' gifts to Caterina: a wax candle, two boxes of sweetmeats, and two sets of twenty-six forks in special cases.[101] Ser Girolamo estimated the weight and value of the boxes and metalware for his records. The wax and sweetmeats were ephemeral. They were immediately put to use, to feed Caterina's many visitors. But the forks were useful and long-lasting gifts. As part of his obligation to the godparents, Ser Girolamo gave a special meal to thank the three men for their service to his family.[102] This may have been a common practice; two months after his daughter Lena's birth, Giovanni Buoninsegni recorded the arrangements for a similar festive meal for Lena's five godparents.[103]

The accounts of Ser Girolamo and his contemporaries suggest that godparents' gifts to a new mother were usually quite predictable. In 1391 Francesco Datini was told by a friend what a godfather should present to his godchild's family: a large sweet cake, a sponge cake, one box of white and one box of red sweetmeats, and a bunch of candles.[104]

Datini was apparently confused over this recommendation, since an earlier letter had emphasized the importance of the sponge cake as a gift to a new mother.[105] Ephemera like sweetmeats, candles, and cakes were the items most commonly listed in accounts throughout this period. The fresco of *The Birth of the Virgin* by Giovanni da Milano and the Rinuccini Master in Florence includes an attendant carrying in a snugly covered form which could be one of these cakes (figure 37). As further testimony to this kind of gift, Giovanni Giraldi made a note of his participation in the baptism of an infant in 1449; he and the other three godparents sent wax, a sweet cake, and a sponge cake to the mother, spending a total of 41 *lire*.[106] These gifts were presented either jointly or individually by the godparents; physical proximity may have determined participation in a joint gift. In Caterina's case, the three men seem to have pooled their resources and sent the gifts as a group. This was fairly common practice. Tommaso Guidetti noted that he and five other men were godparents for a boy in 1489; thirteen days after the baptism they sent a silver spoon holder and a marzipan cake to the new mother as a group.[107] On the other hand, some godparents gave individual gifts, as did four distinguished Florentines to the mother of Cosimo Rucellai, each presenting sweetmeats or lengths of cloth.[108] Like metalware, fabric represented a more permanent gift, and was probably used to make clothing for regular wear. In some cases, the special skills of the godparent resulted in a more personal gift. Vasari described the gift of a drawing, to paint on a birth tray, that the artist Francesco Salviati made for the mother of his godchild.[109] And Guido Reni often gave paintings to the parents of his godchildren.[110]

In some accounts, no gifts were listed at all.[111] Their omission may have been the personal choice of the writer, since it seems that gifts were accepted and expected parts of the ritual. But Lapo de' Sirigatti recorded no gifts from his child's godparents, and noted that these people participated in the ceremony "for the love of God."[112] This seems to imply that they did it out of religious duty. Nevertheless, such pious acts did not always exempt the godparents from the gift-giving obligation. In 1418 Luca da Panzano described his role as godfather for Jacopo di Bonaiuto's son as "for the love of God"; however, four days later he sent a box of sweetmeats and a taper to the new mother.[113] Obviously, the intricacies of baptismal gifts followed their own strict and now often indecipherable etiquette.

Although the baptism was performed soon after the birth, the confinement visits did not end as early. Ser Girolamo continued to buy food and wine until mid-October, occasionally specifying that he did it for the women who came to visit his wife.[114] And there is evidence that Caterina was again having medical difficulties. During this time, the apothecary furnished yellow violet oil, as well as camomile oil, and Ser Girolamo debited Caterina's account for the expenses.[115] Then on October 16, twenty-seven days after Giovanni's birth, Ser Girolamo bought a candle, "for Caterina to enter in Church."[116] This probably referred to a purification ceremony following childbirth and confinement.[117] According to Saint Antonino, the fifteenth-century Archbishop of Florence, the ritual did not have to be observed.[118] Cherubino of Spoleto mentioned purification in his popular treatise on married life, stating that during the days after childbirth and before purification a couple should abstain from sexual relations; in this prescriptive context, he did not describe the nature of the ritual.[119] But the general lack of references to the ceremony in private writings suggests that it was seldom practiced.

Young Giovanni was sent out to a *balia*, or wetnurse, in the Tuscan countryside, a certain Mona Simona. This was the usual practice for those who could afford to do so. Despite the vital importance attached to the birth of an heir, and against the recommendations of contemporary moralists like Dominici, infants were almost always nursed by *balie*. They were generally new mothers themselves, often of a child who had died at birth or who in turn was sent to another, lesser paid woman to be nursed. The practice of wetnursing was also standard at foundling hospitals, where these women played a vital role in the care of abandoned babies.[120] There was a further cost associated with the practice of wetnursing, too; Ser Girolamo paid a woman to help Caterina stop her milk production, since she was not nursing her son.[121]

Once the child was safely ensconced at the wetnurse, and the new mother left her confinement room and fulfilled her sacred obligations, the father's costs lessened considerably. The last expense Ser Girolamo recorded for Giovanni's birth was in late October, when he paid Domenica the *guardadonna* for her five weeks of caretaking. Domenica received only slightly more for these weeks of service than the midwife did for her role in the twenty-two hours of labor and birth.[122] After this payment, Ser Girolamo closed his account of Caterina's expenses. By his own calculations, his total costs for her pregnancy, delivery, and confinement exceeded 280 *lire*.[123] In contemporary exchanges, this was about the annual salary of a master mason, a significant outlay of cash for most people.[124] Since Ser Girolamo was not a member of the wealthiest elite of the city, the money he spent during these months must have been carefully considered and personally justified.

The Birth of Luigi di Ser Girolamo

Ser Girolamo recorded a few further expenses for his first son over the next seven months, which were primarily for Giovanni's wetnurse and clothing. Like many fathers, he assembled a miniature trousseau for the infant, sending him away with several crib linens and articles of clothing, as well as a protective crib covering. He was not as careful in his record of these expenses as he was in recording Caterina's, although it is clear that he spent a considerable amount.[125]

With the newborn in the countryside, household life may have settled into a regular routine. But then in May 1474 Ser Girolamo purchased a flask of white wine and noted that it was "for Caterina. I believe she is pregnant."[126] She did indeed give birth to their second son, Luigi, in January 1475. The popular practice of sending the newborn to a wetnurse eliminated the natural protection against pregnancy nursing women often enjoyed. As a result, many Renaissance women endured several pregnancies with little interval between them. Caterina's eight-month gap was therefore comparatively long.

Following the model of his first son's birth, Ser Girolamo headed a page of his memorandum with the following statement:

> I record here at the foot of the page what I will spend in the second birth of Caterina my wife or for that reason, day by day as it occurs to me.[127]

However, according to Ser Girolamo's accounts, this second birth was not celebrated as generously as the first; after the flask of wine in May, Ser Girolamo bought nothing until November, when he procured eight capons.[128] Following this, he recorded no further costs until a week before Caterina gave birth, when he purchased sweetmeats.[129] No lotions or medications were recorded for this pregnancy, implying that it was a healthier one. Ser Girolamo may not have been as anxious over the whole affair; after all, Caterina had already produced his heir, who was apparently thriving at the wetnurse. Furthermore, Caterina had a great deal of birth objects already, since her clothing, linens, and accessories were all reusable. And finally, Ser Girolamo did not record a wager on this child's sex, perhaps having learned his lesson from the loss he suffered at Giovanni's birth. It was just as well, since Caterina again bore a boy, who had no need for a monetary dowry.

It was thus without much preamble that Ser Girolamo wrote:

> I record how on the 10th of January [1475], at a bit before three in the evening, from Caterina my wife was born to me a beautiful baby boy; thank God both are well. Monna Mathea, who lives in San Lorenzo, delivered him. Caterina had pains for seven hours total, that is from the 20th hour until the 3rd. I gave to the said Monna Mathea eight *lire* for her work. I record how on the 11th at the 21st hour and a half, I baptized my son and gave the names Luigi and Taddeo to the son of Caterina and I. I pray God that He give him life and death always in His sanctity. Amen.[130]

Ser Girolamo called on the same midwife, Monna Mathea, for his wife's second birth. As it was considerably quicker than the first, she received only about half her previous pay.[131] His expenses following the birth included wines, chickens, sweetmeats, and eggs, probably for visitors. Luigi was baptized the day following his birth and Ser Girolamo bought a taper for the ceremony; this time, he listed no gifts from the child's godparents. But there may have been none, since he noted that they carried out their duty "for the love of God."[132] The *guardadonna*, now a certain Theodora, stayed with Caterina for eighteen days, instead of the previous five weeks; like the midwife, she too received about half the previous salary.[133] The changes in wages from the first birth to the second indicate that Ser Girolamo and the attendant women had some sort of understanding about payment based on the time involved.

For Luigi's birth, Ser Girolamo spent a total of 28 *lire*, not a tremendously large amount, and less than a tenth of what he spent when Giovanni was born.[134] Nevertheless, Ser Girolamo's combined cost for the two births was substantial. As a member of the growing professional class, Ser Girolamo had a significant amount of disposable income to spend on a variety of household objects, some of them perhaps as tangible rewards for Caterina. Yet other than the medicines, few of them were absolutely needed for her welfare or that of the babies. These were excessive purchases, indicating both the importance of childbirth during the Renaissance and the density of the material culture that surrounded it.

The Impact of Legislation Governing Childbirth

As the example of Ser Girolamo and his wife Caterina shows, the custom of purchasing both permanent and ephemeral childbirth objects involved great expense. This is equally clear from contemporary images (figure 38). Most men considered it a necessary expense

38 Bartolomeo di Giovanni, *Scenes from the Life of John the Baptist*, 1490–95. The sumptuous and undoubtedly costly green covering on Saint Elizabeth's large bed provides the focal point for her otherwise starkly furnished room. But it is slowly being filled with necessary items: her attendants bring in various accessories and food to accompany the box of sweetmeats and glass pitcher already resting on her headboard. Tempera on panel. Mr. and Mrs. Martin A. Ryerson Collection, Art Institute of Chicago.

to enhance their reputation, doubtless one of the reasons Ser Girolamo spent such a large sum on childbirth objects. He was, of course, pleased to be a father – especially of two sons – and he wanted to provide for his wife. But he profited both socially and politically from being able to purchase and display childbirth objects.[135]

The expense of these items did, of course, create problems in the essentially parsimonious Renaissance city. As discussed in the introduction, San Bernardino condemned luxury goods as representations of worldliness and vanity, and he censured them from a moral standpoint. But he was not the only one to do so. In fact, childbirth and its attendant objects were frequently specified in the constantly recodified sumptuary laws of the period. These laws were largely intended to control the expenses generated by the female population during such rituals as marriage and childbirth. As such they reveal many details about changing ideals. The city of Florence alone witnessed five complete redactions of these statutes before 1600, as well as many less complete variations between major recodifications.[136]

Most citizens were aware of these laws, whether or not they chose to obey them. For example, in 1384 Paolo Sassetti observed that his niece Lena returned to her parental home after her wedding ceremony in the company of a mere two women, since, as Paolo wrote, "by an order newly made by the Commune, no men can accompany her."[137] Concern for the husband was a prominent reason for this legislation, for if the costs of marriage and the subsequent decoration of a wife became excessively expensive – it was argued – men would not marry or, if they did, financial ruin would follow.[138] This then becomes a paradoxical situation. In this family-oriented society, extravagance and the shirking of maternal duties were often connected. But the maternal role was elaborately celebrated at the same time. It is for these reasons that sumptuary laws are important to this examination. In 1433 the Florentine Signoria insisted that sumptuary laws were necessary to control what it described as "the barbarous and irrepressible bestiality of women."[139] In a particularly inflammatory passage, officials observed that:

> [W]omen were made to replenish this free city and to observe chastity in marriage; they were not made to spend money on silver, gold, clothing, and gems. For did not God

39 Workshop of Apollonio di Giovanni, front of a wooden childbirth tray with *The Triumph of Chastity*, c. 1450–60. Like marriage chests, birth trays were often painted with admonitory messages. In the context of childbirth, the iconography of this tray must have been intended as a warning to the pregnant woman to remain chaste in her marriage and ensure the paternity of her children. The reverse of this tray is illustrated in figure 122. North Carolina Museum of Art, Raleigh, Gift of the Samuel H. Kress Foundation.

Himself, the master of nature, say this: 'Increase and multiply and replenish the earth and conquer it.'[140]

The link of chastity and fertility to the enforcement of sumptuary laws is especially relevant. Chastity in marriage was especially critical, since it guaranteed that an heir was, indeed, an heir (figure 39). By controlling expensive feminine display, and relegating women to the role of childbearing, the governing men hoped these laws would help decrease expenses and increase the population. As a result of the social and demographic concerns of the period, an ideology evolved to focus on the family as beneficial to the city; there must be a large population to fight its wars, rent its homes and shops, maintain its low wages, and pay its taxes. But it is clear that an individual man's fear of appearing less affluent than he was, or than he aspired to be, was also a consideration. Despite legal proscriptions, it was important to keep up appearances. This then mitigated the harshly worded precepts of the sumptuary laws, and allowed for, among other things, the extravagant array of marriage and childbirth objects discussed above.[141]

As with all sumptuary restrictions, the ways around the laws regarding childbirth objects were numerous, and the vast number of unspecified luxuries were more than sufficient to create an appropriate setting.[142] There were constant additions to the regulations throughout the period, presumably coming into law when each individual type of transgression approached epidemic proportions. Although some of the fabrics and accessories that made up childbirth objects were restricted by general sumptuary legislation, the city of Florence did not specifically outlaw any childbirth and confinement accessories until the late sixteenth century. There were, however, statutes regarding extravagance at baptism by the early fourteenth century.[143] In 1373 a system by which a tax could be paid to exceed the legal gift expenditure of a florin was instituted; if a godparent or parent paid 20 gold florins, the law could be flouted and any gift could be given.[144] This sum was a significant amount to charge, probably making a legal transgression of the law rare. Clandestine transgressions, on the other hand, were no doubt quite common. In 1388 the law was rewritten, forbidding baptismal gifts of a value exceeding 3 gold florins without the payment of the tax; even the apothecary who sold the extravagant gift could be fined if it cost more. Furthermore, the law stated that there could be no more than three godparents, reinforcing the stipulations of canon law.[145] These laws had so little effect that they were restated in 1402 and 1415.[146] In 1473 the law limited gifts from godparents to two boxes of sweetmeats weighing no more than 12 pounds, 10 pounds of wax, and one white taper weighing less than 6 pounds. Only one florin could be placed in the swaddling clothes. Other gifts could be made only if the total cost did not exceed 2 large florins for each of the godparents.[147] Interestingly, Ser Girolamo's *conpari* were well within the law when they presented Caterina with her gifts, the value and weight of which were in accordance with contemporary legislation. In the sixteenth century, with the advent of ducal society, regulations began to get even more specific. In 1546 Florentine laws dictated that the clothing worn by a child at baptism could not exceed 6 *scudi* in value, and jewelry could not be enameled.[148] Further laws restricting clothing were passed in 1562, forbidding certain linings for cloaks as well as gold and silver ornaments.[149]

These laws seem to have been ineffectual. Many items that could be construed as ostentatious or indicative of sinful expenditures appeared in contemporary inventories. But Florence was not alone in trying to legislate childbirth. The cost generated at confinement and baptism was an issue that occupied many cities throughout the Italian peninsula, and several focused on childbirth and baptism as events in particular need of cost control. Lucca enacted a set of laws regarding baptismal excess in 1362, delineating the godparents' gifts, the accessories of baptisms and confinements, the allowable expenses, and the food permitted at the feast following baptisms.[150] In 1489 the city expanded the laws to specify what type of fabrics and decorations could go on the walls and the bed of the confinement chamber.[151] In Venice in 1542 visitors outside the immediate family were forbidden, as was the use of silk sheets woven with silver and gold threads on the new mother's bed. Midwives had to report the name and address of the new father so that officials could visit the home and ensure that all laws were observed.[152] In 1574 children going to baptism were forbidden from wearing strands of pearls.[153] The Mantuan laws of 1551 banned certain decorations for the rooms, beds, mother, and child.[154] In 1563 the city of Pisa enacted an extensive series of laws that limited a wide range of social activities. This was the most extensive legislation yet; it outlawed the use of gold and silver fabric, as well as jewels and silk, in the room of the new mother, specifying exactly which type of fabric and expenses were legal. Children going to baptism could not wear clothing valued over 12 *scudi*, and could wear only certain types of cloth. And godparents could give only a limited number of coins in the swaddling.[155] Finally, in 1574 Faenza outlawed the use of certain sheets, spreads, and clothes during the visits to the new mother.[156]

The regulations for these cities covered an enormous range of birth-related details directly affecting the appearance of the confinement room. But Florentine law was different. In the late sixteenth century there was increased legal emphasis on the more public and ostensibly sacred ritual of baptism, rather than on the private and domestic ritual of confinement. This may indicate a greater concern with the community as a whole, since baptism had become such an expensive and ostentatious event. The baptism of Filippo de' Medici in 1577, the first and only son of Grand Duke Francesco I de' Medici and his wife Giovanna, was a particularly magnificent example.[157] The need to control such elaborate ceremonies among the general population is therefore important; the court could celebrate with such pomp, but all other citizens needed to be kept in their proper place. On the other hand, what happened in the home, during confinement, was less visibly disruptive to the community and the social order. Of course, the cost of entertaining and providing food for a new mother's many visitors could be quite high, as Ser Girolamo's account book shows. But because these expenses occurred in the domestic realm, and did not pretend to have a sacred or civic purpose, they were less visible and therefore tolerable. Although the importance and worth of a family were clear from the extent of the celebrations, confinement was still, basically, a woman's ritual. To outlaw it may have created more social problems than allowing it to continue.

Ser Girolamo da Colle's great expenditures on childbirth objects for his wife's two pregnancies, births, and confinements were generous, even extravagant, but probably not too unusual. The objects that he purchased granted him respect among other men of the same or higher social standing, all of whom outfitted their wives and their homes in a similar way. The material culture of Renaissance childbirth was dense and rich, and it was made up of a great number of things. The objects examined so far, however, were largely ephemeral. There is no surviving, substantial, material evidence for them. However, Ser Girolamo's account book lacks mention of two more permanent types of object associated with the childbirth ritual – wooden birth trays and bowls and maiolica wares – and these are examined in the next two chapters.

3   Wooden Trays and Bowls for Childbirth

Paolo Uccello's fresco of *The Birth of the Virgin* illustrates a fashionable contemporary interior, full of well-dressed women, carefully accessorized furnishings, and choice edibles (figure 40). The bedchamber of Saint Anne is shown as a warm and comfortable place. It is enclosed with fur pelts and deep coffered ceilings, and it is equipped with large and heavy wooden furnishings. Many of the objects included in this fresco, like those described in the previous chapter, are known only through images, inventories, and account books. This chapter, however, examines a major genre of childbirth art that *does* survive in significant numbers today: the wooden birth tray or bowl. In the background of this fresco one of the attendants standing at Saint Anne's bed is carrying such a tray.

It is usually assumed that there was only one type of wooden childbirth tray, or *desco da parto*, in Renaissance Italy. The modern use of this term to encompass all birth trays, however, is problematic. Surviving examples and documentary evidence indicate that these objects were of four distinct types, of which the first, and the best known, is the painted tray. It appeared around 1370, in the first generation after the Black Death, and continued to be made until the third quarter of the sixteenth century. As the most popular type of wooden birth tray, it is cited in many documents and survives in the greatest numbers. The second type is the inlaid tray, appearing in the late fifteenth century and continuing through the first quarter of the sixteenth century. The third, the simple wooden tray, became popular after the first quarter of the sixteenth century and is mentioned as late as early seventeenth-century inventories. The fourth was more of a low bowl than a flat tray, a hybrid form bridging the gap between wooden trays and maiolica wares (the latter are discussed in the next chapter). These low bowls first appeared in the late fifteenth century and were continually cited in inventories until the late sixteenth century.

Although statistical evidence is not conclusive, largely due to the somewhat haphazard methods employed by the Pupilli officials, inventories assessed by Diane Cole Ahl suggest that nearly half of late fourteenth- and fifteenth-century households had at least one wooden birth tray.[1] Although their popularity lessened in the sixteenth century, they nevertheless persisted even then in significant numbers, as evidence from documents and surviving objects reveals.[2] In fact, wooden trays and bowls were part of birth celebrations at most levels of society for more than two centuries. Fundamental evidence for the popularity of this tradition is the group of approximately eighty wooden trays and low bowls dating from the 1370s to the 1570s that can be identified in public and private collections today.[3]

The most basic role of the wooden birth tray or bowl during the Renaissance was utilitarian; it was used to carry food and gifts into the confinement chamber and to hold items at the new mother's bedside. In his life of Francesco Salviati, Vasari described a drawing by Salviati, which would have been used as a preliminary model "to paint on one of those round panels on which one carries food to confined women."[4] Vasari's emphasis on the inherently functional role of these objects is confirmed in inventories, where they are occasionally specified as items for confined women to use in bed.[5] The estate of

40   Paolo Uccello, *The Birth of the Virgin*, c. 1436. The careful depiction of realistic detail includes an attendant bearing a covered wooden birth tray to the mother in her bed. Fresco. Prato Cathedral. (Scala/Art Resource, New York)

41 Sienese, front of a wooden childbirth tray with a confinement room scene, c. 1520. The back wall of the chamber has both a convex mirror and a painting of the Nativity. Private collection.

Giovanbattista Strozzi included such an object, described as a tray from which confined women ate.[6] And they often appeared in painted scenes of confinement. In Uccello's fresco, for example, the attendant carries a tray bearing two wine carafes to the new mother's bedside. Several surviving trays also include self-referential allusions to their role during childbirth. The example by Bartolomeo di Fruosino depicts a mother sitting up in bed to receive guests with a draped tray on the coverlet beside her (figure 1). Another example shows an eight-sided tray placed on a bedside chest, keeping a bowl and a goblet within the new mother's reach (figure 41).

The emphasis on the utilitarian role of wooden childbirth objects is clear in these images. Their special cloth covers, however, served not only to protect their surfaces but also to reinforce the importance of the objects in the ritualized events of childbirth. They were therefore not entirely utilitarian. The tray in Uccello's fresco is covered with a gleaming white cloth, with the details of its embroidery visible (figure 40). Documents further confirm the existence of such cloths. In 1501 the estate of Bartolomeo Cennini included three small linen covers for a birth tray.[7] The clerk who made the inventory of Lorenzo Vanni's estate in 1429 even took care to note one birth tray without a cover, implying that these covers were expected accessories for the trays.[8] As Uccello's fresco implies, covers were used for protection and for decoration when the tray was in use. But there were also special covers for storage purposes. In 1424 Lodovicho Schiatesi stored a birth tray in its own small bag, while in 1430 Niccolo Peri kept one wrapped in a special cloth.[9] Such accessories for birth trays, which were, in effect, accessories themselves, further indicate the high esteem in which they were held by their owners.

According to inventories, wooden birth objects were occasionally kept in the *antecamera*, the chamber adjoining the *camera*, or bedroom. But most were listed in the *camera* itself. As the most important room of the house, and the one in which large gatherings would be held, the *camera* generally contained the family's most valuable possessions and works of art.[10] Wooden birth trays and bowls were usually listed in the inventories together with paintings or sculptures that hung on the wall or rested in small niches. As John Kent Lydecker has pointed out, the format of the majority of Pupilli inventories suggests that the clerk simply listed all household items in the order in which he saw them as he looked around the walls of the room.[11]

This would imply that, after their initial use in the childbirth ritual, birth trays were hung on the wall; indeed, physical evidence on some of them indicates that they were designed to hang on walls from the start. The backs were often painted with less attention to detail than the fronts, evidence that they had a less visible role in the household. Their often ruinous condition might be a result of several lifetimes of rest and display with the reverse side rubbing against a surface. Some still have their hanging devices; one, painted by the artist Giovanni di Ser Giovanni, has a nail surmounted by a ring driven into its molding on the top of one side (figure 42). Technical examination indicates that this device was inserted before the linen ground was laid on the panel, making the hanger an integral part of the tray.[12] This indicates that the tray was constructed and planned from the outset to have one side facing a wall during display. The more elaborate figural scene, in this case *The Judgement of Solomon*, was then painted on the other side, making it most visible to the viewer (figure 43). Since so few original moldings survive, the frequency of these hooks is difficult to determine. But it does seem logical that birth trays would hang on the walls for a time following their initial use, and that the most complexly painted side would be visible.

As with most types of Italian domestic art, the historiography of wooden birth trays and bowls is relatively limited.[13] The late nineteenth- and early twentieth-century interest in Renaissance decorative arts, stimulated by the renovation of the ancient city center of Florence, resulted in numerous auctions, several articles, and a few books, all of which included wooden birth objects within the larger category of painted furnishings.[14] There are still relatively few studies devoted solely to childbirth trays and bowls.[15] Despite their evident popularity, contemporary literary and visual references to them are comparatively scarce, as was the case with *tondi*, the round, painted, or sculpted devotional panels objects that were also popular at the time.[16] In contrast to some of the items described in the previous chapter, wooden childbirth trays and bowls generated no regulatory laws. Yet

42 Giovanni di Ser Giovanni, back of a wooden childbirth tray with an allegorical figure of Hope, c. 1468. The naked boys surrounding Hope hold heraldic shields to represent Simone di Filippo Lippi-Neri and Ghostanza Buoninsegni, who married in 1467. They were undoubtedly the parents of the child whose birth occasioned this tray. © 1999 Virginia Museum of Fine Arts, Richmond. Museum purchase, The Mrs. Alfred I. du Pont Fund, The General Endowment Fund, and The Art Lovers' Society Fund. (Photo Katherine Wetzel)

they were still important enough to be a part of birth celebrations at most levels of Renaissance society for more than two centuries.

Most of the surviving wooden birth trays and bowls can be attributed to Tuscan artists or associated via heraldry with families from this area. The earliest inventory kept by the Pupilli dates from 1382, and no known example can be significantly earlier than that, although some utilitarian trays, which either do not survive or cannot be identified today, may have been used before this date. Some of this evidence is, however, problematic. Many of the surviving objects have been overpainted, abraded, thinned, cradled, and reframed. And the documentary evidence is incomplete and predominantly patrician in origin. Dating is also perplexing. In many cases, inventories included objects that were kept in the home for a considerable time after their initial usage. These inventories often indicate an awareness of age, suggesting that at some point particular styles fell out of favor. As early as 1403 the estate of Luca Carnasecchi contained what was described as "an old birth tray," indicating an awareness of the stylistic changes that had occurred since this particular tray was produced.[17] When painted trays were described after the beginning of the sixteenth century, by which time fewer of them were being made, such awareness was even greater, and the descriptions were frequently modified. In 1426, for example, Salvestro di Francesco's estate even included a birth tray that was described as *tristo*, or

43 Giovanni di Ser Giovanni, front of the wooden childbirth tray illustrated in figure 42, with *The Judgement of Solomon*.

"sad."[18] In 1533 the estate of Domenico degli Aglie included a tray described as round, painted, and *cattivo*, or "nasty," implying that it was in very bad condition.[19] Terms such as these referred both to the condition and, implicitly, to the age and style of these objects compared with other items in the home. But even birth objects in relatively poor shape were important enough to retain, often for a very long time, and valuable enough to include in an estate inventory. In fact, in the late seventeenth century, Filippo Baldinucci specifically noted that one could still find examples of Renaissance birth trays in contemporary homes.[20]

It is clear that wooden birth objects remained in the home for a long time. Some were included in the list of a newly married couple's domestic furnishings. In 1493 Tommaso and Bartolommea Minerbetti gave their son Andrea and his new wife Maria a number of items to set up their home, including a round painted birth tray with a gold molding.[21] As Maria was not pregnant at this time, the tray was probably handed down to her to make her reflect upon her maternal duties. Many families had more than one birth tray or bowl. For example, in 1469 Piero Cioni's estate included two small painted birth trays, one described as old and the other as new.[22] Such instances negate the traditional assumption that a birth tray was offered only at the birth of the first born.[23] Other families kept them in their homes for decades; years after a child was born, they were still a significant part of the household furnishings. Giulio Gianfigliazzi had a small walnut childbirth tray in his bedroom at his death in 1602, although his youngest child, Lucretia, was already five years old.[24] A few early trays have game boards on the back, a feature which amused the confined woman and rendered the panels useful for years to come (figure 45).[25] These were, above all, necessary items. Even childless couples, like Francesco and Margarita Datini in Prato, had wooden birth trays or bowls.[26]

Personal sentiment and rarity, as well as inherent value and continued usefulness, must have contributed toward the Renaissance practice of preserving household furnishings through several generations.[27] As the confinement ritual grew more elaborate in connection with the increased emphasis on the family in Renaissance society, the wooden birth object was subject to expanded and changing decoration. It became a prestige item, less expensive and less visible but nevertheless similar to a marriage chest in terms of the status it conferred on the owner. All these factors must be kept in mind throughout the following discussion of the four different types of wooden childbirth trays and bowls.

Deschi da parto dipinto

The earliest-known documentary reference to one of the painted wooden trays usually referred to by modern scholars as *deschi da parto* was in the estate inventory of Bartolomeo di Ser Spinelli in 1382.[28] Although limited in description to the fact that it was round, wooden, and painted, this tray belongs to the first type under consideration here. By the early fifteenth century painted birth trays had become very popular and they appeared in a significant percentage of household inventories. The dating of surviving trays is largely based on style, since only one is explicitly dated; it is inscribed "25 April 1428," probably the date of birth of the celebrated child (figure 1). Other trays can be dated by their heraldry; Ellen Callmann has dated a tray from the workshop of Benvenuto di Giovanni and Girolamo di Benvenuto to around 1497, since it bears the coat of arms of Bartolomea Piccolomini and Cristofano Marsili of Siena, who wed in that year (figure 44).[29] It is assumed that they were given the birth tray on or shortly after their marriage, in preparation for future children.

Slightly over half of the known painted birth trays are intact. The others have been thinned or cradled, with several remaining only as front panels and even fewer only as reverse panels. Most measure between 50 and 60 centimeters in diameter.[30] Although contemporary inventories do not provide exact measurements, the existence of some sort of standard is implied by the vocabulary used to describe the trays in documents.[31] The relatively small size of the panels probably made it easy to construct them from a combination of wood remnants in the workshop. An X-ray examination of one early fifteenth-century tray indicates that it was made from two pieces of wood, one much smaller than the other. The join goes from the bottom left corner diagonally up to the right. This neat, dowelless join was covered by four strips of a light, open weave cloth and would have been braced by the original

46 (*above right*) Florentine, front of a wooden childbirth tray depicting a garden of love, c. 1370. Like much sacred art from this period, this tray uses a rich gold ground and complicated punchwork to accentuate the figural scene. The reverse of this tray (including the frame) is shown in figure 45. Musée de la Chartreuse, Douai.

molding.[32] It is probably safe to assume that other trays were constructed in this manner, an economical practice that could be confirmed by further technical examination.

These trays were also easy to produce because their shapes were standardized. They were called *tondi*, *tavole*, *ottongoli* or *quadri da parto*, according to their shape, in contemporary sources. These qualifying terms were more descriptive than the generic noun *desco*, which indicated only the basic use of the panel, not its actual shape. The earliest surviving trays, dating from around 1370, are twelve- or sixteen-sided (figure 46). But documentary evidence suggests that round trays appeared by the late fourteenth century, since by then inventories described trays as *tondi*.[33] But it remains uncertain whether these trays were actually round or whether the clerk was merely hedging in his description of a polygonal panel, since the earliest surviving round tray dates to around 1430 (figure 47).[34] There must have been considerable freedom with shapes, however, since an inventory made of Arrigo Rondinelli's estate in 1418 included a square birth tray.[35]

No matter what the size or shape, the trays were usually painted with egg tempera on both sides and framed with separate gilt or painted moldings.[36] Although

47 (*right*) Master of the Judgement of Paris, front of a wooden childbirth tray with *The Judgement of Paris*, c. 1430. Bargello, Florence. (Alinari/Art Resource, New York)

65

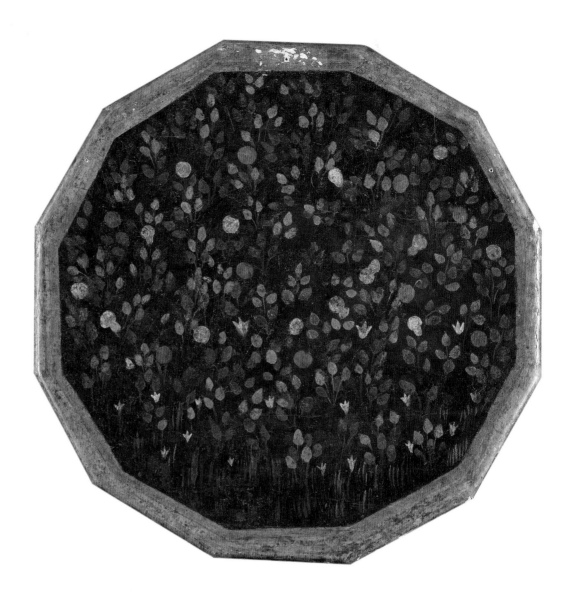

48   Mariotto di Nardo, back of a wooden childbirth tray with a field of flowers, c. 1420. This unique composition relates to tapestry design and may allude to ideas of fertility, which are implicit in the bountiful flowers. Private collection.

relatively few trays still have their original moldings intact, those that do indicate that the moldings were relatively simple strips of gilt wood, attached to one or to both sides of the tray. Evidence of paint overlap on intact moldings, as well as the painted outlines visible on trays that have had their original moldings removed, indicates that childbirth trays were painted with these devices already attached. Although this procedure may have made the panels unwieldy to paint, it was practical, since the carefully executed surface would be damaged if the molding strips were attached later.[37] These moldings helped prevent damage to the painted surface when the tray hung on a wall or rested on a surface.[38] And their raised edges kept small objects from falling off when the trays were carried. The moldings probably sustained considerable stress, resulting in their poor survival rate.

But it is the painted scenes that are the most intriguing aspect of the trays. With very few exceptions, the images on the fronts fall into four general groupings: mythological and classical narratives, contemporary literary themes, confinement scenes, and religious stories.[39] Most of the reverse images, of which far fewer examples survive, also break down into four categories: naked boys, heraldry, game boards, and allegorical figures. There were occasional anomalies, like the reverse of a tray painted with an all-over design of a flowering meadow (figure 48).[40] But this limited range of subjects implies that the iconography of childbirth trays was not gratuitous ornamentation. Each subject must have had a special meaning to contemporaries, hence its recurrence.[41] The same subjects were occasionally depicted on birth trays and marriage chests, a logical overlap given the intimate link between the two events in Renaissance thought.[42] The known intact trays suggest that there was no consistent correlation between the subjects painted on the backs and those on the fronts, resulting in a wide range of possible combinations. The independence of the two sides is not surprising, because the nature of the object did not permit both front and back to be viewed at the same time.[43]

The messages of some of these subjects remain clear. For example, a garden of love alludes to courtly ideals, implying both harmony and fecundity (figure 46). A confinement scene evokes the much sought-after image of a safe birth in a prosperous home (figure 41). But in other cases, the more subtle nuances of meaning may be lost to modern viewers. A tray painted with the story of David and Goliath may allude to a family's wish to associate themselves and their future son with the biblical hero David, whose connection to political power was recognized at that time (figure 50).[44] And it is difficult to reconcile a tray painted with what seems to be scenes from the life of Saint Barnabus to what is known about Renaissance childbirth (figure 49). Yet this tray's shape, size, and reverse image – an allegorical figure – all relate too closely to established examples for it to be anything else.

Two main theories have been suggested to explain the subjects painted on wooden trays, neither of which is completely convincing. The first, offered by Paul Schubring in 1915, involved the division of the genre into birth and marriage trays according to their images: those for birth had confinement scenes, while those for marriage had a variety of subjects ranging from the Judgement of Paris and the Meeting of Solomon and Sheba to the Triumph of Love, the Choice of Hercules, and Diana and Actaeon.[45] Although many scholars continue to assume this, there is absolutely no contemporary evidence that trays were made for marriage during the Renaissance.[46] In my examination of Florentine household inventories from a wide variety of social and economic backgrounds, I never

49   Master of Santa Verdiana, front of a wooden childbirth tray, c. 1370. The scenes have been identified as stories from the life of Saint Barnabus, but the connection between this saint and childbirth has not been determined. Nevertheless, there are no references to the use of painted trays for any occasion other than birth. Pinacoteca, Vatican.

50 Florentine, front of a wooden childbirth tray, c. 1470. This tray depicts a continuous narrative of the story of David and Goliath. As a paradigm of victory over adversity, David was a popular subject in Renaissance Florence and one strongly connected to the ruling parties. Sculptures of David by Donatello and Verrocchio (and, later, Michelangelo) served as political tools in civic propaganda. Painting this subject on a birth tray may have been a way for the parents to associate David's heroic deeds with the futures acts of their unborn child. The Martin D'Arcy Gallery, Loyola University Chicago. (Photo courtesy Christie's, London)

encountered a *desco da nozze* in an estate or a dowry list. Marriage was celebrated with an extensive range of objects, but specific trays were not among them. Even when presented at marriage, as was the Minerbetti tray described earlier, these objects were described as *da parto*, indicating their strong and inseparable identification with childbirth.

A second theory regarding the different subjects divided the iconography according to the child's gender. Writing in 1920, Frank Jewett Mather separated birth trays into male and female subjects: he stipulated that panels with the Justice of Trajan or the Choice of Hercules were presented at the birth of a son, while those with the Judgement of Paris or the Meeting of Solomon and Sheba were given at the birth of a daughter.[47] But, again, there is no contemporary evidence that subject matter was differentiated in this manner. Although the subject painted on the Minerbetti tray is not known, when it was given to them Andrea and Maria had no children; indeed, they were only just married, so there was no way to determine the most appropriate iconography for their future children. This applies equally to inherited or purchased trays. In 1471, a month before his wife delivered, Nicolo Strozzi bought a birth tray from a second-hand dealer.[48] Since he could not know the gender of his future child, he could not have chosen the iconography on that basis. Therefore, it seems that while subject matter was quite important, it depended neither on marriage festivities nor on the gender of the child.

Unfortunately, more specific information about the production and sale of painted childbirth trays is rare. There must have been a considerable demand for them: many artists participated in the profitable domestic art market at this time, making marriage chests, birth trays, and everything in between. Individual trays can be attributed to Masaccio, Giovanni di Ser Giovanni, and Neri di Bicci; a later example, of another type, is attributed to Pontormo.[49] Indeed, Vasari stated that no artist looked upon furniture painting as a shameful activity during the Renaissance.[50]

Nevertheless, few surviving trays can be attributed to specific artists. Many are, of course, in rather poor condition. But the real reason seems to be that most of them were workshop productions, made for sale on the open market. Such a practice provided the workshop with ready-to-sell objects to meet a constant demand. As early as the late fourteenth century, artists displayed ready-made paintings and sculpture in their shops for examination and purchase.[51] For example, in 1383 the wool dealer Benedetto degli Albizzi purchased several panels, including two small birth trays, from the workshop of a deceased painter and then sold them at a profit.[52] The fact that this painter had completed, yet unclaimed, birth trays in his shop when he died indicates that they were executed with no specific buyer in mind. It was apparently common to have them ready for anyone who came to purchase one. In his memorandum Neri di Bicci listed a painted birth tray, made at his own expense, as a stock item.[53] Such practice disproves the assumption that Renaissance art was produced only on commission, for a patron, for a specific reason.

Given the constant demand, the great number of objects that once existed, and the compositional similarities between surviving trays, it is clear that most of them were workshop productions, executed in multiples according to drawn or printed patterns in loose sheets or modelbooks.[54] The availability of these patterns would have facilitated the reuse of specific motifs within the workshop. The iconographic range for birth trays was relatively limited, and almost all known trays can fit into the specific categories outlined earlier. This certainly made their production even easier. Similar serial production is evident in the marriage chest panels and devotional images from Apollonio di Giovanni's and Marco del Buono's popular shop, which made domestic furnishings of all types in the fifteenth century.[55] Motifs were taken from various sources and adapted as necessary to each composition. With this piecemeal method, a shop could keep a staff large enough to complete commissions during busy periods, yet still have enough to do in slower times.[56]

Indeed, a relatively small panel like a birth tray was something that a competent artist could paint in spare moments. Designs were also passed between shops, a practice that is especially noticeable in the group of childbirth trays illustrating Petrarch's *Triumph of Love*.[57] These trays all feature some similar elements, even though they originated in different workshops. The two trays illustrated here (figures 51 and 52), both from approximately the same period, share many of the same motifs. The winged figure of Love holds a bow and arrow, and stands on a globe. The cart is centrally placed, with landscapes to either side and walled cities in the background. Both include Samson and Delilah and

Aristotle and Phyllis in the foreground, cupids on the cart, and an array of fashionably dressed men and women conversing with each other on the sides. But in each case the elements are slightly different, indicating a general dependence on similar models but the hand of at least two different artists.

Unfortunately, only two drawings – one surviving and one now lost – can be associated with painted wooden birth trays. The first, an ink and pencil drawing on parchment of *The Birth and Naming of John the Baptist*, is by Lorenzo Monaco (figure 53). It can be linked to the tray by Bartolomeo di Fruosino, discussed above (figure 1).[58] Bartolomeo was an active member of Lorenzo's workshop, and presumably would have had access to Lorenzo's drawings. A comparison of the drawing and the tray reveals a striking compositional similarity in the architecture, background, and the general placement of the figures. This indicates that Bartolomeo knew either this drawing or one of the other works of art based on it. A few simple alterations rendered the originally sacred composition suitable for the secular birth tray. He removed the haloes and transformed the figure of Zacharias on the left into a procession of gift-bearing attendants. The ostentatious male visitors to the holy confinement room became women in the secular chamber, and anecdotal flowerpots, rolls of swaddling cloth, and trays of food were added to enliven the domestic scene. Nevertheless, Bartolomeo's dependence on the drawing is clear.

The second drawing, mentioned in chapter 2 as an example of a godparent's gift, was mentioned by Vasari as the design for a birth tray by Francesco Salviati in the early 1540s. It fits into none of the iconographic categories common to surviving birth trays. Vasari described it in great detail, indicative of his admiration and, perhaps, his first-hand knowledge of the drawing itself; Salviati was his contemporary, and Vasari may well have been familiar with many of his works. In his discussion of this drawing, Vasari observed:

> Having made friends with the Florentine goldsmith Piero di Marcone, and having become the godfather for his child, he made for his friend and Piero's wife, after her delivery, a present of a beautiful drawing, to paint on one of those round panels which

carry food to the women in birth: the design of the life of man was in sections which held beautiful figures with appropriate festoons that matched the age. In the bizarre composition were two long ovals with the sun and moon, and in the middle was Isais [*sic*], the city of Egypt, asking for knowledge in front of Athena's temple. It shows that for newborns one should pray for knowledge and goodness above every other thing. This design Piero kept as dear as if it was, and it was, a beautiful jewel.[59]

Perhaps the drawing was never executed on a panel. If it had been, it is likely that Piero would have treasured the finished project more than the drawing. Yet, judging by Vasari's comments, the drawing must have been quite an elaborate work of art. Unfortunately, no known drawing by Salviati matches this description.[60] It is especially interesting to note that Vasari emphasized the fact that Piero, rather than his unnamed wife, treasured the drawing. This serves as further evidence that birth trays, like most other items associated with women, were considered the possessions of their husbands.

There were surely many more drawings associated with the production of painted wooden birth trays that simply did not survive. Their use guaranteed a standardization in the final product which ensured that customers received what they wanted. The addition of specific coats of arms at the time of purchase was then all it took to personalize these otherwise stock items. Domestic inventories usually mentioned coats of arms if they were present on an object as a distinctive, identifying characteristic.[61] Heraldry is found on the bases of several reliefs of the Virgin and Child, which were produced in stucco and terracotta by Lorenzo Ghiberti's workshop for domestic interiors (figure 54). These devotional reliefs were made from a two-piece mold that permitted substantial variation in the base design and a certain degree of fashionable assimilation among customers.[62] The molds left space to insert painted coats of arms, making each relief particular to only one marital union.

The use of coats of arms was especially important in the case of birth trays, since they proclaim the major reasons behind the birth celebrations: the new child who extended the lineage, with the two coats of arms representing the *parentado* between the two families. As a result, many childbirth trays have small heraldic shields incorporated into the overall composition in an unobtrusive manner. On a tray by Lorenzo di Niccolò's workshop, the relatively small coats of arms float in the sky above the main scene (figure 55). Such inconspicuous locations allowed for the insertion of heraldic devices on an already painted tray with minimal difficulty once the tray was purchased.

53 Lorenzo Monaco, *The Birth and Naming of John the Baptist*, c. 1422–3. Brown ink and brown and rose pencil on parchment. Formerly Otto Manley collection, Scarsdale, New York.

55 (*below*) Workshop of Lorenzo di Niccolò, front of a wooden childbirth tray, c. 1410, with a scene from Boccaccio's *Commedia delle ninfe fiorentine* (c. 1342). The hunter Ameto and two nymphs judge a musical contest between Alcesto (who advocates a life of leisure) and Acaten (who advocates a life of industry). Boccaccio uses this competition as a moralizing anecdote that helps civilize the formerly rustic Ameto. The celebration of industrious life on this tray was a subtle message to the family who owned it. The Metropolitan Museum of Art, New York, Rogers Fund, 1926.

54 (*left*) Workshop of Lorenzo Ghiberti, *Virgin and Child*, c. 1430. A great number of stucco and terracotta reliefs were produced by Ghiberti's workshop to satisfy the growing market for domestic art during the fifteenth century. The inclusion of heraldry on the base personalized the relief for its purchaser. Polychromed and gilt terracotta. The Art Museum, Princeton University. Bequest of Dan Fellows Platt, Class of 1895.

56 (*above right*) The back of this wooden childbirth tray is dated by its coats of arms to c. 1537, almost eighty years after its front (figure 51). Victoria and Albert Museum, London.

Of course, not everyone purchased birth trays from stock supplies. Some buyers resorted to second-hand dealers: as noted above, Nicolo Strozzi went to a second-hand dealer to buy a birth tray, a nightshirt, and a baby's cloak when his wife was eight months pregnant.[63] While the sale of second-hand childbirth objects was evidently quite common, it is likely that some of them required alterations when they changed hands. Several trays have anachronistic coats of arms, which were probably repainted with a transfer of ownership. Buying used goods and repainting them was a cheaper option than purchasing a new object outright. For example, a tray by Apollonio di Giovanni depicts the Triumph of Love on its front, which is dated to around 1460 (figure 51). But the joined arms on the reverse of the tray are a later type, representing the marriage of the Samminiato and the Gianfigliazzi families in 1537, perhaps when this side was repainted (figure 56).[64]

Unfortunately, payment records for the purchase of used birth trays are rare. Pupilli inventories would, on occasion, provide a valuation of the objects in the estate for sale purposes. Yet it is often difficult to determine if the object was sold at that price or simply appraised for accounting records and left with the heirs. Nevertheless, the cheapest tray listed in the Pupilli was valued at a mere 10 *soldi* in 1418,[65] while the costliest was estimated at 3 florins in 1441.[66] Such a wide range of prices, and the constant demand that created them, indicates an active market.

Despite this market, however, the more prominent – and the more wealthy – Renaissance patrons must have commissioned their childbirth trays directly. One such case appears in the workshop ledger of Apollonio di Giovanni and Marco del Buono.[67] This ledger includes a reference to Giovanni di Amerigo Benci's request in 1453 for a round childbirth tray painted with the story of Solomon and Sheba, which cost him 9 florins.[68] This was no great expense for Benci; he was the general manager for the Medici bank from 1440 until his death in 1455, and as a close colleague of the Medici he was a similarly ostentatious patron of the arts.[69] Because this was a special commission, the 9 florins Benci paid was considerably more than he would have had to spend if he had bought the tray ready-made or from a second-hand dealer.

It is within this context that we must consider the Medici-Tornabuoni birth tray, the best preserved and most extravagant painted birth tray to survive (figure 57).[70] There is a significant amount of information about this particular panel, which makes it possible to reconstruct the circumstances surrounding painted childbirth trays with considerable confidence. Although the Medici family were usually exceptions to the general rules of social life in Renaissance Florence, the history of this childbirth tray provides a wealth of pertinent information that can be applied to other cases.

Evidence indicates that this tray was made to celebrate the birth of Lorenzo di Piero de' Medici, who went on to rule the city of Florence from his father's death in 1469 until his own in 1492. The Medici-Tornabuoni tray is attributed to the prolific Florentine artist Giovanni di Ser Giovanni, known as Scheggia. Scheggia was the brother of Masaccio and a skilled artist in his own right, responsible for a number of other birth trays and marriage chest panels.[71] The tray was presented by Piero di Cosimo de' Medici to his wife, Lucrezia di Giovanni Tornabuoni, at Lorenzo's birth in 1449. Lorenzo was the first-born son, and as such his birth must have been lavishly celebrated, with the full range of childbirth objects in favor at that time. Most of these objects were, of course, ephemeral and they have long since disappeared. However, in 1905, Aby Warburg used the inventory of Medici possessions made at Lorenzo's death in 1492 to establish that the childbirth tray listed in Lorenzo's room at that time was in fact this tray.[72] The inventory describes a round *desco da parto* painted with the Triumph of Fame and valued at 10 florins.[73]

Although household inventories regularly described childbirth trays as painted during the late fourteenth and fifteenth centuries, very few references to their specific figural scenes were supplied. Birth trays and marriage chests were so common and usually so standardized that it was probably enough just to state their presence when compiling an inventory; a contemporary reader would know immediately what was meant by the simple statement "a childbirth tray."[74] This tendency toward simplicity emphasizes the unusual qualities of the Medici-Tornabuoni tray, the iconography of which was so precisely identified in the Medici inventory of 1492.[75] In the sixteenth century, when it was rarer

57   Giovanni di Ser Giovanni, front of a wooden childbirth tray (the "Medici–Tornabuoni tray") with *The Triumph of Fame*, 1448–9. The
Metropolitan Museum of Art, New York, purchase in memory of Sir John Pope-Hennessy: Rogers Fund; the Annenberg Foundation;
Drue Heinz Foundation; Annette de la Renta; Mr. and Mrs. Frank E. Richardson; and the Vincent Astor Foundation gifts, Wrightsman
and Gwynne Andrews Funds, special funds, and Gift of the Children of Mrs. Harry Payne Whitney, Gift of Mr. and Mrs. Joshua Logan,
and other gifts and bequests, by exchange.

58 Giovanni di Ser Giovanni, reverse of the wooden childbirth tray illustrated in figure 57.

to have painted trays, inventories occasionally described them in more detail.[76] But in over two centuries of proceedings, only three descriptions of the actual images on birth trays were provided in the Pupilli, and these were very vague indeed. One referred to a tray painted with a Cupid in 1540,[77] another to a tray with a hunting scene in 1579,[78] and the third simply to a tray painted with six figures in 1581.[79] The occasional inventory made for other reasons was equally prosaic, providing very little information regarding specific iconography. An exception was the inventory of the household of Alessandro Rinuccini in 1518, which included a round birth tray painted with a Roman history scene.[80] On a few occasions beginning in the late fifteenth century, birth trays were described as painted *all'antica* – signifying classical subject matter – as in the case of the

59 Florentine, detail from
the back of a wooden
childbirth tray, c. 1450–75.
The complex device painted
on the back of this tray
includes a garland, a hand,
and a scrolling ribbon
inscribed with the word
Memini. At the top are two
unidentifiable coats of arms.
Galleria Sabauda, Turin.

round birth tray in the estate of Alessandro Borsi in 1497.[81] It is, obviously, impossible to
identify the subjects painted on the trays from these brief descriptions. Each one revealed
very little about the appearance of a particular tray, although each did recall a known type
in general terms.

Clearly the Medici-Tornabuoni tray was a special case. As the inventory stated, the
front depicts the Triumph of Fame, largely based on Boccaccio's *Amorosa visione* (1342)
and Petrarch's *Trionfi* (1354–74), two vernacular texts popular during the Renaissance.[82]
This is the only known tray with this particular subject; it was often represented in a series
with other triumphs on marriage chest panels, but not on its own as an independent
composition.[83]

The reverse of the Medici-Tornabuoni tray is dominated by Piero de' Medici's prominent personal device, made up of a diamond ring, three feathers, and a scroll inscribed
with the motto *semper* (figure 58).[84] On either side of the device, near the top of the tray,
are two coats of arms. On the left are the eight red *palle*, or balls, of the Medici, and on
the right is the rampant lion of the Tornabuoni. The obvious dynastic message this device
carries on the reverse is continued by the garland of red, green, and white feathers on the
elaborate front frame. Such large-scale devices were occasionally painted on the reverse of
childbirth trays. But it is rare to have such a complicated device which can actually be
identified (figure 59).

Piero di Cosimo de' Medici was not the type of man who purchased his art from the
open market or from second-hand dealers. He was a significant art patron with considerable means to satisfy his desire for expensive and glorifying effects.[85] Francis Ames-Lewis
has characterized Piero's taste around the year 1450 as one focused on delicate surfaces,
rich details, bright color, and specific Medicean symbols.[86] All four characteristics can be
seen quite clearly in the Medici-Tornabuoni tray, which must have been commissioned by
late 1448 to be ready for Lorenzo's birth on New Year's Day, 1449. The finely detailed

composition on the front of the tray is carefully designed according to linear perspective. The colors are brilliant, and gold and silver leaf was applied extensively. The Medici-Tornabuoni tray, which is about 30 centimeters wider than most surviving trays, was constructed in an extravagant fashion, making it much too expensive a venture for a mere stock item. And the large-scale device and coats of arms made a deliberate and ostentatious reference to Medicean pride and lineage.

In fact, Piero's public commissions always incorporated his devices and his family coat of arms. He had a great desire to extol his lineage in this public manner.[87] But, as the Medici-Tornabuoni tray indicates, he also had a great desire to surround himself with objects emphasizing that lineage – and its prominence – in his own domestic space.[88] Few other men would have had the means to construct such self-aggrandizing monuments to their lineage, even if they wanted to do so.

There is considerable further evidence for associating this tray with Lorenzo de' Medici's birth. The fact that the Triumph of Fame is a unique subject among surviving and documented childbirth trays implies that it was used in this case by special request. Clearly the image of Fame was an appropriate subject for a child destined to be the leader of the city of Florence. And Piero de' Medici is also known to have had a particular fondness for triumphal imagery. He commissioned an illuminated manuscript of Petrarch's *Trionfi* from Matteo de' Pasti in 1441.[89] Furthermore, to celebrate his wedding to Lucrezia Tornabuoni in 1448, Piero apparently purchased a pair of marriage chests painted with a series of triumphs by Pesellino.[90] Taken together, these factors point to Piero de' Medici as the patron of the Medici-Tornabuoni childbirth tray. He was certainly able to afford such an unusually large and carefully executed object, with its ostentatious metallic leaf and finely detailed figural scene. His Petrarchan manuscripts and marriage chests prove that he was particularly fond of the subject, and his personal devices decorate both the front and back of the tray.

Whether for sentimental, aesthetic, or even political reasons, it seems clear that Lorenzo valued the birth tray given to his mother on the occasion of his birth. It was hanging in his room when he died at the age of forty-three. This was not unusual; there were other cases of men who had what were presumably their own birth trays in their possession well into adulthood. In 1469 the inventory of a certain Frate Floriano, named the new prior at the hospital of Santa Maria della Scala in Siena, included a birth tray.[91] As a monk Floriano would have had no wife or children, so the tray was likely to have been presented to his mother at his own birth and remained among his treasured possessions until his death. Lorenzo's tray is listed between two paintings, implying that it was hung on a wall between them, with its heraldic side hidden from view.[92] This would explain why the clerk taking the inventory did not describe the elaborate device on the reverse; he simply did not see it.

Lorenzo died in 1492, and the Medici were exiled from the city of Florence in 1494. The following year their remaining possessions were confiscated, and the new Florentine government held a sale of Medici property.[93] Officials kept careful accounts of this sale, which indicate that the Medici-Tornabuoni tray was bought by a certain Ser Bartolomeo di Bambello for slightly more than 3 florins.[94] The price is revealing. Without the original commission document, the amount Piero paid for the tray remains unknown. But the inventory of 1492 does reveal that, over forty years after it was made, it was valued at the not insignificant sum of 10 florins. In the three years since Lorenzo's death, and with the subsequent change in government, the tray had depreciated by more than two thirds. The price Ser Bartolomeo paid in 1495 was in accord with the prices of other used birth trays in the late fifteenth century. Given its elaborate nature, the Medici-Tornabuoni tray was a bargain at this price.

Surviving examples and documentary evidence indicate that the production of painted trays had lessened considerably by the sixteenth century, but the birth tray as a genre of domestic art did not disappear. Painted trays were mentioned in household inventories throughout the sixteenth century, no doubt objects handed down from generation to generation. The Medici-Tornabuoni tray was no exception. When Ser Bartolomeo died in 1543, the tray was specifically consigned to his widow, Lucrezia. Like many widows, she received a variety of household goods, perhaps as a way to allow her to set up a home for her children. The consignment of this tray to Lucrezia kept it separate from the wider group of goods from which Pupilli officials pulled saleable objects to raise money to settle the estate's debts. And perhaps these officials, noting the extravagance of the tray, consigned it to her to protect it for Ser Bartolomeo's heirs. By this date, nearly fifty years after the Medici auction, the tray had lost its immediate identification with the Medici family and was described only perfunctorily, as a round, painted, childbirth tray.[95]

The Medici-Tornabuoni tray remained in Ser Bartolomeo di Bambello's family for at least one more generation. At some point after 1543, probably at Lucrezia's death or at Jacopo's marriage, it was passed on to Ser Bartolomeo's son Jacopo. When Jacopo himself died in 1579, the inventory of his estate revealed that he left a round birth tray painted with a hunting scene.[96] Despite that description, this must be a reference to the Medici-Tornabuoni tray. Since painted childbirth trays were relatively rare in the late sixteenth century, they attracted slightly more attention in inventories, including sporadic references to subject matter. With its extravagance and rarity, the Medici-Tornabuoni tray was therefore worthy of special note in the otherwise routine inventory of Jacopo's estate.

The error made by the Pupilli officials in identifying its iconography is understandable; the figures on the front of the Medici-Tornabuoni tray are on horseback, armored and armed, and dogs occupy the front plane, making it appear like a hunting scene (figure 60).

60   Giovanni di Ser Giovanni, detail of the wooden childbirth tray illustrated in figure 57.

61 (*above left*) Florentine, front of a wooden childbirth tray with *The Judgement of Paris*, 1430s. Location unknown. (Photo courtesy Christie's, London)

62 (*above right*) Sienese, front of a wooden childbirth tray with *The Judgement of Paris*, 1550s. Monte dei Paschi, Chigi-Saracini collection, Siena. (Photo Fabio Lensini)

But the mistake indicates several important facts. First, the officials were unfamiliar with Boccaccio and Petrarch, whose texts were no longer as popular as they had been a century earlier. Triumphal imagery, too, had gone out of favor by this time, and was not immediately recognizable to those who saw it. And finally, Jacopo's family, a member of which would have been present when the inventory of Jacopo's estate was conducted, may not have known either the subject or the origin of the tray. This would not be unusual; after all, more than a century had passed since its production, and over eighty years since Ser Bartolomeo di Bambello had purchased it at the Medici auction. It had become a family heirloom, but its provenance and iconography may have been forgotten. As a result, the tray was singled out by the Pupilli officials as something worthy of more than a cursory description, although its importance evidently escaped them.

As already empasized, the Medici-Tornabuoni birth tray is a special case, and its unique nature rendered it identifiable through several owners.[97] But it can serve as an example of the role childbirth trays took in constructing family identity, and as an example of the difficult nature of documentary references to childbirth art. Less extravagant trays probably had a very similar history, but references have not been found to document this.

Although newly painted trays had become increasingly rare by the time of the Medici auction, earlier examples were continually reused by succeeding generations. And they were produced at least through the first three quarters of the sixteenth century, albeit in declining quantity. These later trays were usually larger, with more elaborate frames and more complex scenes. They were competing now with more extravagant home furnishings in general, and so they needed to appear equally ostentatious, while continuing to represent many of the same subjects. If a Florentine tray of the 1430s depicting the Judgement of Paris (figure 61), is compared with a Sienese artist's treatment of the same subject of around 1550 (figure 62), it is clear that the many years separating them resulted in a completely different conception of the narrative. The earlier tray is anecdotal and charming, the static figures have very specific identifying attributes, Venus' nudity is chastely covered, and the scene is self-contained and balanced. In the later tray, the composition is less developed. The figures are more energetic and vital, the scene is more immediate, and it is framed by an elaborate and decorative molding. Such a change is telling. But this tray is one of the latest known of any type. After this date, no surviving wooden tray or bowl associated with childbirth can be identified. Clearly the dramatic changes did not appeal to everyone.

Deschi da parto con tarsie

Despite the declining popularity of the painted wooden tray, this genre did not disappear entirely. A variant arose as early as the fifteenth century, when a taste for decorative woodwork resulted in furnishings characterized by inlaid wood surfaces. This was called *tarsia*, or *intarsia*, and it involved the inlay of small shapes of wood alongside others of different colors to create an elaborate image.[98] This technique was especially popular in the fourteenth century, when Sienese craftsmen working in Orvieto produced figurative intarsia panels for the choir stalls of the cathedral there.[99] It became increasingly popular in the fifteenth century, as evidenced by the commissioning of the sacristy panels in Florence Cathedral.[100] By 1472, over eighty woodworking shops were operating in Florence.[101] Such a large number of artists indicates a lively market fueled by extensive demand. Intarsia produced a durable surface able to withstand wear better than painted wood, thereby making stronger and more resilient objects.

A number of intarsiated chests and decorative panels are known today. In this context, it is important to recall that the didactic and decorative painted marriage chest was replaced in the late fifteenth century by painted *spalliere* panels, which were set higher on the wall and therefore fulfilled Alberti's perspectival prescriptions with greater accuracy.[102] Instead of painted chests, elaborately carved or inlaid chests were now popular, sometimes telling the same story but in three dimensions.[103] Judging from documentary evidence, a similar evolution must have occurred with birth trays, which were certainly produced in the same workshops as the chests and were therefore subject to the same changing aesthetic demands. Inventories reveal that, from the late fifteenth century through the early sixteenth, painted birth trays were at least partly replaced by inlaid trays. In the case of trays, inlay work must have been purposefully chosen over carving, since an ornately carved surface would render a childbirth tray, whose inherent role was functional, practically useless.

To my knowledge, no inlaid birth trays have been identified in any private or public collections.[104] Documentary evidence alone provides clues for this part of their chronology, the earliest reference being an inlaid tray cited in the estate of Benedetto Ubaldini in 1460.[105] This particular tray must have been quite innovative for its time; other references (and there are few overall in comparison to painted trays) date predominantly to the last two decades of the fifteenth century. Elaborate perspectival and figural scenes, using differently colored pieces of wood to construct images similar to those found on surviving sacristy and *studioli* panels, may have decorated these trays. A tray owned by Salvestro di Zanobi at his death in 1496 was described as "intarsiated in the antique style."[106] In other words, Salvestro di Zanobi's estate had a tray intarsiated with some sort of classically conceived scene. The prestige associated with classical subject matter was no doubt still important enough to warrant inclusion on intarsiated birth trays.

Tavolini da parto d'albero

It seems that by the 1530s the plain wooden birth tray became the norm and remained part of birth celebrations through the early seventeenth century.[107] Inventories mention such trays as being made of cypress, walnut, or sometimes simply wood.[108] A tray specified as a certain type of wood was not likely to have been painted, since this would have concealed the identifying grain of the wood. However, they were occasionally ornamented in some way: in 1570, for example, the estate of Carlo Gaetani had a round walnut birth tray with heraldry.[109] These simpler wooden trays were inherently more practical than their decoratively painted or carefully inlaid predecessors. As such, they may have been used with less caution, and discarded when they became too worn. This may explain why none can be identified today.

At this point it is necessary to make a brief digression regarding vocabulary. The variety of terms used in contemporary sources to designate birth trays of these first three types is sometimes confusing. This is heightened by the fact that so few fully intact birth trays of the first type survive, and none at all of the second and third. The three most common terms used to designate childbirth trays, *desco*, *tondo*, and *tavola*, can be defined in several ways. A *desco* was, technically, a tray or panel of any shape. But it was not always childbirth-related. There were kitchen *deschi*, seating *deschi*, writing *deschi*, and chopping *deschi*.[110] A *tondo* was also a tray or panel, specifically a round one; in some cases, however, this term was also used to designate devotional paintings or sculpture.[111]

But a *tavola da parto* is the most ambiguous term of the three. In the most literal sense, a *tavola da parto* would be a table used during the ritual of childbirth. But this was not always the case; during this period many homes had devotional panels that were described as *tavole*.[112] These surely designated flat panels that hung on walls, since there are no indications that painted devotional panels were ever used as trays or tables. But other objects, described as nonspecific *tavole*, often with detachable trestles or legs, appear in inventories from a very early date. For example, there was a table with two trestles in the home of Piero di Sandro in 1418.[113] The detachable fixtures may have been for mobility,

63 Pietro Cavallini, *The Birth of the Virgin*, c. 1295. The round table by Saint Anne's bed serves as an important resting spot for many of the objects associated with childbirth. Mosaic. Santa Maria in Trastevere, Rome. (Alinari/ Art Resource, New York)

storage, or convenience, allowing variety in a room's furnishings. Some of the *tavole da parto* may also, in fact, be properly translated as table tops, either with or without legs. Tables were certainly used in the childbirth ritual: the practice of bringing gifts to the confinement chamber and placing them on a special table dated back to imperial Byzantine ceremony.[114] Italian awareness and adoption of this practice is documented very early, with images like Pietro Cavallini's mosaic of *The Birth of the Virgin* in Rome (figure 63). Cavallini's familiarity with Byzantine art allowed him to adopt this imperial accessory to enhance the status of Saint Anne.[115] However, the gift table soon lost these regal connotations and appeared in simplified form in many Italian Renaissance confinement scenes, where it became the place to put the new mother's food, utensils, and gifts. In a fresco by Ugolino di Prete Ilario, a low covered table rests precisely on the iron-banded bedside chest, affording the mother easy access to the drinks and food placed on it (figure 64). This image presumably mirrored typical practice; a table would clearly

O BEATA ANNA PEDERIT · ET EXEA ORTA EST · BEATA VIRGO MARIA · MATER DOMINI NOSTRI YESU XPI ·

be a helpful piece of furniture, given the variety of objects we know to have occupied the birthing room. The special cover used on the table in Ugolino's fresco further enhanced the special function of the table, as was the case with birth trays.

Despite the clues about tables provided in images of sacred confinements, it is difficult to ascertain whether a documentary reference to a *tavola da parto* signified a table or a tray, unless the reference included legs. For example, in 1584 the estate of Raffaello di Giovanbatista Santacroci contained "a little walnut childbirth table with its feet."[116] Although the legs belonged specifically to this table they were probably detachable and were therefore listed in this manner. The table may have come apart to be used as a tray when necessary, similar to a modern butler's table.

On the other hand, inventories also described *mensini*, or little tables, for childbirth. These surely included legs as an integral part, even though they are not explicitly listed. The earliest such obvious birth table in the Pupilli was inventoried in 1558.[117] Sometimes, *tavole* and *mensini* were interchangeable objects. In 1562 Giovanbattista Villani had six tablecloths for a birth *mensino* in his estate, including one that was so well worn it merited the adjective "nasty" in its description.[118] Although no *mensino* was listed in this estate, there was a walnut birth *tavola*, which in this case probably had legs to make it a table and allow for the use of those six tablecloths.[119]

Without any known objects on which to base this examination, efforts to determine whether an inventory referred to a panel or to a table must depend entirely on context. As the preceding examples indicate, there is not always a clear distinction between the two.

Tafferie da parto

The final type of wooden birth object is represented by a small group of low, painted wooden bowls, two of which have been erroneously referred to as *deschi da parto*. As early as 1890, however, it was pointed out that their unusual shape distinguished them from the larger group of known wooden childbirth trays.[120] These bowls, which have curved walls approximately 2 centimeters thick, were produced by turning on a lathe. Each is approximately 50 centimeters in diameter, and they are gessoed and painted, like the earlier flat trays and indeed like most contemporary panel paintings. Documents indicate that such bowls were used from the very late fifteenth century through to the beginning of the seventeenth, and the few known examples fall well within this period.

The decline in the popularity of painted, figurative birth trays in this period in favor of intarsiated or plain wooden examples is noted earlier in this chapter. But many trays of the painted type were kept in families and handed down for some time thereafter. These were concurrent, then, with some of the bowls. But instead of birth trays, or *deschi da parto*, these bowls seem to be what was referred to in documents as *tafferie da parto*.

The term *tafferia* and its variations generally referred to a low, wooden bowl. Not every one of these bowls was related to childbirth. Some must have been quite plain, purely utilitarian vessels, used for a variety of purposes. For example, in Francesco de' Guanto's estate in 1551, there were three wooden bowls, but only one of them was singled out as childbirth-related.[121] As a rule, childbirth-related trays and bowls have purely formal characteristics that group them with other functional objects. But childbirth objects also have particular iconography that distinguished them from the rest and linked them to the birth ritual.

The earliest reference to a *tafferia da parto* appeared in an inventory of Piero di Nicholo di Panuzio's estate in 1493, when a painted childbirth bowl with heraldry was recorded in his bedroom.[122] This seems to have been a very early example. The next known documentary reference was not until 1518, when the estate of Antonio Veneri included a painted birth bowl.[123] Such bowls were cited most frequently in the 1530s, which is, conveniently, the period to which the surviving examples can be dated; they continued to appear in inventories until the early seventeenth century, when they were often described more particularly as wooden. This suggests that figurative childbirth bowls were made more commonly of another material by that time, as was the case with the earlier trays.[124] And, in fact, during the mid-sixteenth century, their function was largely superseded by that of ceramic bowls, the subject of the next chapter.

The best-known birth bowls are the two nearly identical examples by Pontormo, the

65 Pontormo, concavity of a wooden *tafferia da parto*, c. 1525. This depicts *The Naming of John the Baptist*. Unlike the secular scenes on wooden trays, it includes a man seated in the same room as the new mother. But this follows the iconography, since the man is Elizabeth's husband Zacharias. According to the Bible, he was struck mute for not believing his wife was pregnant and therefore had to write out his new son's name rather than say it aloud to the assembled family and friends. Private collection. (Photo John Blazejewski)

66 Back of the bowl illustrated in figure 65. It is painted with the conjoined arms of Mariano Ughi and Oretta Antinori. They married in 1523 and had their first child in 1525 and their second in 1526, securely dating the bowl to this period. Private collection. (Photo John Blazejewski)

concavities of which depict the Naming of John the Baptist (figure 65).[125] The only
significant difference between these two bowls is in their reverse images. They each have
a similarly composed but differently charged coat of arms, both in an escutcheon surrounded by grotesque motifs (figure 66).[126] Like the earlier examples painted on wooden
trays, these heraldic devices signified the lineage of the two children whose births
occasioned the bowls. Both the scene in the concavities and the presence of conjoined
coats of arms link these bowls to childbirth. The scene is no longer secular, as in the
earlier examples of confinement scenes on flat trays, but this does not exclude it from the
genre. There is still a high degree of intimacy, largely a result of the close proximity of
the figures to the picture plane and the realistic appearance of the confinement room
group.

Two drawings can be connected with these bowls. The first is a preliminary sketch,
presumably from life, of figures in various poses that were later adapted to the scene in
the bowls.[127] The second shows the entire composition, and, like the bowls, it places
the figures in a crowded grouping anchored horizontally by Saint Elizabeth's bed
and vertically by the seated figure of Zacharias (figure 67).[128] The link between the
drawings and the bowls makes it clear that serial techniques were used to create the latter,
suggesting that they were made as workshop products, as was the case with certain birth
trays.

In an interesting change, all known wooden birth bowls are painted with scenes from
sacred history.[129] One of these bowls is especially complex (figure 68). Its general composition is based on Marcantonio Raimondi's print of *Helen and the Vision of the True Cross*
(Bartsch XXVII:460).[130] But the specific subject of the bowl is unknown. A woman sits by
a window in an elaborately appointed interior, her head in her hand and her eyes closed,
while outside a walled city goes up in flames. At her feet is a set of scales, as well as a dog,
a stork, and a small naked child. The meaning behind this is not clear, though a sacred

iconography can be assumed because of the link to the Raimondi print. The exterior of the bowl is painted with an unidentified device; the specificity of the floral motif hanging within the garland probably signified a particular family or individual, although it has not yet been identified (figure 69). This bears some resemblance to the reverse images painted on some of the earlier birth trays. Clearly these personal devices were important additions to childbirth objects.

Small as this group of bowls is, it does indicate that subjects painted on birth bowls were similar to those on the earlier trays, and that the use of heraldic charges or personal devices on the exteriors was still popular. Documentary evidence reinforces this observation. An inventory of 1576 describes a bowl painted with a star and a bell; this motif may have been a device referring to the owner, Ciano, who kept an inn at the sign of the star in Pisa.[131] A bowl in the estate of Galetto Cei in 1579 was described as depicting the tree of the Cei family.[132] This is slightly more obscure; there is no indication that the Cei family arms involved a tree, although Galetto's personal device may have included such a detail.[133]

Like the flat trays, these bowls were probably used to carry foods and gifts to the new mother, and were placed directly on her bed or on a bedside chest. In the early seventeenth century Giulio Mancini noted that the Sienese artist Sodoma made "low things" like "bowls for birthing women to eat from in bed."[134] His statement is as valuable

regarding birth bowls as Vasari's was earlier regarding birth trays. As a contemporary, Mancini knew the relevant vocabulary. Although no birth bowls by Sodoma seem to survive, several trays are associated with his style, thus implying his proficiency in the genre of wooden birth objects.

As was the case with birth trays, a birth bowl could be put on display after childbirth. Antonio di Nicolaio had a large birth bowl attached to the wall of his bedroom in 1570.[135] Such a display signifies that birth bowls had a lasting and commemorative role in the household, in the same way that the trays did. The importance of these bowls is also confirmed by the use of special coverings, like those described for the earlier birth trays and tables. In 1538 Bartolomeo Baldovinetti's estate included a cloth for a birth bowl.[136] Again like the trays before them, such bowls were painted wood and therefore required a certain amount of care to last through more than one generation.

It is probable that these wooden birth bowls developed in Tuscany as a formal response to the newly popular (and probably imported) maiolica bowls discussed in the next chapter. In fact, there is another wooden object that is situated firmly at the intersection of wooden and ceramic childbirth art. It is a shallow painted wooden platter from the circle of Battista Franco (figure 70).[137] Its edge rises abruptly out of the central medallion and then gently curves back on itself, creating an undulating profile more typical of

70 Circle of Battista Franco, front of a wooden childbirth platter, 1530s. The central scene of *The Birth of Hercules* is carefully labeled for the viewer. All the women react in alarm to the snakes, who twine themselves around the child's arms. Victoria and Albert Museum, London.

ceramics than of wood. A scene of the Birth of Hercules is in the center, complemented by a frieze of his labors that runs all around the curving lip. On the reverse of this platter, there are two bands of blue and gold *grotteschi* around a central symmetrical geometric motif (figure 71).[138] The *grotteschi*, reminiscent of statuary, include the usual foliage, masks, drapery swags, satyrs and terms common to the genre. However, in the outer band, there is an anomalous scene of two satyrs terrorizing three small children by holding them in a drapery swag opposite two naked boys who pull on the foliage that grows out of a term. The inclusion of the children may be following the practice of depicting naked boys on the backs of wooden birth trays (and, as we shall see, on birth maiolica). The iconography of the front and back surfaces linked this plate to the genre of wooden childbirth objects.

71 Back of the platter illustrated in figure 70. It is painted with a complex series of *grotteschi*, similar to designs popular on maiolica at that time. Victoria and Albert Museum, London.

But its physical shape relied on a ceramic vocabulary of forms, and Franco was indeed known as a designer of maiolica wares.[139] This places the platter midway in evolution between flat wooden trays and maiolica vessels, which were gaining in popularity during this time.

As these examples have shown, the production and use of wooden childbirth trays and bowls was a long-standing custom. The popularity of these elaborate and often costly objects further emphasizes the importance of childbirth to the Renaissance family. That so much artistic effort was expended on these items reveals much about their dynastic importance and about the ritual of childbirth. But the use of wooden childbirth objects lessened considerably in the early sixteenth century. Neither inlaid nor plain wooden trays, nor wooden bowls, achieved the popularity that figuratively painted trays did in the fifteenth century. This is probably because of the rise of maiolica birth wares, the subject of the next chapter.

4   *Maiolica Wares for Childbirth*

THE WANING POPULARITY of painted wooden birth trays and bowls in the sixteenth century cannot be explained simply as a growing preference for treated wood surfaces. If that had been the case, there would be a more significant increase in the production of inlaid or wooden trays, following the trend observed in the evolution of marriage chests. But surviving objects and documentary evidence reveal that there was an overall decrease in the production of wooden childbirth objects altogether, whether painted, inlaid, or plain wood. And, in fact, beginning in the second half of the fifteenth century, wooden childbirth objects were complemented with, and in some cases substituted by, painted maiolica wares.[1]

Typical of these wares is a maiolica tray, or *tagliere*, from Casteldurante dated around 1525–30 (figure 72). Its edge is painted with a garland of leaves and small berries. Within the garland, a mother sits up in her curtained bed, cushioned by a thick bolster and covered by many bedclothes. Although the setting is, curiously, outdoors, she is surrounded by the comforts of a well-appointed interior. An attendant in a flowing dress rushes up to hand her a bowl. Two young boys are at the foot of her bed; one warms linens at a grand fireplace, and the other covers the swaddled newborn in the crib. The curtained bed and its accessories, the rocking crib, the bedside table, and its many utensils would all be recognizable to Renaissance women as furnishings typical of most homes. The familiarity of the image was intended to engage, and in this way to reassure.

Well over one hundred similar wares, dating from the early sixteenth century to the early seventeenth, are known in private and public collections today. Maiolica childbirth wares existed both independently and in sets and, like wooden trays, were painted with a limited range of figurative motifs. They can be attributed to some of the most important and productive maiolica workshops of the Renaissance, indicating their skill and aesthetic appeal. Individual wares are associated with the workshops of Maestro Giorgio Andreoli, the Fontana and Patanazzi families, and Baldassare Manara, to name only a few. These wares can be considered the final type of functional domestic art relating specifically to Renaissance childbirth. Like the wooden trays and bowls before them, maiolica childbirth wares were functional objects that rewarded the mother and became a pleasingly decorative remembrance of the occasion. During her confinement following childbirth, these wares served a utilitarian purpose which was occasionally described in contemporary inventories. For example, in 1592 the estate of Agostino Contini in Pesaro included "a little [ceramic] tray for a confined woman to keep on the bed."[2] References of this sort are rare, but they do indicate that maiolica wares continued the practice of functional and decorative birth accessories begun by wooden trays.

As especially distinctive objects, these wares have received a certain amount of rather romanticized attention.[3] They were well known to collectors and to scholars; most of the famous ceramic collections of the nineteenth century and the early twentieth included examples of childbirth wares along with the more usual plates, jars, and bowls.[4] Childbirth maiolica even played a part in the early twentieth-century competition between the Italian cities of Faenza and Forlì for preeminence and civic pride.[5] And these wares were revived

72   Casteldurante, top of a maiolica childbirth *tagliere*, c. 1525–30. The exterior of this tray and its matching *ongaresca* is illustrated in figure 96. Umeleˇckoprůmyslové Muzeum, Prague. (Photo Gabriel Urbánek)

with great ceremony during the Fascist era, when they were used as propaganda for the regime's pro-natalist policies.[6]

Development

The evolution of childbirth wares during the Renaissance is complex. They cannot be divided into convenient categories, like the wooden objects discussed in the previous chapter. Instead, their development depended on both the increased production of tin-glazed earthenware, or maiolica, and the changing taste for wooden trays. Ceramics specifically related to childbirth had begun to appear in Tuscan inventories by the mid-fifteenth century, at the time when painted wooden birth trays were most popular. As a result, these first wares did not compete with the wooden birth trays in number or in appearance; they were very different objects. The earliest-known reference to childbirth wares is a pair of lustered – or maiolica – bowls from Spain in the estate of Simone Pagholi in 1457.[7] Lustered ceramics of all sorts were in great demand in Italy at this time, and the vocabulary used in early inventories to describe birth wares of this material indicates that they were imported. A great variety of Hispano-Moresque wares from the Iberian peninsula and the island of Majorca were documented in Italy as early as the turn of the fifteenth century.[8] Prominent Italian families often commissioned ceramics, embellished with their personal coats of arms, directly from Spanish shops.[9] And even modest homes had a number of imported wares.[10] They must have arrived in Italy in significant numbers to be affordable to such a considerable percentage of the population. Largely as a result of this popularity, variations on the term "maiolica" were used in the fifteenth century to designate only these sorts of imported lusterware.[11] Documents reveal that, along with imported lustered plates, bowls, and basins, a significant number of childbirth wares appeared in Tuscan household inventories during this time.[12]

No actual Spanish wares have been linked to the ritual of childbirth in fifteenth-century Italy, so it is difficult to establish what these imported birth wares looked like. But most of the known ceramics of this period were painted in a decorative manner with an emphasis on organic, ornamental design and the effects of luster. The painting of *The Birth of the Virgin* by the Osservanza Master includes an attendant carrying a bowl painted with typical Hispano-Moresque motifs (figure 73). The design on a contemporary but much larger Hispano-Moresque basin has a similar radiating vine, leaf, and flower pattern (figure 74). But these purely decorative designs would not make a birth bowl distinctive enough to retain its link to childbirth for very long after the birth. So the identification of these wares with childbirth in domestic inventories would have depended on the memory of those closest to the event. Alternatively, of course, there may have been more particular imported lustered birth wares that are yet to be identified. But in either case, inventories reveal that the numbers of lustered birth wares were relatively low at this time. Painted wooden trays were still popular, and these trays easily fulfilled the narrative and didactic roles deemed necessary for birth objects.

This did not remain the case in the sixteenth century. The persistent demand for brilliantly colored imported maiolica, not only for childbirth but also for the many routines of daily life, generated sufficient interest in the process among Italian ceramists. And this led, eventually, to the production of lusterware in several central Italian towns in the late fifteenth century. Because of their similarly rich finish, the Italian wares also came to be identified by the term maiolica.[13] But the moment at which the understanding of this word was broadened to include Italian-made wares is not entirely clear. References to birth maiolica throughout most of the fifteenth century surely described imported wares. By the late fifteenth century, however, the word maiolica also began to designate Italian-

made wares: in 1498, for example, the Macci family of ceramists referred to themselves as "labororeria maiolicata," or makers of lusterwares.[14] Further evidence for this is found in various sixteenth-century texts. In Leandro Alberti's discussion of Deruta in his geographical survey *Descrittione di tutta Italia* (1550), he observed that the wares made in that town appeared gilded; Alberti stated that "These vessels are called vessels of Magiorica [*sic*], because this art was found first on the island of Magiorica and brought here."[15] Alberti's text was widely circulated in sixteenth-century Italy, and it went through several editions.[16] The architect and ceramist Cipriano Piccolpasso also meant Italian-produced luster when he used the term maiolica in his treatise on pottery, *I tre libri dell'arte del vasaio* (1557).[17] And this increased production of Italian luster resulted in a decrease in the number of imports.

It is therefore likely that the numerous citations to maiolica birth wares in inventories beginning around the year 1500 were describing Italian luster. It is from this time, too, that surviving objects identifiable with the birth maiolica listed in inventories may be recognized.[18] A number of lustered bowls produced in the town of Gubbio around 1525 are usually identified as childbirth wares (figure 75). All are hemispheric bowls on low feet, or *ongaresche*, with notched edges to facilitate the placement of covers, although no matching covers are known. Their ornamentation, limited to a simply painted roundel in the

concavity, ranges widely from naked boys to profile heads to mere initials, making their iconographic connection to childbirth tenuous. If, in fact, they are birth wares, these *ongaresche* may represent a transitional phase in the development of birth objects.

At the same time, the *istoriato* technique of maiolica painting developed in Faenza and Urbino and became immediately popular for the rest of the sixteenth century. *Istoriato* wares were painted with complex narrative scenes, often derived from widely circulated contemporary prints.[19] Because of this increased production, by the second half of the sixteenth century the word maiolica designated Italian ceramic wares in general, whether or not they were lustered; in many cases, the word was used to refer to these historiated wares. In fact, the modern definition of maiolica relies more on the use of carefully painted, figurative scenes in a variety of colors, fired to a permanent brilliance in tin-glazed earthenware, than it does on the presence of luster. Maiolica production in general allowed for a detailed, finished, and long-lasting appearance, creating an especially

76 Casteldurante, maiolica dish inscribed *Camilla bella*, c. 1530. The inscription may refer to a specific Renaissance woman named Camilla, or it may be meant as a reference to the ancient Camilla, a female warrior who bravely fought Aeneas in *The Aeneid*. Walters Art Gallery, Baltimore.

elegant ware that could also be quite functional. And the vast number of these historiated wares meant that few inventories specified their presence; as was often the case, the popularity of a particular item led to its relative anonymity in estate accounts. There was no need to describe an object in detail if everyone concerned knew exactly what it was.[20]

Once the technical and aesthetic range of maiolica attained these high levels, the technique intruded on the domestic setting in a variety of ways. One of the more personal maiolica objects was the so-called *bella* plate (figure 76). These plates were produced primarily in the town of Casteldurante between 1520 and 1540, and they are notable for their highly individualized portraits of young women surrounded by decorative ribbons inscribed with the word *bella* and a female name.[21] Often they are referred to as betrothal gifts, although it must be pointed out that no known account book from this period detailed their purchase within the larger range of betrothal expenses. Nevertheless, the particular iconography and the inscriptions on these bowls certainly suggests an origin within the courtship and marriage ritual. A lesser known but equally charming object associated with domestic life was the maiolica spindle whorl (figure 77). Small, colorful beads of this type were often labeled, like the plates, with a woman's name or initials and the word *bella*.[22] In all likelihood, they were used as inexpensive love tokens. Contemporary records reveal the practice of presenting a bride with a small box full of personal items like belts and jewels before the wedding, and beads could fit easily into such a box.[23] In addition to these plates and beads, items as diverse as maiolica inkwells were linked in some manner to the marriage ritual.[24]

So it is at this time, and in the company of various domestic objects, that *istoriato* childbirth wares became popular. And once the figurative possibilities were expanded by *istoriato* maiolica, childbirth wares were able to assume the didactic role taken earlier by painted wooden trays (figure 78). The late fifteenth century through the early sixteenth is thus a

78 (*facing page bottom*) Workshop of Nicola da Urbino, interior of a maiolica childbirth *scodella*, c. 1520. The decorative *bianco sopra bianco* design painted on the exterior and rim of this bowl draws attention to the figural scene in the concavity, where a seated woman prepares to swaddle a newborn in bands warmed by her companion at the fire. Victoria and Albert Museum, London.

77 Maiolica spindle whorls, sixteenth century. This group is painted with individual women's names and the word *bella* or simply the letter "B." British Museum, London.

transitional period, during which several types of wooden and ceramic birth object were available at once. It seems that the growing popularity of bowls for childbirth, first from Spain and then from central Italy, actually encouraged the Tuscan production of the wooden *tafferie da parto*. Although the most elaborate *istoriato* wares were not produced in Tuscany, there was a great deal of contact between that market and the central Italian towns best known for their maiolica production.[25] As discussed in the previous chapter, wooden birth bowls combined the shape of ceramics with the detailed figurative scenes typical of painted wooden trays. Because they were made of wood, *tafferie* could not incorporate all the decorative details of ceramics, and their painted decoration could not achieve the luster of metallic oxides.[26] Their painted surfaces could not withstand any prolonged contact with food, rendering them much less practical, and perhaps less popular, than maiolica wares in general. Overall, few wooden birth bowls survive, and comparatively few were listed in inventories in relation to wooden birth trays or even maiolica.

It was as a composite form, then, that *tafferie da parto* attempted to reconcile the two major genres of childbirth art in the mid-sixteenth century, a combination also evident in the wooden platter from the circle of Battista Franco (figure 70), which synthesized a detailed figural scene with an undulating shape typical of ceramics. It is evident again in a maiolica platter of around 1545 by the so-called Painter of the Coal-Mine Dish (figure 79).[27] This unique plate adopts the size and flat profile more typical of the wooden birth trays examined in chapter 3.[28] However, its iconographic complexity makes it unlike any other known birth object in any medium. The central medallion has an elaborate childbirth scene partially adapted from woodcuts of the Birth of Hercules from various editions of Ovid's *Metamorphoses*.[29] But, even more so than the woodcuts, this platter is crowded with the intimate details of daily life. The actual birth is occurring, and a

79 Painter of the Coal-Mine Dish, front of a maiolica childbirth platter, c. 1545. No satisfactory explanation has been given for the many details of this complex platter. It does seem clear, however, that it relates to childbirth. The inscriptions on the tablets on either side translate, "Without virtue, illustrious valor, and art, the seed of Minerva and Mars is not born" and "He whom you plainly see here is born to be the flower of our age." Victoria and Albert Museum, London.

80 Back of the maiolica platter illustrated in figure 79. Victoria and Albert Museum, London.

crowd of women surround the seated and straining mother, carrying helpful items and comforting her as best as they can. Drawers are left open, to help free up passages and aid the birth in a sympathetic fashion. The innermost frieze around this scene depicts personifications of the planets and Fortune, and the outermost has cupids, a rooster, and personifications of the virtues.[30] Two tablets on each side of the composition extoll the birth of the child the plate was made to celebrate. The reverse is painted with an intricate interlacing motif inside geometric and organic garlands (figure 80).[31] The elaborate narrative scene on this platter, together with its utilitarian shape and durable surface, represents a combination of the best features of wooden and maiolica birth objects.

At this juncture, it is important to emphasize that, as maiolica birth wares became more narrative, wooden birth trays became more decorative, with a greater reliance on intarsia scenes or even plain wood over complex figure painting. Although painted trays were made through the third quarter of the sixteenth century, their numbers had lessened considerably by that time. But the variety of wooden and maiolica objects for childbirth during the late fifteenth century and the early sixteenth shows that there was easy exchange between materials and shapes. Historically this is notable, since it means that, from the late fourteenth century until at least the early seventeenth, there was always a childbirth object with narrative decoration available for those who wanted to acquire one. It is thus probable that the early, decoratively ornamented birth wares, similar to the Hispano-Moresque example depicted in the painting by the Osservanza Master, were discarded in favor of new objects as styles changed. The figurative possibilities of maiolica became more clearly articulated with the advent of *istoriato* maiolica wares. And documents confirm that some women used wooden trays, wooden bowls, and maiolica concurrently during childbirth. For example, in 1471 the estate of Bartolomeo di Piero included a painted wooden birth tray and five ceramic birth bowls, three of which were specified as imported lusterwares, as well as a birth mantle and a birth cloth.[32] His wife was, it seems, particularly well equipped, though it can be assumed that many women were surrounded by a similar variety of objects for the occasion, given the large quantity available at the time.

Terminology

The appropriate name for maiolica childbirth wares is a matter of some debate. With very few exceptions, most contemporary sources used the phrase *da parto* to designate specific maiolica wares as birth-related, consistent with the use of the phrase noted earlier in relation to the wooden birth trays, bowls, and various allied objects.[33] Alternatively, and with some historical accuracy, a number of modern scholars refer to birth wares as *impagliata*, a term that dated back to at least the early sixteenth century. Various linguistic sources have been sought for this word, usually focusing on its proximity to *paglia* (straw). Gaetano Guasti, for example, stated that a parturient rested on a straw mattress.[34] Yet contemporary household inventories rarely included straw mattresses; most are described as full of flax or wool. Straw was probably not nearly so pleasant, and could not have sustained repeated use. In fact, the only example of such a mattress found in a Pupilli inventory was described as "nasty."[35] This may be why so few were cited in household inventories. Alternatively, Francesco Cioci suggested that straw was placed in the wall crevices to stop unhealthy drafts from entering the confinement room.[36] But neither of these explanations is definitive; in fact, *impagliata* may have been used in a more colloquial manner simply to signify the idea of being in bed. It was common enough to be included in John Florio's Italian–English dictionary of 1611, in which the verb *impagliare* was defined as "to lye in child-bed" and the noun *impagliuola* designated "a woman laid in child-bed."[37]

Whatever the derivation, as an adjective identifying the wares in question as childbirth related, *impagliata* was used as a synonym for the more common *da parto* among certain locales in central Italy. The relative scarcity of this word in documents from Florence, for instance, indicates that the term was rarer in Tuscany. It appeared very infrequently in the Florentine Pupilli, with all but one of the references in the same volume.[38] This may suggest that the clerk responsible for that particular volume was from another area and was thus more familiar with the term than a Tuscan clerk would have been.[39]

The earliest reference to maiolica described as *impagliata* seems to be from a Pesaro inventory of 1528, which cited an *impagliata* bowl without a cover.[40] Dating to approximately the same time is a maiolica fragment from a Deruta workshop, which provides critical evidence for the use of the term (figure 81). Once part of an indeterminate larger ware, this fragment is painted with a decorative motif overlaid by the inscription *Anita alinpaliata bella* or, roughly translated, "beautiful pregnant Anita."[41] The original object must have been a birth ware of some sort, personalized for this particular Anita in a manner similar to the *bella* plates discussed earlier.

Notwithstanding its rather circumscribed use during the Renaissance, the popularity of the word *impagliata* among scholars today is largely due to a much-cited passage in Cipriano Piccolpasso's treatise on pottery. Piccolpasso's discussion of what he called *schudelle dal impagliata* implied that childbirth wares were common items by his time. But what, exactly, did he mean by *schudelle dal impagliata*?[42] The word *scodella* (in a variety of spellings) was rather ambiguous, and was not necessarily related to childbirth at all; in fact, the term was used as early as the fourteenth century to identify imported lusterware of unspecified shapes.[43] The ceramist Bartolomeo di Giovanni was identified as a *schodellaio* in Florence in 1423, implying that he specialized in making many types of ceramic ware.[44] And Florio's dictionary defined a *scodella* most generally as "any kind of dish or potanger."[45] In addition to his *schudelle da impagliata*, Piccolpasso used the terms *scudelle da l'orlo*, *schudelle s'utili*, and *schudelle alla foggia*;[46] the distinctions between them must have been as obvious to his audience as they were to Piccolpasso himself.[47] As was the case with wooden trays and wooden bowls, the *scodelle* for childbirth must have had particular characteristics that identified them as birth-related. And these characteristics, at least in the case of the *istoriato* examples, were probably based on iconography.

Piccolpasso described two types of *schudelle dal impagliata*. The first consisted of two separate pieces, a bowl and its lid. Piccolpasso observed, "Among these [wares made on the wheel] are two kinds that are made in two pieces: [the first is] the *schudelle dal impagliata*, on which goes its *coperchio*."[48] Unfortunately, he did not illustrate these two-piece sets, but physical and visual evidence for them exists in certain surviving maiolica wares and the confinement room scenes depicted on them. For example, a *tagliere* from Urbino shows an attendant holding a two-piece set high in the air (figure 82). This representation is especially significant because the painter deliberately altered the original engraved source for this scene, a popular print of *The Birth of Joseph* by Bernard Salomon, substituting this set of vessels for Salomon's flat plate (figure 83). Such self-referential images were as important here as they were with the wooden birth trays; the element of recognizability, and thus personal identification, was critical for these objects, so the artist needed to make the scene believable.

Monumental images followed the same logic. An altarpiece made for a church in Faenza by Giovanni Battista Bertucci the younger includes a two-piece set of birth wares among the many details of Saint Anne's confinement (figure 84). The set is offered to Saint Anne as she reclines in bed, and it seems to be made up of a low rounded bowl with a sloping cover topped by a small finial. A two-piece set by an artist in the Patanazzi workshop, also from the 1580s, has a similar profile, painted with elaborate *grotteschi* designs on a white ground (figure 85). The bowl has smooth walls but the precisely fitted cover has an

81   Deruta, maiolica fragment, sixteenth century. The inscription translates "Beautiful pregnant Anita." Mario Bellucci collection, Perugia.

82 Urbino, top of a maiolica childbirth *tagliere* with a confinement room scene, c. 1570–80. The figural scene is painted in a blue grisaille, which is rare for childbirth maiolica. The outer rim has an odd assortment of musical instruments, shields, and quivers in trophy-like arrangements. For a similar scene on an *ongaresca*, see figure 112. Museum für Kunst und Gewerbe, Hamburg.

83 Bernard Salomon, *The Birth of Joseph*, woodcut from Damiano Maraffi's *Figure del Vecchio Testamento* (Lyon, 1544). (Photo author)

84 Giovanni Battista Bertucci the younger, *The Birth of the Virgin*, 1586. In addition to the covered maiolica bowl, Bertucci includes such now-recognizable details as the plate of poultry, the basin and ewer for washing hands, and the roll of linens to swaddle the newborn. Oil on panel. Pinacoteca Comunale, Faenza.

interior ring that prevents it from sliding off the top; inside the bowl is an image of a seated woman and child (figure 86). An artist like Bertucci, working in a region known for its maiolica production, is likely to have been familiar enough with these objects to know how – and when – to best represent them in paintings.

Piccolpasso followed his brief description of two-piece sets with a more detailed discussion of the second type of *schudella dal impagliata*, the one most often cited by modern scholars. According to Piccolpasso, it consisted of five or nine functional wares stacked one on top of the other to form an elaborate vase-like assemblage:

85 (*above left*) Workshop of the Patanazzi family, maiolica bowl and matching cover, 1580s. An examination of maiolica from this period indicates the extent to which Bertucci's painting (figure 84) was based on fact. Württembergisches Landesmuseum, Stuttgart.

86 (*above right*) Interior of the bowl illustrated in figure 85. The scene depicts a seated woman holding a swaddled child in an interior. Württembergisches Landesmuseum, Stuttgart.

You must know then that the five pieces that make up the *schudella da donna di parto*, all 5 have their function and all 5 are put together to make a vessel. But to be better understood we will look at the drawing. These are all 5 pieces of the *schudella*. The way to make a complete vessel is this: the *taglieri* is turned upside down on the *schudella*, that is the flat piece where the number 2 is, goes turned on the hollow of the *schudella* marked number 1, the hollow of the *ongaresca* goes turned on the feet of the *taglieri*, the *saliera* is put thus on the foot of the *ongaresca*, above which goes its *coperchio*, as can be seen here. See how all together they make one vessel like this, a thing of no small ingenuity. There are others who make them of 9 pieces, keeping always the same order, and these are called *schudelle* of 5 or 9 pieces.[49]

From this description, it can be deduced that the singular noun *scodella* – already defined as a two-piece set – was also the term for a five-piece assemblage, as well as for a single bowl on a high foot. In the five-piece model, a *tagliere* was a tray that was placed on the *scodella* as a lid. The *ongaresca* was a low bowl, which rested, reversed, on the *tagliere*. The *saliera* was a small salt placed on the foot ring of the *ongaresca* and topped by its own *coperchio*. Piccolpasso included carefully labeled drawings of the five-piece *schudella dal impagliata*, with the different wares shown both separately and assembled together (figure 87). In this drawing of the five-piece set, the *scodella*, *tagliere*, and *ongaresca* fit together by means of interlocking rings. The *tagliere*, in fact, rests on this ring on the fictitious ground line in Piccolpasso's sketch.

Most of the surviving childbirth wares from the sixteenth century, as well as most of the documentary references, fall into Piccolpasso's five typological categories. The largest number of known wares are what Piccolpasso described as *scodelle*, or bowls on raised feet. But there are also a significant number of known *taglieri*, several *ongaresche*, and even one *saliera*.[50] Unfortunately, however, it is not possible to link these disparate pieces into complete multi-ware sets; the sets may have been rare and were certainly expensive, as well as prone to loss and breakage. No more than two pieces from any one set seem to survive intact. A *saliera* (figure 89) and a *scodella* (figure 90) from Casteldurante, ornamented in the same manner with a blue ground and white *grotteschi*, represent one

ti mano alle Talle io no ragionero de gli Coperchi da schudelle
+ Eb questi nano tutti a ui mndo eccetto quelle di 5
pelli delle quai prima Eb io nadi piu oltre intedo ragio
nare e dungg da sapere che gli cinqui pelli de Eb si compo
ne la schudella da dona di parto tutte 5 dico fano
le me operationi e poste tutta 5 in siemi formanonn
Vaso ma p esseve inteso meglio ueremo al disegnio

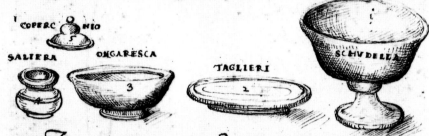

29   COPERC NIO   SALIERA   ONGARESCA   TAGLIERI   SCHVDELLA

questi sono tutta 5 gli pelli della schudella. lordine di
farne tutto u Vaso e questo il Taglieri si riuersa su la
schudella cio e quel piano done il numero. 2. na nolto
sopra al concauo della schudella al n° i. il concano de
longaresca na nolto sul uiedi del Taglieri la saliera
na posta eoui impiedi nel pie de longaresca sopra la qua
le na il mo Coperchio come qui si uedera ecoui che tutte
fano u sol Vaso come il   presente cosa no di
poco ingegnio altri sono   che le fano di 9
pelli tenedo sempre il   medemo ordine
e queste si chiama   no schudelle
de 5 pelli onero   di 9

30

88 Casteldurante, exterior of a maiolica childbirth *scodella* and *tagliere*, c. 1530. The coordinating decoration, identical style, and secure fit make it clear that these two pieces were intended to be together from the start. The raised ledge on the top of the *tagliere* indicates how the original *ongaresca* would have been secured. The top of the *tagliere* is illustrated in figure 17. Walters Art Gallery, Baltimore.

such grouping. Although they have been separated and are now in different collections, their size and appearance indicate that they once were together, probably as part of a five-piece set like the one described by Piccolpasso. Unfortunately, the other pieces remain untraced. More commonly, either a *scodella* or an *ongaresca* and its matching *tagliere* survive together, kept as a set through the intervening centuries (figure 88).

Inventories attest to the existence of such multi-ware sets, in an even greater variety of numbers than those Piccolpasso mentioned.[51] In 1558 the estate inventory of Matteo di Matteo in Pesaro included a four-piece birth *scodella*.[52] This four-piece ensemble was considered a unit, and was referred to as a single item in the inventory. In 1573 Cardinal Ferdinando de' Medici purchased a small, nine-piece maiolica birth service decorated with *grotteschi* from the ceramist Flaminio Fontana.[53] Was this the sort of nine-piece set to which Piccolpasso referred, or is that reference mere coincidence? Yet more fantastic, an inventory of the Palazzo Ducale in Urbino made in 1609 included an historiated birth *scodella* decorated with *grotteschi* and made up of fifty-three pieces.[54] Since Urbino was a leading maiolica-producing center, it is understandable that such an elaborate service would be recorded there; either the Duchess of Urbino, or some other prominent court woman, would have had the most extravagant item possible to celebrate a childbirth.

In addition to the drawing by Piccolpasso, there is only one other certain representation of a multi-ware childbirth set. It is part of a confinement room scene painted inside an *ongaresca* (figure 91).[55] A woman is shown about to present a fully assembled five-piece set to the mother in bed. The similarity between the appearance of this set and the one in Piccolpasso's manuscript is striking, and it may attest to the practice of standardizing shapes in Italian maiolica production.[56] It also makes it clear that Piccolpasso's text was based on his observations of actual practice.

These examples illustrate the problematic nature of the word *scodella*, which referred more to a general concept – a birth ware – than it did to any certain number of wares arranged in any certain manner. The documentary sources for birth wares further

87 (*facing page*) Cipriano Piccolpasso, *I tre libri dell'arte del vasaio* (1557) folio 11r. Victoria and Albert Museum, London.

89 Casteldurante, *saliera*, c. 1525. One of the components of Piccolpasso's *scodella da impagliata* was the *saliera*, which formed the finial of the set. Victoria and Albert Museum, London.

perpetuate this. Despite the references cited above, documents yield very little information regarding the number or type of birth wares. Most inventories simply cite *scodelle* for childbirth, likely designating high, footed bowls. But, as discussed above, such bowls may have been outfitted with a cover, or they may have had a number of other wares associated with them.[57] In inventories, birth bowls were often described as a *paio* (pair), or even as multiple pairs. In 1475, for example, Andrea Bucelli had three such pairs of maiolica birth *schodelle*,[58] while in 1531 the estate of the brothers Salvi and Aghostino Bardegli included a single pair of *schodelle*.[59] The word "pair" probably designated two identical but autonomous objects that came together as a set. It was used in this way to describe the sets of marriage chests that carried the bride's trousseau; each chest was a separate entity, although both were similar in shape, size, function, and ornamentation.[60] This definition probably applies to birth wares, too. An example of this type of pairing may be seen in a manuscript illumination of *The Birth of the Virgin* by the miniaturist Antonio di Niccolò di Lorenzo (figure 94): an attendant brings the new mother a tray bearing a knife and two footed bowls, presumably of lustered, imported, maiolica, one with a rim and one without. Specific documentary references to paired and multiple wares had decreased by the mid-sixteenth century, when inventories tended to list such items more ambiguously as "una scodella."[61]

This very indeterminate vocabulary makes a modern discussion of childbirth wares extremely difficult. And variations in details make it clear that Piccolpasso's description was

90 Casteldurante, *scodella*,
c. 1525. This *scodella* is
painted with the same colors
and motifs as the *saliera*
(figure 89), and they
presumably belonged to the
same five-piece *scodella da
impagliata*. Petit Palais, Paris.
(© Photothèque des Musées
de la Ville de Paris/Cliché
P. Pierrain)

not universal. Birth wares varied not only in number, but also in shape and size. An *ongaresca* could have a profile distinctly different from Piccolpasso's drawing, as evidenced by a bowl from Casteldurante, which has a bulbous shape that swells out between rim and foot (figure 92). It could also have handles: a vine-like appendage is attached to both sides of a *scodella* from the Fontana workshop (figure 93). These wares could be ovoid, rather than circular, as seen in a *tagliere* attributed to the Patanazzi workshop (figure 95). Either an *ongaresca* or a *tagliere* could have a curving lip, which was usually painted differently to frame the central image. When these two pieces were placed one on top of the other, the lips produced a gradually sloping profile like that on a paired *ongaresca* and *tagliere* attributed to the town of Casteldurante (figure 96). The sizes of birth ware also varied. In 1479 Francesco Ducci's estate distinguished between a pair of lustered childbirth bowls and a pair of small lustered childbirth bowls,[62] and in 1483 the estate of Giovansimone Tornabuoni included a group of six birth bowls of various sizes.[63] This evidence for relative shapes and sizes is confusing, but it indicates the flexibility maiolica shops had in the production of birth wares.

Notwithstanding the variations, the production of different childbirth wares over a long period of time in a number of maiolica centers suggests that each type of ware had a particular purpose. In fact, Piccolpasso indicated that each object in his *schudella dal impagliata* had an individual, although unspecified, function.[64] Logically, each would have carried some sort of sustenance to the new mother. For liquids and broths, there were

91 (*right*) Workshop of Orazio Fontana, interior of a maiolica childbirth *ongaresca*, c. 1540. This fascinating bowl shows the mother and her child in bed, about to be presented with an assembled *scodella da impagliata*. Location unknown. (Photo John Blazejewski)

92 (*below left*) Casteldurante, exterior of a maiolica childbirth *ongaresca*, mid-sixteenth century. Painted with a delicate landscape scene, this *ongaresca* has a profile that gradually undulates from foot to rim. It may have been made as a single piece, independent of any other elements, or it may have had a *tagliere* to cover it, with an interior ring to hold it in place. The interior of this *ongaresca* is illustrated in figure 10. Iparmüvészeti Múzeum, Budapest.

scodelle and *ongaresche*. To hold more solid foods, there was a *tagliere*. And the *saliera* provided salt, which acted as both a flavoring and a preservative. Even the most elaborately painted wares must have been used in this practical manner during childbirth, or the genre could not have attracted such a large audience.

★ ★ ★

106

94 (*right*) Antonio di Niccolò di Lorenzo, illumination from a choir book depicting the Birth of the Virgin, c. 1475. One of the attendants carries in a tray with two low *ongaresche*, which may have been made of lustered maiolica. Library of the Convento dei Servi, Santissima Annunziata, Florence. (Scala/Art Resource, New York)

93 (*facing page bottom right*) Workshop of the Fontana family, exterior of a maiolica childbirth *scodella*, c. 1540–50. The fragile handles and elegant, narrow foot of this bowl, together with its flange-like rim, make it likely that it was an independent ware. Kunstgewerbemuseum, Staatliche Museen zu Berlin, Preussischer Kulturbesitz.

96 (*below right*) Casteldurante, *ongaresca* and *tagliere*, c. 1525. In some cases, it seems that maiolica childbirth wares were made to emulate more costly metalwork objects. This bowl and cover fit together snugly and are painted with a simulated gadrooning that would have been more typical of contemporary metalwork. The top of the *tagliere* is illustrated in figure 72, and the interior of the *ongaresca* in figure 155. Uměleckoprůmyslové Muzeum, Prague. (Photo Gabriel Urbánek)

95 (*above left*) Workshop of the Patanazzi family, top of a maiolica childbirth *tagliere*, c. 1580. Kunstgewerbemuseum, Staatliche Museen zu Berlin, Preussischer Kulturbesitz.

Iconography

The elaborate ornamentation found on childbirth wares seems to negate the possibility that they had a utilitarian role. It is difficult to imagine that such carefully painted objects were used to serve something as simple as soup. Yet the same paradox arose in the context of the elaborately painted wooden trays. As Vasari stated, magnificent yet eminently functional objects were common in Renaissance domestic interiors.

97 Faenza, interior of a
maiolica childbirth *ongaresca*,
early seventeenth century.
This delicate handled bowl
is painted in the *compendario*
technique, using orange,
blue, brown, and yellow but
allowing the overall white to
dominate. Museo
Internazionale delle
Ceramiche, Faenza.

Although documents provided only minimal information regarding the shapes and
numbers of maiolica birth wares, they gave even less information about iconography. As
was the case with the wooden birth trays, the range of words and phrases used to describe
the majority of maiolica birth wares was extremely brief and visually limited. There are a
few ways to circumvent this problem. By the late sixteenth century some inventories had
begun to include information on the place of manufacture for individual wares. This
indicates a contemporary awareness of the style of Italian maiolica from various production
centers. The inventory of the Medici *guardaroba* of 1588 listed two birth bowls from
Urbino.[65] Urbino was particularly noted for its high quality *istoriato* wares, which, by this
time, often included *grotteschi* on exteriors and rims. Another birth bowl, cited in a
Florentine inventory of 1594, was from Montelupo, a small town near Florence that had
produced a significant amount of distinctive, brightly colored maiolica since the fourteenth
century.[66] Other citations referred to wares from Faenza, including the Medici inventory
of 1588, which listed four birth wares from this city.[67] These wares probably had much in
common with the white birth bowl listed in the estate of Domenico di Tommaso Fagiuoli
in 1617.[68] White wares, or *compendario*, evidently developed as an alternative not only to
the complex *istoriato* wares being produced in many other maiolica centers in the early
sixteenth century but also to the costly porcelain imports from the East. Faenza wares are

identifiable by their heavy, white glaze and minimal, sketchy compositions, usually outlined in only a few colors.[69] The technique was introduced in the 1540s, and soon dominated production in Faenza. It was quicker to paint than *istoriato* ware, due to its less detailed appearance. Eventually the style was imitated in other regions and exported all over Italy and Europe.[70] An estate inventory of 1612 distinguished a birth bowl painted in many colors from another, which was not.[71] The special reference to multicolors (presumably signifying an *istoriato* ware) separated these two references, and probably identified the second bowl as a white ware.

Several white ware birth bowls can be identified, and, again, it is their imagery that links them to the birth ritual. One example, roughly contemporary with Fagiuoli's estate, has a squat profile with elegant curving handles. The interior is painted with a scene of a woman seated in a bed, her body a bit disproportionate to the furnishings (figure 97). The scene has a sense of energy, with minimal details and an emphasis on the white ground. But the imagery, and even the overall shape, recalls the earlier *istoriato* birth wares.

Although references to place of origin yield information about overall appearance, they reveal little about the actual images painted on the wares. As was the case with wooden trays and bowls, discussion of the iconography must rely primarily on surviving examples. In every case, the exteriors and edges of birth wares were painted with the same sort of ornamentation as was found on contemporary maiolica made for a wider variety of uses. In the second quarter of the sixteenth century, when *istoriato* birth wares became popular, this usually meant landscape scenes. By the middle of the century, however, the fanciful *grotteschi* popular among maiolica artists became the more typical ornament (figure 98), as discussed above in connection with the nine-piece set purchased by Cardinal Ferdinando de' Medici and the fifty-three piece set in the Palazzo Ducale in Urbino. Painting the exteriors in this manner allowed for a certain degree of consistency with the other wares made in the workshop. And it made the birth object look like an average piece of maiolica to the casual viewer.

98   Workshop of the Patanazzi family, maiolica childbirth *scodella*, late sixteenth century. Although the exterior is painted with a complicated arrangement of *grotteschi*, the interior depicts a seated woman and a swaddled child, very similar to the scene illustrated in figure 86. Location unknown. (Photo courtesy Phillips, London)

But the main interest here is in the parts of the ware that were not visible to the casual viewer. The concavities of maiolica birth bowls or the tops of maiolica birth trays – many of which would have been covered, in turn, by an *ongaresca* – almost always have images that link the wares conclusively to childbirth. Some of the subjects painted on *istoriato* wares were similar to the subjects used earlier on wooden trays, indicating that maiolica childbirth wares represented a continuation of the same ideologies and traditions.[72] By far the vast majority of these wares depict confinement room scenes, usually showing the mother or child. The next largest group has images of an actual birth (figure 99). And a small number have images of family life, presumably shortly after the birth. Only occasionally do wares of the shapes described by Piccolpasso as childbirth-related have historical or mythological scenes, which were otherwise the most common narratives illustrated on contemporary maiolica. Mythological scenes, in

99 Urbino, interior of a
maiolica childbirth *scodella*,
c. 1570–80. The woman
seems to be going into labor
in an open-roofed court.
High demand for childbirth
maiolica meant that
compositions were repeated
on a number of pieces; for a
similar scene, see the
ongaresca illustrated in the
frontispiece. Louvre, Paris.
(Photo © RMN)

100 Workshop of the
Fontana family, interior of a
maiolica childbirth *ongaresca*
with a confinement room
scene, c. 1560–70. Museum
für Kunst und Gewerbe,
Hamburg.

101 Workshop of the Fontana family, top of a maiolica childbirth *tagliere* with a confinement room scene, c. 1550–70. Howard I. and Janet Stein collection. (Photo Graydon Wood)

particular, often appear on wooden birth trays. But these trays were prominently displayed on the walls of the home following a birth, linking them to the larger tradition of painted panels. The audience for childbirth wares was different; they were smaller and more portable, and their audience was therefore more intimate, made up almost exclusively of the pregnant woman or new mother. Erudite themes seem to have had relatively little use on most birth maiolica, implying their more private role.

The confinement room scenes painted on maiolica are composed in a deliberate manner. An *ongaresca* from the Fontana workshop fits the figures into the curve of the bowl and places the action against the surface (figure 100). The immediacy of the scene is emphasized by the way in which the bed curtain hangs into the viewer's space, an effect enhanced by the graceful, muscular figure of the woman on the right. The action is pulled closer to the viewer, eliminating the need for a contrived architectural construction like the diorama-type boxes that often contained the birth scene on earlier wooden trays. This compositional immediacy is typical of maiolica birth wares: with their small size and intimate scenes, they seem to demand a close connection to the viewer.

The settings for these scenes further personalized the images, locating the world of childbirth in a distinctly well-off environment filled with a wealth of recognizable details of daily life. This is much more obvious on maiolica birth wares than it was on wooden trays or monumental paintings. An image on a maiolica *tagliere* from the Fontana workshop thus provides extensive information about late sixteenth-century interiors (figure 101). The bare wooden floor is made of long planks, and the ceiling is coffered wood. The brick walls extend almost to the ceiling, where a molded cornice line divides the wall. Above is a grisaille *spalliera*, painted with a battle scene to resemble relief sculpture. The bricked fireplace has classically inspired pilasters with capitals, and a hook hangs in it to roast food in the flames. The large canopied bed has white sheets and a floral coverlet. It rests on six sculpted feet, and its orange curtains twist around the bedposts. A convex

102 Forlì, interior of a maiolica childbirth *scodella* with a confinement room scene, c. 1549. Museo delle Ceramiche, Forlì. (Photo Giorgio Liverani)

103 Workshop of the Patanazzi family, interior of a maiolica childbirth *ongaresca* with a scene of a woman nursing, c. 1580–1600. Kunstgewerbemuseum, Staatliche Museen zu Berlin, Preussischer Kulturbesitz.

mirror in an elaborate tabernacle frame hangs above a sarcophagus-style chest. Such specificity made an immediate link between the viewer and the object itself, insisting on personal identification.

These wares also give clues about the activities that took place during the confinement period, which are shown with incredible specificity and charm. The inside of a *scodella* from Forlì depicts a classically inspired, busy confinement chamber (figure 102). To the left, in her elegantly curtained bed, a mother sits up as an attendant serves her. To the right, another attendant warms linens for the baby's swaddling. Her cloak billows out in the back, indicating her rapid movement from crib to fire. In the center foreground, in a miniature intarsiated bed with stately head and footboards, a tiny baby, with only the head visible, is tucked under a patterned blue coverlet by a third attendant.

In other examples, women are shown nursing (figure 103). An activity with highly charged connotations, nursing was usually depicted in monumental art in a detached, asexual, and theologically implicit manner involving the Virgin and Child.[73] The comparison of the intimate moment between mother and child depicted on the maiolica, and the iconic representation of the same activity in countless sacred paintings, makes the different audiences for these works apparent. There was certainly a doctrinaire quality about these idealized nursing scenes, since moralists of the Renaissance strongly advocated that mothers nurse their own children, despite the overwhelming preference for wetnurses at that time (see p. 52 above). There was no genre of maiolica wares for a wetnurse; these wares were for the mother, and the image must have been an attempt to encourage the practice. Of course, mixed messages were also sent, acknowledging the problematic role of the wetnurse in Renaissance society. A *scodella* from Casteldurante includes both a mother in bed and a wetnurse on the floor with the child (figure 104). Nevertheless, while these specific details drew the viewer into the scene, they also had a didactic function, with clear depictions of the specifics of confinement room care that made them especially appropriate on objects for new mothers.

104 Casteldurante, interior of a maiolica childbirth *scodella* with a confinement room scene, c. 1530. The mother sits up in bed, ready to receive the food carried in by her attendant, while her young son plays with a pinwheel. A wetnurse sits on the floor, nursing the newborn in a rocking crib. The Art Museum, Princeton University. Museum purchase. (Photo Bruce M. White)

105   Urbino, top of a maiolica childbirth *tagliere*, c. 1525–30. This tray, which has been trimmed all around, is based on a popular woodcut of *The Birth of Hercules* from Ovid's *Metamorphoses*. A jealous Juno flies in on the left; Jupiter had betrayed her again, this time with Alcema, and Juno wanted to ensure that Alcema would not give birth. To do so, she instructs the goddess Lucina to crouch with her legs crossed nearby. But the maid Galanthis, taking pity on Alcema, tricked Lucina into believing the birth had already occurred, and the goddess changed her position. The impediment removed, Alcema delivered Hercules, whose head pokes out from under her skirts on this tray. Foreshadowing Galanthis' punishment, a weasel runs across the floor; Juno transformed Galanthis into a weasel for her trickery. Despite the mythological basis, the events occur in a Renaissance domestic interior amid all the details of daily life. Animals from the weasel family become important in Renaissance childbirth (see figures 132, 134, and 135). Victoria and Albert Museum, London.

106 Casteldurante, top of a maiolica childbirth *tagliere* with a birth scene, c. 1525–30. Victoria and Albert Museum, London.

This is particularly obvious in the context of wares depicting childbirth. These scenes are executed with what seems to be a high degree of accuracy, despite the fact that the painter was most probably a man unlikely to have witnessed the event himself. For example, the central fragment of a *tagliere* from Urbino shows the newborn's head peeking out from between the mother's skirted legs, while her female friends run about carrying various necessary accessories (figure 105). Another maiolica *tagliere*, this time from Casteldurante, also depicts a woman giving birth. The midwife sits on a low stool in front of her, and an attendant reaches forward to smooth back her hair in a concerned gesture (figure 106). An astrologer stands at a window behind the group, casting the chart of the coming newborn child. This motif serves as a reminder that astrology was an important part of Renaissance society; household inventories, in fact, reveal that many homes contained astrology books.[74] Such birthing scenes (as opposed to confinement scenes) are without precedent in either monumental or decorative Western art, yet they appear in considerable numbers on maiolica birth wares.

From where, then, did these images come? Prints from popular Ovidian texts inspired certain details, as noted above. In addition to these, related scenes occasionally appear in contemporary obstetrical texts. Written in the vernacular, these were intended to provide midwives with guidelines for the event. But the texts themselves dealt largely with herbal remedies and natural techniques that had been part of the tradition for centuries. Only a few texts dealt directly with obstetrics in any detail. Even the two more reputable ones, by Michele Savonarola and Scipione Mercurio, were based on comparatively little practical experience and still relied heavily on antique precedent.[75] Both can serve as evidence, however, that men were beginning to get a grip on this apparently profitable profession. And, appropriately, their illustrations serve as revealing contrasts to the images on maiolica wares. A woodcut from the 1559 edition of Savonarola's *Practica major* (1440) depicts a woman on her birthing stool, a particularly formidable-looking seat shown both in use and

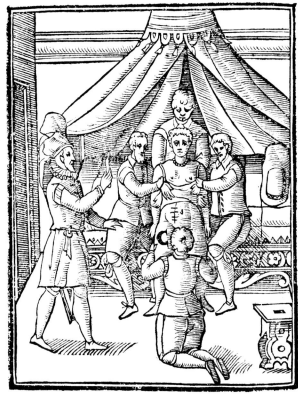

on its own; she is held from behind by the midwife, who is herself braced by another female attendant (figure 107). Although the artist included several domestic details, such as the paned windows, the chests under the canopied bed, the trellis garden, and the wooden bucket in the foreground, there is a certain clinical detachment that makes the scene neither encouraging nor comforting. The purpose was clearly educational.

This is even more obvious in the illustration of a Caesarian section from a 1601 edition of Scipione Mercurio's *La commare o riccoglitrice* (1596), in which a woman is held down by four fashionably attired men (figure 108). She wears nothing but a cloth about her waist and a beaded necklace. The approaching surgeon is dressed at the height of fashion as he advances with his scalpel held high in the air. Despite the richly carved and canopied bed, this is not a pleasant image and could not possibly serve to reassure an expectant mother. Instead, it is part of a series of illustrations intended to demonstrate proper surgical procedure. During this time, Caesarean sections were a last resort, intended to extract the trapped infant, not to save the suffering mother.

The audience for such an illustration was the male doctor. After all, he was the hero of the event. In Mercurio's image, he shows off his surgical prowess. But even in Savonarola's, where there is no man present, the relatively stark scene and the emphasis on the configuration of the stool was more practical than comforting. Clearly obstetrical illustrations were vastly different from the images on birth wares, where the audience was the pregnant woman or new mother. Birth wares rendered childbirth in especially intimate and comforting detail. The images were both recognizable and plausible to the women who looked at them. They suggested a pleasant experience, no matter what the physical reality of birth entailed. A maiolica artist could paint the mother at the very peak of her labor (figure 109). But she is always surrounded almost exclusively by female friends and professionals who take care of her needs, often in a setting of unusual architectural grandeur. In this *scodella*, despite the presence of the well-dressed male doctor, the

117

109 Workshop of the Patanazzi family, interior of a maiolica childbirth *scodella* with a birth scene, c. 1580–1600. A man stands on the left and helps to brace the laboring woman during her contractions. His presence is intimate, implying that he is her husband rather than her doctor. In fact, the protagonist of this scene is the kneeling midwife who will conduct the delivery to the best possible conclusion. Uměleckoprůmyslové Muzeum, Prague. (Photo Gabriel Urbánek)

impression is still positive and encouraging. The doctor conducts himself very differently from the one in Mercurio's illustration: his presence is positive, intended to encourage and pacify women in difficult situations. And it is important to recall that such scenes were typically portrayed in hidden and discreet locations on maiolica wares, aimed primarily toward the mother herself.

These very personal compositions, together with the popularity, durability, and functionality of maiolica, generated a great demand for historiated childbirth wares, a demand that had a direct effect on production techniques. A number of surviving pieces are painted with almost identical scenes, indicating serial production within the maiolica workshops. For example, the confinement scene painted in the concavity of one *scodella* (figure 110) is closely replicated in at least two other examples.[76] The artist, in this case a painter associated with Fra Xanto Avelli, must have used model drawings to create a number of near-identical vessels to fulfill a strong demand.

Serial production was also aided by the widespread use of printed sources. Maiolica scholars have long pointed out how popular engravings by Marcantonio Raimondi and others were used in sixteenth-century maiolica shops to inspire certain iconography and compositions. The *scodelle* cited above are indeed based on sections of Raimondi's scandalous *I modi* prints (figure 111):[77] the woman's pose has been twisted to convert her

110 Workshop of Fra Xanto Avelli, interior of a maiolica childbirth *scodella*, c. 1535. The boisterous boy, whose lively pose prohibits the attendant from swaddling him, seems older than a newborn. The exterior of this *scodella* is illustrated in figure 124. Victoria and Albert Museum, London.

111 Marcantonio Raimondi, *I modi*, 1527. The pose of the noticeably nude mother painted in figure 110 is derived from one of Raimondi's engravings after designs by Giulio Romano. These prints, which were combined with infamous sonnets by Pietro Aretino, were almost completely destroyed by the offended public during the sixteenth century. Only one later set and a few relatively innocuous fragments seem to survive, of which this is one. In an interesting twist, the maiolica artist has turned what must have been an extremely erotic pose into one of casual domesticity. British Museum, London.

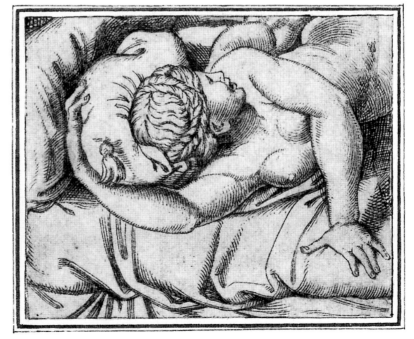

from a sexually uninhibited and potentially dangerous female to a devoted mother. Around mid-century, artists expanded their range and used various popular woodcut volumes as compositional sources. The importance of various editions of Ovid's *Metamorphoses* has already been noted, as has that of Bernard Salomon's Old Testament woodcuts. Another bowl, from the Fontana shop, also derives, ultimately, from Salomon's print, although there is a notable shifting and substitution of certain figures and motifs (figure 112). But overall, most artists working on birth wares made only partial reference to printed sources, adding instead details based on first-hand observation of the domestic interior and the activities in it. But these details were often reused in multiple wares, implying that there were model sources for them, as well.

The workshop nature of these objects is further indicated by the fact that very few of them have heraldic details. They were probably purchased as needed from workshop stock. However, while the painters responsible for wooden trays could add a coat of arms to the small area reserved for this purpose on a newly purchased stock item, the manner in which maiolica was produced prohibited ceramists from making spontaneous personalization of this sort. The ornamentation on a maiolica ware had to be fired, and painted coats of arms could not be added at a later date to an already fired ware. So it is probable that a patron commissioned a birth ware only in rare and special cases. One such case is a matched *scodella* and *tagliere* painted by Baldassare Manara, which has a coat of arms on the side of the *scodella* representing the Viarani and the Benini families of Faenza (figure 113).[78] These two items are among the very small percentage of birth wares depicting mythological narratives: the interior of the *scodella* illustrates Aeneas fleeing Troy, one side of the *tagliere* depicts Pyramus and Thisbe, and the other has Hercules and the Nemean lion. All are surrounded by laudatory inscriptions. They probably once belonged to a larger ensemble, as Piccolpasso's five-piece model dictated. The heraldic device and inscriptions make these two wares remarkably elaborate. This is further enhanced by their iconography, perhaps best interpreted as an allegory of virtue.

Examples as fine as these are relatively rare. The vast majority of childbirth wares were skillfully executed and aesthetically pleasing, but they seem to have been workshop pieces, executed using serial production techniques. And in every case, other wares, which have nothing to do with childbirth, were produced by the same workshops. This indicates that childbirth wares were made in productive workshops that created a variety of wares for the demanding domestic market. Whether made of wood or maiolica, childbirth objects probably provided a lucrative and assured side business for an artist's workshop, which in turn further stimulated their serial production.

Although their workshop production confirms the fact that they were in demand, specifics regarding the purchase and presentation of maiolica birth wares remain uncertain. The use of the phrase *da parto* links these wares to the childbirth objects discussed so far, all of which were given by men, most likely by the woman's husband. In most cases they would remain in his estate, and it seems logical to associate their purchase with him as part of his financial and social obligations surrounding childbirth. I have found only one reference specifying the purchase of childbirth maiolica: in 1490 Tribaldo de' Rossi spent 16 *soldi* on a pair of maiolica birth bowls three weeks before his wife, Nanina, gave birth to their first son.[79] Tribaldo does not state where he purchased the bowls; at this date they were likely imported lusterware, probably sold by merchants who imported them for the demanding market.[80] Interestingly, Tribaldo included this purchase within a long list of his expenses for the occasion, in between purchases of grain to fatten Nanina's chickens and special treats from the apothecary. The cost was 2 *soldi* more than he paid to refill the box of sweetmeats for his wife's visitors, and over twice as much as he paid for a flask of wine for them to drink. But, of course, the sum of 16 *soldi* was insignificant compared with the 10 florins assigned to the wooden birth tray in Lorenzo de' Medici's estate in 1492.

112 Workshop of the Fontana family, interior of a maiolica childbirth *ongaresca*, 1560–70. The scene ultimately derives from Bernard Salomon's woodcut of *The Birth of Joseph* (figure 83). For another maiolica ware based on this composition, see figure 82. Louvre, Paris (Photo © RMN)

113 Baldassare Manara, maiolica childbirth *scodella* and *tagliere*, c. 1530–40. The inscription around the scene of Pyramus and Thisbe on the top of the *tagliere* refers to the virtues of both Hercules and Aeneas; as such, it may have been a compliment to the father, or to the hoped-for heir. It translates, "He who wanted to conquer Paradise, he who slew Cacus, who was possessed by the fury. He who made his way through the fire like a salamander with Julius and Anchises." The Metropolitan Museum of Art, New York.

114   Workshop of the Fontana family, back of a maiolica childbirth *tagliere*, second half of the sixteenth century. This little boy, carrying an overflowing basket on his head, was taken from a print of *Alexander and Roxanne* by Gian Giacomo Caraglio. However, here he is presented as an independent entity, and his naked body and overflowing basket are symbols of fertility. Civiche Raccolte d'Arte Applicata, Castello Sforzesco, Milan. (Photo Saporetti)

Maiolica birth wares thus enjoyed considerable popularity among Tuscan households by the second half of the fifteenth century, although they neither equaled nor usurped the popularity of the various wooden birth objects. Whether a single bowl, covered with a matching lid or complemented by multiple related wares, maiolica described as *da parto* or a variation on this phrase remained in wide use throughout Tuscany and much of central Italy until at least the early seventeenth century. This time span emphasizes the continuing importance attached to figurative objects as part of the birth ritual, which also helps to explain the limited use of simpler wooden trays. The painted scenes of confinement and childbirth on maiolica, like those on the earlier wooden birth trays and bowls, would have provided positive reinforcement for Renaissance women in a far more intimate and constant manner than the sacred confinement scenes painted in their churches. But such objects could also play another, rather mysterious, role in the ritual of childbirth. The images of naked boys painted on the undersides of wooden trays or maiolica wares (figure 114) evidently carried a quasi-magical symbolism and were used as mediating devices, both before and during birth. Only the mother, who interacted with the object most intimately, would have seen these images. The next chapter examines this mediating role in greater detail.

5 *Maternal Mediators*

CHILDBIRTH IN RENAISSANCE ITALY was surrounded by objects and rituals designed to keep it under control. This control was necessary, if somewhat illusory, given the tragic mortality rates in this post-plague society. As a result, anything that could provide women with a certain amount of protection and mediation – whether real or imagined – was clearly desirable. With such an advantage, a woman could consider herself less susceptible to the machinations of nature and society; she could regulate her reproductive power and even the gender of her children. The contemporary belief in sympathetic magic and the mediating force of specific objects and rituals promised a greater personal control over pregnancy and birth than was medically possible at that time.[1]

This mediating force took many different forms. Monumental confinement scenes in churches, which idealized the events in the bedchamber following the birth of the Virgin or of John the Baptist, are important evidence for the practices and ideas surrounding childbirth in Renaissance Italy. By situating these events in a contemporary setting, the artists created particularly strong paradigms for female behavior. Furthermore, there was a certain comfort and familiarity in these images that would have reassured apprehensive or frightened women. In Ghirlandaio's fresco of *The Birth of the Virgin*, the orderly and richly appointed room is filled with visiting patricians and doting caregivers who tend to every need of the mother and child (figure 115). These details of daily life doubtless reflected the habits and tastes of the wealthy merchant patrons, who seem to have wanted the works of art they commissioned to include the same type of furnishings and accessories that they had in their own households. As we have seen, many of the special objects that appear in confinement scenes were listed in contemporary inventories. They were particular enough to retain their birth-related identity, signified by their common designation *da parto*, years after the actual event. Although relatively few survive today, their frequent inclusion in paintings and documents attests to the elaborate furnishings of the typical Renaissance birth chamber, with its embroidered sheets and pillows, painted tables and birthing chairs, and special clothing and amulets. Such objects assisted, celebrated, and rewarded the successful birth by decorating the mother, the child, and the bedroom in honor of the event, and their actual presence in the home encouraged the maternal role. The Renaissance emphasis on childbirth, in fact, appeared in its most tangible form in the production and promotion of these varied aids to pregnancy and childbirth.

There were many mediating devices, both domestic and sacred, that addressed the maternal imagination and bridged the gap between real and ideal birth in this demographically depressed society. Some items, such as amulets and herbal remedies, were typically recommended by the community of women who dominated the actual birthing process.[2] On the other hand, in the public and officially sanctioned sphere of religious worship, prayers, relics, and votive offerings were created and sanctioned by the dominant male authorities – whether Church, state, or familial – that controlled much of Renaissance society.

It is important to examine this entire range of material culture when analyzing the manner in which Renaissance society reacted to childbirth.[3] A broad approach is essential

115 Domenico Ghirlandaio, *The Birth of the Virgin*, c. 1490. Fresco. Santa Maria Novella, Florence. (Alinari/Art Resource, New York)

in order to determine contemporary attitudes to childbirth and the meaning behind the art associated with it. This is particularly important since most childbirth art was associated with the domestic realm. The wooden birth trays and bowls, maiolica, and even clothing and accessories examined so far are all examples of domestic art. As such, they have only recently received any mention at all in scholarly literature. But taken together they reveal much about Renaissance childbirth. These aids, both domestic and sacred, served as necessary mediation between real and ideal birth in the post-plague society.

Domestic and Sacred Mediators

The images painted on birth-related trays and bowls are particularly important in the context of mediation. The scenes of confinements and childbirths are positive, festive, and often quite cluttered. In the concavity of an *ongaresca* from the workshop of Orazio Fontana, the curtained bed in the corner is unoccupied (figure 116). But the mother may be one of the two women in the foreground, who, together with a small boy, busy themselves with the newborn child. One woman is seated on the tile floor, her legs straight out in front of her to support the baby. The other is on a low chair. Both are engaged in swaddling the newborn, who is already a healthy and impossibly large child. They use a roll of white swaddling and a larger cloth square, which the boy has probably just warmed at the nearby hearth. Careful details provide recognizable touches for the viewer. There is a chest against the back wall, a mirror above it, and an elaborate metal vessel on the ledge above that. The viewer is pulled into the scene by the two watching pets, and by the vivid nature of the relationships between the figures. Clearly the little boy is eager to play with the baby, and he leans forward excitedly with a rattle. But the women are intent on their duties, and on the comfort of the baby, whose head rests on a soft pink pillow. These details made the scene both engaging and reassuring to a Renaissance woman, and the mood is much more intimate than that of Ghirlandaio's fresco.

The scenes on many trays and bowls also emphasize the congenial aspects of confinement room visits. The wooden tray by Bartolomeo di Fruosino includes visitors who converse to the accompaniment of a harpist (figure 1). A maiolica bowl from the Fontana workshop illustrates a nursing mother interrupted by a group of well-wishers (figure 117). Renaissance notions of the proper role for women, and an especially sentimental attitude toward children, are evident in these images. The new mother is celebrated; she is dressed in fine clothing, supplied with special accessories, and honored by visits from friends and relations. These scenes, albeit idealized, echoed the experiences of many Renaissance women. Their lively narrative quality was instructive. Before childbirth, such images were encouraging and exemplary; after, they were celebratory. In this manner, they mediated between the actual and the ideal event in an important way.

The images of naked boys painted on the reverse of wooden and maiolica birth objects, where they are not visible to the casual observer, are very different from the confinement scenes on the front. The children fly, squat, sit, box, and urinate; they hold drums, small animals, pinwheels, and hobby horses. Those carrying a bow and arrow are clearly identifiable as Cupid (figure 118). Others bear laurel branches or garlands, symbolic of future fame for the newborn (figure 119). With their variations in poses and accessories, naked boys endured on the backs of birth objects from the 1420s to at least the 1580s. Their appearance is so variable that it is unlikely that they were meant to be heraldic. And it is particularly significant that most, if not all, of these children are male, a fact made obvious because most are naked. Frolicking boys of a similar type appear quite often in the borders of contemporary manuscript illuminations. In these cases, they seem to be merely

116 Workshop of Orazio
Fontana, maiolica childbirth
ongaresca, scodella, and *tagliere,*
c. 1560–70. Although the
scodella and *tagliere* fit
together in the way
Piccolpasso describes, the
curving lip of the *ongaresca*
(here shown on its side
facing the viewer) make it
too large to fit on top of
them. Perhaps it was
originally meant as an
independent ware? Founders
Society Purchase, Mr. and
Mrs. Henry Ford II Fund,
Detroit Institute of Arts.

decorative details. But when they appear on domestic objects made for marriage and childbirth, they have a more magical resonance. They seem to foreshadow, by their very presence, the much-desired child.

Similarly active boys were popular subjects for many Renaissance artists. Contemporary statuettes by the so-called Master of the Unruly Children represent little boys in analogous poses (figure 120).[4] Several of these figures were painted or gilded, though few traces of their original coloration remain. Their small size and secular subject matter insist on a location within the domestic setting. And such objects do appear in contemporary household inventories; they may be what was described in one inventory as "two gold babies hugging each other."[5] These statuettes have a striking resemblance to some of the boys painted on birth objects. One, in fact, can be linked quite closely to the boxing pair on the back of a wooden birth tray from the workshop of Apollonio di Giovanni (figure 121).

There must have been some underlying reason for the persistent popularity of this subject on domestic art. The most logical explanation is that the little naked boys acted as

117 (*right*) Workshop of the Fontana family, interior of a maiolica childbirth *ongaresca* with a confinement room scene, c. 1550–70. Howard I. and Janet Stein collection. (Photo Graydon Wood)

118 (*facing page top left*) Workshop of the Fontana family, bottom of a maiolica childbirth *tagliere* with a Cupid, c. 1550–70. This *tagliere* is the companion piece to the *ongaresca* in figure 117. Howard I. and Janet Stein collection. (Photo Graydon Wood)

119 (*facing page top right*) Workshop of Orazio Fontana, back of a maiolica childbirth *tagliere*, c. 1550. A naked boy is holding laurel branches; the traditional association of laurel with victory made an auspicious claim for the future child. The *tagliere* is illustrated with its possible companion pieces in figure 116. Founders Society Purchase, Mr. and Mrs. Henry Ford II Fund, Detroit Institute of Arts.

120 (*facing page bottom left*) Master of the Unruly Children, *Two Boys Fighting*, terracotta, late fifteenth century. (Photo courtesy Altomani & Co., Pesaro)

121 (*facing page bottom right*) Workshop of Apollonio di Giovanni, back of a wooden childbirth tray, c. 1450. Note the similarities in both mood and pose between the boys on this tray and the statuette illustrated in figure 120. Location unknown (Photo John Blazejewski)

fertility symbols. This is suggested from the many texts then in circulation that discussed the influence of the maternal imagination on the unborn – or even unconceived – child.[6] The power of image magic during pregnancy and childbirth was well established throughout Renaissance Europe. The belief can be traced as far back as the Old Testament, with the story of Jacob and Laban in Genesis (30:25–43). In order to best his father-in-law Laban, Jacob peeled branches and placed the mottled boughs in front of Laban's strongest animals while they mated. As a result, they produced lively speckled and spotted offspring, which Jacob obtained for his own flock. Similar powers were also attributed to statues and paintings in antiquity. The early second-century gynecological treatise of Soranus and the fifth-century treatise *Against Julian* by Saint Augustine, both known to Renaissance readers, described a disfigured Cyprian tyrant who made his wife look at beautiful statues during intercourse to ensure that he would not father an equally disfigured child.[7] This pseudo-scientific tenet was adopted from a number of classical texts and held to tenaciously in the Renaissance, even in educated circles. In a lecture on Genesis, for example, Martin Luther cited the case of a woman who gave birth to a mouse after one surprised her during her pregnancy.[8] The theory continued into the realm of obstetrical science. In *La commare o riccoglitrice* (1596), Scipione Mercurio cited a wide range of references to this

type of occurrence, all within a learned discussion of ancient authors that gave both a seriousness and a certain justification to his text.[9]

Other writings also reveal a belief in images as impulses to conception. In his astrological treatise *Liber de vita* (1489), Marsilio Ficino extended the power of the imagination to the father as well as to the mother: "people who are making babies often imprint on their faces not only their own actions but even what they were imagining."[10] Such a statement suggests the importance attached to controlling the imaginative parameters of potential parents by presenting desirable images, in important locations, at key moments. Furthermore, if care was not taken to avoid undesirable images, there could be negative effects.[11] Bestiaries, for example, warn pregnant women to keep away from grotesque beasts:

whatever [women] view, or even if they imagine it in their mind during the extreme heat of lust while they are conceiving, just so do they procreate the progeny.[12]

Horrific sights thus had to be concealed in order to procreate perfect children. Benedetto Varchi, a historian and humanist at the court of Duke Cosimo I de' Medici, read his treatise *Della generazione de' mostri* to the Florentine Academy in 1548; it includes a reference to the maternal imagination as one of the main causes of monstrous births.[13] A few years later the Parisian surgeon Ambroise Paré devoted a chapter of his *Des monstres et prodiges* (1573) to the subject. Paré stated that anything the mother looked at during conception could influence her offspring. As an example, he cited a hairy girl, conceived while her mother gazed at an image of Saint John in his hair shirt. Paré's advice followed that of the earlier bestiary: "Women – at the hour of conception and when the child is not yet formed . . . – should not be forced to look at or to imagine monstrous things."[14] Certain images and objects were therefore best concealed. Otherwise, they could contaminate the mother's imagination and, consequently, her womb.[15]

Since the maternal imagination was susceptible to these influences, it was important to stimulate it by the sight of beautiful things. Leon Battista Alberti confirmed this belief in his architectural treatise, *De re aedificatoria* (1452). In reference to the use of painted portraits in the bedchamber, he wrote:

> Wherever man and wife come together, it is advisable only to hang portraits of men of dignity and handsome appearance; for they say that this may have a great influence on the fertility of the mother and the appearance of future offspring.[16]

Although the roots of this theory can be traced back to antiquity, it carried particular weight in the Renaissance and was diffused into popular culture in various ways, one of which was the representation of naked and cavorting boys on the back of birth trays and bowls. They functioned as birth talismans to stimulate the mother's imagination towards the procreation of healthy, hearty sons.

As observed in earlier chapters, only three explicit references to the purchase of birth trays and bowls are known. All three document their acquisition at some time before childbirth. Other examples were inherited or consigned, further evidence of their presence in Renaissance homes long before childbirth and even before conception. The talismanic role of the urinating boy on the back of the wooden tray by Bartolomeo di Fruosino is made explicit by the partly obliterated inscription around the salver's rim, which Laurence Kanter has translated: "May God grant health to every woman who gives birth and to their father . . . may [the child] be born without fatigue or peril. I am an infant who lives on [an island?] and I make urine of silver and gold" (figure 2).[17] The wish for good health and safety was clearly important in this era of high-risk childbirth. The silver and gold urine, on the other hand, could be viewed both as a sign of fecundity and prosperity. In a similar ritual, a coin was placed in a new bride's shoe, symbolizing the hope for future wealth. Francesco Datini's illegitimate daughter received such a coin in her shoe on her wedding day in 1407.[18] The importance of sympathetic magic is again apparent in such a ritual.

No other wooden or maiolica birth object has such an explicit inscription, but details common to this group of painted boys suggest that they all had a similar talismanic role. On the back of a wooden tray from the workshop of Apollonio di Giovanni, two boys play with what seems to be poppy seed capsules while one of them urinates beneath three coats of arms (figure 122). Bursting, fruitful poppy seed capsules were obvious symbols of fertility. They appear again as weapons swung by the two naked boys on the reverse of a birth tray (figure 123), as decorative motifs on the exterior of a maiolica childbirth *scodella* (figure 124), and in a garland on the back of another birth tray (figure 56). On

three of these four objects, poppy capsules are placed in physical proximity to heraldic devices, making a deliberate link between fertility and lineage. Furthermore, the combination of objects like seed capsules and urine was critical to the overall message of fertility that so many birth objects emphasized. Keith Christiansen has securely placed such images within the context of traditional marriage imagery and poetry, based on his study of Lorenzo Lotto's *Venus and Cupid* (figure 125).[19] The details of this compositon make the connection to pregnancy and childbirth is then made even clearer.

Another wooden tray, this time from Ferrara, depicts a winged boy holding overflowing cornucopia, obvious symbols of plenty and fertility (figure 129). Here nothing is left to chance. The child wears a coral bracelet around each wrist and two coral necklaces; from one of these necklaces a coral branch hangs. Coral was thought to ward away evil,

126 (*right*) Florentine, back of a wooden childbirth tray, c. 1450. The two boys, naked but for flowing sashes and coral amulets, play a tambourine and sing in a flowering meadow. The front of this tray is illustrated in figure 18. Ca' d'Oro, Venice. (Photo Osvaldo Böhm)

127 (*far right*) Masaccio, detail of the front of the wooden childbirth tray illustrated in figure 24. Gemäldegalerie, Staatliche Museen zu Berlin, Preussischer Kulturbesitz. (Photo Jörg P. Anders)

and it is in this apotropaic role that branches of it are included on many of these little boys (figure 126). Paintings of the Christ Child often include coral, as indeed do the infants included in confinement room scenes on birth trays (figure 127). This practice was extremely popular in daily life; in 1472 Nicolo Strozzi bought ninety pieces of coral to make a necklace for his six-month-old son Carlo.[20]

Naked boys can be connected with other objects and images, all of which served as suggestive fertility devices in the Renaissance. Perhaps the most common such object was the marriage chest. Depending on the narrative they depicted, the painted panels on the fronts of these chests could also emphasize demographic renewal. A chest with an image of the Rape of the Sabine women, for example, can be seen as a way to encourage new wives to have children for the sake of their husband's lineage. This ancient tale of taking brides from a neighboring country to ensure the continuation of the Roman race must have had special meaning in Renaissance Italy, where the plague had devastated a significant percentage of the population.[21]

Not all of the painted encouragement on marriage chests was as obvious. The reclining men and women painted underneath the lids could have had a similarly suggestive power, but they were simply seen much less frequently (figure 128).[22] Although they now seem far from erotic, their transparent gossamer veils and body-hugging stockings may have contributed toward setting the desired mood for marital consummation. A representation of what may be a bridal procession from the front of a marriage chest by Giovanni di Ser

128 Florentine, inside lid of a marriage chest with a reclining nude woman, c. 1465. Tempera on panel. Gift of the Associates in Fine Arts, Yale University Art Gallery, New Haven.

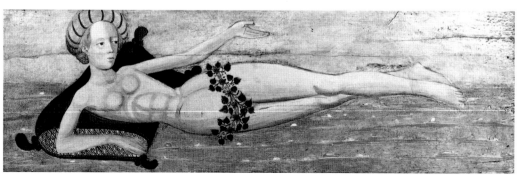

129 Ferrara, back of a wooden childbirth tray, c. 1460. Gift of Mrs. W. Scott Fitz, Museum of Fine Arts, Boston.

Giovanni demonstrates how these chests were transported through the city (figure 130).[23] In this scene the coffer is closed and carried on the back of a household servant. The figures painted within were therefore safe from the inquisitive (and impressionable) eyes of the general public. But they were seen by the bride in her bedroom each day, as she used the linens and other items stored in the chests. Such images therefore encouraged sexuality and its only acceptable end, procreation.[24]

The concealment of such sexually charged images and their role in procreation was advocated by Giulio Mancini in his treatise *Considerazioni sulla pittura* (c. 1621). He wrote that lascivious images should be covered and placed in private rooms for selective viewing.

130 Giovanni di Ser Giovanni, detail from a marriage chest panel, c. 1470. This is presumably a wedding procession, and the painted *cassone* at the far right is carried on the back of a burly retainer. The painted horse on the side of that chest accords well with known *testate*. The artist's delight in detail is evident throughout the panel: note, for example, the iron rings and bars that support the festive tapestries hung on building façades. Tempera on panel. Alberto Bruschi collection, Florence.

131 Florentine, side panel of a marriage chest, c. 1450–75. Tempera on panel. National Gallery, London.

They were especially appropriate in the bedroom, Mancini observed, "because such sights help excite the parents and make beautiful, sound, and healthy children."[25] Such an impetus was important, since it was commonly believed that both the male and the female had to achieve orgasm in order for conception to occur.[26] These were therefore extremely powerful images which should be concealed from, as Mancini put it, "children or old maids, or strangers and scrupulous persons."[27]

The smaller side panels, or *testate*, on marriage chests are also important in this context. They usually depicted heraldic devices, allegorical figures, or smaller narrative scenes; the example on Giovanni di Ser Giovanni's panel has a rearing horse, perhaps the heraldic device of a particular family. A significant group of these side panels depict naked boys, similar to the ones on birth objects; some even carry the ubiquitous poppy seed capsules (figure 131). One of the most interesting *testate*, however, does not survive as an actual panel. Instead, it is depicted in an *Aeneid* manuscript illuminated by Apollonio di Giovanni (figure 133).[28] The *testata* in this illustration depicts a kneeling boy playing with a small animal. Apollonio's productive workshop specialized in domestic art; he would have been aware of the meaning of this odd pair, and he would have known where it would be most appropriate and most believable to his patrons. In fact, a

134

132 Masaccio, back of the wooden childbirth tray illustrated in figure 25. The mysterious pair on the back of this tray bear a strong resemblance to the duo on the chest illustrated in figure 133. Gemäldegalerie, Staatliche Museen zu Berlin, Preussischer Kulturbesitz. (Photo Jörg P. Anders)

133 Apollonio di Giovanni, *The Ghost of Sichaeus Visiting Dido* from an illuminated *Aeneid*, c. 1460, folio 67v. This ancient scene is set in a Renaissance interior. Such a large bed and its surrounding chests could be found in many homes of the time. Biblioteca Riccardiana, Florence. (Photo Donato Pineider)

134 Venetian, marten head made of enameled gold, ruby, garnets, and pearls, mid-sixteenth century. Since martens were thought to conceive their young without sexual intercourse, and to give birth miraculously, they became symbols of Christ's conception and birth. This link between martens and the Incarnation is made clear by the enameled dove on this animal's snout. Walters Art Gallery, Baltimore.

135 a (*facing page*) and b (*detail, above*) Paolo Veronese, *Countess Lucia da Porto Thiene and her Daughter Porzia*, c. 1551. At this date, the Countess was pregnant, a condition alluded to here by her large form, loose clothing, and the marten head on her fur piece, similar to the one illustrated in figure 134. Oil on canvas. Walters Art Gallery, Baltimore.

strikingly similar pair appears, almost thirty years earlier, on the back of the wooden birth tray painted by Masaccio (figure 132).

Such similarities cannot be coincidental. It has been suggested by several scholars that this animal, with its lithe body and pointed snout, is a marten, a fur-bearing carnivore often confused with the weasel or the ferret in the Renaissance. Its importance here lies in the fact that contemporary bestiaries stated that it either conceived or gave birth through the ear.[29] This ability linked the marten, in the medieval and Renaissance mind, to the mystery of the Incarnation, and made it a type of talisman to help pregnant women have easy deliveries. In fact, elaborate marten heads made of costly metalwork and jewels were fastened to fur pieces worn by women (figure 134).[30] These furs had two distinct functions. First, they were practical. In an era of relatively poor hygiene, they were thought to draw vermin away from the wearer's body. But, depending on the animal, furs could also be apotropaic. The popular link between martens and the Incarnation made wearing marten fur particularly significant for pregnant women. The addition of elaborate metalwork heads, attached first to the fur and then to the woman's girdle to secure it in place, made the fur a prominent accessory with highly charged connotations (figure 135).

Given the connection between martens and pregnancy, it seems likely that the image of a boy with a small animal was widely understood and accepted by contemporaries as a childbirth talisman. The pairing may have illustrated a popular adage no longer known. Marriage chests, with paintings on front panels, side panels, and inner lids, therefore provided the bride with a constant reminder of her childbearing duty. Depicted both on marriage chests and on childbirth trays, these little boys, regardless of their activities or accessories, must have been related to fertility, providing a stimulant for the mother's impressionable imagination. Such ideas persisted even up to the nineteenth century: a popular maxim recorded in the 1870s, "quel che se fissa, se fa" ("what she looks at, she makes"), indicates a continuing belief in sympathetic magic.[31]

136

Other sympathetic devices were also employed during the marriage ritual, probably to alert the participants to the goal of the imminent union. For example, a real child was placed in a new bride's arms as part of the marriage ceremony, symbolizing the hoped-for baby.[32] And among the new dresses, jewels, and prayer books in her trousseau, a bride also received special linens and swaddling bands; in 1490 Alessandra de' Rossi's trousseau included two little tablecloths for childbirth.[33] These served as unmistakable encouragement for her to ponder her future role. Other women received charms for the use of their future infants. In 1502 Caterina Bongianni's trousseau included three gold and pearl charms for babies.[34] Such a charm may have resembled the one represented in Bernardino di Antonio Detti's *Madonna della Pergola*, in which John the Baptist offers an elaborate contraption to the Christ Child, made up of a branch of coral, a cross, an Agnus Dei medallion, and an animal tooth, all mounted in metal and attached together by a chain (figure 136).[35]

In many cases, the trousseau also contained life-size terracotta or stucco dolls, sometimes dressed as the Christ Child or a saint, in elaborate and expensive gowns. As Christiane Klapisch-Zuber has shown, such dolls were probably played with and cared for like real children, not only prompting devotion to the holy figures but also nurturing the maternal instinct.[36] In 1486 Marietta Strozzi's trousseau included a figure of Christ wearing a brocade garment and a crown of gold and pearls.[37] Despite this elaborate and probably costly dress, the doll was part of the unestimated portion of her trousseau, which usually included the personal accessories and toiletries of value only to the bride. Thus the doll was intended for Marietta's personal use, rather than to fulfill the monetary obligation her father and future husband had negotiated. In some cases, however, these dolls were so valuable that they were part of the estimated trousseau.

Paul Barolsky has suggested that Donatello's mysterious bronze *Genius* (figure 137), who stands jauntily with pants lowered to expose his penis, could have been executed to celebrate a marriage.[38] Having such a statue present in the home would be a logical development from the custom of placing a child in the bride's arms, all practices that can be linked with the naked boys on the backs of birth trays and bowls. Donatello's statue,

136 a (*right*) and b (*detail, below*) Bernardino di Antonio Detti, *Madonna della Pergola*, late fifteenth century. Note the special attention accorded the sacred and secular charms that John offers to the Christ Child. Tempera on panel. Museo Civico di Pistoia. (Photo M. Tronci)

137 Donatello, *Genius*, c. 1440. This enigmatic figure may have been a fertility device. Surely the frank pose and joyous demeanor of the laughing boy indicate an origin in a domestic setting. Bronze. Bargello, Florence. (Alinari/ Art Resource, New York)

along with the more ephemeral terracottas by the Master of the Unruly Children, can then be interpreted as three-dimensional versions of two-dimensional fertility images.

Other images on childbirth trays and bowls were suggestive, rather than sympathetic. Erotic iconography was very popular during the Renaissance, in a tradition that culminated in the 1520s with Marcantonio Raimondi's sexually explicit illustrations for Pietro Aretino's *I modi*.[39] But even a century before Raimondi, covertly suggestive images were painted on childbirth objects. For example, on the front of a Florentine wooden tray, a young man slowly and provocatively lifts away the outer dress of the lady by his side (figure 138). Another Florentine tray includes a charming trio, with a male lute player favored by the attentions of two ladies; one places her arm about his shoulder while the other rests her hand on his belt (figure 46). In a maiolica *ongaresca* from Forlì, a couple lie naked in bed, hidden but for a gap in the curtains (figure 139). The fact that so many images of this type were painted on the backs of birth trays, the undersides of ceramic vessels, and the sides or insides of marriage chests, demonstrates that they were intended to be privately enjoyed. They were not prominently positioned in full view of anyone who might enter a room, and even when they were used, they could be covered with special cloths, a practice so common that it often appeared as a detail in monumental paintings (figure 40). Of course these cloths protected the painted surfaces from spills and abrasions. But they also hid the images from inappropriate eyes in the same way that closed marriage chest lids hid the nudes depicted within them. Their secret and privileged locations controlled their potent effects on the imagination in the manner advocated by Mancini for lascivious paintings. Here too, visual access was limited until it was deemed necessary or proper.

The idea of limiting visual access was also advocated by the Church for particularly important works of art believed to have miraculous powers. As a result such images as the Virgin of Impruneta were seen only on special days and only for compelling reasons.[40] Even private devotional paintings came equipped with curtains. These not only protected the images from candle drippings and smoke, but also limited accessibility. For example, in 1482 Tommaso Guidetti bought a painting of the Virgin, and then purchased several lengths of white taffeta to make a curtain to cover the image.[41] Inventories frequently describe paintings with similar accessories; in 1512 the estate of Chimenti Selaio included a painting of the Virgin with its own curtain and brass candleholders.[42] Such elaborate and costly accessories emphasize the sacred nature of the painting, and, when necessary, limit its visibility. This type of control was imitated by the makers of birth objects, but for very different reasons.

Popular behavior suggests that ephemeral objects, as well as images, were also employed to assist parents in procreation. In fact, the entire practice of obstetrics was dominated by a wide range of folkloric procedures that both derived from and appealed to a primarily female population. These generally focused on the employment of specific, tangible talismans in a magical or supernatural manner to generate a positive response in the user.

Such objects were apparently so common that they required little explanation when cited in inventories and letters. In 1393 Margarita Datini's sister suggested a cure for Margarita's childless situation that involved "a plaster that they put on their bodies . . . but . . . it smells very strong, and [the maker] says that there are some husbands who throw it away."[43] Homemade, generally herbal, concoctions were mysterious even to contemporaries; they were made only by certain people, or at certain times of the year. Too little information is available to determine their constituent elements, or even how they were used, with any certainty. However, it is known that at his death in 1421 Bartolomeo de' Rossi's estate included a box full of birth spices.[44] Antonio de' Nobili was possibly alluding to his wife's use of a herbal treatment when he wrote to Lucrezia Tornabuoni in 1473, to inform her that "this day at the tenth hour, thanks to the grace

138 (*right*) Florentine, detail from the front of a childbirth tray, early fifteenth century. The couple is depicted in a garden of love. The Art Museum, Princeton University. Bequest of Professor Frank Jewett Mather, Jr.

139 (*far right*) Forlì (signed A.L.), interior of a maiolica childbirth *ongaresca* with a confinement room scene, dated 1549. Museo delle Ceramiche, Forlì. (Photo Giorgio Liverani)

of God and to your remedy, I have had a beautiful baby boy."[45] In 1461 Penelope Orsini wrote to Ginevra de' Medici:

> I am sending you a prescription to get pregnant, praying to God that it will be good for you. It cannot harm you, and all who have tried it have all found it good, that is those who were not able to make children . . . I believe that it will be good especially for you, because your body is suitable for it.[46]

How unfortunate that the prescription was not preserved along with the letter.

It is clear that remedies of the kind recommended by Lucrezia Tornabuoni and Penelope Orsini were quite popular. The extensive library that formed part of the estate of Niccolo Peri in 1431 included a large volume of these medical remedies.[47] The book was probably similar to the *Tesoro de' poveri*, a fourteenth-century collection of remedies which included a number of aids for pregnancy and childbirth.[48] Popular texts described several remedies for both encouraging and impeding childbirth, most of which employed various plants and minerals.[49] A popular ingredient in these remedies was the mandrake root, which was thought to be shaped like a human, and had therefore long been considered an aid to conception. It was even mentioned in this capacity in the book of Genesis (30:14–17).[50] In his early sixteenth-century play *La mandragola*, Niccolò Machiavelli invoked the use of the mandrake as a fertility aid on which the entire plot turned. In Act II, Callimaco tells Nicia, "there is no more certain way to get a woman pregnant than to give her an infusion of mandrake to drink."[51] It may also have been used in the fertility plaster recommended by Margarita Datini's sister. Although the maker did not disclose the ingredients in her noxious concoction, she stated that it could be made only after October.[52] According to the *Ricettario fiorentino* (1499), the official pharmacopeia of the Guild of Doctors and Apothecaries, mandrake was a November crop, so it could have been the major ingredient in the plaster.[53]

Other natural items were used to assist in childbirth. For example, coriander seed was popular for its ability to insure a fast delivery; an illumination in a manuscript of Pseudo-Apuleius' *Herbarium* shows the midwife placing a coriander seed under the mother's skirts to help force out the infant (figure 140).[54] Among the items listed in the inventory of the Frescobaldi confinement room cited earlier was a number of packets of spices and sugars, no doubt meant for medicinal purposes.[55] The specific ingredients could be very exotic: in 1563 the physician Giovanni Marinello cited concoctions made of pulverized snake skins, rabbit milk, and crayfish as aids against miscarriage.[56]

Stones were also used for such purposes. For example, Marinello advocated carrying diamonds to prevent miscarriage.[57] A more popular (and perhaps more affordable and accessible) mineral employed in childbirth was the aetite, alternatively called an eagle stone or aquiline.[58] Like the mandrake root, aetites were associated with childbirth because of their physical characteristics: they are a type of hollow geode, with small pieces loose inside them that rattle when shaken. According to the logic of sympathetic magic, aetites therefore recalled the child in the womb. Ruberto Bernardi's collection of popular medical lore of 1364 cited the aetite, and recommended that pregnant women carry it on their right sides.[59] In 1494 the Marchesa of Mantua, Isabella d'Este, wrote of her great faith in such stones, although she noted that her delivery was so easy that they had no chance to demonstrate their efficacy.[60] In his *Liber de vita*, Ficino attributed the stone's power to hasten delivery to the planet Venus and to the Moon.[61] Although Ficino wrote erudite, scholarly prose for a largely male audience, he may have been influenced by the popular and no doubt female practice of using aetites to aid in childbirth. Given its popularity as a birth charm, the childbirth stone mounted in gold mentioned in the estate of Giuseppe Coscietti in 1602 is likely to have been an aetite.[62] The value of this stone as a birth aid would justify such a rich setting; indeed, prophylactic stones and gems were often

140 Pseudo-Apeleius, *Herbarium*, thirteenth century. This manuscript illumination shows the kneeling woman on the right delicately placing a coriander seed under the birthing woman's skirts. Österreichische Nationalbibliothek, Vienna.

mounted for protection or display.[63] It is not always easy to link documentary references to tangible items. In 1479, for example, the estate of Albertaccio Satini included a rose of Jerusalem for childbirth.[64] This may have been a clerical error for the rose of Jericho, a cruciferous plant thought to help pregnant women by enabling them to give birth as easily as a plant blooms.[65]

In 1388 the estate of Deo del Beccuto included a silver-mounted stone of Saint Margaret; this too may have been a birth-related item.[66] The virgin martyr Margaret of Antioch was a patron saint of childbirth, and this role made her representation on domestic art particularly important.[67] Next to the Virgin Mary, who appeared in innumerable household paintings and sculptures, Saint Margaret was one of the most popularly represented saints in domestic art. Among the many inventories referring to works of art with her as the subject is that of Andreuolo Zati's estate, which contained a painted wooden statue of Margaret.[68] Books of the legend of Saint Margaret were also popular, like the little one found in Filippo Sapiti's estate in 1424.[69] The connection between childbirth and Saint Margaret was often made explicit. For example, Tribaldo de' Rossi's wife, Nanina, gave birth at the end of September 1493; two weeks later, Tribaldo purchased an illuminated manuscript of the legend of Saint Margaret.[70] In addition, the text of her legend could be used as a birth talisman. Anthonius Guainerius, a professor of medicine at the University of Pavia, recommended in his *Tractatus de matricibus* (1481) that Margaret's story be recited during labor.[71] Guainerius wrote his Latin text to assist male practitioners, but it is likely that he was responding to common superstitious practices in a profession dominated by midwives. In fact, the preface to a sixteenth-century version of Margaret's legend stated that the text should be read to the laboring woman or even placed on her stomach to aid her.[72]

Illuminated scrolls, based on the length of the body of Christ and inscribed with prayers to the Virgin or Saint Margaret, were used as girdles for pregnant women, and were actually wrapped around their bodies during labor.[73] But other girdles were even more mysterious; the childless Margarita Datini was instructed by her sister to wear a special fertility belt that had to be placed around her waist by a virgin boy, with its inscription against her skin, after which she was instructed to say three paternosters and three Ave Marias. But her brother-in-law advised Margarita's husband, "I believe that it would be more useful and much better for her if she fed three poor men on three Fridays and did not listen to the words that women say."[74] His response indicates that these charms and amulets were considered female aids, inferior to the methods sanctioned by men and not to be taken seriously.

Texts, whether or not they could be read, carried an enormous amount of weight. The underside of a maiolica *tagliere* attributed to the workshop of Nicola da Urbino displays the word MASCHIO (male), suggesting its use as a verbal rather than visual augury (figure 141). Similarly, an *ongaresca* from Urbino has the name SILVIA painted in its concavity (figure 142), and the word PIENA (pregnant) hidden under the foot ring (figure 143).[75] These hidden words may have been credited with quasi-magical properties to produce the desired result. Furthermore, the inclusion of these words on maiolica provides further evidence that the birth objects were given to a woman before her confinement. The verbal augury would do no good after she had given birth and the sex of the child was established. It is only before birth, during pregnancy, that such auguries could have an effect. Similarly suggestive is the scene on a Sienese wooden tray, which includes an inscription on the headboard above the new mother that reads *Bevis laboru quies* (figure 145).

Whether in the form of books, girdles, or inscriptions, the written word was considered both mysterious and powerful by many at this time. This belief resulted in a certain amount of exploitation for profit. When Giovanni Boccaccio visited the monastic library of Montecassino, he was said to have been dismayed that many ancient manuscripts had been destroyed. They were torn apart by the monks to make, among other things, charms for women, a product that was clearly in demand.[76] These charms, called *brevi*, were small pouches that held bits of inscribed texts. Mysterious fragments of text, no matter what they said, were held in great awe by the illiterate and were commonly employed as aids against physical ailments. Franco Sacchetti described how one entrepreneurial friar sold *brevi* of his own making, which he alleged assisted women in childbirth.[77] At his death in 1571 Poggio Morelli's estate included a little box full of *brevi* and other things for birthing women.[78] *Brevi* were also common objects to send with newborns to the wetnurse; in 1524 Ser Piero Bonaccorsi's daughter Clemenza took two with her to her wetnurse, along with more standard items such as a crib, sheets, and swaddling.[79] These

141 (*right*) Workshop of Nicola da Urbino, maiolica childbirth *tagliere*, c. 1530. Within a decorative border the artist has painted the word MASCHIO, surely an invocation for the conception and delivery of a son. Museo Civico Medievale, Bologna.

142 (*below left*) Urbino, interior of a maiolica childbirth *ongaresca*, c. 1530–40. The name SILVIA is inscribed in the center of the bowl. Location unknown. (Photo courtesy Bonhams, London)

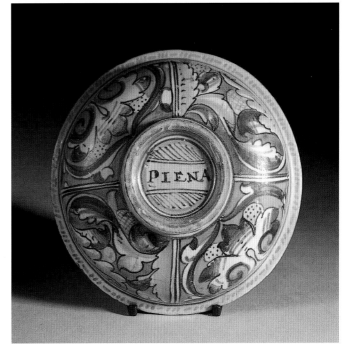

143 (*above right*) Urbino, exterior of a maiolica childbirth *ongaresca*, c. 1530–40. The word PIENA (pregnant) is inscribed under the foot ring. Location unknown. (Photo courtesy Bonhams, London)

objects combined religion with more supernatural elements, and were therefore often scorned for their folkloric nature; witness Margarita Datini's brother-in-law's response to the fertility girdle that his own wife recommended. And yet, the fact that these objects were included in estate inventories lends credence to both their value and their vast popularity.

The institutional Church endorsed its own methods of mediation, perhaps in direct opposition to the quasi-magical objects described above. For example, special masses could be said for a pregnant woman. One late fifteenth-century text calls for a week's worth of masses for a woman in her ninth month of childbearing. Beginning on Sunday, with the mass of the Nativity of Christ, the list continued on Monday with the mass of the Nativity of John the Baptist, on Tuesday with that of Saint Leonard, and on Wednesday with that of the Virgin. On the next four days the masses of the Holy Ghost, Saint Margaret, the Virgin, and the 11,000 Virgins were read.[80] The text does not specify the cost of this

144   Piero della Francesca, *Madonna del Parto*, c. 1455. This image of the Virgin, her pleated dress emphasizing her physical condition, was an important devotional site for pregnant women. Fresco. Santa Maria a Momentana, Monterchi. (Alinari/Art Resource, New York)

145 (*facing page*)   Sienese, detail of the front of the wooden childbirth tray illustrated in figure 41, c. 1520. Private collection.

personalized litany of masses. However, commemorative masses for the souls of the deceased cost relatively little at this time; Giovanni Tornabuoni paid a mere 5 *lire* in 1485 for a commemorative mass in honor of his deceased wife.[81] It is therefore safe to assume that many could afford to commission masses, providing an inexpensive and Church-sanctioned alternative to mysterious rocks and garbled texts on girdles.

Holy objects also served similar purposes. The hat of Archbishop Antonino of Florence was thought to have powers to aid women during delivery.[82] The use of relics was, in fact, recommended by Guainerius, who suggested that women keep saints' relics by their side in a delivery.[83] Again, his advice probably echoed what was already a popular practice; at her husband's death in 1471 Madelena Inghirammi had a crystal, a reliquary ampule, and a hanging relic, to be worn by a birthing woman, all in a small painted box.[84] Further assistance could be provided by threads which had touched the Virgin's girdle in Prato, a relic considered an aid for women in labor. Depictions of the pregnant Virgin, such as Piero della Francesca's *Madonna del Parto* (figure 144), may have been special devotional sites for pregnant women or new mothers.[85]

It was relatively common for a woman to make an offering after delivery, and this could take many forms. Usually, the woman had prayed for a particular saint's assistance in conception or delivery, promising an offering to persuade the saint to grant her wish. Following a safe birth, which indicated the saint's divine intervention, the mother was obligated to present her offering. Tribaldo de' Rossi's wife, Nanina, prayed for a safe birth by giving a large candle and money for a mass to the church of Santa Maria Impruneta

144

shortly before she delivered in 1490.[86] The wife of Pietro Vettori gave the chapel of San Alberto, in the church of the same name, an embroidered altar cloth when her wish for a son was fulfilled.[87] In 1451 Giovanni Giraldi's wife Brigida gave birth to a son whom they named Francesco Benedetto, because Brigida had prayed to Saint Francis and promised to name the child in his honor.[88] Sadly, however, the saint did not intervene to prevent the death of his namesake at the age of only five days. Other vows were more inventive. Caterina Antinori had prayed for a son. After her infant Tommaso was born in 1433, she was obligated to dress him in a white monk's habit for five years and to provide an annual feast for a group of monks to show her gratitude.[89]

Placing costly silver or wax votive offerings in churches to give thanks for a favor received from a saint was another popular practice.[90] It was important for these ex-votos to be in the shape of the person or thing affected by the vow.[91] Numerous silver offerings in the shape of various body parts and human figures are listed in the periodic inventories made by the Servite priors at Santissima Annunziata in Florence during the fifteenth and sixteenth centuries. In 1578 the Grand Duke Francesco de' Medici gave the Annunziata a silver ex-voto of a life-size swaddled baby representing his son Filippo.[92] Filippo was Francesco's first son and sixth child by his first wife, Giovanna of Austria; the offering worked for a few years, but the boy died in 1582. Many other ex-votos were given by the general public in relation to fertility and childbirth. Inventories of the Annunziata describe silver offerings in the shape of swaddled babies, breasts, and even the Virgin Mary giving birth.[93] Surely these were presented in hopes of, or in gratitude for, a successful childbirth or a recovery from a birth-related illness.

Even more offerings of this sort must have been made in wax. Purchased from the waxworkers who lined the via de' Servi (the street that led up to the Annunziata), these cheaper ex-votos were ephemeral and rarely inventoried. But they were often executed with great skill. The most famous waxworkers were members of the Benintendi family of Florence.[94] Numerous references to this family in memoranda of the period indicate their interaction with a large segment of the population. In 1476, for example, Nicolo Strozzi recorded a payment to Orsino the waxworker for an image offered by his wife to the Annunziata on behalf of their son.[95] In 1483 Lorenzo Morelli baptized Orsino's son Priore; Morelli was a man of significant standing in society, indicating the important connections the Benintendi had with the Florentine elite. These connections were no doubt fostered by the nature of their business and its supposed beneficial effects.[96] The market for these wax offerings was constant and profitable, and several generations of the Benintendi made their living in this profession.

At the end of the period under discussion, other offerings were made in the form of painted panels, usually depicting the supplicant in some form of distress. In 1588 the Dutch traveller Arnout von Buchell made special note of the painted panels in the Annunziata which showed "the wounded, the hanged, the tortured, the shipwrecked, the imprisoned, the sick, the pregnant lying in bed."[97] It is not surprising that such practices were so common. With few other inexpensive options for Church-sanctioned aid, fearful mothers probably placed a great deal of hope in the accepted practice of vow and ex-voto.

This wide range of mediating objects and images stimulated the imagination of the Renaissance woman, emphatically encouraging her to fulfill her societally sanctioned maternal role. Since both marriage and childbirth were critical to the continuation of the family, the inclusion of birth-related objects in a dowry or the purchase of them before or during a pregnancy was used to focus a woman on motherhood. Looking at suggestive paintings in the privacy of her bedchamber would ready her for the procreative act. Playing with baby dolls and receiving a small child into her arms at her wedding ceremony would encourage her to imagine the desired child. Even sacred recourse could be found in special prayers, votive offerings, and monumental paintings. The disporting naked boys

on the undersides of childbirth objects provided an even more positive (and gender-specific) encouragement to procreation (figure 146). All of these maternal mediators responded to the needs of Renaissance women by idealizing and encouraging this vitally important but potentially dangerous event.

Conclusion

WHAT DOES THE INFORMATION presented in this book contribute to the study of Italian Renaissance art? Much of it might seem tangential: after all, small utilitarian objects in varying stages of conservation and personal accessories known primarily through documentary references are not the usual subjects of art history. But in order to do justice to such a socially significant event as Renaissance childbirth, it is vital to explore the entire range of material culture, monumental and domestic, surviving and ephemeral, sacred and especially profane. And such a range is demonstrated by the profusion of objects discussed throughout this study (figure 147). From this wide-ranging examination, one fact should have become obvious: childbirth was an event which affected not only the family but also the economy and the appearance of society in general.

To use a term popularized by the French anthropologist Arnold van Gennep, childbirth was a liminal event.[1] At the threshold between childhood and matronhood, it may be defined as a rite of passage that marked a woman's fulfillment of her expected role. Both because of this liminal nature and because of the many risks surrounding it, Renaissance childbirth generated the variety of objects examined in this book. Italy was not necessarily unique in this respect. Other societies, in other times, also used objects and images as part of their birth rituals. Enamel and silver medallions, decorated with frightening gorgon heads, were used as protection for pregnant women and infants in the Byzantine east (figure 148).[2] Women in Baroque Holland had special drinking glasses with folkloric fertility motifs.[3] Their fantastic dollhouses, the pride of many wealthy merchant wives, often included a special room that was furnished as a confinement chamber (figure 149).[4] And tapestries made for the Tsaritsas of Russia in the early sixteenth century emphasized the importance of their role in producing future rulers.[5]

But childbirth culture and childbirth objects were even more extensive in the plague-decimated Italian peninsula, a fact made evident by any examination of birth-related trays and bowls (figure 150). A family was a mark of honor and prestige, as well as a sure way to perpetuate one's name and one's wealth. The mediating objects and images used at this time are indicative of the overwhelming emphasis placed on fertility and childbearing in Italian Renaissance society. The particular role of art in promoting the importance of the family in this devastated population has been an underlying theme of much of this study. But it is one in which intentions and meanings must be largely hypothetical, a drawback of discussing any past society.

Furthermore, it is difficult to examine marriage and childbirth in the Renaissance because of the intimate connection between these rituals and the world of women. Many aspects of women's history remain in the shadows despite the valuable discoveries of recent years. Part of this is due to the nature of women's identities. Contemporary men had a wide range of identities. Inside the home, they were husbands, fathers, and widowers; outside the home, they were merchants, statesmen, artisans, and members of guilds and confraternities. They came and went as they pleased, making money, crafting goods, and influencing the state with little impediment. They carried the same name throughout their lives, and this name referred back to any number of male relations before them. Because

147 Giovanni di Ser Giovanni, front of a wooden childbirth tray, c. 1440. This scene depicts events directly following childbirth: the mother reclines in bed and attendants bring her trays heaped high with various fruits. Institut de France–Musée Jacquemart-André, Paris.

148 Eastern Mediterranean, Medusa pendant, ninth century. Such apotropaic devices were used to assist pregnant women. The inscription around the edge of the reverse translates, "Womb, dark [and] black, eat blood [and] drink blood," and, in the center, "As the serpent you coil, as a lion you roar, as a sheep, lie down; as a woman . . ." Asking the womb to "eat blood [and] drink blood" was a way to ward against miscarriage. Silver. Menil Collection, Houston.

149 Dollhouse of Petronella Oortmans-de-la-Court, late seventeenth century. The confinement room is filled with miniature versions of the childbirth-related items used by Dutch merchant wives during the late seventeenth century. Centraal Museum, Utrecht.

these men could take on so many roles, in and out of the home, sometimes within the course of a single day, they had virtually limitless lifestyle options.

But Renaissance women had to adopt a more constricted range of identities.[6] A few were members of religious groups, and the archives of certain convents yield useful information about them. But most Renaissance women remained in the secular and domestic world, living inside the home and being defined by it. At any given juncture, most women were wives, mothers, or widows. Their names revealed their role; unmarried girls appended their fathers' names to their given names, while married women appended their husbands'.

One way to examine these female identities is through the objects that helped construct them. Marriage, childbirth, and widowhood were key rites of passage for the typical Renaissance woman. And each of these rites was marked by specific domestic objects. Inventories made this especially clear; most of the objects specifically designated for lay women were labeled in their husband's or father's estate inventories with the identifying adjectival phrases *da donna novella* (for a bride), *da parto* (for a mother), or *da vedova* (for a widow).

During the marriage ritual, new brides wore special embroidered shirts and caps and silver belts; they had finely worked sheets and painted or stucco trinket boxes, and they kept them all in large, historiated chests.[7] The objects associated with widows consisted primarily of clothing for public use, such as veils, cloaks, and handkerchiefs.[8] Widows wielded slightly more power than did other women. But the widow's sexual identity, always a problematic issue, was vague. Neither a virgin nor a married matron, she occupied a slightly anomalous position in society, although it was occasionally one of respect. Alessandra Strozzi, for example, ran her home and her husband's estate with alacrity while her sons were in exile. But most widows did not have such independence. If they were still young, they quickly remarried, or they were shuttled back to their father's home until a suitable new husband was found.

150

150 Urbino, top of a maiolica childbirth *tagliere*, c. 1540–50. The large, muscled boys are not newborns, and the loosely robed, barefoot women do not seem like the usual birth room attendants. But the interior is grand and the bed is heavily cushioned, making the scene a comforting one to its pregnant viewer. Kunstgewerbemuseum, Staatliche Museen zu Berlin, Preussischer Kulturbesitz.

151 Andrea del Sarto, *The Birth of the Virgin*, c. 1513. This painting places the holy event in an elaborate sixteenth-century secular space. Fresco. Atrium of Santissima Annunziata, Florence. (Alinari/Art Resource, New York)

This leaves us with one final identity, which is, of course, the one I have sought to examine: mothers. The objects designated *da parto* in inventories are specific to childbirth and confinement. It is clear that the setting for childbirth had to be festive. Visitors arrived in glorious garments and costly jewels, so the new mother had to look magnificent as well. Many of these items are visible in contemporary paintings of sacred births. In Andrea del Sarto's fresco of *The Birth of the Virgin* (figure 151), for example, the attendants caring for the newborn are almost as elegantly dressed as the visiting matrons who sweep into the foreground of the painting, wrapping their long trains around their arms to protect the rich fabric from the dirty city streets. The mother, who sits up to wash her hands in a metal basin, wears a special cap and collar, and an attendant offers her a birth tray. Her bed has a bright blue coverlet, trimmed with a long fringe at the edges. The fresco would lose much of its immediate and personal effect if these intimate details were omitted.

Although designated in inventories as objects specific to brides, mothers, or widows, these items did not belong to the woman in question. In fact, apart from her monetary dowry and the personal accessories she brought with her into the marriage, most objects described as hers were absorbed into her husband's estate and considered in the estimation of his net worth. For example, four small birth mantles were in Benedetto degli Albizzi's home at his death in 1401; a notation in the inventory next to them stated that these items were Benedetto's and that they were sold.[9] Although worn by his wife during her confinement, the mantles were considered part of Benedetto's estate, to dispense with as necessary.

152

But regardless of ultimate ownership, many of these objects were used to construct a woman's identity both within and without her home. The figuratively painted items, whether marriage chests, wooden birth trays and bowls, or maiolica, provided specific didactic and suggestive images that were intended to help her fulfill her very circumscribed tasks inside the house as wife and mother. And her clothing and accessories identified her to the outside world as bride, widow, or mother.[10]

Why were these objects associated only with women? No objects were specifically designated as a groom's or father's or widower's. It seems that, for men, these personal identities were a matter of course; there was no need to emphasize them, and they required no physical trappings, whether he was in his home or outside it. And a man, of course, owned almost everything. There were very few household items he could not lay claim on should he desire to do so. A woman, however, was accessorized according to her status as bride, mother, or widow. The objects themselves retained their special associations for many years. The young bride may have become a matron or even a widow, and the new mother may have become a grandmother, but she still had bridal or childbirth objects in her home. These objects helped establish her identity as a member of a certain house, and they served a commemorative purpose at the same time.

As a result, the wide variety of objects that surrounded childbirth became necessities, and most families were reluctant to be without at least a few of them. Furthermore, as material buffers in the face of mortality, these objects provided encouragement and assistance during a particularly risky period. Both their presence and their imagery were of immense importance to the Renaissance woman.

The critical nature of the images on many of these objects may help explain why there is so little metalware related to childbirth. Most metalware could not be decorated with complex narrative scenes. Perhaps as a direct result, there are only occasional references to metalware in the birth ritual. There are a few examples: in the early fifteenth century, Francesco Castellani gave two silver salts to a woman following childbirth.[11] But in most cases the metalware associated with women is simply referred to as *da donna*, as in the five small silver spoons described as *da donna* in the estate of Chanbio Petrucci in 1530.[12] It is most likely that these spoons, and other similarly designated metalware, were part of the bride's trousseau, probably included as special tokens for her new role. But metalware was almost never described as childbirth-related.[13]

Given the exhaustive list of objects related to childbirth, the paucity of birth-related metalware is puzzling. In chapter 1 we saw how Renaissance families of varying social levels had extensive collections of plate, and how they displayed it on important occasions (figure 13).[14] Much of the impetus behind the birth ritual was to display a family's wealth and social standing, and families presumably would have purchased plate for so important an occasion had it been the custom to do so. As Christiane Klapisch-Zuber has shown, many families did mark childbirths by exchanging metal goblets filled with sweetmeats and decorated with heraldry.[15] But evidence indicates that these were primarily dynastic objects, given to a certain woman when the occasion demanded it, kept for a period of time, and then given to the next woman in the extended family who gave birth.[16] These goblets were not meant for one specific mother, nor were they intended to be part of her surroundings for an extended period. They were only temporary gifts.

So it is difficult to account for the virtual absence of special metalware for childbirth, metalware that would have remained as part of a woman's surroundings and would have reminded her of her identity within the family. The high cost of metalware may have been a factor in some cases. But the main reason does seem to be the unsuitability of metalware for elaborate narrative scenes. The ideal birth object was both useful and didactic. Indeed, the popularity of figural scenes on surviving wooden and maiolica birth objects indicates that their narrative capabilities took precedence over the long-term investment potential of metalware. The appearance of these objects and their ability both to function in the ritual and to make clear and positive statements on Renaissance family life was what made them unique and long-lasting domestic items.

The relative scarcity of porcelain for childbirth can be explained along similar lines. The documentary references to porcelain of any sort are so minimal that it is often difficult to tell if the object listed was a locally produced, tin-glazed earthenware painted white and blue, or a coveted, expensive, and rare work of true porcelain from the East.[17] For example, in 1620 Domenico Bruni and his wife Lisabetta had what was described as a fine porcelain birth bowl and plate.[18] It is impossible to establish whether this was a local piece or an imported one. But it is interesting to note that "porcelain" wares were often described with laudatory adjectives that did not accompany the more common maiolica birth objects. This may have been due to their rarity, their cost, or their highly coveted decorative motifs. An earlier reference, of 1543, reveals how, following the birth of her son Don Giovanni, Duchess Eleonora de' Medici requested two porcelain childbirth *scodelle* for soup.[19] It is certain that she did not dine on mere earthenware. But the first Italian porcelain was not produced until the 1570s, when Grand Duke Francesco I de' Medici sponsored a limited series of experiments that are represented today by fewer than sixty various pieces of soft paste porcelain.[20] So it must be assumed that Eleonora was referring to imported wares.

Medici porcelain, in fact, has an indeterminate role in this discussion. Shapes of known pieces range from low bowls or plates to flasks and ewers. Most are painted in underglaze blue, with motifs from Chinese, Iznek, and contemporary Italian *grotteschi* wares. None can be identified, by shape or by iconography, as specific childbirth wares. Yet a great number of historiated maiolica birth wares are dated to the late sixteenth century, guaranteeing an awareness of the genre among those ceramists making Medici porcelain. In 1940 Giuseppe Liverani associated a painting by Alessandro Allori with Medici productions (figure 152).[21] Some of the blue and white wares Allori depicts in this painting may in fact be Medici porcelain; his altarpiece is contemporary to the porcelain experiments in Florence, and he was a favorite artist of Francesco I, who honored him with various commissions. This painting, then, may be Allori's acknowledgement of porcelain production under the Medici. The two plates with low rims and the water

153 (*right*) Workshop of the Ferniani family, maiolica childbirth set, mid-eighteenth century. This set, one of several from the Ferniani workshop in Faenza, consists of a tray, a low bowl, an egg cup, and its cover. Each piece is painted with elaborate decorative designs, imitating costlier imported porcelain. Victoria and Albert Museum, London.

154 (*far right*) Pesaro or Urbania, interior of a two-handled maiolica childbirth bowl, eighteenth century. The exterior is painted with elegant, stylized *grotteschi*. But the inscription in the concavity of the bowl translates "godmother's soup" or "mother's soup," linking the bowl to the childbirth ritual. © Fitzwilliam Museum, University of Cambridge.

152 (*facing page*) Alessandro Allori, *The Birth of the Virgin*, 1595. As a court artist for Duke Francesco I de' Medici, Allori must have known of Francesco's attempts to produce porcelain, which resulted in the soft paste wares now called Medici porcelain. This altarpiece seems to include several pieces of Medici porcelain, used as a set for the new mother and as the basin and ewer with which she washed her hands. Oil on canvas. Santa Maria Nuova, Cortona. (Alinari/ Art Resource, New York)

basin seem to be more utilitarian overall; their shapes and decoration link them closely to contemporary Medici wares. But the low covered bowl with its ornamental knob seems more distinctive. It is similar to the set shown in the painting by Bertucci (figure 84), and it is therefore similar to the actual two-piece maiolica set from the Patanazzi workshop (figure 85), both of which are examined in chapter 4 in relation to maiolica childbirth wares. This may have been a particular shape used for birth wares, whether maiolica or porcelain. It was certainly functional and well suited to carrying the broth recommended for new mothers.

Definite porcelain-inspired birth wares appear some time after the period discussed here.[22] Although still technically maiolica, they are considerably more elaborate than the earlier narrative examples. Some are complex, multi-piece sets (figure 153); others are simpler, handled bowls (figure 154). Notably, they are not painted with narrative scenes. These later examples have decorative designs, or at the most clichéd vignettes, following the current styles for porcelain production; they therefore carry none of the same associations as the earlier figurative maiolica wares. The contrast between the two types is quite clear, in fact, and the absence of a narrative tradition for these porcelain-inspired wares removes them from the didactic, suggestive roles of earlier birth objects. Now, they may still be functional, but the emphasis was on decoration over didacticism.

Why would this occur? Here it is important to review the demographic situation. Population levels slowly began to climb again in the late sixteenth century and the early seventeenth, although they did not reach pre-plague levels for some time. Concurrent with this growing population, there was a significant drop in the numbers of wooden and ceramic birth objects; both the variety of objects and their popularity had decreased considerably by this time. This was no coincidence.

The art of childbirth – from wooden trays and bowls and maiolica to sheets, clothing, and charms, as well as monumental scenes of confinement – manifested Renaissance attitudes towards childbirth and childbearing. All of these artifacts exemplified the family-centered ideology that characterized Italian society following the disastrous population decline after the Black Death. Even as the population slowly grew, reminders of the plague and the need for larger numbers were a constant part of everyday life. But by the late sixteenth century, with the burgeoning population, the popularity of these objects as a group waned.

What is considered a quintessentially Italian focus on the family must have grown out of the demographic catastrophe that occurred during the Renaissance. Such a connection was clearly made by the officials in Benito Mussolini's Fascist government, when they

155 Casteldurante, interior of a maiolica childbirth *ongaresca* with a confinement room scene, first half of the sixteenth century. The exterior of this *ongaresca* and its matching *tagliere* is illustrated in figure 96. Uměleckoprůmyslové Muzeum, Prague. (Photo Gabriel Urbánek)

156 Luigi Servolini, maiolica *scodella da impagliata*, 1940. The five-piece set, based on Piccolpasso's drawing, was given to Princess Maria Josè of Italy by the city of Forlì when she gave birth to her third child. The set was painted with symbols of the region and the House of Savoy. Location unknown. (Photo author)

engineered the revival of maiolica birth wares in the late 1930s (figure 156). In this interesting twist, they focused on the actual object, rather than on its ornamentation. Maiolica was seen as a traditional Italian product, and the revival of kilns in central Italy under Mussolini's dictatorship cannot be denied. The focus on childbirth, and therefore on motherhood, was considered a long-standing value, to be emphasized for the good of the state. In the face of a new demographic crisis – brought on by the flu epidemic, the disasters of World War I, a declining birth rate, and high infant mortality – it was difficult to fulfill Mussolini's doctrinaire demographic agenda. But the Fascist revival of birth wares was one way the government tried to encourage it. This revival, however, resulted in decorative childbirth wares, very different from the explicitly narrative and compellingly didactic Renaissance wares (figure 155). Nevertheless, the Fascist hope that such an object could help encourage procreation in their decimated country was a conscious return to Renaissance ideals.

It seems clear that these ideals were an important part of Renaissance society. As symbols of fertility, birth objects and images encouraged pregnancy. As rewards for procreation, they tangibly congratulated the new mother. And as physical manifestations of the attitude towards childbirth and childbearing, this wide range of objects and images illustrates the strong bond between the art and rituals of childbirth in Renaissance Italy.

Appendix A   The Estate of Francesco Inghirrami

THE FOLLOWING INVENTORY of the estate of Francesco di Baldino Inghirrami was made by Ser Benedetto da Staggio for the Florentine Ufficio dei Pupilli on November 8, 1471. Inghirrami left four sons and three daughters, and there must have been considerable concern regarding the fair and equitable settling of his extensive estate. The following transcription is excerpted from *MPAP*, 173, 265r–273v.

[265r] Rede di Franciescho di Baldino Inghirrami cittadino fiorentino

Apresso inventario di beni mobili e d'inmobili e prima:
Uno chasa grande dov'era la sua abitazione posta in sul chanto de lana dela stufa da lato di San Lorenzo chon un altra chasetta da lato a picchata chon essa che non qui sua apertenenza confinate
E prima masserizie trovate in dette chase e prima:

NELA VOLTA DELA CHASA GRANDE

1ᵃ botte de barili 32½ di vino vermiglio piena; 1ᵃ botte di barili 21½ di vino vermiglio piena; 1ᵃ botte di barili 20½ di vino vermiglio piena; 1ᵃ botte vota di barili 6 in circha; 1ᵃ botte vota di barili 3 in circha; 1ᵃ botte di barili 10 di vino vermiglio piena; 1ᵃ botte di barili 9 di vino vermiglio piena; 1ᵃ botte di barili 7 di vino vermiglio piena; 1ᵃ botte di barili 10 di vino vermiglio piena; 1ᵃ botte di barili 10 di vino vermiglio piena; 1ᵃ botte di barili 8 di vino vermiglio piena; e i sedili apertenenti a dette botte; 1ᵃ bighoncia danne de mania; 1ᵃ penera

NELA VOLTA DELA CHASA PICCHOLA E PRIMA

1ᵃ botte di barili 30 in circha entrovi barili 24 di vino in circha; 1ᵃ botte di barili 5 di vino vermiglio piena; 1ᵃ botte di barili 6 di vino vermiglio piena; 1ᵃ botte di barili 10 di vino vermiglio piena; 1ᵃ botte di barili 9 di vino vermiglio piena; 1ᵃ botte di barili 19 di vino vermiglio piena; 1° bighonciuolo; e più sedili apertenenti a dette botte

IN TERRENO NELLA CHASA PICCHOLA

1ᵃ botte vota di barili 3 in circha; 1° chassonaccio d'entrovi più schritturaccie; 1° paio di ceste da portare fanciugli; 1ᵃ tavola da mangare regholata di noce di braccia 7 in circha buona; 1° bighonciuolo da dare bere a chanagli con 2 manichi; 1ᵃ lettiera al'antica di braccia 4½ in circha vecchia; più some di fraschoni cioè fastella 16 in circha e più fastella 5; charrate 2 di vinciglie in circha; 1ᵃ piana di chastagnio di braccia 6 in circha

NELLA CHAMERA TERRENA DELLA CHASA PICCHOLA

1° chassone grande a 2 serami cho' libri e schritture; 1° paio di trespoli di noce da tavola; 1° chorbello grande entrovi più libri e schritture; 2 tinelle, 1ᵃ da charne insalata e l'altra no; 12 horcia da olio salde e piene, 11 di barili 2 l'uno in circha [blank]; 1° descheto da sedere di noce; 7 pezi di charne seccha cioè 7; 1° pezo di lardo; 1ᵃ seggiola grande d'arcipresso buona; 1° paniere grande da pane entrovi schritture; 1° chassone di braccia 3 in circha pieno di schritture intarsiato di noce; 5 fiaschi schiacciati

NELA CHORTE DELLA CHASA PICHOLA

Legnie chataste 3½ in circha; 1ᵃ charriuola nuova di braccia 3; 1° chorbellino voto; 1ᵃ schuricina; 3 palaccie da chalcina; 1° panchaccia trista di braccia 5

NEL TERRENO DELLA CHASA GRANDE

3 targhoni cho' l'arme sua; 1ᵃ tarcietta cho' l'arme del parto e del chomᵉ; 4 panche, 1ᵃ nuova e l'altre vecchie, in tutto braccia 20 in circha; 4 rastregli a picchati da tenere aste; 1° pezo d'asse a picchata al muro per credenziera

NELLA STALLA DELLA CHASA GRANDE

1° ronzino baio cho' suoi fornimenti; 1ᵃ mangiatoia e 1ᵃ rastelliera; 1° forchone di ferro; 1° vaglio; 1° chorbellino da biada

NELA CHAMERA TERRENA NELLA CHASA GRANDE

2 charrategli di barili 3 da tenere malvagia cioè dua; 1° letuccio salvaticho di braccia 3 al'antica; [265v] 1ᵃ bighoncia da biada; 1ᵃ lanterna choperta di panno; 1° chorbello da tenere biada; uno mezo quarto da biada; 4 horcie vote salde da olio; 1ᵃ chassaccia vechia di braccia 2 di noce sancha coperchio; 4 telaia da finistre inpannate; un mezo usciaccio vechio tristo

NELA CHORTE DELLA CHASA GRANDE

1ᵃ tinella lungha da bangniare; 1° chatino di rame mezano di libbre 8 in circha; 2 trespoli di noce da tavola buoni; 1ᵃ finestra d'abeto dala stalla; 1ᵃ streghia e 1° pettine da chavallo

NELLA SALA DELLA CHASA GRANDE

1ᵃ finestra inpannata; 1ᵃ tavola di braccia 7½ in circha regholata di noce; 1ᵃ seggiola da donna di stranba; 1° paio d'alari di libbre 46; 1° sechione d'aquaio di libbre 6; 17 horciuoli cho' l'arme tra piccholi e grandi; 3 chandellieri d'ottone a 4 nodi cioè tre; 1° armario a uso di credenziera chon più serami; 1ª bandinella da mano usata di braccia 6

NELLA CHAMERA DELLA CHASA GRANDE

1° cholmo di Nostra Donna di rilievo in uno tabernacholo; 1ª lettiera vechia dipinta di braccia 5 ingessata con sacchone in 2 pezi e trespoli e channaio; 1ª materassa di bordo piena di lana; 1ª choltrice usata di piuma San Giovanni; 2 primacci in tutto chola sopradetta coltrice in tutto libbre 120 in circha; 1° paio di lenzuola usate a 4 teli di panno forestiera; 1° choltrone di banbagia di braccia 4 di libbre 20 in circha; 1ª sargia verde d'un pezo di braccia 6 in circha; 3 ghuancali con federe; 2 chassapanche con tarsia a 4 serami con toppe e chiave; 2 forzieri dipinti begli all'usanza cho' l'arme; 1° lettuccio [e] 1° chapellinaio begli di noce con tarsia di braccia 4; 2 materassini da letuccio con pelo di bordo; 1ª choltre biancha da letuccio usata a detto letuccio; 1° forziere da soma usato entrovi libbre 26 di chandele di cera di più ragoni

NEL PRIMO FORZIERE GRANDE IN DETTA CHAMERA

2 tappeti nuovi di braccia 3 l'uno; 1° usciale d'arazo chon fighure e cho' l'arme; 1ª spalliera d'arazo di braccia 9 in circha; 1ª sargia rossa a teli dipinta di braccia 7 in circha; 1° chapone rosato usato doppio di panno monachino loghoro; 1ª cioppa paghonaza da uomo loghora foderata ½ di dossi e ½ di panno rosso e filettata di dossi maniche strette; 1ª cioppa di bigio fiandrescho da uomo scienpia cho' maniche strette; 1ª coppa rosata da uomo scienpia cho' maniche strette loghora; 1ª coppa rosata da uomo scienpia maniche strette; 1° mantellino di bigio fiandrescho da fanciugli foderato di pelle nere; 1° mantellino rosato da fanciugli foderato di chodioni di dossi; più pezi di fodere di pancie e di dossi vecchi; 1° sachetto di più filetti neri; 1ª chovertina azurra da chavallo foderata di tela azurra

NEL SECONDO FORZIERE IN DETTA CHAMERA

1° farsetto di veluto nero da uomo usato; 1° farsetto di ghuarnello nero raso cho' maniche e cholaretto di veluto nero; 1° farsetto di ghuarnello nero cho' maniche e cholarino di raso nero; 1° farsetto di ghuarnello bigio cho' maniche e cholarino di raso nero usato; 1ª saia rossa e nera da donna sanza maniche usata; 1° lucco luchesino cho' maniche a mantellini foderato di taffeta di gª e le maniche di taffeta chermuxi; 1ª ghamurra di panno verde da donna usata sanza maniche; 4 giornee di marezato nere da fanciulle nᶜ; 1ª coppa rasata da uomo sanza maniche scienpia; 1° lucchetto di rosato da uomo foderato di taffeta di gª usato; 2 maniche di rosato a mantellini usate; 1° lucco rosato chiuso foderato di taffeta di gª; 1° mantello luchesino da uomo usato buono; 1° lucchetto rosato piccholo da uomo foderato di taffeta di gª; 3 giornee di rascia biancha richamate da fanciulle; 2 coppette azurre da fanciulle tonde cho' maniche strette; 1ª ghamurra azurra da fanciulle non fornita sanza maniche; 1ª coppetta di bigio fiandrescho da fanciulle cho' maniche strette; 1ª coppetta di bigio fiandrescho chiaro da fanciulle cho' maniche strette tonda; 1ª coppetta di bigio fiandrescho da fanciulle cho' maniche strette; 3 ghamurre di rascia biancha melanese sanza

maniche richamate a fiori di seta cholorate foderate di tela biancha; 1ª ghamurra di rascia detta cho' manicha richamate chome di sopra; 1° mazo di pienne di paghone; 1ª coppetta di bigio fiandrescho da fanciulle cho' maniche strette; 1ª coppetta paghonaza da fanciulle scienpia e meze maniche; 1ª chotta a uso di saia di seta rossa e nera sanza maniche; 1ª ghamurra paghonaza di saia da donna cho' maniche di raso nero; 1° chapello nero da uomo di pelo; 1° paio di chalze di perpingniano nero da uomo usate e solate; 1° matellino di ghuarnello biancho chon cholarino d'ariento con traffatto; 1ª ghamurra di panno paghonazo da donna sanza maniche chon una tira di veluto nero da piè; 1ª coppa da fanciulle richamata di chalisea biancha chon oro e seta; 1ª coppa di bigio fiandrescho da donna maniche strette scienpia

NELA PRIMA CHASSA A PIÈ DEL LETTO IN DETTA CHAMERA

1ª tovaglia di braccia 11 ala parigina nuova; 1ª ghuardonappa nostrale con buchi di braccia 6 in circha nuova; 1ª tovaglia nostrale con buchi di braccia 6 nuova; 1ª ghuardonappa ala parigina di braccia 11 nuova; 1ª tovaglia nostrale usa di braccia 10; 1ª ghuardonappa nostrale usa di braccia 10; 1ª tovaglia grossa usa di braccia 5 nostrale; 1° mantile chome tovaglia di braccia 4 grosso uso; 1ª tovaglia nostrale con buchi usa di braccia 9; 1ª ghuardonapa chon buchi di braccia 6 usa e nostrale; 1° mantile di braccia 4 uso; 1ª tovaglia con buchi nostrale di braccia 6 usata; 1ª ghuardonappa con buchi nostrale di braccia 6 usata; 1ª tovaglia con buchi nostrale usa di braccia 7; 1ª tovaglia con verghe usata di braccia 7; 1ª tovaglia nostrale con buchi usata di braccia 6; 1ª ghuardonapa nostrale con buchi loghora di braccia 8; 1ª ghuardonappa nostrale con buchi usata di braccia 8; 1ª tovaglia ala parigina usata di braccia 9; 1ª ghuardonappa ala parigina nuovi di braccia 9; ½ tovaglia di braccia 4 con buchi usata; 5 bandinelle da mano usate di braccia 6 l'una; 2 tovagliuole chapitato con buchi usate sottile; 1° mantile da tavola uso di braccia 4; 1° mantile da donna di parto loghoro; 4 tovagliuole usate a chapi bianchi triste; 8 chanovacci d'aquaio usi; 6 tovagliolini da mano usi; 22 tovagliolini leghati insieme vecchi ch'erano 6 chole verghe [266r]

NELA SECONDA CHASSA A LLATO AL LETTO

2 lucchetti da fanciugli di saia paghonaza foderati di taffetta verde nuovi; 4 ghonnellini da fanciugli paghonazi ala lonbarda usi; 2 ghonnellini rosini da fanciugli usati; 3 ghonnellini cioè ghamurrini di saia paghonazi da fanciugli chole maniche e cholarino di raso verde; 4 ghamurrini di rascia bianchi da fanciugli chon cholarino di raso nero usi; 1ª giornea da uomo di tela nera marezata nuova; 1ª giornea da uomo di raso nero chola frangia all'anticha; 2 chatelani di panno paghonazo d'oricello da fanciugli nuovi; 2 ghonnellini da fanciugli di bigio fiandrescho usati; 1° chamiciotto da fanciugli; 1ª chamigia da donna usata per choperitura de'panni

NELA ⅓ CHASSA A PIÈ DEL LETTO

1ª fodera da cioppa da schrittoio di fianchi di volpe e nel busto pelle biancha; 1° fodera da cioppa di fianchi di volpe da uomo dal mezo in su pelle biancha; 4 quarti di fodera di dossi di vaio da cioppa da uomo da piè cioè dal mezo in giù

NELA ¼ CHASSA A PIÈ DEL LETTO

6 tovagliolini a picchati insieme grossi sanza verghe; 4 tovagliuole chapitate nuove chon buchi; 2 tovaglie usate ala parigina di braccia 10 l'una; 1ª ghuardonappa chon buchi ala parigina di braccia 6 usata; 1ª tovaglia ala parigina chon buchi usata di braccia 10; 1ª ghuardonapa nostrale chon buchi di braccia 10; 2 bandinelle da mano use di braccia 6 l'una; 2 tovagliuole chon buchi ala parigina usate; 3 tovagliolini sottili con verghe; 1ª tovaglia ala parigina nuova di braccia 8; 1ª ghuardonappa ala parigina nuova di braccia 8; 1ª tovaglia ala parigina usata di braccia 9; 1ª ghuardonappa ala parigina usata di braccia 9; 1ª tovaglia ala parigina usata di braccia 9; 1ª ghuardonappa ala parigina di braccia 9 nuova; 1ª tovaglia ala parigina usata di braccia 10; 1ª ghuardonappa ala parigina usata di braccia 9; 1ª tovaglia nostrale nuova di braccia 10; 1ª ghuardonappa di renso di braccia 11 con verghe nere usata; 1ª tovaglia di renso usata di braccia 14 in circha; 1ª ghuardonappa di renso usata di braccia 14; 1ª tovaglia di renso di braccia 14 usata; 1ª ghuardonappa di renso di braccia 14 usata; 1ª ghuardonappa con buchi nostrale di braccia 9 usata; 1º tovagliolino sottile con verghe; 4 berette da nnotte da uomo, 2 nere e 2 bianche; 1º chandelliere di ferro a picchato a 1ª ghocciola; 1ª ghuardonappa ala parigina di braccia 11 usata

NELO SCHRITTOIO IN DETTA CHAMERA

1º rinfreschatoio da maiolicha piccholo; 1º rinfreschatoio di vetro piccholo; 1ª mezina invetriata dipinta; 1ª lucerna d'ottone; 3 choltellesse vechie con ghuaina; 1ª tafferia da maiolicha picchola; 1º libereto di reghole coperto d'asse in charta pechora; libbre sei di più aghuti e altri ferri vecchi; 1º paio di tanaglie picchole; più libereti e quadri e altre schritture vechie; 1º chorbelletto piccholo; 1º piè d'archolaio

NEL NECESSARIO

1º paio di bisaccie vecchie; 2 fiaschetti

NELA SECONDA CHAMERA DOV'ABITAVA FRANCESCO NELA CHASA GRANDE

1ª Vergine Maria dipinta in piano in uno tabernacholo chon i sportegli nel muro; 1ª lettiera di braccia 5 con tarsia; 1º sachone e trespoli e channaio e pancha; 1ª materassa di bordo cho' lana e tela azzurra; 1ª choltrice con 2 primacci di penna San Giovanni di libbre 160 in circha; 1º paio di lenzuola a 4 teli usate di panno forestiero; 1º choltrone di braccia 4 di banbagia di libbre 25 in circha; 1ª sargia verde di braccia 7 in circha usata; 1º ghuancale con federa; 1º chortinaggio da 3 lati di tela forestiere con cielo e pendenti usato; 2 chassapanche a 4 serami con tarsie intorno a detto letto; 1º lettuccio [e] 1º chapellinaio con tarsie di braccia 4; 1º materassino di tela azzurra chon chapecchio; 1º choltrone da charriuola di braccia 3; 1º tappeto di braccia 4 vecchio; 1º paio di ghuancali da

lettuccio foderati di domaschino alessandrino con fodere lavorate; 1º ghuancale con mostre di taffeta di gª con federa lavorata; 1º ghuanciale con federa da lettuccio; 2 ferri di chiaverine all'anticha; 1º paio di chassoni dipinti in detta chamera cioè forzieri; 1ª tavola tonda dipinta da donna di parto; 1ª rosta di penne di paghone; 1º San Girolamo in uno tabernacholino con vetro dinanzi con più relique; 1ª Piatà dipinta in tavola; 1º San Francesco dipinto in un tabernacholino; 1ª palla di specchio di vetro; 1º lucerniere chol piè di marmo; 1ª chassettina d'un braccio entrovi 1º paneruzo lino con più aghuti nuovi

NEL PRIMO CHASSONE DIPINTO NELA SECONDA CHAMERA DETTA

12 chamicie da uomo usate; 2 sciughatoi con verghe da donne vedove sottile in un filo; 1º sciughatoio con verghe nere da donna vedova nuovo; 1ª chamicia tagliata da donna sottile; 2 braccia di panno lino sottile; 3 sciughatoini in un filo da chapo con verghe nere; 2 fazoletti in un filo sottili da mano; 12 mutande usate da uomo; 1º sciughatoio con verghe nere largho da letuccio usato; libbre 3½ di refe biancho sottile; 38 fazoletti sottili da mano da donne novelle in un filo rinvolti in una bandinella; libbre 3½ di più pezi di veletti di Bolognia; 50 tovagliolini in uno filo nostrali; 1º fardellino di libbre otto di più pezi di veletti di Bolognia; 1º leghato entrovi 3 chamicie da uomo di panno forestiere nuove; 1ª peza di pannolino di bordato di libbre sei; 6 chamicie nuove da donna novella; 8 sciughatoi grossi in un filo grossi da piè; 1º sciughatoio piccholo a picchati a detti; 1ª pezetta di panno lino forestiere di libbre sei oncie 4; 1ª pezetta di panno lino forestiere di libbre quatro oncie 8; 1ª peza di panno lino grosso nostrale ripieno di stoppa di libbre 38; 1º leghato entrovi più fazoletti di fiore in pezi 9 di libbra 1ª oncie 11; 6 sciughatoi con verghe nere di fiore sottile in 3 pezi; 1º sciughatoio d'accia sottile chon verghe nere nuovo; 4 benducci con verghe nere da fanciugli; 32 fazoletti tra da mano e da chapo ~~da uomo~~ per donne novelle; 33 benducci in un filo da donne novelle con verghe nere; 7 benducci in un filo da donna con verghe nere; 2 benducci con verghuccie da donna in un filo; 7 benducci da donna sottili con verghe nere in un filo; 11 benducci da donna sottili chon verghe nere in un filo; 15 chamicie nuove grande da donne novelle lavorate; 4 chamicie da fanciulle nuove lavorate; 6 chamicie da uomo nuove 3 chucite e 3 a chucire; 1ª choltruccina d'azzurra a bottoncini biancha; 3 sciughatoi di fiore fini con verghe nere; 5 chuffie da donna cho' recitelle usate; 3 pezi di nastri sottili churati da donna novella; [266v] 1º benduccio da donna novella chole verghe bianche; 2 pezi di bende di fiora grosse; 7 chuffie da donna lavorate tra usate e nuove; 2 pezi di reticelle strette da chamicie; 2 fazoletti da mano in un filo grossi; 3 federe da ghuanciagli nuove da letuccio; 4 sciughatoi sottili da donne vedove usati; 3 fascie nuove da fanciugli; 2 benducci da donna sottili in un filo con verghe nere; 3 benducci da donna in un filo sottili; 2 fazoletti da mano sottili in un filo; ½ sciughatoio di fiore con 1ª vergha nera sottile; 1º fazoletto di fiore da chapo nuovo cioè 1º; 1º sciughatoio di

fiore sanza verghe nuovo; 1° velo da donna vedova nuovo; 1° fazoletto di fiore da chapo nuovo; 1° benduccio nuovo da donna con verghe nere; 1ª fascia sottile da fanciugli; 1° sacchetto entrovi 17 chuffie da donne novelle tra nuove e usate; 4 fazoletti di renso usati da donna; 3 veletti di Bolognia da chapo; 1° sachettino entrovi mozature di panno lino e lett^e; braccia uno $\frac{1}{3}$ in circha di veluto piano paghonazo chermusi; 6 pezi di veluto piano verde di braccia 8 in circha di peso di libbre dua oncie 6 usato; 1° ghuardaquore bigio da fanciugli foderato di pelle bianche e 1ª chamicina; 2 peze di reticele da ghuanciali di peso di libbre 1ª oncie 4; 2 federe a reticele da ghuancali; 5 benducci da donna vedova con verghe bianche; 4 paia di maniche di seta da fanciulle cholorate e richamate; 11 maniche da fanciulle richamate di saia e di bocchaccino rinvolte in un pezo di tela; 1° sacchettino d'accia sottilissima biancha tra un matasse e inghomitoli libbre 8 oncie 10 chol sachetto; 4 paia di maniche di seta da donna usate di più cholori; 17 oncie xvii di banbagia nera in uno sachetto filata; 6 oncie vi di banbagia biancha filata in uno sachettino; libbre 3 oncia 1° di pepe sodo in uno sachettino; 5 oncie cinque di zafferano in uno sachetto di chuoio chol sacchetto; 8 charte di pilletti cioè 4; 13 aghoraiuoli di seta e bochato di più cholori in una schatolina; 2 berette in tela richamate chon orpegli e più 1ª meza beretta; 1° cinto biancho di braccia 1° di raso; 1ª schatola tonda grande entrovi più segnialetti d'oro buono ed orpello e frangie e alchuna perluzza da fanciugli; 1° chasetino piccholo entrovi 1ª peza di nastro sottile di refe, 1ª chuffia richamata chon oro e seta in pezi, 1° libriccino di Nostra Donna chovertato di raso paghonazo fornito d'ariento con più mini forestieri, 1ª beretta da donna di veluto verde chon i schaglie d'ariento dorate, 1ª beretta di bocchato chermisi d'oro alto e basso, 1° anello da chucire d'ariento, 2 collari da fanciulle con 47 bottoni grossi d'ariento dorati con 2 pendenti con 6 perle per uno e 1ª rubino nel mezo in bocchetta, 3 altri chollari con 28 bottoni per chollare sanza pendente, 1ª chatenuzza d'ariento dorata di $\frac{2}{3}$ di braccio, 3 paia di ghuanti di chamoscio bianchi da fanciulle

NEL SECONDO FORZIERE OVERO CHASSONE NELA DETTA CHAMERA DIPINTO

1° fardellino entrovi braccia 31 di rascia biancha in 2 tagli; 1° fardellino entrovi braccia 13 di saia tinta in grana fine; 1° fardellino entrovi braccia 11 di chalisea biancha; 1° fardellino entrovi braccia 17$\frac{1}{4}$ di saia bigia; 1° fardellino involto in una choltricina da zana entrovi braccia 3$\frac{1}{2}$ di panno di Londra paghonazo e braccia 13 di rascia tinta in grana; 1° fardellino entrovi 1° taglio di braccia 10$\frac{3}{4}$ di panno nero di Firenze; 1° fardellino entrovi 2 tagli, 1° di braccia 29$\frac{3}{4}$ di saia verde e 1° taglio di braccia 48 anche verde in tutto braccia 77$\frac{3}{4}$; 1° fardellino entrovi 2 tagli di suantone, 1° bianco l'altro bigio di braccia 3 l'uno in tutto braccia 6; 1° fardellino entrovi 2 ghonnellini di panno lino forestieri dipinti; 1° fardellino entrovi 2 peze di cianbellotti paghonazi fini; 1° fardellino entrovi 1ª coppetta verdebuna vechia da donna; 1° fardellino entrovi schanpoletti di bigio fiandrescho di più fatte di peso di libbre cinque oncie sei; 1° rinvolto di paia 4

di maniche paghonaze e 1° busci e altri pezuoli di panno paghonazo; 1° rinvolto di 4 chordovani da stivaletti, 2 rossi e 2 azurri; 1° rinvolto entrovi x berette di grana cioè 10 e 1ª paghonaza augho; 1° rinvolto entrovi 4 quartieri di 1ª coppa e 4 quartieri d'una ghamurra paghonaza; 1° rinvolto entrovi 1° coppone bigio di panno fiandrescho tagliato e non chucito; 1° rinvolto entrovi 4 berette nere; 1° rinvolto entrovi 2 chapucci rosati 1° di panno e 1° di saia melanese; 1° rinvolto entrovi braccia 2 di saia tinta in oricello in 3 taglia l'altro taglio biancho di braccia 7 e l'altro di braccia 4 paghonazo di g^a; 1° rinvolto entrovi 2 paia di chalze verde e 1° schanpoletto verde di perpingniano di braccia 2 in circha; 1° rinvolto entrovi schanpoletti 3 di saia biancha e azurra e rascia biancha; 1° rinvolto entrovi più schanpoletti di panno bigio di più ragioni; 1° rinvolto entrovi più schanpoletti e ritagli di panno azurro; 1° rinvolto entrovi 1° pezo di cioppa vecchia bigia d'araconciare altre; 1° rinvolto entrovi inbusti e tagli di saia azurra e biancha; 1° paio di maniche nere da donna; 1° sachetto entrovi più pezi di saia rossa e nera e altri pezuoli di panno di più cholori; 1° sachetto entrovi più ritagli di panni bigi; 1° pezo di nuoglia da nuolgere panni; 2 sciughatoi vecchi al chapellinaio; 1ª beretta a aghomischiata di più cholori nel forziere detto

NELA PRIMA CHASSA A CHAPO A LETTO IN DETTA CHAMERA

1° rinvolto entrovi 3 paia di lenzuola di panno forestiere a 4 teli; 1° sachettino entrovi 13 paia di mutande da fanciugli e 4 chamicie da fanciugli e 9 fazoletti da mano e 1° grenbuole da fanciugli e 1ª schatolina chon aghora, tutte le chose line usate; 1° sachettino entrovi 18 benducci usati; 1° schatolino dipinto entrovi 1° tondo di cristallo e 1ª anpollina di relique e 1° chordiglia biancho e 1° nastro di seta biancho con orlique a picchato da porre a dosso a donna di parto; [267r] 2 chamicie da donna, 1ª da donna novella nuova e l'altra no; 4 chamicie vecchie da donna; 11 chamicie da fanciugli usate; 17 ~~segniale~~ sciughatoi usati di più sorte; 3 sciughatoi sottili con verghe bianche da donna vedova; 2 sciughatoi sottili con verghe nere da donne vedove; 3 sciughatoi da chapo usi; 2 pezi di teli di lenzuolo; 2 federe da ghuancali; 8 benducci usati da donna; 1° sacchetto entrovi 2 veli da donne vedove; 1° sciughatoio di fiore sottile e 1° sciughatoio nostrale con verghe nere usati; 1° sachetto entrovi 4 federe da ghuanciali usate e 1° fazoletto ~~da donna~~ cioè 1° fazoletto di mano e 2 sciughatoi usati da donna vedova e 3 veli sottili e tre mezi sciughatoi sottili e 1° sciughatoio da donna vedova di fiore con verghe bianche e 1° fazoletto d'accia sottile da chapo e 1ª meza federa da ghuancali a reticella tutta; 1° sachettino entrovi pepe pesa libbre tre oncie 2; 1° sachettino entrovi 4 benducci da donne usati e 2 bende e 1ª chuffia e 1ª beretta biancha di panno da donne tutte use; 1° sachetto entrovi 9 chuffie nuove e 2 testiere da fanciulle grosse e 8 chuffie sottile da donna use e 3 chollarini da fanciulle chon reticelle; 1° sachettino entrovi più chartocci di pepe e zafferano e libbre 4 oncie 4 di mandorele nostrale; 1ª chucchiaiera cho' la chassa chon otto chuchiai, 7 cho' lioncino e 1° no, e otto forchette cho' lioncino che vene 1ª rotta; 1° sachettino di pepe e zafferano e grengiovo libbre dua; 1° sachettino entrovi uno anello d'ariento da chucire da donna e più ritagli di velluto e 2 bende e 3 sogholi e 2 benducci da fanciugli e 4 nappe da ghuanciali di grana di seta

NELA SECONDA CHASSA IN DETTA CHAMERA

1° rinvolto entrovi tre lenzuola grande e 1° forestiere a 4 teli l'uno in tutto lenzuola quatro; 1° lenzuolo di 4 teli usato a reticelle di panno forestiere; 1° lenzuolo nuovo a 4 teli di panno forestiere; 3 lenzuola di panno forestiero da fante; 1ª coltre scienpia a verghe da letto di braccia 4; ¼ di chortina da letto biancha con frangie; 7 berette da nuotte di panno usate di più cholori; 2 chuffioni di ghuarnello; 4 chandele bianche benedette di peso di libbra 1ª in circha

NELA ⅓ CHASSA IN DETTA CHAMERA

1° choltellino d'ariento cho' l'arme; 10 chamicie da donna tagliate di panno forestiere; 1° sachettino entrovi più ritagli di panno lino tra grandi e picholi e nastri e altri sachetti; 1ª ghamurra mormorina usata da donna vechia; 1ª coppa di rascia nera da donna vedova usata; 1ª coppa da donna vedova di saia melanese nera chiusa dinanzi e nuova; 1ª coltricina da lettuccio a bottoncini di braccia 4; 1ª coppa nera usata da donna vedova; 1° pezo di panchale di braccia 8 sopannato di tela verde cho' l'arme; 1° pezo di spalliera di braccia 3 sopannato di tela verde cho' l'arme; 1° mantello monachino da uomo fine usato

NELA ¼ CHASSA IN DETTA CHAMERA APERTA E VI PANNI DE' FANCIUGLI PER LORO VESTIRE E QUALI AL PRESENTE PERTANO

NELA ⅓ CHASSA CH'ERA RIMASTA A DRIETO IN DETTA CHAMERA

1ª coppa nera ritinta sdrucita [e] 1° ghonnellino nero usati

NELLO SCHRITTOIO DELA CHAMERA DOV'ABITAVA FRANCESCO

1ª Vergine Maria in uno tabernacholuzzo; 1° bacino nuovo chon chonpasso e altro lavoro d'ottone; 2 bacini d'ottone usati cho' l'arme di Francesco e dela donna; 1ª miciroba nuova grande; 1ª miciroba usata cho' l'arme di Francesco; 6 chandellieri d'ottone chol piè alto nuovo; 8 chandellieri chol piè basso afoggia nuova d'ottone; 1° schaldaimiande d'ottone; 4 chandellieri da torchietti ala domaschina; 1ª miciroba a boccha aperte grande d'ottone; 1° chandelliere domaschino chola lucernuza d'ottone; 1° rinfreschatoio di vetro chol piè; 1° rinfreschatoio da maiolicha chol piè; 1° rinfreschatoio di vetro sanza piè; un paio di rinfreschatoi da maiolicha da donna ~~di parto~~ cioè novella; 1° piatello da maiolicha piano; 1° chalamaio da maiolicha; 1° chalamaio di chuoio dipinto; 1° specchio chol piè alto a fiori di seta; 1° chornetto di vetro; 1° specchio chon altri specchi dintorno dipinto; 1ª fiaschetta di vetro cho' lavori; 1° stangnione mezano pieno d'utriacha; 1° orciuolo di rena; 2 teste di terrachotta da donna dal busto in su; 1° tavoliere e schacchiere picholo chole tavole e schacchi;

1° panno in tavola dipinto fiandresco con 2 teste cioè Nostro Singniore e Nostra Donna; 1ª sportellina chon aghuti e 1° martellino; 1° Giesu dipinto in tavola; 1° bacinetto di rame chon più sugegli d'ottone; 3 pugniali al'anticha e 1ª choltella melanese; 1ª chatelana cho' l'arme dorata; 1° stoccho ingniudo; 1ª forchetta da rostire chacio; 4 falcholette di cera di libbre tre in circha; 1° libro biancho segnata A [e] 2 quaderni di chassa [e] 4 quadernucci di richordi lunghi [e] 2 libri di richordanze, apertenenti a Francesco Inghirami e Giovanni di Nuto quand'erano conpagni; 1° libretto di richordi apertenente a Madonna Maddalena propria; 1ª filza di più schritture e 2 bolle con sugegli di pionbo; 1ª chassetta di Levante chon chonpassi d'avorio entrovi 1° paio di choltellini forniti d'ariento da fanciulle; 1° paio di choltellini cho' l'arme d'ariento di Franciescho; 2 punteruoli d'avorio l'uno fornito d'ariento e 1° no; 1° paio di smocholatoie d'ottone; 1ª ghuaina chon tre choltellini fiandreschi; 1° tondo di bionbuove la testa di Chosimo; 1ª schodella [e] 2 schodellini di lattimo; 4 saliere di lattimo di mistura da Murano; 6 saliere di vetro cristallino; 2 saliere chol piè di vetro cristallino; 2 taze e 1° bicchiere di vetro cristallino; 2 bossoli da spezie di vetro azurri e bianchi; paneruzolini di vetro azurri e bianchi; 1ª anpolluza picchola di vetro; 1° bossolo di vetro chol choperchio; 1ª saliera di vetro dipinta; 3 saliere di vetro azurro; 1ª choppa di legnio fatta nell'Amangnia; [267v] 1ª schatolina dipinta entrovi 1ª anpollina in che è chome balsimo; 2 sugegli e 1° scuzichatoio da orechi d'ariento e sugegli cho' l'arme; 2 tenperatoi Tedeschi; 1° paio d'ochiali fini; 1° pettine d'avorio dipinto; 1ª chiocciola marina; 1° choltello da charne secha nuovo sanza maniche

1ª CHASSETTA ENTROVI

2 chassettini di chuoio entrovi suoi brunlegi; 8 quadri di fogli fini da schrivere; 1° libriccino di Lalde e altre chose choverte d'asse di ¼ foglio; 1° libro d'asse di charta pechora in Latino titolato Rosa Bella overo Rosa Novella; 1° librodone la legenda di San Nicholo choverte d'asse; 1° libro di musicha in chavretti choverta d'asse; 1° libretto d'asse dela passione di Cristo; 1° vilume di Boezio coverte d'asse in banbagia; 1° libro di strologia in charta pechora choverto di charta; 1° libro in charta pechora sanz'asse trata di più chose in Latino; 1° libro in francioso lapidario in chavretti choverte di charta pechora; 1° libretto d'asse coperto di chuoio rosso in charta banbagina di versi miniato volghari; 1ª scharsella che portava Francesco chon chatenelle d'ariento entrovi 2 brunlegi; 1ª meza madre perla

IN DETTO SCHRITTOIO NELA CHASSETTA DOVE SI SIEDE PIÙ MAZI DI LETTIERE DI PIÙ TENPI

1° chandelliere d'ottone grande da pichare al muro nuovo; 1° mazo di chontratti in charta pechora di numero xxii; 1° libro di charta pechora di chanto fighurato miniato tutto coverto d'asse e veluto chermisi con serami d'ariento; 1° libro di chanto fighurato in charta banbagina choperto di chuoio paghonazo; 1° mazo di più schritture; e'l piè del chandelliere grande da pichare al muro e con più rami d'ottone

SOTTO LO SCHRITTOIO

2 rinfreschatoi grandi da maiolicha piani; 2 piategli grandi da maiolicha piani; 4 piategli da maiolicha grandi; 2 piategli di detta ragione

SOPRA LO SCHRITTOIO

1° bacino d'ottone grande rotto di libbre xiiiiᵒ; 1ᵃ acetta a una mano; 1ᵃ spada al'anticha; 1° paniere entrovi 8 mezette cho' l'arme

A LATO A LO SCHRITTOIO

1ᵃ chassettina entrovi più schriture vechie; 1ᵃ chovertina nera da chavallo

IN DETTO LUOGHO

una chassa vechia entrovi più mazi di lettere di più tenpa; 1ᵃ chasetta da fuse piena di lettere; 1° sachetto verde pieno di chontratti a numero xxv; 1° libro biancho segnato C titolato in Giovanni e Francesco di fogli mezani in schritto da carta 1 a carta 238 e in detto libro 5 quadernucci di richordi; 1° libro rosso segnato B di fogli reali titolato in Francesco proprio entrovi 1° chanpione di richordi; 1° leghato di 4 quaderni e più altri fogli di bilancio di ragione; 1° leghato di più fogli di schritture; 1° sachetto entrovi più mazi di schritte e più quadernucci; 1° sachetto con più lettere; 1° mazo di 2 libretti e 1° quaderno e altri straccia fogli; 1° descho da donne di parto rotto dipinto; 1° choltelliera sanza choltegli cho' l'arme; 1° marchietto; 1° martellino; 1° paio di tanaglie

NEL NECESSARIO

1° orcio da olio entrovi 20 chaci marzolini in circha; 1° bighoncione da chruscha voto; 1° raniere lungho; 1ᵃ archetina entrovi 1° saccho grande nuovo e più cenci; 1° saccho da farina; 1° sachetto di susine secche d'un quarto; 1ᵃ chassetta salvaticha sanza coperta d'abeto; 1° paio di staffe chon i stafili piccholi; 1° paio di pianelle frateghe; 1° paio di sproni

NEL'ANTICHAMERA DELLA DETTA CHAMERA

1ᵃ Vergine Maria al'anticha chon i sportegli; 1ᵃ Vergine Maria dipinta in un tabernacholetto; 1ᵃ lettiera di braccia 4 chorniciata di noce; 1° sachone trespoli channaio e pancha; 1ᵃ materassa di bordo e tela rossa; 1ᵃ choltricie chome nuova con 2 primacci a detto letto di libbre 100 in circha; 1° paio di lenzuola di panno forestiero a 3 teli; 1ᵃ choperta di saia biancha e verde di braccia 5 a detto letto; 3 ghuancali sanza federa; 1° chortinaggio ala Franzese a 3 lati chol sopracielo e pendenti; 2 chassapanche basse a 4 serami; 1° chapellinaio di braccia 3; 1° forziere dipinto a ucellini al'anticha; 1° orcio da olio saldo; 1° chonchone e cholatoio grande; 1° chatino di rame grande di libbre 17 cioè xvii; 1° forzeretto da soma; 1ᵃ fiaschetta schiacciata dipinta chon aqua arzente

NELA PRIMA CHASSA IN DETTA ANTICHAMERA
A LATO AL POZO

1° ghamurrino biancho da donna usato; 1° paio di stivaletti usati

NELA SECONDA CHASSA NON NULLA

NELA ⅓ CHASSA [ ] DI NON STIMA

NELA ¼ CHASSA

1ᵃ chaperuccia di romangniuolo; 1° pezo di ferro da schaldaletto di libbre 5; 4 chamiciottini di chanavaccio loghori e tristi

NEL FORZIERE IN DETTA CHAMERA

1ᵃ choltre biancha bella con più lavori di braccia 7 pero filata di refe nero; 1ᵃ choltre biancha a bottoncini di braccia 7 in circha; 1° sachetto entrovi 1ᵃ coppa monachina da donna foderata di pelle bianche di Madonna Maddalena; 1ᵃ coppa monachina da donna vedova loghora; 1ᵃ giornea di ghuarnello nero da uomo loghora; 1ᵃ giornea di rascia rosina scienpia loghora; 1ᵃ coltretta da letuccio di braccia 4 in circha; 1° sachetto entrovi lino pettinato pesa in tutto libbre xiiiiᵒ oncia viᵒ [268r]

NEL FORZERETTO DA SOMA IN DETTA ANTICHAMERA

1° paio di lenzuola nostrale a 3 teli e mezo rotte; 4 chamici da fanciulle usati di tela forestiere; 2 chamicie grosse da fanciulle; 1° taglio di tela forestiera stretta di braccia tre; 2 chamicie da fante nuove grosse; 1ᵃ chamicia tagliata da uomo nuova di panno nostrale; 1° pezo di tela forestiera di braccia 1½; 4 paia di chalze di panno lino da fanciulle rotte; 1° pezo di fiangone di refe da chortina libbre tre in circha; 1° paio di maniche di panno biancho da fanciulle usate; 1° sachetto lungo entrovi più ritagli e pezi di panni lini e di rascia e altri cenci; 1° sachettino chon refi di più chori di libbre dua oncia viii; 1° gharzo da donna di 4 mari; 1ᵃ doppia verde da mettere a 1ᵃ donna da piè a una coppa [ ]; 1° paio di maniche di perpingniano nere da fante; 1ᵃ doppia di chalisea biancha da coppa da donna; 1° paio di brodoni di chalisea biancha da fanciulle; 2 ghuarnellucci usati da fanciulle; 4 paia di scharpettine nuove da fanciugli, 2 bianche e 2 rosse; 2 fascie tagliate grosse da fanciugli; 1° sachetto entrovi più frastagli di più ragoni e pezuoli di panno verde e altri chori e cholarinuzzi di seta e chalcetti vechi; 1° inbusto con bordoni da ghamurrino e pezi di ghuarnello da fodera in detto sachetto di sopra; 1ᵃ berettaccia bigia da nuotte; 1° sachettino entrovi bottoni 14 d'ariento e ghangheri 22 d'ariento e altre magliette in arientate e ghangheri; 6 rochetti da setaiuoli suvi ariento fine e oro e orpello e 1° leghatuzo entrovi più chordelline chon punte d'ariento in detto sachetto; 1° panno di tela lina dipinto vechio e rotto a pichato presso al pozo in detta antichamera

NELA CHASA PICCHOLA E NELA PRIMA SALA

1ᵃ tavola regholata con filo di tarsia di braccia 5 con trespoli; 1ᵃ tavoletta da fante d'albero con trespoli; 1ᵃ chassetta da pane; 1ᵃ pancha regholata vechia di braccia 3; 8 seggiole di stranba da sedere; 3 deschetti tondi; 1° paio di trespoli da tavola; 1ᵃ predella; 1ᵃ paletta da fuoco; 1° paio d'alari di libbre xlviii; 3 lucernieri di legnio; 1° cestino da pescie

marino; 1ᵃ channa da misurare; 2 finistre inpannate nuove; 1°
paio di forbice; 1° schannello da serare e da schrivere

NELA PRIMA CHAMERA DI DETTA CHASA DETTA CHAMERA BUIA IN SULA SALA

1ᵃ Vergine Maria dipinta in uno tabernacholo quadro; 1ᵃ
letiera di braccia 5 con tarsia chon sachone di 2 pezi e trespoli
e channaio e pancha; 1ᵃ materassa di bordo e chanovaccio
rosso cho' lana; 1ᵃ choltrice di penna San Giovanni amezata;
2 primacci chola sopradetta choltrice in tutto libbre 150 in
circha; 1° paio di lenzuola a 4 teli usate di panno forestiere; 1°
choltrone chon banbagia di braccia 5 di libbre 25 in circha;
1° panno biancho da letto con verghe nere di braccia 7; 1°
ghuancalino piccholo sanza federa; 2 chassapanche a 4 serami
con tarsie; 1° lettuccio di braccia 3 salvaticho; 1° materassino
di chanovaccio chon chapecchio per detto letuccio; 2
choltricine da zana di braccia 1½ l'una con penna di ghallina;
1° pannetto da letuccio di più cholori vechio; 1°
chapellinanizo di braccia 2; 1° pettine da lino nuovo; 2
forzieri dipinti all'anticha; 1ᵃ chasettina di braccio 1° picchola;
1° paniere di veture chol manicho

NEL PRIMO FORZIERE DIPINTO A LATO ALA VERGINE MARIA ENTROVI

1° sacheto entrovi libbre 21 di lino pettinato scio; 1° sacheto
entrovi libbre 25 di lino pettinato vernio; 1° sacheto
entrovi libbre 17 di lino fine pettinato; 1° sacheto piccholo
entrovi libbre 7 di lino vernio pettinato; 1° sacheto
lungo entrovi libbre 32 di lino pettinato vernio; 1° mazo di
lino sode di libbre 5 oncie 5; 1° sacho entrovi accia biancha
di lino e di stoppa di libbre 31½ lorda

NEL CHASSONE DI PIERO INGHIRRAMI ENTROVI IN DETTA CHAMERA

2 pannetti d'arazo azurri e chochani usati di braccia 6 l'uno;
1° panno d'arazo averzura di braccia 8 in circha usato
bernolto; 1° panno d'arazo averzure usato di braccia 7 in
circha; 1° tapeto vechio di braccia 4; 1ᵃ sargia verde usata di
braccia 8 in circha; 1° usciale di panno nero chon richami
cho' l'arme vechio; 1ᵃ coltre biancha a chonpassi da letto di
braccia 7 buona; 1ᵃ coltre sottile a chonpassi da letto di braccia
7 usata; 1ᵃ choltre biancha grossa di braccia 5 usata; 1° chap-
erone paghonazo da uomo usato soppannato di verde; 1°
ghonnellino di panno nero da uomo sopannato e usato; 1ᵃ
copetta romangnuola da fante usata; 2 leghati entrovi 1ᵃ
coppaccia di ffatta nera con suoi sopanni; 1° sachetto entrovi
cine secche libbre 34½ tonde

IN DETTA CHAMERA NELLA CHASSA DELA FANTE ENTROVI

7 sachetti con civaie di più ragoni

NEL SECONDO FORZIERE IN CHAMERA DETTA AL'ANTICHA

1ᵃ choltre biancha a gigli di braccia 7 in circha usata; 1ᵃ
ghamurra di saia verde sanza maniche usata; 1° pezo di
panchale vechio di braccia 8; 1ᵃ spalliera di braccia 4 foderata
di tela verde; 1° chanezo di valescio di braccia 4 verde; 2
pezi di spalliera di braccia 3½ l'una fodera verde; 2 pezi di
spalliera di braccia 3 l'uno; 1ᵃ ghamurra di bigio fiandrescho
cho' maniche nere da donna foderata di volpe; 1ᵃ giornea
monachina da uomo vechia sopannata di valescio

NELA PRIMA CHASSA A LATO A LETTO IN DETTA CHAMERA

1ᵃ paniera moresca da donna grande nuova; 3 pezi di
foderacci; 1° sachettino entrovi più pezami di 4 mari e dossi
di vaio e lanzi

NELA SECONDA CHASSA A PIÈ DEL LETTO

1ᵃ chornamusa sanza saccho; 3 paniere moresche; 2 paniere di
paglia; 1ᵃ sportellina moresca; 1ᵃ schatola piena d'occhi di
paone; 1° sachettino entrovi alume in tutto libbre 7½; 1ᵃ
chassettina da fusa; 2 rocche moresche in più pezi; 1°
chassettino di ½ bracccio da serare entrovi più fusa; 1°
sachettino entrovi libbre 5 d'alume di roccho; 2 aspi lavorati

NELA ⅓ CHASSAPANCHA

1° sachettino di mandorle chol ghuscio di libbre undici; 1°
farsetto da uomo di ghuarnello nero cho' maniche e cholarino
di veluto paghonazo chermisi e manichini di rosato; [268v] 1°
farsetto di ghuarnello bigio cho' maniche e cholarino di
veluto nero; 1° farsetto di chamoscio nero chol cholarino
rosato sanza maniche; libbre 68 d'accia grossa biancha di più
ragone; 1° sacheto entrovi frangie di seta nera e altri stracci
vechi; 1° papaficho bigio frastagliato ala Franzese; 6 manili
foderati da fanciulle chome ghuanti

NELA ¼ CHASSAPANCHA ENTROVI

mazi 31 di lino sodo di libbre 165½ vernio

NELA CHASSETTINA IN DETTA CHAMERA DI BRACCIA 1°

1° libro di charta pechora choverto d'asse e di chuoio
paghonazo che si chiama il Salterino di San Girolamo; 1ᵃ
anchudine e martello da mettere punte d'aghetti; 1° paio di
forbice mezane; 1° choltellino chon ghiera d'ariento cho'
l'arme del popolo (tienne la chiave l'Antonia sua figliuola)

NEL'ANTICHAMERA DELA CHASA PICCHOLA

1ᵃ Vergine Maria dipinta in piano in uno tabernacholo chon
chamiconi dorati; 1° quadretto dov'è dipinto l'Anunziata [ ];
1ᵃ lettiera di braccia 5 ingessata; 1° sachone di 2 pezi e trespoli
e chamaio e pancha; 1ᵃ materassa di bordo e tela azurra con
lana; 1ᵃ choltrice con dua primacci di penna San Giovanni di
libbre 130 in circha; 1° paio di lenzuola a 4 teli di panno
forestiero; 1° choltrone chon banbagia di braccia 4; 1°
pannetto d'arazo a chani azurro; 1° ghuancale con federa; 1ᵃ
spalliera di giunchi moresca di braccia 8 in circha; 2
chassapanche con tarsie a 4 serami; 2 forzeretti da soma
coverti di chuoio; 1° forziere dipinto all'anticha; 1° chassone di
braccia 3 in circha; 1° chassone con tarsia di braccia 3; 1ᵃ
chassetta a 1° serame di braccia 2½ senprice; 1ᵃ archetta di
braccia 1½; 1° sciughatoio vechio a Nostra Donna; 2 tavole

schrittovi su il chalendario e i chomandamenti; 1ª chassa da choltegli; 1ª chassa da chuchiai; 2 palette da fuocho nuove; 1° paio di molle grande; 1° paio di molle picchole; 1ª forchetta da fuocho nuova; 2 forchette da fuocho vecchie; 1ª forchetta da rostire chacio; 1° paio d'alari chon palla di sopra di libbre 36; 1° schannellino da schrivere e serare; 1ª zanellina; 3 paia di lenzuola a 4 teli l'uno in tutto 6 lenzuola; 4 paia di lenzuola a 3 teli l'uno in tutto 8 usata; 1° lenzuolo grosso da fante a 3 teli; 3 bandinelle triste; 3 chanovacci da mano; 1ª ghuaina da taze; 1ª chorazina choperta di fustano nero; 2 seggiole; 1° monachordo cho' la chassa; un paio d'orghanetti chola chassa; un bacinetto da danari; 1° salterino di San Girolamo in charta pechora; 1° dialogho di San Ghraghoro e lo Specchio dela Chrocie in uno volume choverto d'asse e di chuoio verde; 1° stangnione d'utriacha; 1° libro di più legende di santi coverto d'asse e chuoio biancho; 1° libro che tratta de' Romani choverto d'asse in charta banbagina; 1° libro Ninfale di Fiesole in charta banbagina coverto d'asse; 1° libro di chantari dela Reina d'Oriente ed altri coverto d'asse di chuoio; 1° libro de' Trionfi del Petrarcha in charta banbagina converto d'asse; 1° libro di rapresentazioni di più santi di charta banbagina coverto d'asse; 1° libro di chanto fighurato coverto di chuoio paghonazo; 1° donadello usato e vechio; 1° libro di legende di santi di charta pechora; 1° libro dela rapresentazione d'Abram sanza coverta; 1° libro di sonetti rotto; 1° libro cho' legende di più santi coverto di charta pechora vechio; 1° quaderno di chanto fighurato coverto di chuoio azurro; 3 paneruzoli; 2 alberegli invetriati; 2 paniere da chucire di vetrice; 1ª chassettina da fusa; 1° forzerino vechio da donne novelle; 1° chapello di pelo foderato di veluto nero; libbre xvii d'accia cruda tra grossa e sottile tra di lino e di stroppa; 1° chapellinaniozo stretto di braccia 3; 1° telanizo da richamare suvi uno pezo di domaschino biancho; 3 paia di pianelle con ghiggie bianche [e] 2 paia di pianelle rosse nuove

NEL CHASSONE IN DETTA CHAMERA

1° bereniale porteraccio nuovo di pregio di barili 30 in circha barili trento; 6 paia di ghuanti da uomo bianchi; 2 scharselline franzese; 1° paio di maniche azurre e inbusti alucio lati; braccia 1½ di tela nera marezata; 1° leghato di maniche di seta da fanciugli vechie di più cholori; 1° alberello di vetro azurro entrovi manea; ½ braccio di saia di seta rossa e nera; 2 berrettine turchiesche da fanciugli; 1° leghato di più pezuoli di taffetta di grana; 1ª chapellina rosata scienpia da donna; 1° pungniale; 1° trafiere; 1° quartiere di trippa nera usata; 1° sachettino nero che ne più ritagli di veluti di più cholori e chollarini vecchi; 2 paia di brodoni di saia rossa; 1° paio di maniche di tela marezata nera da fanciulle usate; 1ª chapellina di veluto chermisi con chopette d'ariento da donna usata; 2 chapelline di veluto chermisi con luciole d'ariento dorate; 1ª chapellina di veluto chermisi e biancho usata; 2 berette di veluto chermisi vechie; 2 brodoni di sfatti di veluto chermisi; ⅓ di braccio di zetani chermisi; ½ braccio di raso biancho disegniato per richamare; ¾ di braccio di taffetta nero; [269r] 1° leghatuzo di più pezi di drappi di più cholori; 1ª schatola con 5 salierine di vetro entrovi sapone moschadato; 1° leghato di 3 pezi di panno monachino fine nuovo di braccia 2 in

circha; 3 paia di chalze solate da fanciugli paghonaze; 1° rinvolta in uno chanovaccio; ½ cinto di braccia 1° di raso verde con maglietti; 1ª schatola entrovi frangie e chollarini di seta e ghuanti da fanciugli e 1° choniglio dattimo; 1ª chasettina dipinta Morescha entrovi 1° cholarino biancho richamato d'argento buono; 2 berette a reticelle richamate d'oro e di seta; 1° ramo di chastagnio richamato di seta e d'oro in su taffeta; 2 richamuzi richamatori su libbre dua di perle; 1° chasettino traforato d'arcipresso entrovi 1ª manicha d'ariento da choltellino dorata; 2 paia d'ochiali chole chaselle; 1° paio sanza chasella; 1ª beretta di rete di seta; 1° anello d'ariento da chucire; 1° leghato entrovi oncia una in circha d'ariento vechio di più sorte; 1° leghato entrovi perle cinquanta di più sorte d'arento; 1° leghatuzo di perle di più sorte di peso di libbre dua in circha; 1ª scharsella di raso nero; 1° pezo di bocchaccino biancho usato; 5 bavagli cioè schapolari 3 bianchi e 2 bigi da banbini; 1ª chasetta entrovi più seta da richamare; 1ª setola coverta di chuoio rosso; 1° rinvolto di domaschino biancho e azurro nuovo di libbre dua; 1° sacheto di ritagli di più drappi; 1° paio di chalze nere da uomo nuove di stameto di Molano; 1° chasettino coverto di noce entrovi 2 paia di choltellini forniti d'ariento chole forchette d'ariento; 1° paio di choltellini con ghuaina nera chon un pocho dichiera d'ariento; 2 pezi di cinti neri larghi di braccia 4 rasi; 2 berette di raso biancho richamate d'ariento contrafatto; 1° aghoraiuolo chol torsello di veluto chermisi richamato di perle; 2 aghoraiuoli richamati chon ariento buono; 1° di veluto alesandrino e 1° paghonazo; 1° cinto biancho usato stretto di braccia 1¼; 1° cinto di raso verde punteggiato d'ariento; 1° cinto di raso verde di braccia 1°; 1° cinto chermisi nel mezo oro usato di braccia uno; 1ª anpolla di muscho picchola; 2 beretini a dagho scienpi di grana; 1° berettino scienpio di panno paghonazo; 2 anpolline lunghe di polvere di cipri; 1ª schatola biancha entrovi 1° mazochio richamato chon oro buono a seta usato e più pezi di nastri di seta e frangie; 1° sacheto di polvere di violetta; 1ª mano di chanto fighurato in charta pechora; 1° sacheto entrovi intagli e tire da piè a cioppe usate; 1ª chapellina di chalisea biancha da donna sopannata di rosato; 1ª berettina di veluto verde chon arienti buoni; 1° sachettino nero entrovi 6 berettini da fanciugli di più cholori; 1ª berettina scienpia di panno paghonazo; pezi di richami chon oro fine vechi; 1° pennoncino di bocchaccino cho' l'arme loro; 1° sachettino chon una tirella di taffeta verde cho' richami; d'argenterie chattive; 4 pezi di domaschino biancho richamati d'ariento chativi; 1° pocho di raso biancho disegniato e richamato di seta; 3 anime di bocchaccino bianche richamate chon ariento chativo; 1° pezo di tira richamato chon orpello; 1ª tira chon orpello e seta biancha intera; 1° pezo di tira cho' nastro d'orpello largho e intorno frangioline verde; 12 braccia in circha di nastro d'orpello largho; 1ª giornea di domaschino biancho cho' mostre di domaschino verde e biancho usata rinvolta in un telo di lenzuolo; 1° sacheto di fusaiuoli di vetro

NEL SECONDO CHASSONE IN DETTA CHAMERA

52 schodellini di stangnio nuovi libbre xliiii° netti; 58 schodelle a orlo largho nuove libbre lxxii nette; 68 pezi di stagnio di più ragoni vechio di libbre c°xi° ½ netto; 3 ghuaine

da chuchiai e forchette; 1ª schatola entrovi più spezierie in chartocci pesa chola schatola libbre dua ½; 1ª schatola di tregiea piena e 3 pezi di morsellatti di libbre nove ½; 1° cinto verde con puntale di rame dorato; 5 tra forzierini e chasettini entrovi 3 cholarini richamati d'oro e seta da fanciulle; 3 paia di ghuanti a agho da fanciulle bianchi e paghonazi; 2 paia di ghuanti di chamoscio sottili da fanciulle; 1ª beretta di raso bianco richamata; 7 cinti di seta di più cholori sanza ariento stretti; 1° cinto verde d'un braccio punteggiato d'oro; 5 ghorgias di veluto di più ragone chon paia dodici di ghangheri d'ariento; 1° pennaiuolo di chuoio dipinto; 2 paia di cesome chatelane dorato; 1° paio di choltellini da fanciulle con ghuaina nera e ghiera d'ariento e 1° di rizatoio di ferro; 1° paio di scharsellini da uchiegli dorati nuovi; 2 charte di spilletti; 1° scharsellina di chamucha azurro; 4 borsotti da fanciulle a dagho lavorati cho' nero e ariento 1° verde 1° azurro e 1° rosso e 1° nero bellissimi tutti nuovi; 3 borse d'Inghilterra lavorate chon oro e seta; 3 borsotti da uomo 2 neri e 1° rosso chon oro; 1° chollarino di bocchatello verde e bianco sanza arento; 1ª beretta chermisi da fanciulle chon 1ª rosa di perle; 2 berette e 2 chuffie da fanciulle richamate le chuffie; 1° cholarino d'oro tirato chon una crocellina e parechi perluze; 1ª scharsellina di raso verde ala Franzese; 6 cinti da fanciulle usati di seta di più cholori sanza ariento; 1° borsotto e 1° aghoraiuolo d'oro e seta richamato; 2 paia di ghuanti da fanciulle a agho; 6 rete di seta richamate chon oro e seta; 1ª beretta richamata chon oro e seta cholorata; 1ª cintola in fetta nera largha ripezata con fibia e puntale di rame dorato; 1ª fetta di raso nero largha da donna con fibia e puntale di ferro nero; 1° leghatuzo dov'è più ritagli di bochato e 1° chordiglio bianco 1° segnialetto chon oro e 1ª scharsellina di raso verde in detto forziere; 1ª coppa da uomo paghonaza sopannata di panno bigio usa; 1° ghamurrino di bianchetta foderato di pelle bianche da donna usate; 1ª coppa paghonaza da uomo cho' maniche e ghozi filetata di dossi e foderata di dossi e panno; 1ª ghamurra di perpingniano nero da donna vechia; 1ª ghamurra di panno azurro da fanciulle sanza maniche; 1° saia da fanciulle paghonaza picchola maniche di bocchaccino nero con ghangheri 52 cioè 26 choppie a magliette d'ariento; 1° saia da fanciulle bianca cho' maniche di bocchaccino nero; 1ª ghamurra di panno azurro da fanciulle sanza maniche; 1° libriccino in charta pechora da donna bello basso letera parigina chon fibia e puntale d'ariento dorato; 1° fodero da uomo bianco aperto dinanzi; [269v] 1° ghamurrino cioè ghuardaquore bianco cho' maniche; 1ª ghamurra di panno bigio fiandresco cho' maniche di panno nero usata, 1ª ghonnella bigiella grossa nuova, 1° chamiciotto di chanovaccio nero, 1° ghuarnello bigio da donna usato cho' maniche nere, 1ª cioppa bigiella usata, 1° ghuarnello bianco da donna usata (tutte da fante); 7 charte di spilletti

1° paio di cesoie da sarti; 1° pezuolo di choltre rotta; 3 ghuanciali sanza federe; 1ª giornea di rascia verde trista; 1ª ghamurra azurra vechia da fanciulle sanza maniche; 1° ghamurrino azurro vechio da fanciullo sanza maniche; 1ª ghamurra azurra vechia cho' maniche nere; 1ª sanza paghonaza vechia da fanciulle chon 48 maglie d'ariento; 1ª cioppellina nera vechia da fanciulle; 4 busti di saia a ucellini neri e rosse cho' magliette 100 d'ariento in circha cioè cento; 1° paio di maniche di veluto chermisi vechie da donna; 1° ghamurrino nero da fanciugli di panno; 1° ghamurrino di rascia nero vechio da fanciullo; 1° rinvolto chon più pezi di sopanni vechi lini; 1° ghamurrino da fanciullo vechio bigio cho' maniche e cholarino nero; ½ braccio di rascia nera; 1° paio di chalze di soantone bianco da donna; 1° paio di maniche di rascia biancha da fanciulle nuove; 1° paio di brodoni paghonaza da fanciulle; ¼ di coppa paghonazi vechia da donna

NEL PRIMO FORZERETTO DA SOMA SOTTO IL CHAMINO ENTROVI

1ª coppa da schrittoio romangnuolo foderata di chastroni bianchi; 1ª coppettina bigia da fanciugli foderata di pelle biancha usata; 3 copette da fanciugli bigi sopannati di panno biancho; 3 ghamurrini di bianchetta da donna sanza maniche usate cioè sono tre; 1ª coppa mormorina da uomo dopia di panno usa; 1° mantellino di panno bigio foderato di pelle biancha da fanciugli vechio; 5 ghamurrini da fanciugli di più cholori vechi; 1° paio di maniche di panno bigio vechie da fanciulle; 2 paia di chalze nere da fanciugli usate; 1ª ghamurra azurra da fanciulle maniche di tela nera usata; 1ª coppetta di rascia nera usata da fanciulle; 1° giorneino nero e 1° ghuardachulo di ghuarnello

NEL SECONDO FORZERETTO NONN È NULLA

NELA PRIMA CHASSA A LATO A LETTO ENTROVI NULLA

NELA SECONDA CHASSA A PICHATA NULLA

NELA TERZA CHASSA ENTROVI

1° schatolone grande dipinto ala Morescha entrovi 1° banbino ala viniziana di legnio dipinto cinto chon una pallina d'ariento cioè bottone grosso; 1ª Vergine Maria di gesso dipinta; 1° leghato di grenbuili azurri e neri; 2 braccia 2 di tela marezanta nera; 1ª chovertina di panno nero ala Franzese; 1° paio di maniche di rascia paghonaza richamate con seta biancha; 1° sopanno di ghamurra vechia da fanciulle; 2 paia di chalze di rascia bianche da fanciulle usate; 1° paio di maniche vechie di chermisi da fanciulle cho' manichini rosati; 2 chamicie vechie da donna; 3 paia di maniche vechie da fanciulle di rascia paghonaza e biancha; 1° ghuarnelluccio bianco da fanciugli; 5 chamiciottini usati da fanciugli; 8 paia di chalze line vechie da fanciugli

NELA ¼ CHASSA VOTA

UNO FORZERINO CHOPERTO D'OTTONE ENTROVI

2 vezi di choralli chon 8 bottoni d'ariento dorati; 1° pezo di domaschino biancho chon uno fiore; 1ª brochetta d'oro leghatovi drento 3 diamanti in punta e 3 perle grosse e 1° balascio in mezo distima di fiorini; 1ª brochettina con 4

perluzze d'ariento e 1ª dopia in mezo; 1º libriccino di salmi penitenziali vechio (messo detto forzerino nel primo chassone di detta chamera)

NEL'ARCHETTA IN DETTA CHAMERA

4 pezi di cielonaccio rotti

NELA SALA DI SOPRA NELA CHASA GRANDE IN PRIMA

1ª tavola regholata di noce di braccia 4 in circha con trespoli vechi; 1ª tavola vechia di braccia 4 in circha con trespoli; 2 chassapanche vechie al'anticha con sei serami; 1ª chassa vechia di braccia 2; 1ª segiola di stranba da sedere; 1º uomo di legnio chol piè; 1ª sciugha taglieri; 4 pezi di charne seccha vechia; 2 saccha grande di grano sugellate entrovi staia xxxvii; 1ª panchettina da schrivere

NELA PRIMA CHASA IN SALA ENTROVI

1º saccho rotto pieno di minudello di stoppa

NELA SECONDA CHASSA

staia 3 di panicho in circha

NELA $\frac{1}{3}$ CHASSA

1º inbottatoio da barili

NELA $\frac{1}{4}$ CHASSA VOTA

NELA $\frac{1}{5}$ CHASSA

1ª pentola di lardo strutto libbre 4 in circha

NELA $\frac{1}{6}$ CHASSA

36 taglieri usi; 1º pestello nuovo da mortaio; 1º alberello invetriato

NELA CHASSA VECHIA DI BRACCIA 2 ENTROVI

1º sacheto d'accia biancha di stoppa in matasse libbre 26½ chol saccho; 1º sacheto d'accia biancha in matasse e ghomitoli grossa di stoppa libbre xxiii lorda; 1º sacheto d'accia bianca in matasse e ghomitoli libbre 31 lorda

NELA CHAMERA IN SULA SALA DI SU DELA CHASA GRANDE

1ª lettiera di braccia 5 ingessata suvi 1º sachone in 2 pezi e trespoli e channaio e pancha; 1ª materassa di bordo cho' lana vechia; 1ª choltrice con 2 primacci piena di penna San Giovanni di libbre 150 in circha; 1º paio di lenzuola a 3 teli grosse; [270r] 1ª charpita bigia con verghe di braccia 4; 1º panno vermiglio stracciato in pezi; 1º paio di chassapanche al'anticha a 5 serami vechie entrovi 1º bighoncione da chruscha

NELA PRIMA CHASSA

1º sacho di stoppa di libbre 32 lordo

NELA SECONDA CHASSA NULLA

NELA $\frac{1}{3}$ CHASSA NULLA

NELA $\frac{1}{4}$ CHASSA

52 schodelle di legnio use; 10 taglieri nuovi; 1ª chassetta da fusa

NELA $\frac{1}{5}$ CHASSA PANNI DELA FANTE

NEL AGIAMENTO NULLA

NELA CHUCINA DELA CHASA GRANDE

2 saccha grande con grano sugellate di staia lvii; 1º botticello pieno d'aceto di barili 3 in circha; 1º barile d'aceto entrovene ½; 1ª asse da pane; 1º fochone da berbiere di terra chol choperchio; 1º trepie da chaldaia di libbre 14 di ferro; 1ª ghabia da putte; 1ª mina da misurare di legnio vechia; 2 chorbellini tristi; 2 fochoni da berbieri cho' choperchi nuovi; 5 pentole grandi; 1º vasetto da buchato rotto; 1ª staia entrovi 6 chapponi e 2 doccie da bechare di legnio; 1ª segiola d'anfermi ferrata grande; 1º chorrente di braccia 3; 1ª choncha da buchato entrovi 6 staia di veccie; 1º chassonciello di braccia 1½ entrovi; 1ª palla di marmo da stare in sula schala; 1ª staia; 1º chianistello piccholo; 1º uncino da pichare al palcho; 1º descho da schodelle di braccia 2½; 1ª tafferia di legnio grande; 1º fornellino di terra

IN SUL PALCHO DI CHUCINA

1ª botte di mena entrovi barili 11 d'aceto; 1ª botte di barili 6 in circha entrovi barili ½ d'aceto; 2 pezi d'uscio vechio; 15 pezi tra piane e asse vechie; 1º chorbellino mezano; 1º fastello di minudello di libbre xxx in circha di stoppa; 24 polli tra ghalline e pollastre

NELA CHAMERA DELA CHUCINA DOVE SI FA IL PANE

1ª letiera salvaticha di braccia 4; 1ª materassa di chanovaccio rosso piena di chapechio; 1ª choltrice e 1º primaccio vecchie piene di penna di pollo di libbre 100 in circha; 1º chopertoio azurro di braccia 4; 1ª charpita con verghe di braccia 4; 3 cholatoi sotto letto; 1ª zana entrovi 1º archuccio da fanciugli; 1ª testa di lietiera vechia suvi 1º sachone di paglia dove si pone il pane; 1º celone di libbre 3 in circha da choperire il pane; 1ª panchetta vechia di braccia 2; 1ª madia da pane vechia; 1º donadello da fanciugli messo nelo schritoio; staia 2½ di farina nela madia; 1º staccio; 1º bighoncione da chruscha; 1ª bighoncia da vendemia; 1ª archetta da farina entrovi staia 6 di farina; 1ª madia grande chome nuova; 1º bighoncione pieno di cruscha di staia 4; 1º chonchoncino di terra pieno di stacciatura; 1ª predella; 1ª panchetta bassi di braccia 1½; 3 fusa d'archolaio chol pie; più archolai di channa

NEL'ANTICHAMERA DELA CHUCINA

1ª chassapancha vechia a 3 serami vota; 1ª chassa di braccia 3 a 1º serame; 1º schannello da schrivere; 1ª seggiola di stranba; 1ª chaldaia chol manicho di libbre 34; 1º telaio da nastri; 3

orcia da olio salde; 2 segiolaccie di stranba vechie; 1° choperchio da fochone da berbiere; 2 schidoni di legnio chol manicho di ferro; 8 pezi d'arme vechie innastre; un paio di sechie di rame con chatene charuchola e fune al pozo di detta chamera

NELA CHASA DI BRACCIA 3 A 1° SERAME ENTROVI

1ª sachetto·entrovi sei 1° di ceci in circha; 1° paniere entrovi 3 paneruzoli e $\frac{1}{2}$ quarto di ceci; 1ª tafferia di legnio nuova; 1° segholo vechio sanza manicho; 1° pezo di stangha da finestra di braccia 6

NELA CHOLONBAIA DEL'ANTICHAMERA ENTROVI PIPIONI [e] TORRAIUOLI

16 paia in circha di pipioni torraiuoli; 1ª abeneratoio

NELA CHUCINA DELLA CHASA PICCHOLA

1ª chassapancha vechia a 2 serami entrovi; staia 3 di spelda in circha; 6 fiaschi e 1° fiaschetto schiacciati entrovi sapa e agresto; 1ª archa grande da farina entrovi staia 15 in circha di spelda; 1ª staia da chapponi di braccia 3 rotta; 1° piè d'archolaio; 1° botticino d'un barile entrovi agresto; 1° paio d'alari da volgere arosti di libbre 28; 1° fochone da berbiere chol choperchio vechio; 5 schidoni tra grandi e piccholi sanza piè; 1ª chassetta di braccia 1° in circha entrovi 4 paniere di veture, 3 schodelle di legnio e 4 taglieri; 1ª chassetta di braccia 2 rotta cioè vota; 1° forzeretto da soma vechio ferrato di braccia 2 entrovi 1° sachetto di [ ] di fave [ ]; 4 schodelle da maiolicha e 4 taglieri; 2 asse da pane di braccia 3 l'una; 1° chorbelletto vechio; 1° paio di molle; 1ª alare di libbre 15; 2 alari picchioli di libbre 15; 1ª chatena da fuocho; 1° trepie da pentole grande; 1° trepie da teghia picchiolo; 1° vaso da buchato rotto grande; 1ª gratichola di ferro; [270v] 3 padelle di ferro chol manicho; 3 teghie di rame 2 picchiole e 1ª mezana di braccia 9½; 1° schaldaletto di rame chol manicho libbre 7; 1ª gratugia; 1° tozzo da buchato; 1ª teghia di rame grande di libbre 7; 10 lucerne usate; 1ª padellina pichina ratta e 1° romaiuolo e 1ª paletta forata; 1ª predellina forata; 3 predelle da sedere; 3 peze d'ase vechie di braccia 2 l'una; 1° lucerniere vechio; 1° letuccio vechio al'anticha di braccia 4; 1° descho da schodelle di braccia 2 tristo; ii ª seggiola da sedere e 1ª picchina; 1ª panchetta lungha bassa di braccia 2 forata; 3 choltegli da tavola vechi con ghiera d'ariento; 5 chotegli da tavola di più sorte; 2 choltellacci da chucina

NELA CHAMERETTA DELA CHUCINA DELA CHASA GRANDE

1ª schianceria di legnio sanza armadura nuova a 4 gradi; 1ª asse da pane di braccia 3; 1ª finestruzza vechia; 3 pezi da saccie vechia strette di braccia 3 l'una

NEL'ANTICHAMERA DI DETTA CHUCINA

1° bacino grande d'ottone chol piè di libbre xi ½; 1° paiuolo mezano di libbre 10½; 1° paioletto di libbre 7½; 1° paiolino di libbre 6; 1° paiolino rotto di libbre 3½; 1° orciuolo di rame grande rotto di libbre 5½; 1° coltellaccio di ferro; 1° vassoio di

legnio fesso; 32 pezi di stagnio tra schodelle e schodellini e piategli libbre 33; 1ª schala apiuoli di braccia 4; 6 pezi di maiolicha rotti; 1° deschettino picchino; 1ª chonchetta da buchato; 1° chorbello mezano; 1ª travaccia vechia di braccia 4; 1ª tavola vechia con trespoli per descho da schodelle; 2 ramaioli di ferro; più pentole grande e mezane e picchole; chatini e piategli e chatinelle e teghami mezine e schodelle e schodellini di terra per uso dela chucina e più taglieri; 1ª stadera pesa da lato grosso libbre 40; 2 sechie con chatene e charuchola e fune; 1ª tovaglia da tavola picchola nostrale di braccia 3½; 1ª bandinella da pane di braccia 4; 1ª tovaglia di braccia 9 nostrale; 1ª ghuardonappa di braccia 9 nostrale; 10 tovagliolini sudici; 1° chanovaccio quadro da mano; 1° libricino da donna con serami d'ariento ch'era di Mona Maddalena nelo schritoio; 29 chiavi tra picchole e mezane di più serami di dette chasse ne quali serami sono le dette chose ecetto le chose lasciate fuori de seramie più 7 sciughatoi grossi da chapo ch'erano molli; braccia 2 in circha di panno nuovo monachino bangniato e cimato in chamera di Francesco nela ⅓ chassa messo ch'era al cimatore; 1° paio di stivaletti a ½ ghanba di chordovano di levanto rossi; 1° paio di stivaletti biancho di chuoio di levante; 1° fermagliuzo d'ariento con 4 perle e 1ª dopia in mezo, 2 berette di veluto chermisi con 2 rose di perle, 1ª schatoletta piena daghora da domascho, 3 charte di spilletti, 1° stuzichatoio d'ariento da orecchi, 5 paia di ghuanti di chuoio bianchi da 5 fanciulle, 1° ghorgiasdraso chermisi con 6 ghangheri d'ariento, 1ª grillandina d'oro da testa con 18 perle, 1ª frangia d'orpello, più segnialetti d'oro e d'ariento, 6 cholaretti richamati con trafatti, 3 cinti d'ariento chon trafatti richamati, 1ª beretta di raso nero chon una croce d'ariento (tutte le chose leghate insieme messe in uno sachetto nel secondo forziere in chamera di Franciescho); in uno sachetto più panerate di seta di diversi cholori pesano chol sachetto libbre cinque oncia 2

CHOSE ERONO NEL BUCHATO

1° sciughatoio grande da zana; 8 sciughatoi tra grossi e sottili da chapellinaio; 1° chamice grosso; 1° pezo di chortina; 2 sciughatoi grossi pichini; 8 teli da letuccio e da forzieri grossi e sotili; 2 lenzuola a 4 teli di panno nostrale usato cioè 1° a 4 e l'altro a 3 teli; 2 lenzuoline triste; 2 tovaglie a buchi [e] 2 ghuardonappe di braccia 6 l'uno a buchi vechie; 4 mantili [e] 26 tovagliolini [ ] vechie; 1° mantiluzo da parto; 1ª tovagliuola ala parigina usata; 8 federe da ghuancali; 1° chamice grosso da fanciugli; 1° tovagliolino; più cenci cioè 1° monte di chamiciarie rotte

NON CI SONO LE CHOSE CH'ERANO IN BUCHATO CHE'ANNO AUTO E FANCIUGLI E FANCIULLE SEGHUONO CHOSE ERANO IN BUCHATO

5 chamicie vechie usate da fanciulle; 2 chamici da fanciulle; più nastri grossi; 3 grenbiuli tristi 3; 4 federe da ghuancali; 4 benducci da lato; 18 chamicie da fanciugli; 4 chamici grossi da fanciugli; 12 fazoletti da mano; [271r] 5 benducci da lato; 8 mutande; 1° paio di chalze line; 3 bariagli da fanciugli

Tutte le chose erono nel buchato sono nela chamera dele fanciulle nela prima e seconda chassa a piè da letto . . .

1° chassone ferrato entrovi uno chassoncino e uno forzerino
in che sono le chose a piè e prima nel chassone grande: 4
lenzuola nuove a reticelle nostrale a 4 teli; 2 lenzuola da parto
nuove nostrale fine lavorate e belle chogli orli lavorati a 4 teli
l'uno; 1° lenzuolo fine lavorato a 3 teli e mezo nuovo
forestiere; xxiiii° chuchiai begli nuovi di peso di libbre dua e
oncie tre denari venti di stima di lire 3 soldi 12 l'oncia; 2 dua
chuchiai da schatola avite chon i smalti pesono oncie tre ½ di
stima di lire tre soldi 12 l'oncia d'ariento; xii forchette belle
nuove chon uno Erchole di sopra d'ariento di peso d'oncie
sette di stima di lire tre soldi 12 l'oncia; xvii cintole di più
cholori fornite d'ariento di peso in tutto di libbre quatro e
oncie cinque e denari xviii di stima l'ariento libbre tre e oncie
tre e di lire tre e mezo l'oncia tutte stimate lire centotrentasei
e soldi x piccioli e in detta stima eruno granachuore ch'era
con dette chose venderonsi per libbre 4 oncie 5; 1° pezuolo
di tela di renso molto fine di braccia sei; 1° pezo di panno
forestiere fine di braccia xli ½ a punto; 6 sei tazze d'ariento
fiorentino di peso di libbre quatro e oncie quatro ½ di stima
di fiorini dieci . . . 1° nappo d'ariento dorato grande di peso di
libbra una e oncie quatro cioè libbra uno oncie quatro denari
quindici ne una smalto in mezo; 1ª coltelliera entrovi quatro
choltella fornite d'ariento e dua pichole chon ghiera e
chaperozolo d'ariento di stima di fiorini tre; 1° libro in uno
sacchetto nel forzerino grande di Giovanni Inghirrami
seghuito per Franciescho iscrittoivi su da carta 2 a carta 79 e
chovertato di chuoio rosso; 2 brievi da fanciugli e 2 Angnius
Dei e 1ª crocellina d'ariento e 1ª brancha di chorallo in tutto
di stima di fiorini dua; 1° libro bianco segnata B di
Franciescho proprio schritto da carta 1 a carta 36; 1ª chiave al
forziere ferrato

1° fermaglio da testa chon uno ucello filicie smaltato di
bianco entrovi cinque perle e uno diamante in punta e uno
rubino ciottolo in mezo di stima di fiorini 18 larghi cioè
diciotto; 1ª altra brochetta da testa tonda con cinque perle e
uno diamante in punta e uno rubino ciottolo in mezo di
stima di fiorini xii larghi; 1° pendente chon tre perle con 2
foglie smaltate e uno balascio forato di stima di fiorini diciotto
larghi; 1ª perla leghata in uno anello in ghanbo smaltato di
stima di fiorini xiiiiª larghi; 1° rubino cioè 1° rubino leghato
in ghanbo a chanali di stima di fiorini sei larghi cioè fiorini sei
larghi; 1ª turchina grande leghata in ghanbo d'oro a chanale di
stima di fiorini 6 larghi cioè di fiorini 6 larghi; 1ª turchina
picchola in ghanbo d'oro a chanale di fiorini cinque larghi; 1°
diamante in tavola leghato in ghanbo d'oro nuovo a chanali
con granatura di stima di fiorini cinque larghi; 1° diamante
schudo chon una schiena leghato chome di sopra di fiorini
quatro larghi; 1° diamante tavoletta leghato chome di sopra
fiorini quatro larghi; 1° diamante nuovo mandorla leghato
chome detto di fiorini sei larghi; 1° diamante nuovo tavola
leghato chome detto di fiorini quatro larghi; 1° diamante
schudo leghato chome detto di fiorini tre larghi; 1° diamante

tavola con traffatto in ghanbo d'oro fiorini uno largho; 1°
diamante tavoletta leghato a detto modo in ghanbo d'oro di
stima di fiorini cinque larghi; 1° diamantuzo tavoletta leghato
ala parigina di fiorini tre larghi; 1° rubino ciottolo leghato in
ghanbo pulito usato di fiorini dieci larghi; 1° diamantino
tavoletta leghato in ghanbo usato di fiorini quatro larghi; 1°
annello da sugellare cho' l'arme di chalcidonio di peso di
denari dieci e ⅔ di stima di fiorini dua e mezo larghi 3
verghette d'oro di denari quatordici per tutto fiorini tre e
mezo larghi; 1ª perluza leghata in ghanbo d'oro pulito a
mulinello di stima di fiorino uno e mezo largho; 4 diamanti
sciolti 3 tavola e 1° schudo di fiorini cinque larghi tutti; più
arienti rotti vecchi di più ragoni con putatori diretto più
spranghe d'ariento in tre pezi di fette di libbre dua e oncie
dua netto in uno sachetto di stima di lire tre e mezo l'oncia
in tutto stimato lire novantaquatro soldi x piccioli; 1°
sachettino entrovi più leghati di perle e richami sugellato di
peso lordo d'oncie diciannove e denari ventidua . . .

2 peze di tele forestiere strette di panno lino pesorono chol
chappio libbre quarantasei e grosso; 3 peze di panno lino
forestiere stretto e grosso pesorono libbre settanta chol
chappio; 3 peze di panno lino bordati d'una medesima
largheza pesorono chol chappio libbre ventotto; 2 peze di
panno lino nostrale mezano peso chol chappio libbre
cinquantatre; 1ª peza di panno lino nostrale finissimo di libbre
diciassette e oncie quatro chol chapio; 3 lenzuolette forestiere
a tre teli l'uno a reticele; 1° lenzuolo di panno forestiere a 4
teli uso a reticele; 1° lenzuoletto di panno nostrale a 3 teli; 2
lenzuola di panno nostrale usato a 4 teli; 5 lenzuola di panno
nostrale a 3 teli e mezo l'uno cho' reticele; 1ª tela di 3
ghuardonappe in un filo nostrale di libbre dieci ala parigina; 1ª
tela di ghuardonappe in un filo nostrale di libbre nove e mezo
ala parigina; 3 tovaglie in un filo di braccia dieci l'una nuove
ala parigina; 36 tovagliolini in un filo nostrali nuovi ala
parigina; 2 tovaglie in un filo nuove nostrali a buchi di braccia
dodici l'una ala parigina; 3 tovagliole ala parigina nuove in un
filo; 7 tovagliolini con verghe nere in un filo nostrali ala
parigina; 4 tovaglie nuove ala parigina nostrale pesano libbre
diciannove e oncie dieci; 4 tovaglie nuove in un filo nostrali
e alla parigina pesorono libbre diciotto oncie quatro; 2
ghuardonappe nuove nostrale spicchate 1ª con buchi bella di
libbre quatro oncia dua ala parigina; 2 tele di ghuardonappe
nostrale nuove con buchi ala parigina pesano libbre dodici
oncia sei; 3 mantili nuovi in un filo di braccia quatro l'uno
in circha di stoppa ala parigina; 2 peze di panno lino nostrale
in uno rinvolto pesa libbre cinquantaquatro chol chapio;
5 pezuoli di sciughatoi nuovi in un filo chole verghe
nere rinvolti in uno chanovaccio di libbre dodici oncia sei; 2
tele di fazoletti da mano in un filo rinvolto in panno lino di
libbre quatro oncia otto; 2 ghuancali lavorati con federe a
reticelle di baldachino chon mappe di seta e botoni d'oro
begli da donne di parto rinvolti in un telo; 1ª chiave al detto
chassone . . .

4 mantegli neri lunghi; 4 chapucci monachini; 2 ghabanelle nere sopannate di biancho chole chaperuccie usate; 2 ghonnellini di rascia nera usati per detti; 3 ghonnellini, 2 azurri cho' maniche e 1° bigio sanza maniche, tutti foderati di pelle biancha; 1° ghonnellino nero sanza maniche foderato di panno lino; 2 paia di scharpette di chalisea bianche da fanciulle; 4 gornee nere di bocchaccino da fanciugli; 1° paio di manichuccie nere da fanciullo; 2 ghonnellini neri foderati di pelle biancha da fanciugli; 2 ghonnellini neri sanza maniche usati da fanciugli vechi; 2 chatelanuzi neri vechi da fanciugli; 4 paia di chalze di perpingniano nere usate; 1° ghonnellino bigio cho' maniche nere scienpio; 2 farsettini di ghuarnello nero cho maniche nere di panno; 3 paia di chalze vechia da fanciugli usate; 4 ghonnellini neri sanza maniche triste; 2 ghonnellini neri in pezi cioè di sfatti e sopannati di verde da fanciugli; più pezi di ritagli per rachonciare e panni a fanciugli; 1° libriccino da donna al'Antonia chon serami d'ariento vechio; 1° libriccino da donna ala Lisabetta chon uno serame d'ottone vechio; 1° libriccino ala Fiammetta da donna con 2 serami d'ottone; 1° pettine grande d'avorio che non era in sul inventario . . .

NOTA DELE CHOSE CH'ERANO FUORI DI CHASA CHE NON ERA FATTO INVENTARIO VERUNO E PRIMA

1° paio d'orghanetti a una mano chola chassa rossa e quali a Bernardo d'Inghilese Ridolfi disse gli aveva i nulla; staia 50 di grano era in chasa Benedetto Ciciaporci; staia 12 di grano ebe Chimenti lavoratore di Francesco in presta . . .

[272r] SEGHUE INVENTARIO DELE MASERIZIE E NETUNAGLIE TROVATE A CHAREGGI NELA CHASA DELA SUA ABITAZIONE E PRIMA NEL CHORTILE DI DETTA CHASA

1° paio di sechie con chatene e charuchola e fime al pozo

NELLA LOGGIA A MANO RITTA

1ª tavola di braccia 7 regholata di noce e quasi nuova; 4 panche di braccia 6 l'una in circha; 2 saccha da grano vote; 2 pezi d'asse d'albero triste di braccia 5 in tutto

NELLA LOGGIA A MAN' SINISTRA

1ª pancha intorno d'albero chola rinvolta in tutto braccia 14 in circha; 10 fastella di fiaschoni

NELLA SALA TERRENA

1ª tavola regholata di noce di braccia 4 in circha nuova; 4 panche intorno a detta di braccia 20 in circha; 1ª panchetta senprice di braccia 4 in circha; 1ª botte vechia di braccia 5 in circha

NELLA DISPENSA DIRIETO ALLA SALA

10 fastella di fiaschoni; ½ chatasta di legnie grosse di querciuolo; 1ª seggiola da donna di parto; 1° choperchio di fochone da berbiere frusto; 1° vaso da buchato rotto

NELLA CHAMERA DELA DETTA SALA A MAN' SINISTRA

1ª lettiera di braccia 4½ con tarsie; ½ sachone di chanovaccio e trespoli e channaio e pancha; 1ª materassa di bordo e chanovaccio con chapechio; 1ª coltrice con dua primaccia nuove di libbre 140 in circha; 1ª coltre biancha di braccia 8 in circha sottile usata; 1ª chassapancha cioè 1ª a dua serami vota; 1° letuccio e chapellinaio con tarsia di braccia 3½; 1° forziere dipinto vechio al'anticha entrovi 2 mantili da pane e 1° paneruzolo di vetuce; 1° telaio di chortinaggio sopralleto; 1° materassino da letuccio di bordo e chanovaccio usato con chapecchio; 1° rastrello spicchato con 4 piuoli; 1° telanizo da richamare usato; 2 asse vechie da pane di braccia 3; 1° paio d'alari di libbre 48

NELA CHAMERA A MARITTA DI DETTA SALA

1ª letiera di braccia 5 regholata di noce chome nuova; ½ sachone e trespolo e pancha e channaio; 1ª materassa di bordo e chanovaccio con pelo; 1ª coltrice con 2 primacci di libbre 150 in circha; 1° telaio sopra a letto da chortinaggio; 1° paio di chassapanche a 4 serami 1ª regholata di noce e l'altra no; 1° coltrone di banbagia di braccia 5; 3 ghuancali sanza federe, 2 picholi e 1° mezano; 1ª charriuola di braccia 4 con mezo sachone e channaio; 1ª coltricetta con 2 primacci grandi di libbre 80 in circha; 1° lettuccio al'anticha di braccia 4; 1° chapellinaio di braccia 3 salvaticho; 1° materassino da letuccio di bordo e chanovaccio di pelo; 1° chassone a lato a letuccio di braccia 3 a uno serrame entrovi 2 quancali di chuoio dorati tristi; 2 chassoni di rinpetto al'uscio di braccia 3 l'uno usi; 1° paio di vanghamole nuove da peschare; 1° chorbelletto usato; 1° choperchio di fochone da berbiere vechio; 1ª seggiola rotta; 1ª chaldaia sanza manicho di libbre 18; 1° paiuolo grande di libbre 16 chol manicho; 1° trepie grande da chaldaia di libbre 15; 2 padelle col manicho 1° grande e 1ª picchola; 7 lucerne usate; 1° paio di molle picchole; 1° fuso d'archolaio

NELA PRIMA CHASSA A PIÈ DEL LETTO

7 piatelletti invetriati di terra; 2 piatelletti da maiolicha; 28 taglieri usati; 2 saliere e 1° bossolo di vetro azurro e biancho; 1° paio di cinbamelle d'ottone picchole

NELLA SECONDA CHASSA

2 piategli invetriati di terra; 7 horciuoli cho' l'arme; 1ª chasettina vechia da fusa sanza conperchio

NELLA ⅓ CHASSA

1° libricino in chavretti choverto d'asse di Dante vechio; 1° libro di lalde in chavretti coverte d'asse vechio; 1° schatola dipinta vota; 1° paio di forme da palotole di cierbottana rotte; 1ª tascha di chuoio biancho da danari; 1° libretto di chanto fighurato in charta banbagina choperto d'asse; 1° Isopo in chavretti Latino choverte d'asse; 1° donadello tristo in chavretti choverto d'asse; 1ª setola nuova choperto di chuoio rosso; 1° paio di maniche triste da fanciulle e bianche di chalisea; 1ª paneruzoletta di vetrice; 2 pentole grande di terra

1° giuocho da vossi; 1° giuocho di rulli; 1° schachiere chogli schachi uso; 1° cinbolo uso; 1ª setola vechia; 3 paneruzolini di vetrice e 1ª paneruzola a uso di confettiera; 1° tavoliere di noce con tavole; 1ª cierbottana chola choverta; 1° specchio tondo dipinto sanza banbola; 1ª rostra di brucioli; 1ª palla di mistura di vetro; 2 sacchetti di sale e salina e l quale si porto a Firenze per loghorare peso in tutto libbre 35 cho' sachetti; 1° paio di stadere

IN UNO CHASSONE DE DUA DI RIMPETTO AL'USCIO

1ª choltre da letto usata con conpassi di braccia 7; 1ª choltre chon chonpassi usata di braccia 6; 1° pezo di fune nuova da rangnia di libbre 4½; 56 pezi di stagnio usato di libbre 63; 1ª paniera di vetrice

NELL'ALTRO CHASSONE

8 pezi di chortinaggi usati di borbati cioè sopracieli e per dintorno; 4 pezi di pendenti con frangie di refe; 1° pezo di lenzuoletto; 1° stangnione d'utriacha di libbre cinque e oncia 4; libbre 2½ di lino vernio sodo; 1ª paneruzolina di vetrice; 1ª schatolina di nove entrovi 1° rascio e 1° paio di forbice lavorate nuove; 2 chapegli di paglia nuovi da uomo

NEL NECESSARIO DELLA DETTA CHAMERA

7 orcia da olio, entrovi in uno aceto negli altri barili nove d'olio; 12 chopie di chacio marzolino; [272v] 1° cholatoio d'aranno; più pezuoli di charne seccha meta di libbre v; 1° pezo di dopiere di libbre cinque di cera; 1° descho di braccia 3 in circha chon trespoli; 1° rinfreschatoio da maiolicha piano grande; 1° rinfreschatoio chol piè da maiolicha; 1° Infreschatoino di maiolicha; 1° paio di mantaci d'orghano con 2 pezi di pionbo di libbre 14; 1° rinfreschatoio di vetro chol pie; 6 fiaschi che ne malchimi acque; 7 paia di zocholi da fanciugli vechi; 4 archolai di channa

NEL'ANTICHAMERA DELA DETTA CHAMERA

2 Vergine Marie d'orpello e contraffatte; 1ª letiera di braccia 4½ chon uno mezo sachone di tela rossa e trespolo e channaio e pancha; 1ª predella a piè del letto; 1ª tavola chon trespoli d'albero vechia di braccia 6; 1° paio d'orghani grandi di braccia 2 in circha sciolti; 1° charratello dagresto pieno di barili uno; ½ barile entrovi agresto; 1° bariglione piccholo pieno d'aciesto; 1° chapellinaio di braccia 2 salvaticho; 3 chapegli da rinbiondere fanciulle; 1° paneruzolino di vetro piccino; 16 granate nuove

SEGHUITE NELA CHAMERA DELLA LOGGIA A MAN' DESTRA

1ª Piatà dipinta in tavola; 1ª letiera ingessata biancha vechia di braccia 4½; 3 trespoli di noce da tavola; ½ sacchone di chanovaccio biancho e trespolo e channaio e pancha sanza piè; 1ª coltriccetta vechia con piuma di pollo trista di libbre 40 in circha; 1ª altra choltrice a detto letto con 2 primacci di libbre 80 e vechia piena di penna bologniese; 1° lenzuolo a 3 teli e mezo di tela forestiera nuovo o chome nuovo; 1° altro lenzuolo a 3 teli e mezo di tela forestiera vechio; 1° panno rosso vechio di 2 pezzi; 1° celone bigio verghato di braccia 4 in circha usato; 1° pannaccio biancho da letto stracciato

IN SUL VERONE SOPRA A LA LOGGIA

1ª pancha di braccia 4 d'albero salvaticha

IN SALA DI SOPRA

1ª tavola regholata di noce di braccia 4 in circha con un paio di trespoli; 1° deschetto chola spalliera cho' l'arme; 3 deschetti tondi; 1° secchione daquaio di rame di libbre sette; 1° armario a uso di schianceria entrovi 15 taglieri di legnio usati; 1° piatello da maiolicha fesso; 2 fiaschi nuovi pieni d'aceto; 2 horciuoli di terra da olio; 2 horciolini da olio e aceto; 1° tagliere grande da migliacci; 1° armarietto aperto suvi 1° bacino d'otone chon i smalto d'ariento cho' l'arme cola misciroba sanza smalto; 1° paio d'alari di libbre venti; 1° trepie da teghia piccholo; 1° paio di molli; 1° chatino e 2 mezine di terra; 1° piccholo lucerniere; 1° monte di vinacciuoli per colonbi

NELA CHAMERA IN SU DETTA SALA A MAN' SINISTRA

1ª lettiera vechia al'anticha di braccia 5; ½ sachone di chanovaccio e trespolo channaio e pancha; 1ª coltrice con 2 primacci penna bologniese libbre 140 in circha; 1° ghuancale con federa; 3 chassapanche vechie a 6 serami; 1ª archetta grande chome nuova; 1° letuccio vechio tristo al'anticha di braccia 4; 1ª madia da pane; 1ª chassaccia vecchia sanza coperchio; 2 ghabie da pippioni

NELA PRIMA CHASSA DI DETTE

3 bavagli da fanciugli; 5 sachettini tristi da cinaie; 18 chanovacci da chucina di più ragoni; 1° sachetto cinto da chacio; 2 pezi di matili tristi da chucina; 1° chamiciottino tristo di chanovaccio

NELA SECONDA CHASSA

4 pentole, 2 piene di mostarda e sapa

NEL AGIAMENTO IN DETTO CHAMERA

2 botticelle triste con aceto in tutto barili 3 in circha

IN CHUCINA SU DETTA SALA

1ª chanpana da stillare di pionbo con rame libbre 28 col fondo; 1° orciuolo di rame grande di libbre xii; 1° paioletto chol manicho di libbre vii ½; 1° ramaiuolo da buchato di libbre iiii°; 1ª padelletta chon manicho di ferro; 2 trepie da pentole; 1° trepie da teghie; 2 schidoni, 1° col piè l'altro sanza, di ferro; 1ª chatena da fuocho di braccia tre in circha; 1ª paletta da fuocho; 2 ramaiuoli di ferro; 1ª mestola forata di ferro; 2 lucerne vechie; 1° paiolino rotto di rame di libbre cinque; 14 taglieri di legnio; 1ª tafferia di legnio; 16 pentole di terra tra grandi e picchole; 1° trepie da chaldaia di libbre sette; 1° tondo di legnio da choprire il vaso del buchato; 1ª panchetta dala choncha da buchato; 1ª predellina picchola di legnio; 1° mortaio di pietra e 1° pestello; viiii° chatini di terra grandi e mezani; 2 chatinelle invetriate

IN CHAMERA SULLA CHUCINA IN PALCHO

1ª lettieraccia trista di braccia iiii°; 1ª materassaccia trista con chapecchio; 1ª madia da pane buona; 1° bighonciuolo da chruscha; 1ª pala di ferro trista; 1ª chonchetta da chruscha fessa e trista; [273r] 2 tapetuzzi vechi e tristi di braccia 2 in circha l'uno; 1ª chassaccia vechia a 2 serami braccia 5 in circha; 1° lucerniere di legnio tristo; 1° pezo di panchalaccio verghato di braccia 6 in circha; 1ª chassapancha a 3 serami vechia e vota; 1° descho da schodelle di braccia 3; 1° fochone da berbiere grande con choperchio; 2 predelline triste; 1° schannello da schrivere tristo; 5 seggiole vechie; 1° staio di ferro di libbre 16 buono; 1° chatinetto di rame di libbre 3½; 1ª ghabia da ucellini con filo di ferro; 1° deschuccio quadro di ½ braccio tristo; 1° alaruzo vechio; 1° manicho di paiuolo; 1ª rasiera da madia

IN CHAMERA GRANDE DI SOPRA IN SULA SALA A MAN' RITTA

1ª lettiera d'albero di braccia 5½ biancha; ½ sacchone di chanovaccio con channaio trespolo e pancha; 1ª materassa di bordo e tela rossa piena di pelo; 1ª coltrice con 2 primacci di libbre 160 in circha; vi° ghuancali 3 con federe e 3 sanza; 1ª sargia rossa di braccia viii usata; 2 chassapanche a detto letto a 4 serami; 2 forzieri vechi al'anticha; 1° lettuccio e 1° chapellinaio al'anticha di braccia 4; 1° forzeretto da soma; 3 chassette d'albero di braccia 1½ l'una cioè tre; 2 seggiole e 1ª predelluzza; 1ª lettiera nuova d'albero senprice di braccia 4½ con channaio; ½ sacchone di chanovaccio biancho; 1ª coltrice chome nuova con 3 primacci di penna bologniese di libbre 100 in circha; 1ª chassapancha a 2 serami vota; 1ª Vergine Maria chon i sportellini; 1ª tavola dipinta suvi la Piatà

NEL FORZIERE AL'ANTICHA PRIMO DI RINPETTO AL'USCIO

6 staia di mandorle in circha

NEL'ALTRO FORZIERE

2 sachetti entrovi staia 3 di mandorle in circha

NEL FORZERETTO DA SOMA

1° monachordo dipinto bello cholla chassa; 1° vasetto di vetro verde dorato; 12 coltegli da tavola usati di più ragoni; 1° cenbolo vechio chon sonagli; 1° ghuancale chon federa; 1° pennaiuolo rosso uso; 1ª setola vechia; 1ª tafferia di vetro fessa; 18 chiave vechie

NELA PRIMA CHASSA DEL LETTO GRANDE

4 staia di fichi secchi in circha neri

NELA SECONDA CHASSA

1ª rangnia da ucellini sanza sachetto usata; 1° tovagliuolino sottile da mano; 2 rangnie, 1ª da tordi e una da' ucellini, usate; 1° paio di sproni usati

NELA ⅓ CHASSA A PIÈ DEL LETTO

1° sachetto entrovi più cenci vechi di panno; 2 bossoli rossi da spezie; 3 chandellieri d'ottone piccholi; 1ª coltre biancha di braccia 8 usata

NELA ¼ CHASSA

1° celone verghato rotto; 1° forzerino da donna novella vechio voto; 2 charegli a schachi di panno vechi; 1° sachoncino da letuccio di chanovaccio e chapechio; 1° materassino di bordo e tela rossa con chapecchio; 1° tanburino; 2 paneruzole di vetrice e 1° paneruzolo chol manicho entrovi vue secche; 2 grenbiuli verdi usi; 1° deschetto tondo da sedere; 1° descho da schrivere; 20 libbre di ferramenti vechi; 1ª gratugia nuova; 1° chatino da gelatina dipinto; 1ª pentola grande e 13 teghami e 1ª chatinella di terra; 1° paniere di vetro chol manicho uso entrovi più ghuastade e bichiere di vetro; ½ cerbottana; 2 paia di forbice vechie; 2 telai da richamare; 1° fuso d'archolaio chol piè; 1ª chasettina d'uno braccio vota; 4 chatinelle di terra e 2 testi grandi; 1° telaio da richamare suvi 2 pezuoli di domaschino

NEL NECESSARIO DI DETTA CHAMERA

panicho staia sei; orzo staia dodici; vena staia sette; fave staia [e] veccie staia dieci e più nera di veccie staia quatro in tutto staia xiiii°; sagina staia dodici; 1° schaldaletto di rame; 1° bighonciuolo di farina; 1ª chassa salvaticha di braccia 2; 2 predelline forate; 1° pettine da lino; 16 tra fiaschi e fiaschetti; 1° chapello da uomo chattivo; 1ª ghabia da chacio a 2 palchi; 1ª zanellina picchola

NELL'ANTICHAMERA DI DETTA CHAMERA DOV'È IL GRANO

un monte di grano di moggia/fimoggia ventuno staia iii e l quale grano e sugellato nel granaio detto/mª ventuno staia iii; 30 granate nuove in circha; 3 pezzi d'usci vechi e tristi; 1° pezo d'asse tristo; 1ª pala da grano di legnio; 1° deschetto tondo da sedere

NELA VOLTA DELLA DETTA CHASA

7 horcia cho' choperchi da olio vote; 1ª botte di tenuta di barili 14 vota; 1ª botte di tenuta di barili 25 in circha piena di vino vermiglio; 1ª botte di tenuta di barili 25 vota; 1ª botte di tenuta di barili 25 in circha piena di vino vermiglio; 1ª botte di tenuta di barili 5 piena di vino vermiglio; 1ª botte di tenuta di barili 10 in circha piena di vino vermiglio; 1ª tinella da suinare di tenuta di barili 8; 1ª penera; 12 cerchi nuovi di più sorte; e più sedili per le dette botte

NELA VOLTA PICCHOLA A PIÈ DELLA SCHALA

2 orcia da olio usate cho' choperchi vote . . . [273v] 1ª botte di tenuta di barili 9 vota; 1ª botte di tenuta di barili 5 piena di vino vermiglio; 1ª botte di tenuta di barili 11 e piena di vino vermiglio che è di Giorgio lavoratore; 1ª botte di tenuta di barili 5 piena di vino biancho; 1ª botte di tenuta di barili 4 piena di vino biancho; 1° botticino di tenuta di barili 2½ piena di vino biancho; 1° charratello di tenuta di barili 1°

entrovi $\frac{1}{2}$ barili di biancho; e più sedili apertenenti a dette botte; $\frac{1}{2}$ barile da vino; 1ª cholonbaia entrovi più cholonbi e cestoncini a picchata cholla detta chasa

NELLA DETTA CHASA 1° STRETOIO DA VINO CHO'SUOI FORNIMENTI

1° tino di tenuta di barili 45 in circha; 1° tino di tenuta di barili 35 in circha; 1° tino di tenuta di barili 20 in circha; 1ª tinella di tenuta di barili 14 in circha; Le dette maserizie apartenente al podere che lavora Chimenti a lato alla chasa; 1ª mangiatoi e rastelliera di braccia 5 in circha; 1° pezo di saccia di braccia 12 in circha

NELA CHASA DEL PODERE DI GIORGIO

1° tino di tenuta di barili 40 in circha; 1° tino di tenuta di barili 28 in circha; 1° tino di tenuta di barili 16 in circha; 1° tino di tenuta di barili 15 in circha; 1ª tinella di barili 8; 1ª tinella di barili 10; 1° pezo d'uscio vechio; 3500 mezane e mattoni e pianelle in circha per murare; 70 hontani lunghi; 2 bighonciuoli e 2 bighoncie e pezze di piane; 1ª mangiatoia e rastelliera di braccia 5 in circha; 500 mattoni in circha dirieto alla chasa grande; 1° botte che a Chimenti di Simone lavoratore di barili 8; 1ª botte che a Giorgio di Martino lavoratore di barili $6\frac{1}{2}$; 100 melarancie in circha insu melaranci dela chorte; 1° barile da vino; 2 marrette da lavorare la vingnia

COSE RIMASE A DRIETO

20 tapetuzi vechi tristi di braccia 2 in circha l'uno; 1ª chassaccia vechia a 2 serami di braccia 5 in circha; 1° lucerniere di legnio tristo; 1° pezo di panchalaccio verghato di braccia vi in circha; 1ª chassapancha a 3 serami vechia ruota; 1° descho da schodelle di braccia 3; 1° fochone da barbiere grande con choperchio; 2 predelline triste; 1° schannello da schrivere tristo; 5 seggiole vechie; 1° staio di ferro di libbre 16 buono; 1° chatinetto di rame libbre tre $\frac{1}{2}$; 1ª ghabia da ucciellini con filo di ferro

Appendix B   Antonio Castellani's Wedding Expenses

THE FOLLOWING ACCOUNT IS TRANSCRIBED from a loose folio in *Acquisti e doni*, 302, insert 1. It contains information on the guests and the festivities surrounding the wedding of Antonio Castellani in 1416. The folio is folded in a complex fashion; the order presented here seems the most logical way to read it. The first group of names, forty-six women (with three crossed out), seem to be the guests invited to one or more of the celebrations. Several are identified only by their status as daughter or daughter-in-law of prominent men (the daughter-in-law of Giovanni di Bicci – presumably Giovanni di Bicci de' Medici – may have been Contessina de' Bardi, the wife of Cosimo di Giovanni, or Ginevra Cavalcanti, the wife of Lorenzo di Giovanni). Forty-three youths (again with three crossed out) were invited to accompany these women. Castellani often included several from one family identified only by a single man and a number next to his name, perhaps to represent sons or brothers. Judging by the number of plates prepared for each meal, the guest list varied for each event. There were six meals planned: one on Saturday evening, two each on Sunday and Monday, and a morning meal on Tuesday. Castellani provides a menu for each meal, and lists the necessary ingredients and serving items. This litany is briefly interrupted by a list of the ten women who made up his bride's court. He concludes with lists of items procured from two apothecaries, three poultry vendors, and a butcher, and a list of the various plate and silverware necessary. The document provides significant information about the planning of wedding festivities among prominent Florentines.

Antonio di Niccholo Chastellani meno la donna a dì 24 di gennaio in domenicha 1416

Madonna Francescha di Messer Vanni
Monna Andrea di Tedeldo
Monna Tadea d'Aghabito
Monna Madalena di Papi
Monna Sandra di Michele Chastellani
Monna Alessandra d'Alamano
Monna Pippa d'Antonio di Fronte
Monna Chosa di Bernardo di Salvestro Nandi
Mona Nana di Scholaio Salteregli
Monna Chaterina di Giovanni di Nofri
Monna Bice figliuola di Giovanni di Nofri
Monna Tance d'Antonio di Serristoro
Monna Picchina di Filippo Guagni
Monna Chaterina d'Andrea del Polagno
Monna Nanina di Tedaldo

Monna Tita di Nanni da Chastello Fiorentino
Monna Nanna di Messer Matteo
Monna Chaterina di Baldassare Macingni
Monna Nanna di Lorenzo di Totto
Monna Violetta di Bernardo Ridolfi
Monna Chaterina di Giovanni Bischeni
Monna Pippa di Filippo Ghuidetti
Monna Lena d'Arigho Rondinelli
Monna Tita d'Andreuolo Sacchetti
Monna Chaterina di Papi di Gileo
Monna Sandra d'Antonio Bonbeni
Monna Piera di Fronte
Monna Neca di Niccholo di Marcho
La nuora di Niccholaio Davanzati
Monna Lena d'Iachopo Ghuidetti
Monna Oretta di Messer Riccardo
Monna Checha degli Alessandri
Monna Milia d'Angnolo di Sale
~~Monna Odetta d'Alberto Chastellani~~
Monna di Messer Palla
La nuora di Giovanni di Bicci
Monna Antonia di Niccholo del Palagio
~~Monna Mea di Messer Tommaso Sacchetti~~
La dona di Migotto de' Bardi
~~Monna Barda di Messer Lorello~~
Monna Tommasa di Pierozo
La fanculla di Piero di Ser Antonio
Monna Antonia di Berrnardo Lanbertischo
La Cice
Monna Maria di Niccholo di Francho
La figliuola di Filippo di Messer Uberto

Giovani ivitati:
3 Damiano d'Antonio di Iacopo
Pandolfo d'Angnolo
1 Bocchacco Alamani
1 Niccholo Chavalchanti
2 Giovanni Ghuiccardini
Papino Velluti
5 Simone Tornabuoni
3 Jachopo di Bartolino
2 Domenciho Lanbertoschi
4 Doffo Arnolfi
Niccholo Macingni
5 Checcho dello Strinatio
Vespucco
3 Giovanni Niccholini

Bernardo Arighi
Chastello Quratesi
Pagholo Malasalsa
4 Charlo di Marchucci
Niccholo de Nici
Tinoro Ghuaschoni
Batista Ghuiccardini

Vicini per la domenicha sera
[blank]

Per sabato sera (16 taglieri): insalata d'erbe; pesce d'uovo; pesci d'Arno e tenche fatte; frutte

Per la domenicha mattina (40 taglieri): pinnocchiato orato; 1 peza di vitella di libre [ ]; 1 tagliere di ravioli; 1 chappone 2 starne 1 pezo di torta per tagliere; delle pere ghuaste; de' chonfetti

Per domenicha sera (30 taglieri): 1 tagliere di gelatine; 1 chappone 1 starne 2 pippioni per tagliere; pere ghuaste; tregieia

Per lunedi mattina (30 taglieri): 1 pezza di vitella; 1 chappone 1 starne 1 pippione per tagliere; delle pere ghuaste; de' chonfetti

Per lunedi sera (25 taglieri): 1 tagliere di gelatine; 1 chappone 1 starne 1 pippione per tagliere; delle pere ghuaste; delle tregeia

Per martedi mattina (10 taglieri): 1 cenvellata 1 chappone 2 starne per tagliere; chonfetti

Per 60 taglieri de raviuoli: 200 uova; 60 chaci; 20 libre di parmigano

Per 20 teghami di gelatina: 60 chapponi; 600 libre di porcho; 1000 piedi di chastrone; 20 oncie di zafferano; 60 oncie di pepe pesto; 3 barili d'aceto forte

Per 60 taglieri di torta: 30 libre di charne di porcho in lonbo; 10 libre di rancate; 5 libre di cediate; 18 oncie di vue di choranto; 2 oncie di gherofani pesti; 16 oncie di pepe pesto; 18 oncie di spezie fine; 18 oncie di pinocchi mondi; 2 oncie di zafferano; 8 libre di frengniacco frescho

Somma chaponi per li taglieri:	135
per la gelatina:	60
starne in tutti paia:	93
pippioni paia:	58
vitella libre:	500

Chosa bisongna ala detta festa: panchali per dì la e dopa; 12 bacini cholla miscirobe; 80 forchette; 30 choltelle da tavola; 2 bacini grandi; 12 mezine; 4 chonfettiere; 12 orciuoli di chuarto; 12 di mezo quato; 300 bicchieri; salira; 200 fiaschi in prestanza; tovaglie ghuardanappe e mantili; taglieri schodelle e masserizie di chucina; 16 famigli per servire; 25 chandellieri per le tavole; 400 melarance; 20 granate; pera ruggire; charboni; pane biancho

Chorteo:
Monna Chaterina d'Andrea de' Pazi
Monna Albiera di Ghuiglielmo di Giuliano
Monna Maria di Salvestro
Monna Sandra di Giuliano d'Averardo de' Medici
Monna Tita di Gonnozo Gianfigliazi
Monna Alessandra di Bingieri Rucellai
Monna Orsina d'Andrea di Soldo
Monna Piera di Piero Vespucci
Monna Vagga di Bernardo di Bonachorso
Monna Maria di Nani di Marcho di Ghondi

Piero di Giovanni speziale de' avere: 20 torchi innaste di peso libre 72; 20 oncie di zafferano per gelatine; 60 oncie di pepe pesto per gelatine; 5$^1/_1$ libre di torchetti ansitti; 8 libre di chandele moze; 17 libre di treggea biancha; 5 libre di treggea di pere per vescholare; 2 libre 1 torchietto per la dona novella; 10 libre di cancate; 5 libre di cedriate; 18 oncie d'uva di choranto; 2 oncie di gherofani; 16 oncie di pepe pesto; 18 oncie di spezie fine; 18 oncie di pinocchi; 2 oncie di zafferano

D'Antonio di Giovanni la sangio pollaiuolo: 12 chapponi da gelatine; 53 starne; 22 chapponi; 2 chapponi da charulia

Da Papi pollaiuolo: 12 chapponi da gelatine; 22 chapponi; 50 starne

Da Marietto: 12 chapponi; 24 starne

libre 57 pinocchiati lire	57
libre 67 tregea lire	80
libre 57 di cera lire	31
in torchi e altre chose dallo speziale lire	~~65~~ 80
	~~233~~
	248

D'Algnasso, speziale in Porta Rossa, libre 50 di pinocchiati

Dal Pago: libre 400 di chapi; libre 237 di spalle; libre 12 di sciugnaci; libre 32 di lonbi; libre 125 di lardo

Ariento e bacini: 4 chonfettiere; 3 bacini 3 miscirobe d'ariento; 6 bacini 6 miscirobe da domascho; 5 bacini 5 miscirobe d'ottone; 6 chandellieri d'ottone; 20 chandellieri di domascho; 77 forchiette; 40 choltelle; 9 chucchiai

Appendix C   The Frescobaldi Confinement Room

THE FLORENTINE UFFICIO DEI PUPILLI CONDUCTED an inventory of the extensive estate of Girolamo di Lionardo di Stoldo Freschobaldi in 1529. It began with his house in the via del Fondaccio, in the area of Santo Jacopo sopr'Arno in Florence. A room in this house was described by the clerk as "the room where the woman was confined." This woman was not named, and the room in which she was confined was not Girolamo's bedroom, as this was listed separately. Although many of the objects in this room may have been part of its regular furnishings, others were probably brought in especially for the event. This is excerpted from *MPAP*, 191, 130r–131r.

Apresso le masserizie della chamera dove era la donna del parto:
uno usciale di rovescio n° per la donna del parto
uno bernia nera, dicie era di Madonna Nannina de' Strozzi
una gamurra di saia azurra chole maniche
uno gamurrinno di rovescio rosso foderato di pelle bianche chole maniche
uno gamurrino di rovescio azurro
uno gabbano di Girolamo di panno tane
uno gabbano di fregio nero
uno guanciale grande da lettuccio in fodera biancha
una paniera chol cierchio da chucire
uno tondo da mangiare chon arme di Freschobaldi e Taddei
una chamiciuola di suontone biancho
uno archucio da zana
uno aspo
uno sciuguatoio chole verghe azure da chapellinaio
uno paio di lenzuola da famiglia usata
2 paia di lenzuola [ ]
una paniera grande di vetricie entrovi una peza lina
una choltre da letto a botoncini, dicie è achattate
uno guanciale sanza federa
uno chavello da segiole a schache
uno paio di pianelle da donna
uno forzeretto dipinto cho' l'arme di Freschobaldi
In detto le infrascripte chose:
3 tovagliolini in fondo a pichati insieme
uno rinvolto di più schampoli di panno
una peza bigia da zana sempricie
una peza di panno bigio fine chon 1° profilo di dossi intorno foderato di rovescio bigio
uno panno bigio fine per l'archucio chon orli di dossi
uno mantellino di panno bigio fine foderato di dossi
uno mantellino di panno bigio fine foderato di pelle bianche

uno mantellino di panno bigio foderato di rovescio
3 peze bige dichono a usono a essere 5
uno paio di chalze bianche di Madonna Lena
2 rinvolti, cioè 1° grande e 1° mezano entrovi più pelle di lupi e chapri
una paniera
uno cholletto di taffetta nero chon una trine d'oro intorno sopannato di tela
2 chuchiai e 1ª forchetta d'ariento e uno choltello cholle maniche d'ariento
uno mazo di chandele gialle chon una falchola gialla di libre 1
2 tovagliolini
più chartocci di spezie e zuchero
uno rinvolto d'orli di velluto nero
una guardanappa
una paniera entrovi una bandinella da 1° tondo di rensa
uno tovagliolino di rensa
4 chuffia di panno lino
uno torsello di raso nero
Una paneruzola di paglia entrovi:
4 palle da chortinagio dorate
uno grembiule azurro
3 ghomitoli di refe
4 rinvoltuza di tela
2 paia di forbicie
Una chasetta d'albero di braccia 2 in circha entrovi:
18 peze lina da banbino
4 pezaccie chattive line
19 peze pichole usate
11 fascie grande da banbini
2 fascie pichole
5 federe da guanciali picholi
2 federa da guanciali grandi
5 paia di chalcietti da donna
uno fazoletto da chapo
4 teli da zana
5 chamiciacie
uno paio di chalze di panno lino
uno grenbiule di panno lino
6 chamicie da donna
5 sciuguatoi da viso grandi
uno sciuguatoi da piè
3 sciuguatoi da pettinare picholi
uno tovagliolino di rensa
Uno sachetto lino entrovi:
uno telo da zana chole reticielle
una fasciuola di rensa lavorate

una peze da archucio lavorata
Uno sachetto lino entrovi:
7 chuffie line chon 2 nastri
4 chuffie, 2 di rensa, 2 di panno lino sottile
uno benduccio da lichare il chapo
una pezuola orlata
16 fazoletti da mano da huomo
17 pezuole da soffiare il naso

uno chassettino d'avorio entrovi 2 penne di struzolo, 2
    torsigli, uno brieve
uno lettuccio di nocie chon chasse
2 tappeti usati in chamera di Madonna Lena
2 paia di bolgetta di quoio in chucina
2 chandallieri di ferro al chamino di sala
uno chandelliere di ferro in chapo di sala
uno chandelliere di ferro nel'androne di sale

Appendix D   Antonio Rustichi's Supplies for the Wetnurse

IN HIS MEMORANDUM, Antonio di Lionardo Rustichi kept careful note of the objects he sent with his fifteen children when they went to their wetnurses. When they left their nurses (whether because of death, a change in nurse, or weaning), he ensured that he got each object back; when it was returned, he crossed it off his list. Rustichi records that he reused items for more than one child. He made the following list when his first son, Lionardo, was sent to the wetnurse on March 9, 1417. It is transcribed from *Carte strozziane*, II, 11, 11r.

E lle chose ch'io mandai chol fanciullo sono queste, cioè, e
   son' tutte nuove:
uno mantelino bigio nuovo foderato di pelli bianche
una ghamurra nuova
uno mantellino nero di berettino foderato di peli
vi pezze lane nuove (riebi ne 2)
vi fascie nuove
xii pezze line vechie, e più poi vi pezze
uno teletto vechio per in sula zana
una zana vechia
uno brieve di domaschino azurro
una brancha di chorallo chon una ghiera d'ariento, uno dente
   chon detta brancha, uno brieve di scamito nero cho'
   l'arme, chon detta

iiii peze di gharnello nuove (riebbi 2)
uno mantellino di gharnello nuovo cho' uno aghetto
   d'ariento sopanato di valesco
3 chamicuze pichine
una gubba biancha di panno lino vechio
una cioppolina paghonazza doppia
una chuffia bella richamata di seta
uno mantellino verde sopanato di bianchetta
una berettina rosata chon chopette
una beretta grande di domaschino sbiadato su vi uno bottone
   grande di perle belle
una ghamura nova di scharlattino foderata
una cioppa rosata aghozzi vechia chon chopette a frastagli
   degni e bottoni 14 dinazi
iiii bagluzzi di panno lino doppi
una cioppa bigia nuova asettata
uno gharnello biancho asettato vechio
uno ancho di ghuarnello nuovo biancho
uno ghuarnello biancho asettato nuovo
una ghamura usata fu della Mattea
uno fodero nuovo assettato
una ciopa usata asettata fu dela Mattea
una beretta alla gienovese di domaschino di grana
una ghamurra nuova

Notes

Introduction

1 On this, see Marvin Eisenberg, *Lorenzo Monaco*, Princeton, 1989, 84–6.

2 For this particular tray, see Laurence B. Kanter *et al.*, *Painting and illumination in early Renaissance Florence 1300–1450*, New York, 1994, 311–14.

3 For further information on this bowl, see Carmen Ravanelli Guidotti, *Donazione Paolo Mereghi*, Bologna, 1987, 205–7.

4 For the statutes defining the Pupilli, see Francesca Morandini, "Statuti e ordinamenti dell'Ufficio dei Pupilli et Adulti nel periodo della Repubblica Fiorentina (1388–1534)," *Archivio storico italiano*, CXIII, 1955, 522–51; CXIV, 1956, 92–117; CXV, 1957, 87–104. For this study, I examined *MPAP*, 1–25, 27–94, 151–88, and *MPP*, 2645–58, 2660, and 2662–71: a total of 157 volumes, spanning the years 1381–1620. No ledgers survive for some years, others are haphazardly documented, and some estates are recorded several times, prohibiting any conclusive dating boundaries.

5 One example of an estate designated as a woman's is found in *MPAP*, 170, 190v (Mona Betta, the widow of Niccholo di Filippo di Banchozzo in 1443). For further information on women and their legal position, see Thomas Kuehn, *Law, family, and women: Toward a legal anthropology of Renaissance Italy*, Chicago, 1991.

6 *MPAP*, 41, 154r: "1 schiava che'a nome Maddalena."

7 The only study of this cycle is Tommaso Rosselli Sassatelli del Turco, "La chiesetta di San Martino dei Buonomini di Firenze," *Dedalo*, VIII, 1928, 610–32. For a brief reference to the iconography of this fresco, see Silvia Meloni Trkulja, "Due opere di misericordia rettamente interpretate," *Paragone*, 479–81, 1990, 110–14.

8 Attilio Schiaparelli, *La casa fiorentina e i suoi arredi nei secoli XIV e XV*, ed. Maria Sframeli and Laura Pagnotta, Florence, 1983, and E. Polidori Calamandrei, *Le vesti delle donne fiorentine nel quattrocento*, Florence, 1924.

9 Christian Bec, *Les livres des fiorentins (1413–1608)*, Florence, 1984; see also A.F. Verde, "Libri tra le parete domestiche: Una necessaria appendice a lo studio fiorentino 1473–1503," *Memorie domenicane*, XVIII, 1987.

10 John Kent Lydecker, *The domestic setting of the arts in Renaissance Florence*, unpublished doctoral dissertation, The Johns Hopkins University, 1987.

11 Richard Goldthwaite, *The building of Renaissance Florence: An economic and social history*, Baltimore, 1980, esp. 317–50, and his *Wealth and the demand for art in Italy 1300–1600*, Baltimore, 1993.

12 The definitive study of Renaissance marriage chests remains that by Paul Schubring, *Cassoni: Truhen und Truhenbilder der italienischen Fruhrenaissance*, Leipzig, 1915 and 1923. But more recently see Paul F. Watson, *Virtù et voluptas in cassone painting*, unpublished doctoral dissertation, Yale University, 1970, and Ellen Callmann, "The growing threat to marital bliss as seen in fifteenth-century Florentine paintings," *Studies in iconography*,

v, 1979, 73–92. Thematic studies on marriage chests link many diverse subjects to contemporary marriage ideology. See, for example, Cristelle L. Baskins, "Griselda, or the Renaissance bride stripped bare by her bachelor in Tuscan *cassone* painting," *Stanford Italian review*, X, 1991, 153–75, and Christiane Klapisch-Zuber, *Women, family, and ritual in Renaissance Florence*, trans. Lydia G. Cochrane, Chicago, 1985, 213–46, for two examinations of marriage panels with the story of Griselda and their implications for the Renaissance bride.

13 For possible interpretations of this story on marriage chests, see Jerzy Miziolek, *Soggetti classici sui cassoni fiorentini alla vigilia del Rinascimento*, Warsaw, 1996, 25–44, and Cristelle L. Baskins, "Corporeal authority in the speaking pictures: The representation of Lucretia in Tuscan domestic painting," in *Gender rhetorics: Postures of dominance and submission in history*, ed. Richard C. Trexler, Binghamton, 1994, 187–200.

14 *MPAP*, 171, 183r: "uno forziere dipinto di storia di Lucrezia."

15 Iris Origo, *The world of San Bernardino*, London, 1964, 52.

16 Most of these have been destroyed. For further information, see Monika Dachs, "Zur ornamentalen Freskendekoration des florentiner Wohnhauses im späten 14. Jahrhundert," *Mitteilungen des kunsthistorischen Institutes in Florenz*, XXXVII, 1993, 71–129.

17 Giorgio Vasari, *Le vite de' più eccellenti pittori, scultori ed architettori*, ed. Gaetano Milanesi, II, Florence, 1882, 148–9: "usandosi in que' tempi per le camere de' cittadini cassoni grandi di legname a uso di sepolture, e con altre varie fogge ne' coperchi, niuno era che i detti cassoni non facesse dipignere . . . E che è più si dipignevano in cotal maniera non solamente i cassoni, ma i lettucci, le spalliere, le cornici che ricignevano intorno; ed altri cosí fatti ornamenti da camera, che in que' tempi magnificamente si usavano, come infiniti per tutta la città se ne possono vedere."

18 Richard Goldthwaite, "The empire of things: Consumer demand in Renaissance Italy," in *Patronage, art, and society in Renaissance Italy*, ed. F.W. Kent and Patricia Simons, Canberra, 1987, 153–75. For a broad survey, see Lisa Jardine, *Worldly goods*, London, 1996.

19 See Susan M. Pearce, *Museum studies in material culture*, London, 1989, on the essential dilemma between objects traditionally considered part of the decorative or applied arts and those associated with the fine arts.

20 For a partial list of these sources, see Gian Mario Anselmi *et al.*, *La 'memoria' dei mercatores: Tendenze ideologiche, ricordanze, artigianato in versi nella Firenze del quattrocento*, Bologna, 1980, 93–149.

21 Gene Brucker, ed., *Two memoirs of Renaissance Florence*, trans. Julia Martines, New York, 1967, 115.

22 *Acquisti e doni*, 18, 50r: "A dì 6 di giugno 1509 in circha a ore 14 mi naque della Bendeta mia donna e figliuola che fu di Barone di Bernardo di Ser Salvestro di Ser Tommaso di Ser Salvestro uno figliuolo al quale posi nome Giovanfrancescho Domenico et Romolo. Battezzossi in San Giovanni deto dì a

ore 22 in circha. Conpari furono Ser Nicholaio di Silvestro Salamoni et Nofri di Francesco di Baldo di Nofri. Era mercedi et la vigilia del Corpus Domini. A dì 9 di deto nelo posto a balia Monna Dianora donna di Batista di Domenico Bargiani che sta a Pizzulaticho, lavoratore di Ser Bastiano da Sitengnola per pregio ciaschuno mese di lire 4 piccioli . . . morì a dì 28 d'aghosto 1509 a hore 9½ e sottrato in San Piero Scheraggio."

23 On the practice of naming in the Renaissance, see Klapisch-Zuber, 1985, 283–309; for the use of the names Romolo and Romola, see esp. 293.

24 For examples of this, see Klapisch-Zuber, 1985, 310–29.

25 Michael Baxandall, *Painting and experience in fifteenth-century Italy*, Oxford and New York, 1972, 2/1988, repr. 1989, 45–8.

26 Although manuscript illuminations of the birth of Caesar also depict an actual birth, these are, of course, Caesarian sections, performed on a dead mother. See Renate Blumenfeld-Kosinski, *Not of woman born: Representations of Caesarian birth in medieval and Renaissance culture*, Ithaca, NY, 1990.

27 See, for example, Robert Müllerheim, *Die Wochenstube in der Kunst*, Stuttgart, 1904, and Volker Lehmann, *Die Geburt in der Kunst*, Braunschweig, 1978. Both discuss childbirth throughout the world and throughout history using images, but their analysis largely ignores the material and social ramifications of childbirth.

28 Dora Thornton, *The scholar in his study: Ownership and experience in Renaissance Italy*, New Haven and London, 1997.

29 Much of his wealth came from his involvement in the Medici bank; see Raymond de Roover, *The rise and decline of the Medici bank 1397–1494*, Cambridge, 1963, 17, 71–2, and 235.

30 *MPAP*, 173, 265r–274r. See Appendix A for a partial transcription of this inventory.

31 Marco Spallanzani and Giovanna Gaeta Bertelà, ed., *Libro d'inventario dei beni di Lorenzo il Magnifico*, Florence, 1992, 27, 80, 103, 104, and 152. See pp. 73–9 above for a discussion of one of the trays, which was certainly made on the occasion of Lorenzo's birth.

32 *MPP*, 2650, 153v.

33 *Carte strozziane*, V, 1751, 125r. For more information on this case, see Jacqueline Marie Musacchio, "Pregnancy and poultry in Renaissance Italy," *Source*, XVI, 1997, 7–8.

34 ASP, *Ceppi*, 211, 32 right: "per lo amore di Dio."

35 *MPP*, 2650, 339r.

36 *MPAP*, I, 234r.

37 *Carte strozziane*, IV, 418, 20v.

38 *Carte strozziane*, IV, 71, 22v.

39 Marriage objects, too, seem to have had resale value; see Mark Phillips, *The memoir of Marco Parenti: A life in Medici Florence*, Princeton, 1987, 44.

40 See, for example, *MPAP*, 171, 208r, where a birth tray was among the objects from the estate of Pellegrino Vinacciesi and his brothers that were sold to a second-hand dealer named Sano di Filippo.

41 *MPAP*, 175, 115r.

42 *MPAP*, 166, 97v: "uno mantiletto tristo da donna di parto."

43 *Carte strozziane*, III, 275, 76v.

44 *MAP*, CXXXVI, 10r. My thanks to Gino Corti for this reference.

Chapter 1

1 See especially the essays in Klapisch-Zuber, *Women, family, and ritual*, and Samuel K. Cohn Jr., *Women in the streets: Essays on sex and power in Renaissance Italy*, Baltimore, 1996. Also important is the ground-breaking study by Joan Kelly-Gadol, "Did women have a Renaissance?," in *Becoming visible: Women*

in European history, ed. Renate Bridenthal and Claudia Koonz, Boston, 1977, 137–64.

2 *Acquisti e doni*, 302, insert 1, loose folio. For a transcription of this document, see Appendix B.

3 On the theory that the panels in this cycle represented an injunction against contemporary excess, represented in part by this elaborate setting, see Christina Olsen, "Gross expenditure: Botticelli's Nastagio degli Onesti panels," *Art history*, XV, 1992, 146–70.

4 Herbert Horne compared this representation to the account Giovanni Rucellai provided of the wedding of his son Bernardo to Nannina di Piero de' Medici in 1466; see Herbert P. Horne, *Alessandro Filipepi, commonly called Sandro Botticelli*, London, 1908, 133.

5 On the importance of the dowry see Julius Kirshner and Anthony Molho, "The dowry fund and the marriage market in early quattrocento Florence," *Journal of modern history*, L, 1978, 403–38, and Anthony Molho, *Marriage alliance in late medieval Florence*, Cambridge, 1994. For a discussion of the issues of honor, marriage, and shame in connection with the growing costs of dowries during the early fifteenth century, see Michael D. Taylor, "Gentile da Fabriano, Saint Nicholas, and an iconography of shame," *Journal of family history*, VII, 1982, 321–32.

6 *MPAP*, 53, 37r: "per l'amore di Dio e per l'anima del detto testatore fiorini trenta d'oro a fanciulle povere e bisognose per maritarsi."

7 Cited in Roberto Rusconi, "San Bernardino of Siena, the wife, and possessions," in *Women and religion in medieval and Renaissance Italy*, ed. Daniel Bornstein and Roberto Rusconi, Chicago, 1996, 187–8.

8 Leon Battista Alberti, *The Albertis of Florence: Leon Battista Alberti's Della famiglia* (1430s), ed. Guido A. Guarino, Lewisburg, 1971, esp. 27.

9 Cherubino da Siena [*sic*], *Regole della vita matrimoniale*, ed. Francesco Zambrini and Carlo Negroni, Bologna, 1888, 61–2.

10 *Acquisti e doni*, 302, insert 1, loose folio: "uno libro di Fra Cherubino in forma coperto di cordovano azuro." Although Fra Cherubino wrote several other texts, it seems most likely that this one on marriage would be the one included in Caterina's marriage goods.

11 Paolo da Certaldo, "Libro di buoni costumi" (1370), in *Mercanti scrittori*, ed. Vittore Branca, Milan, 1986, 15–17 (no. 91).

12 Alberti, *Della famiglia*, 121. His second consideration was her family, and his third, of course, was her dowry. One might wonder, however, whether the order of these considerations was followed in real-life situations.

13 Alessandra Macinghi Strozzi, *Lettere di una gentildonna fiorentina del secolo XV al figliuoli esuli*, ed. Cesare Guasti, Florence, 1877, 527–31. Also observe the comments made about a prospective daughter-in-law transcribed in Lucrezia Tornabuoni, *Lucrezia Tornabuoni: Lettere*, ed. Patrizia Salvadori, Florence, 1993, 64.

14 Cited in James Bruce Ross, "The middle-class child in urban Italy, fourteenth to early sixteenth centuries," in *The history of childhood*, ed. Lloyd de Mause, New York, 1974, 206.

15 On this, see Heather Gregory, "Daughters, dowries, and family in fifteenth-century Florence," *Rinascimento*, XXVII, 1987, 235–7.

16 *MAP*, LXXVI, 239: "la Piera [his wife] . . . questa nocte passata a hore sei partorì una bambina femmina . . . Tiene per certo che io non ne sono mancho lieto che si fussi stato maschio." I am grateful to Gino Corti for this reference.

17 *Carte strozziane*, III, 178, 6: "Parmi che avendone uno maschio, e visto tanto quant'egli è, che non meno ti debbi rallegrare di questa sendo femina, che se fussi maschio, perchè

prima comincerai a trarre frutto che del maschio, cioè, ne farai prima um bello parentado." Lorenzo di Pierfrancesco de' Medici sent a similar condolence letter to Isabella d'Este's husband after the birth of their first daughter in 1494; see Alessandro Luzio and Rodolfo Renier, *Mantova e Urbino: Isabella d'Este ed Elisabetta Gonzaga nelle relazioni famigliari e nelle vicende politiche*, Turin, 1893, 68–9. There is evidence that Isabella, too, was disappointed, since she did not use the special cradle her father had given her until her first son, who was her third child, was born; see Edith Patterson Meyer, *First lady of the Renaissance: A biography of Isabella d'Este*, Boston, 1970, 66.

18 Phillips, *Marco Parenti*, 44.

19 *MAP*, XXVII, 192: "Et a vostra moglie dicete che lei se è portata molto meglio che non ha facto mia moglie, la quale benchè habbia facto questo maschio al presente, ne ha facte octo femine primo che habbia facto questo maschio." My thanks to Gino Corti for this reference.

20 See both Richard C. Trexler, "The foundlings of Florence, 1395–1455," *History of childhood quarterly*, I, 1973, 259–84, and Klapisch-Zuber, *Women, family, and ritual*, 132–64.

21 A few women did react against this; for examinations of these exceptional women, see Paul Oskar Kristeller, "Learned women of early modern Italy: Humanists and university scholars," in his *Studies in Renaissance thought and letters*, Rome, 1985, II, 189–205, Lisa Jardine, "Isotta Nogarola: Women humanists – education for what?," *History of education*, XII, 1983, 231–44, and Margaret King and Albert Rabil Jr., ed., *Her immaculate hand: Selected works by and about the women humanists of quattrocento Italy*, Binghamton, 1983.

22 ASP, *Archivio Datini*, 1103, loose folio (19 August 1381): "La Francesca dicie tu dicha alla Margherita che uno o due fanciulli de' suoi le prestava, ma donarglile no, perch'ella non'a provato come si fanno."

23 Several rather romanticized biographies have been written about Cappello. One of the best accounts based on documentary evidence is Guglielmo Enrico Saltini, *Bianca Cappello e Francesco I de' Medici*, Florence, 1898; see also Maria Luisa Mariotti Masi, *Bianca Cappello: Una veneziana alla corte dei Medici*, Milan, 1986.

24 Regarding Bianca's purported pregnancies, see the series of letters by Simone Fortuna, the Duke of Urbino's agent in the Medici court, in *Archivio di Urbino*, Appendix I and II, as well as Roberto Cantagalli, "Bianca Cappello e una leggenda da sfatare: La questione del figlio supposto," *Nuova rivista storica*, XLIX, 1965, 636–52. A similar incident is described in Alberto Chiappelli, "Di un singolare procedimento medico-legale in Pistoia nell'anno 1375 per supposizione d'infante," *Rivista di storia delle scienze mediche e naturali*, X, 1919, 129–35.

25 *MPAP*, 176, 88r: "1ª Nuziata dipinta in tela fiandrescha."

26 *Prestanze*, 1322, 22r. My thanks to Gino Corti for this reference. For reference to another male practitioner, see the letters from Agnolo Poliziano to Lorenzo de' Medici discussing the health of Lorenzo's pregnant wife Clarice and the care she received from her male physician, in Agnolo Ambrogini Poliziano, *Prose volgari inedite e poesie Latine e Greche edite e inedite*, ed. Isidoro del Lungo, Florence, 1867, 59–63.

27 *Carte strozziane*, V, 22, 97 right: "A dì XXIII detto piaque a di Dio chiamare asse la benedetta anima della Fiametta mia donna . . . Il male suo fu che nel parto di sopra non purghò bene e niente di meno. Anchora che avessi auto in detto parto qualche dì uno poco di febre e alchune doglie di 4 dì era stata bene ed era levata e stavasi per chasa. El dì sulle 21 hora li chominciò una doglia grande intorno al quore. Girossi sul letucio e di qui si fecie portare ne'letto, ramarichandosi sempre grandemente del chuore. E per molti ripari vi si faciessino per

donne e per medici nulla govo. Che circha a hore XXIII finì." For another example of such a tragedy, see *Carte strozziane*, III, 108, 77r.

28 For the case of Bartolommea, the wife of Bernardo Rinieri, who died of "mal di matrici" in 1496, according to the autopsy done on Bartolommea's own wishes, see *CRSGF*, 95 (212), 171 right. This case and others are cited as evidence for the importance of autopsies as standard medical and legal practices in Katharine Park, "The criminal and saintly body: Autopsy and dissection in Renaissance Italy," *Renaissance quarterly*, XLVII, 1994, 1–33.

29 *CRSGF*, 102 (356), 41.

30 For midwives, see Merry E. Wiesner, "Early modern midwifery: A case study," in *Women and work in preindustrial Europe*, ed. Barbara Hanawalt, Bloomington, 1986, 94–113, and Nadia Maria Filippini, "The church, the state, and childbirth: The midwife in Italy during the eighteenth century," in *The art of midwifery: Early modern midwives in Europe*, ed. Hilary Marland, London, 1993, 152–75. When questions were raised regarding pregnancy, legitimacy, or succession, midwives could serve as legal witnesses; see Monica H. Green, "Documenting medieval women's medical practice," in *Practical medicine from Salerno to the Black Death*, ed. Luis Garcia-Ballester et al., Cambridge, 1994, 338–40.

31 *MAP*, XXXII, 285. I am grateful to Gino Corti for this reference.

32 For a later example of their often extraordinary competence, see Laurel Thatcher Ulrich, *A midwife's tale: The life of Martha Ballard, based on her diary, 1785–1812*, New York, 1990.

33 Trotula, *Sulle malattie delle donne* (1577), ed. Pina Cavallo Boggi, Turin, 1979, and Trotula, *Medieval woman's guide to health*, ed. Beryl Rowland, London, 1981. It has been suggested that these texts were written by a man and later attributed to a female author for credibility; see John F. Benton, *Trotula, women's problems, and the professionalization of medicine in the Middle Ages*, Pasadena, 1984.

34 In the late first century AD, the Greek physician Soranus wrote his extremely influential *Gynaecia*, a work dealing with obstetrics, pediatrics, and gynecology. Along with a similar treatise by Galen, this work served as the source for most of the later texts on the subject. Monica Helen Green analyzes the early texts in *The transmission of ancient theories of female physiology and disease through the early Middle Ages*, unpublished doctoral dissertation, Princeton University, 1985, 269–94. For a summary of ancient medical ideas on children and child care, see Robert Etienne, "Ancient medical conscience and children," *Journal of psychohistory*, IV, 1976, 144–50.

35 Giovanni Boccaccio, *The Decameron* (c. 1350), trans. Guido Waldman, Oxford, 1993, 565.

36 Bernardino da Siena, *Le prediche volgari di San Bernardino da Siena dette nella Piazza del Campo l'anno MCCCCXXVII*, ed. Luciano Banchi, II, Siena, 1884, 116–17: "Se ella è gravida, ella sura fadiga ne la sua gravidezza; ella ha fadiga in parturire e'figliuoli; ella s'affadiga in governarli, in allevarli, e anco ha fadiga di governare il marito, quando egli è in nissuno bisogno e infermità: ella dura fadiga in governare tutta la casa. E però, come tu vedi che in ogni modo ella dura fadiga, così tu, marito, quando la tua donna ha niuno caso, fà che tu l'aiti a portare la fadiga sua. Se ella è gravida o in parto, aitala in quello che tu puoi, perocchè quello è tuo figliuolo . . . Tutta questa fadiga vedi che ella è sola della donna, e l'uomo se ne va cantando."

37 David Herlihy and Christiane Klapisch-Zuber, *Tuscans and their families: A study of the Florentine catasto of 1427*, New Haven and London, 1985, 277.

38 See, for example, *Ufficiale della Grascia*, 188, unpaginated (17

July 1430): "Monna Pina di Giuliano, popolo San Piero Gattolino, in via Vechia, riposta in detta chiesa, sopra parto."

39 *Ufficiale della Grascia*, 188, unpaginated (7 October 1430): "Monna Giulia di Lodovicho Cieffini, popolo San Simone, riposta in Sancta Croce, sconciossi."

40 See especially the discussion on death by age and gender in Herlihy and Klapisch-Zuber, *Tuscans*, 270–79.

41 See Strozzi, *Lettere*, 59–60.

42 Stanley Chojnacki, "Dowries and kinsmen in early Renaissance Venice," *Journal of interdisciplinary history*, v, 1975, 587.

43 *Acquisti e doni*, 301, insert 1, loose folio: "el più iscontento uomo di Firenze."

44 For further information on this popular practice, see Klapisch-Zuber, *Women, family, and ritual*, 283–309.

45 Julia Cartwright, *Beatrice d'Este, Duchess of Milan 1475–1497: A study of the Renaissance*, New York, 1903, 305–6.

46 Luigi Samoggia, "Lodovico Bonaccioli medico ostetrico di Lucrezia Borgia in Ferrara," *Atti della Accademia dei fisiocritici in Siena*, XIII, 1964, 513–31.

47 Maddalena's death in 1519, two weeks after she gave birth to Caterina de' Medici, the future Queen of France, was due to post-partum infection. Apparently this was quite common at the time; Goro Gheri, the Medici secretary, wrote, "questo anno ne sono morte assai qui in Firenze, come è la verita, delle donne di parto" (Andrea Corsini, *Malattie e morte di Lorenzo de' Medici, Duca d'Urbino*, Florence, 1913, 105).

48 Gaetano Pieraccini, *La stirpe de' Medici di Cafaggiolo*, II, Florence, 1925, 128–31.

49 *Carte strozziane*, I, 32, 247v: "che fusse meglio lasciarla vivere quel poco di vita che gli restava senza più travagliarla."

50 ASP, *Archivio Datini*, 1103, loose folio (7 November 1388): "La serva vostra è stata da martedì sera in qua sopra partorire, ed è lla magiore pietà che mai si vedesse. Che mai no fu femine contantri e non si a si duro chuore che no piagnesse vedendola. E conviene che ssia tenuta, altrimenti s'ucciderebbe; era vi donne ch'à parte a parte di loro la guardano. Stamano dichono che temono che lla criatura nella sia morta in chorpo."

51 Herlihy and Klapisch-Zuber, *Tuscans*, 273.

52 See, for example, *Ufficiale della Grascia*, 188, unpaginated (15 August 1524): "Uno fanciullino di Giandonato di Miniato riposto in San Piero Ghattolino nata innanzi al tempo."

53 *Ufficiale della Grascia*, 188, unpaginated (1 May 1425): "Un fanciulo d'uno Tedescho popolo Sancto Lorenzo riposto a Sancto Bernaba di tre dì."

54 *Carte strozziane*, II, 17, 66r: "anchora si sconcio la Sandra in uno fanciulo maschio era grosa di mesi cinque."

55 *Carte strozziane*, II, 16 bis, 6v: "si sconcio in 3 fanciulli di mesi 2 o circha. Di 2 si vide ch'erano maschi, e'l $\frac{1}{3}$ non si scorgira che fussi. Comincio a hore di $\frac{1}{3}$ o ciercha, e l'altra sconciatura fu dopo none. Stette a pericolo di morte pure a Dio gratia rimase libera. Ma durolle il male grande più di 15 dì, Idio lo dato di tutto." See also Filippo Strozzi's description of his wife Clarice giving birth to stillborn twins in 1525 (*Carte strozziane*, III, 108, 77r–77v).

56 My thanks to Dr. Krystin Bandola for clarifying this point for me.

57 *Archivio Gherardi Piccolomini d'Aragona*, 326, loose folio: "ii fanciugli maschi ebbe a uno chorpo."

58 Philippe Ariès, *Centuries of childhood: A social history of family life* (1960), trans. Robert Baldick, New York, 1962, and Danièle Alexandre-Bidon and Pierre Riché, *L'enfance au moyen age*, Paris, 1994. For a critique of Ariès' methodology see Adrian Wilson, "The infancy of the history of childhood: An appraisal of Philippe Ariès," *History & theory*, XIX, 1980, 132–53.

59 See Margaret L. King, *The death of the child Valerio Marcello*,

Chicago, 1994, and Giovanni di Pagolo Morelli, *Ricordi* (1393–1421), ed. Vittore Branca, Florence, 1956, esp. 455–9. An analysis of Morelli's account is in Richard C. Trexler, *Public life in Renaissance Florence*, New York, 1980, 159–86.

60 See, for example, the record of Girolamo di Bartolomeo Bartolomeo, who lists the birth of thirteen children. Of these thirteen, four live, but nine die, all before the age of five and the majority much earlier, as recorded in *Archivio Bartolomei*, 274, 79v, 83v.

61 Cited in Park, "Autopsy and dissection," 9.

62 On these, see especially Sharon T. Strocchia, *Death and ritual in Renaissance Florence*, Baltimore, 1992.

63 For my understanding of the Tornabuoni, I am especially grateful to Rab Hatfield, who generously shared his own unpublished observations with me and willingly discussed my ideas. I am also indebted to the dissertations by Sheila McClure Ross (*The redecoration of Santa Maria Novella's Capella Maggiore*, unpublished doctoral dissertation, University of California, Berkeley, 1983) and Patricia Simons (*Portraiture and patronage in quattrocento Florence with special reference to the Tornaquinci and their chapel in Santa Maria Novella*, unpublished doctoral dissertation, University of Melbourne, 1985), both of whom likewise benefited from Hatfield's generosity. Studies of the Tornabuoni have focused primarily on issues of patronage, and the family's role in the artistic and political circles of Renaissance Florence has been well established, especially by Simons's work. The focus here is on the manner in which Giovanni Tornabuoni commemorated his dead wife and child. Although there is no conclusive physical evidence that Francesca's tomb was placed in the Minerva chapel, other facts build a compelling circumstantial case. For the relevant literature, see the thorough summation in Shelley Elizabeth Zuraw, *The sculpture of Mino da Fiesole (1429–1484)*, unpublished doctoral dissertation, New York University, 1993, 952–71.

64 *MAP*, XXXV, 746: "Carissimo mio Lorenzo. Son' tanto oppresso da passione e dolore per l'acerbissimo e inopinato chaso della mia dolcissima sposa che lo medesimo non so dove mi sia. La quale chome durai inteso ieri, chome piacqui a Dio, a hore XXII sopra parto passò di questa presente vita, e lla creatura, sparata lei, gli chavamo di chorpo morta, che m'è stato anchora doppio dolore. Son' certissimo che per la tua solita pietà avendomi chompassione marai per ischusato s'io non ti scrivo a longho."

65 Poliziano, *Prose volgari*, 62: "Madonna Clarice s'è sentita da iersera in quà un poco chioccia. Scrive lei a Madonna Lucretia, che dubita di non si sconciare, o di no avere il male che ebbe la donna di Giovanni Tornabuoni."

66 The Bargello relief (and thus the tomb) has been associated with the circle of Andrea Verrocchio at least since Vasari's time, and with the Tornabuoni family since at least 1836. For pertinent bibliography on this complicated issue, see Zuraw, *Mino da Fiesole*, 952–71 (where the tomb is attributed to Mino).

67 This is different from representations of Caesarian sections, a common illumination in manuscripts of the life of Caesar; for these, see Blumenfeld-Kosinski, *Not of woman born*. It is not until seventeenth-century England that tombs for women who died in childbirth begin to approach the intensity of the Tornabuoni relief; see Judith W. Hurtig, "Death in childbirth: Seventeenth-century English tombs and their place in contemporary thought," *Art bulletin*, LXV, 1983, 603–15.

68 James Beck, *Jacopo della Quercia*, I, New York, 1991, 142–8.

69 It has been observed that the general composition and the figures themselves have much in common with Roman reliefs of the Death of Meleager or the Death of Alcestis, both of which were well known in the Renaissance. See Frida

Schottmüller, "Zwei Grabmäler der Renaissance und ihre antiken Vorbilder," *Repertorium für Kunstwissenschaft*, XXV, 1902, 401–8. Similar motifs were also utilized for the bronze relief of *The Death of a Hero* on Francesco Sassetti's tomb in Santa Trinita in Florence; on Sassetti, who was a colleague of Giovanni Tornabuoni's in the Medici banking enterprise, see Aby Warburg, *Gesammelte Schriften*, I, Leipzig, 1932, 127–58, and Eve Borsook and Johannes Offerhaus, *Francesco Sassetti and Domenico Ghirlandaio at Santa Trinità, Florence: History and legend in a Renaissance chapel*, Doornspijk, 1981, 25–6.

70 See Zuraw, *Mino da Fiesole*, 952–71. This relief is the only object that can now be associated with Francesca's tomb with any certainty. It was removed from the Minerva before 1666, when it was cited in the estate of Cardinal Carlo di Ferdinando de' Medici (*Guardaroba*, 758, 18). The relief became part of the ducal holdings on the cardinal's death at seventy-one on June 19, 1666; for the date of his death, see *CRSGF*, 119 (55), 96r. Various features mentioned in the *Guardaroba* description but no longer with the relief were probably independent features of the original monument that have been destroyed or disassociated with the relief over time.

71 See Hermann Egger, *Francesca Tornabuoni und ihre Grabstätte in Santa Maria sopra Minerva*, Vienna, 1934.

72 For a case of baptism in the womb during delivery, see *Carte strozziane*, I, 32, 246r.

73 This tomb is discussed in Roberta Sulli, "Il monumento funebre a Pereyra-Camponeschi: Contributo allo studio della cultura antiquariale a L'Aquila nel secondo quattrocento," *Bullettino della Deputazione abruzzese di storia patria*, LXXVII, 1987, 207–28.

74 For the most thorough examination of the plague, see Jean-Noël Biraben, *Les hommes et la peste en France et dans les pays européens et méditerranées*, 2 vols., Paris, 1975–6, as well as the new interpretations offered by David Herlihy, *The Black Death and the transformation of the West*, ed. Samuel K. Cohn Jr., Cambridge, Mass., 1997. Of course, the plague was not the only problem facing the population at this time, as analyzed by Hans Baron, *The crisis of the early Italian Renaissance*, Princeton, 1966.

75 Ann G. Carmichael, *Plague and the poor in Renaissance Florence*, Cambridge, 1986, 60–61.

76 For information on the different circuits, see Paula Lois Spilner, *Ut civitas amplietur: Studies in Florentine urban development 1282–1400*, unpublished doctoral dissertation, Columbia University, New York, 1987.

77 For an analysis of the changes in Florentine population from 1300 to 1550, see Herlihy and Klapisch-Zuber, *Tuscans*, 60–92.

78 Matteo Villani, *Cronica* (1348–63), ed. Francesco Gherardi Dragomanni, I, Florence, 1846, 9: "la sterminio della generazione umana." For a summary of contemporary statements on the epidemic, see Millard Meiss, *Painting in Florence and Siena after the Black Death*, Princeton, 1951, 65, n. 24.

79 For a study of the Black Death of 1348, see Robert S. Gottfried, *The Black Death: Natural and human disaster in medieval Europe*, London, 1983; demographic examinations include David Herlihy, "Population, plague, and social change in rural Pistoia," *Economic history review*, XVIII, 1965, 225–44; for a more environmental approach (but one with a perhaps problematic conclusion), see Graham Twigg, *The Black Death: A biological reappraisal*, London, 1984.

80 See, for example, Paul Binski, *Medieval death: Ritual and representation*, London, 1996; Samuel K. Cohn Jr., *The cult of remembrance and the Black Death: Six Renaissance cities in central Italy*, Baltimore, 1992; and Strocchia, *Death and Ritual*.

81 Meiss, *Painting . . . after the Black Death*. For revisions to this thesis, see Henk van Os, "The Black Death and Sienese

painting: A problem of interpretation," *Art history*, IV, 1981, 237–49, Bruce Cole, "Some thoughts on Orcagna and the Black Death style," *Antichità viva*, XXII, 1983, 27–37, and above all Cohn, *Cult of remembrance*, 271–80.

82 Louise Marshall, "Manipulating the sacred: Image and plague in Renaissance Italy," *Renaissance quarterly*, XLVII, 1994, 485–532.

83 See Paul Heitz, *Pestblätter des XV. Jahrhunderts*, Strassburg, 1901, Raymond Crawford, *Plague and pestilence in literature and art*, Oxford, 1914, and Comune di Venezia, *Venezia e la peste, 1348–1797*, Venice, 1980.

84 Strocchia, *Death and ritual*, 64.

Chapter 2

1 *CRSGF*, 111 (140), 76v and 165r.

2 For further information on this tray, see Luciano Berti, *Masaccio*, Florence, 1988, 197–201.

3 These could also be illusionistically painted. Walls frescoed with fur hangings were documented during the destruction of the city center of Florence during the nineteenth century; see Dachs, "Freskendekoration."

4 Little is known about this all-female event in the Italian Renaissance, prohibiting the sort of informative analysis put forth for seventeenth- and eighteenth-century England; see Adrian Wilson, "The ceremony of childbirth and its interpretation," in *Women as mothers in pre-industrial England: Essays in memory of Dorothy McLaren*, ed. Valerie Fildes, London, 1990, 68–107.

5 Microhistory has received a considerable amount of attention in recent years. The potential to learn more about a particular society by examining one component of that society in depth has proved particularly successful for scholars discussing personal events, such as marriage, or female activities, such as convent life. Studies dealing with Italy include Judith C. Brown, *Immodest acts: The life of a lesbian nun in Renaissance Italy*, New York, 1986; Gene Brucker, *Giovanni and Lusanna: Love and marriage in Renaissance Florence*, Berkeley, 1986; and Carlo Ginzburg, *The cheese and the worms* (1976), trans. John and Anne Tedeschi, Baltimore, 1980. For a cogent analysis of this method, see Lawrence Stone, "The return of narrative," *Past and present*, LXXXV, 1979, 3–24.

6 *CRSGF*, 111 (140), 76r: "Ricordo come a dì 19, a hore venti et tre quinti in circa, per lo Iddio gratia e della Beata Vergine Maria e di sancto Niccolò nostro protectore e advocato e di tucti gli altri sancti e sancte di Dio, mi naque della Chaterina mia donna uno fanciullo maschio con tucte sue menbra et bene proportionato, Iddio lodato. Et decta Chaterina et el fantino stanno bene. Allevollo una Monna Mathea, sta a chasa dal bottaio di Sancto Lorenzo dalla porta del fianchio che va nella via della Stufa ala quale io decti et Monna Lena mia suocera. Per me e di mia danari per sua faticha perchè ci stette circa a hore 22 in circa per durarci molte sua faticha fiorino uno largho, cioè lire 5 soldi 10. E domani di buona hore lo farò batezare e faro gli porre il nome del padre mio, cioè Giovanni, et perchè naque in domenicha faro gli porre nome Giovanni e Domenicho et perche non abbia quello benedecto nome Romolo, prego Iddio e la sua madre madonna sancta Maria, Sancto Niccholò, e tucti gli altri sancti di Paradiso die lo facino buono fanciullo nella gratia di Dio."

7 See, for example, the description of the birth of a son in 1499 to Giovanni di Ser Bernardo Buongirolami in *Carte strozziane*, II, 23, 131v.

8 *CRSGF*, 95 (212), 159 right: "come l'ordinario."

9 *Archivio Gherardi Piccolomini d'Aragona*, 139, 2 left: "per provedere a bisogni della donna ch'aveva a partorire." Another

example would be Chanbio Petrucci, who wrote that he was paid by Piero da Chanpi "per chonperate alchune chose per la dona sua ch'era in parto" (*Carte strozziane*, II, 10, 22r).

10 *CRSGF*, III (140), 37v: "Ricordo di tutti i denari spenderò per la Caterina mia donna nel parto et in sua grossezza." Other men listed their expenses in a more abbreviated fashion. For example, in 1457 Carlo di Messer Palla Strozzi wrote: "E a dì xv d'ottobre lire quatordici s.viiii piccioli, sono pe'l parto della Lucrezia, cioè lire 2 s.5 a monna Antonia la levò, el batesimo chol torchietto s.12, e s.33 ala detta, e lire 6 s.16 per 4 paia di chaponi e 2 paia di polle grose e altre chose, e lire 5 s.8 per libre 6½ di tregiea e libre 1½ di chandele di ciera. In tutto, quanto detto lire 14 soldi 9" (*Carte strozziane*, V, 13, 55 right). These were the only costs Carlo designated as birth related; his 14 *lire* were negligible compared with Ser Girolamo's final expenditures.

11 *CRSGF*, III (140), 37v. A covered urinal was included in the inventory of Francesco Datini's rented home in Florence in 1400 (ASP, *Archivio Datini*, 236, 26 July 1400 inventory, 3r).

12 *CRSGF*, III (140), 37v.

13 *CRSGF*, III (140), 37v. Dragonwort was a common ingredient for prescriptions listed in the Florentine pharmacopeia of 1499; see *Ricettario fiorentino* (1499), ed. Luigi Crocetti, Florence, 1968, unpaginated.

14 *CRSGF*, III (140), 37v.

15 *CRSGF*, III (140), 60r.

16 The materials for these items, and some of the items themselves, are listed in *CRSGF*, III (140), 37v, 60v, 61v, 69r, and 71v.

17 A fascinating reconstruction of sixteenth-century ducal costumes is given in Kirsten Aschengreen Piacenti and Caterina Chiarelli, *Moda alla corte dei Medici: Gli abiti restaurati di Cosimo, Eleonora e Don Garzia*, Florence, 1993.

18 On the cloth industry see Jacqueline Herald, *Renaissance dress in Italy 1400–1500*, London, 1981, 66–96, and Aurora Fiorentini Capitani and Stefania Ricci, ed., *Il costume al tempo di Lorenzo il Magnifico: Prato e il suo territorio*, Milan, 1992.

19 *MPP*, 2656, 511r.

20 *MPAP*, 49, 225r.

21 *MPP*, 2655, 581r.

22 For an overview of special childbirth-related clothing, see Sara Piccolo Paci, "Le vesti della madre: Considerazioni socio-antropologiche dalla preistoria al XX secolo D.C.," in *Da donna a madre: Vesti e ceramiche particolari per momenti speciali*, Florence, 1996, 7–54.

23 *MPAP*, 151, 73r.

24 The different materials are listed in *CRSGF*, III (140), 37v.

25 *MPAP*, 152, 38r.

26 *CRSGF*, III (140), 37v.

27 *MPP*, 2649, 631r.

28 *MPP*, 2651, 190r.

29 *MPAP*, 68, 81r.

30 *MPAP*, 172, 264r.

31 *CRSGF*, III (140), 37v and 65v.

32 William Boulting, *Women in Italy, from the introduction of the chivalrous service of love to the appearance of the professional actress*, New York, 1910, 161.

33 *MPP*, 2649, 670v.

34 *CRSGF*, III (140), 71v.

35 These laws are recorded in Lorenzo Cantini, ed., *Legislazione toscana*, Florence, 1800–08, II:171–2, 353–4; V:64–6; VII:256; and XI:353.

36 *Notarile antecosimiano*, 14623, 5v–6v. My thanks to Gino Corti for this reference.

37 See, for example, the case of 1585 involving wagers on the gender of children due to five different women in *Acquisti e*

doni, 302, insert 2, loose folio. I am grateful to Elaine Rosenthal for referring me to this document.

38 *MPP*, 2653, 93v. See also Piero Calamandrei, "Il totocalcio demografico di Benvenuto Cellini," in *Scritti inediti celliniani*, ed. Carlo Cordié, Florence, 1971, 149–64.

39 Calamandrei, "Totocalcio demografico," 163.

40 *CRSGF*, III (140), 37v and 73v.

41 For comparative costs see the tables in Goldthwaite, *Renaissance Florence*, 430 and 438.

42 *CRSGF*, III (140), 75v: "Ricordo come a dì 18, a hore XXIII in circa cominciorono le doglie alla Chaterina, e per decta cagione conperai... uno pippione grosso... oncie ½ di margheritoni... 3 uova fresche."

43 *CRSGF*, III (140), 67r, 71v, and 74r.

44 *MPAP*, 178, 162v.

45 *Carte strozziane*, V, 13, 55 right.

46 For comparison, see the account of wetnurse expenses in *Panciatichi*, 49, 31r.

47 Michele Savonarola, *Il trattato ginecologico-pediatrico in volgare: Ad mulieres ferrarienses de regimine pregnantium et noviter natorum usque ad septennium* (c. 1460), ed. Luigi Belloni, Milan, 1952, 69 and 131.

48 See Musacchio, "Pregnancy and poultry," 3–9. For the longevity of this symbol in the context of fertility, see Lorrayne Y. Baird, "Priapus gallinaceus: The role of the cock in fertility and eroticism in classical antiquity and the Middle Ages," *Studies in iconography*, VII–VIII, 1981–2, 81–111.

49 *CRSGF*, III (140), 75v.

50 Further information on this guild is found in Raffaele Ciasca, *L'arte dei medici e speziali nella storia e nel commercio fiorentino dal secolo XII al XV*, Florence, 1927.

51 For information on this text see Luigi Crocetti, "Nota sul Ricettario fiorentino," in *Ricettario fiorentino* (1499), Florence, 1968, unpaginated.

52 For a recipe for *treggea*, see ASP, *Archivio Datini*, 1093, loose folio.

53 *CRSGF*, III (140), 74r and 75v. *Confetti* were also bought for weddings; when Bernardo Rinieri got married in 1459, he paid Mariotto the apothecary "per più confetti auti dal loro quando menai la donna" (*CRSGF*, 95 (212), 22 left).

54 *Carte strozziane*, II, 16 bis, 4r. Sets of forks and spoons, sometimes with coats of arms, were popular gifts for both childbirth and marriage. In 1447 Francesco Chastellani bought "dodici forchette d'ariento picchole alla viniziana" to give to Messer Benedetto d'Arezzo on his wedding day (*CRSGF*, 90 (84), 31v).

55 ASP, *Ceppi*, 211, 33 right. This was a common practice among various governmental and religious charities. In 1458 the *Camerlingo* of San Lorenzo gave a box of sweetmeats to Piero delle Pietre Buone when his wife had a son; see Biblioteca Laurenziana, Florence, *Archivio capitolare di San Lorenzo*, 2310, 113v. My thanks to Jonathan Davies for the latter reference.

56 BNCF, *Fondo nazionale*, II, II, 357, 59r.

57 *CRSGF*, 90 (84), 51r.

58 *CRSGF*, III (140), 74r and 77r. Two boxes were given to him by an acquaintance, Maestro Ugolino, but Ser Girolamo entered their value as a debit in his account of birth expenses. He stated that Maestro Ugolino gave him these boxes because he wanted Ser Girolamo to tend to some documents for his daughter. Ser Girolamo was probably intent on providing only the amount of professional services equivalent to the worth of the boxes and he debited Caterina's account for these services accordingly.

59 *CRSGF*, III (140), 74r.

60 Savonarola, *Trattato*, 131, and Paolo da Certaldo, "Libro," 35 (no. 154). Such precepts were clearly practiced as part of

everyday expectations. A letter to Lorenzo di Piero de' Medici from a certain Alessandra requested Lorenzo's financial assistance in her forthcoming birth. Alessandra was impoverished, and described herself as "sanza vino," implying that this fact constituted a major difficulty for a woman in her condition (*MAP*, XXV, 631: my thanks to Gino Corti for this reference).

61   *CRSGF*, 111 (140), 74r and 79v.

62   *Carte strozziane*, IV, 71, 24r. When Lucrezia Tornabuoni assisted at her daughter-in-law Clarice's confinement in 1471, she brought two flasks of wine with her (*MAP*, XXVII, 31).

63   Vasari, *Vite*, ed. Milanesi, III:267.

64   *MPAP*, 160, 430r.

65   *MAP*, XXI, 55: "le vicitationi alla Laudomina per tua parte si sono facte, et quanto si richiede intorno a cciò." For a discussion of confinement room visits in the seventeenth century, see Tommaso Rinuccini, *Le usanze fiorentine del secolo XVII*, Florence, 1863, 24.

66   See the discussion of this paradoxical attitude in Goldthwaite, *Wealth*, esp. 204–12.

67   This splendor is a characteristic many have found typical of the Venetian Republic; see Edward Muir, "Images of power: Art and pageantry in Renaissance Venice," *American historical review*, LXXXIV, 1979, 16–52.

68   Edmond Bonnaffè, *Voyages et voyageurs de la Renaissance*, Paris, 1895, 56–7.

69   Francesco Sansovino, *Venetia: Città nobilissima et singolare*, Venice, 1581, 402.

70   Lorenzo Lotto, *Il "libro di spese diverse" con aggiunta di lettere e d'altri documenti (1538–56)*, ed. Pietro Zampetti, Venice, 1969, 237.

71   The Milanese priest Pietro Casola described how visitors to a Venetian confinement room left unfed, contrary to the vast and expensive feasts common in Milan; see Mary Newett, *Canon Pietro Casola's pilgrimage to Jerusalem*, London, 1907, 341. Casola's differentiation indicates his opinion that money spent on clothing, jewels, and furnishings was money well spent, while funds spent on perishables like food and drink were not.

72   *CRSGF*, 102 (356), 28 right.

73   Klapisch-Zuber, *Women, family, and ritual*, 213–46.

74   *Carte strozziane*, IV, 418, 8v.

75   *Carte strozziane*, IV, 418, 11v.

76   Salvagia Strozzi received a goblet full of pine-nut sweetmeats from her son-in-law when she had a daughter in 1487. The next year Salvagia's husband sent another goblet, also full of sweetmeats, to his daughter when she had her first son (*Carte strozziane*, V, 41, 164 left; see Klapisch-Zuber, *Women, family, and ritual*, 237, n. 77). Although these goblets were frequently exchanged, they are not readily identifiable in inventories. One exception was in 1522, when the estate of Gherardo Charnesechi included "1° nappo d'argento choll'arme" (*MPAP*, 185, 228v). It may be because they were exchanged so frequently, and were not permanent possessions, that so few were kept in a home long enough to be listed in an estate.

77   *Archivio Gherardi Piccolomini d'Aragona*, 139, 161r: "Io donai in nome dela Vaggia [his wife] ala Marietta sua sorella donna di Lionardo Ridolfi che avea partrito un figliolo maschio domaschino tane per una chotta chon maniche di tragittato."

78   Strozzi, *Lettere*, 80.

79   *MPAP*, 191, 130r: "le masserizie della chamera dove era la donna del parto." See Appendix C for a transcription of this document.

80   Leon Battista Alberti, *De re aedificatoria* (completed 1452, published 1485), trans. Joseph Rykwert *et al.* as *On the art of building in ten books*, Cambridge, Mass., and London, 1988, 149.

81   Cherubino da Siena [*sic*], *Regole*, 62–3.

82   Gino Capponi, *Storia della repubblica di Firenze*, I, Florence, 1876, 250.

83   The San Gallo hospital in Florence assumed that foundlings up to the age of fifteen days needed to be baptized, and that those aged twenty or more days had already received the sacrament; see Richard C. Trexler, *Dependence in context in Renaissance Florence*, Binghamton, 1994, 241. On the other hand, confirmation occurred some time later; Francesco Giovanni makes note of six of his children being confirmed on the same day in 1435, when the oldest child was ten, and the youngest was about thirteen months (*Carte strozziane*, II, 16, 3v, 4r, 4v, 5r, 8r). This rite is mentioned only rarely, however, and its details are therefore uncertain.

84   *Carte strozziane*, II, 9, 123r. Concern with the child's state at birth led to confusion over burial; if the child was not baptized, it could not be buried on sacred ground. For Giovanfrancesco Mazinghi's account of a stillborn child and the subsequent dilemma faced at burial, see *Acquisti e doni*, 301, insert 1, loose folio. On some occasions, midwives determined that a child, though seemingly dead, was in need of baptism, and they performed the rite immediately at the home; for the case of Paolo Sassetti's nephew, who died shortly after birth but was nevertheless baptized, see *Carte strozziane*, II, 4, 46v.

85   Louis Haas, "*Il mio buono compare*: Choosing godparents and the uses of baptismal kinship in Renaissance Florence," *Journal of social history*, XXIX, 1995, 341–56.

86   *CRSGF*, 111 (140), 74r.

87   *Carte strozziane*, IV, 71, 30v.

88   *Carte strozziane*, IV, 418, 18r.

89   See Girolamo Cardano, *Della mia vita*, ed. Alfonso Ingegno, Milan, 1982, 121: "secondo le usanze." For another example, see Brucker, *Giovanni and Lusanna*, 99. A similar custom occurred in both the seventeenth and nineteenth centuries; see Rinuccini, *Usanze fiorentine*, 9.

90   For more information on the role of the godmothers, see Haas, "Choosing godparents," 341–56.

91   *Carte strozziane*, II, 11, 31v, 45r, and 61r.

92   *Carte strozziane*, II, 17, 46v.

93   *Carte strozziane*, V, 22, 94 left.

94   *Carte strozziane*, V, 22, 90 right.

95   Giovanni Dominici, *Regola del governo di cura familiare* (1403), ed. Donato Salvi, Florence, 1860, 139–40.

96   Haas, "Choosing godparents," 341–2.

97   *Carte strozziane*, II, 16, 8r.

98   *MPP*, 2652, 490v.

99   *MPP*, 2657, 3v, and *MPP*, 2660, 74r.

100 For further information see Joseph H. Lynch, *Godparents and kinship in early medieval Europe*, Princeton, 1986. On the transgression of this law see Rosario Ferreri, "Rito battesimale e comparatico nelle novelle senesi della VII giornata," *Studi sul Boccaccio*, XVI, 1987, 307–14.

101 *CRSGF*, 111 (140), 79r.

102 *CRSGF*, 111 (140), 79r.

103 *CRSGF*, 102 (356), 28 left.

104 ASP, *Archivio Datini*, 1092, loose folio (20 January 1391).

105 ASP, *Archivio Datini*, 1092, loose folio (31 July 1390).

106 *Acquisti e doni*, 301, insert 1, loose folio.

107 *Carte strozziane*, IV, 418, 9v.

108 Alessandro Perosa, ed., *Giovanni Rucellai e il suo zibaldone I: Il zibaldone quaresimale*, London, 1960, 35.

109 Vasari, *Vite*, ed. Milanesi, VII:20–21.

110 Scott Schaefer, "*Io Guido Reni Bologna*, man and artist," in *Guido Reni 1575–1642*, ed. Susan L. Caroselli, Los Angeles, 1988, 14.

111 For example, *Carte strozziane*, V, 41, 161 left.

112 *Carte strozziane*, II, 6, 19r: "per amore di Dio."

113 *Carte strozziane*, II, 9, 11r. This is contrary to the analysis of Louis Haas, who contends that a godparent relationship contracted "for the love of God" did not entail a gift-giving obligation; see Haas, "Choosing godparents," 344.

114 *CRSGF*, III (140), 79v.

115 *CRSGF*, III (140), 75r. Both oils were mentioned by Scipione Mercurio as aids for pregnant women; see Maria Luisa Altieri Biagi *et al.*, ed., *Medicina per le donne nel cinquecento: Testi di Giovanni Marinello e di Girolamo Mercurio*, Turin, 1992, 106.

116 *CRSGF*, III (140), 79v: "per la decta per entrare in Sancto."

117 In the fourteenth-century village of Montaillou in France, purification ceremonies seem to have taken place in a local shrine to the Virgin; see Emmanuel Le Roy Ladurie, *Montaillou: Cathars and Catholics in a French village* (1975), trans. Barbara Bray, London, 1978, 207, n. 1.

118 Saint Antoninus, *Confessionale volgare intitolato spechio di coscienze*, Florence, 1490, unpaginated.

119 Cherubino da Siena [*sic*], *Regole*, 62–3.

120 For information on foundlings, see Klapisch-Zuber, *Women, family, and ritual*, 103–5, and Trexler, "Foundlings of Florence," 259–84. I am grateful to Steven Bule for sharing his knowledge about foundlings at the Ospedale di San Luca in Lucca with me; the situation in Lucca seems similar to that in Florence.

121 *CRSGF*, III (140), 79v. In a society that depended so heavily on wetnursing, this may have been a common expense; see also *CRSGF*, 102 (489), 69 left. There was a certain consciousness of abnormalities of the breast. In fact, if abnormalities occurred, votive offerings in silver could be made; an inventory of 1441 listing the silver offerings at Santissima Annunziata included "due poppe di peso d'once due" (*CRSGF*, 119 (48), 36v).

122 *CRSGF*, III (140), 79v.

123 *CRSGF*, III (140), 74r.

124 For equivalences, see Goldthwaite, *Renaissance Florence*, 348.

125 For one father's particularly lengthy account of the items he sent with his first son when he went to the wetnurse, see Appendix D.

126 *CRSGF*, III (140), 127r: "per la Chaterina credo sia grossa."

127 *CRSGF*, III (140), 163r: "Ricordo qui da pie di quello spenderò nel secondo parto della Chaterina mia donna o per cagione di quello, dì per dì come m'accadrà."

128 *CRSGF*, III (140), 163r.

129 *CRSGF*, III (140), 163r.

130 *CRSGF*, III (140), 165r: "Ricordo come a dì 10 di gennaio, a hore tre di notte, pocho prima, dalla Chaterina mia donna mi naque una bello fanciullo maschio, che per la Dio gratia l'uno e l'altro stanno bene. Allevollo Monna Mathea sta a Sancto Lorenzo. Ebbe la doglia in tutto hore 7, cioè da hore 20 in sino a hore 3. Decti alla decta Monna Mathea per sua faticha grossoni otto lire ... Ricordo come a dì 11 a hore XXI et ½ feci batezare mio figliuolo e posili nome Luigi e Taddeo per el fanciullo dalla Chaterina e mio, che pregho Iddio che li dia gratia viva e muora sempre nel Suo Sancto Amen."

131 *CRSGF*, III (140), 163r.

132 *CRSGF*, III (140), 165r.

133 *CRSGF*, III (140), 163r.

134 *CRSGF*, III (140), 163r.

135 Casola believed that the visit he made to a Venetian confinement room had been arranged specifically to showcase his host's magnificence; see Newett, *Casola's pilgrimage*, 339. This type of display also occurred in the homes of French merchants; see Christine de Pisan, *A Medieval woman's mirror of honor: The treasury of the city of the ladies* (1405), trans. Charity Cannon Willard, New York, 1989, 194–5 (and 236 for further bibliography).

136 Although the first comprehensive set of laws date to 1281, there is no record of them. For the redaction of 1356, see Andrea Lancia, "Ordinamenti contro alle soperchie ornamenti delle donne e soperchie spese de' mogliazzi e de' morti," *Etruria*, I, 1851, 370–82 and 429–42. In 1388 the laws were restated with slight revisions; see Dominici, *Regola*, 221–37. They were then codified twice more: in 1415 (*Statuta popoli et communis Florentiae: Publica auctoritate, collecta, castigata, et praeposita anno salutis MCCCCXV*, Friburgi [*sic*], 1778, II:381–2); and in 1562 (Cantini, *Legislazione*, IV:402–10). For a revisionist analysis of the implications of sumptuary legislation, see Lynn Laufenberg, *The legal status of women in trecento Florence*, unpublished doctoral dissertation, Cornell University, 1999.

137 *Carte strozziane*, II, 4, 70r: "per uno ordine nuovamente fatto per lo Chomune che non vadino huomini."

138 The most recent general information is in Alan Hunt, *Governance of the consuming passions: A history of sumptuary law*, New York, 1996. On sumptuary laws as social controls, see Diane Owen Hughes, "Sumptuary law and social relations in Renaissance Italy," in *Disputes and settlements: Law and human relations in the West*, ed. John Bossy, Cambridge, 1983, esp. 74. Investigations of these laws have indicated some of the ways men controlled women through the clothing and accessories that they permitted their wives, sisters, and daughters at the key moments of their lives. Female appearance ranked with procreation as a great concern of the writers, moralists, and politicians of the period. In 1416 the Venetian Francesco Barbaro agreed with widely held beliefs when he wrote in his *De re uxoria* that excessive dress and accessories "lead not only to the ruin of a marriage but often to the squandering of a patrimony as well ... Wives ought to care more to avoid censure than to win applause in their splendid style of dress." (Benjamin G. Kohl and Ronald G. Witt with Elizabeth B. Welles, *The earthly republic: Italian humanists on government and society*, Philadelphia, 1978, 206). The idea of expensive feminine frivolities contributing to a husband's financial ruin also appears in sumptuary legislation; see Stanley Chojnacki, "The power of love: Wives and husbands in late medieval Venice," in *Women and power in the Middle Ages*, ed. Mary Erler and Maryanne Kowaleski, Athens, Georgia, 1988, 131.

139 Translation from Gene Brucker, ed., *The society of Renaissance Florence: A documentary study*, New York, 1971, 181.

140 Translation from Ronald E. Rainey, *Sumptuary legislation in Renaissance Florence*, unpublished doctoral dissertation, Columbia University, 1985, 479.

141 For further information, see Catherine Kovesi Killerby, "Practical problems in the enforcement of Italian sumptuary law, 1200–1500," in *Crime, society and the law in Renaissance Italy*, ed. Trevor Dean and Kate J.P. Lowe, Cambridge, 1994, esp. 118–19. Killerby's analysis of sumptuary legislation, which emphasizes the fact that such laws were not the appropriate tool for controlling luxury consumption and that there was, in the end, little desire to condemn this consumption, is particularly relevant here.

142 For a much-cited example of the ingenious ways women avoided sumptuary regulations, see Franco Sacchetti, *Il trecentonovelle*, ed. Antonio Lanza, Milan, 1993, 275–7.

143 Romolo Caggese, ed., *Statuti della Repubblica fiorentina*, I, Florence, 1921, 222–31.

144 Transcribed in Rainey, *Sumptuary legislation*, 256.

145 Transcribed in Dominici, *Regola*, 234–5.

146 Information on the law of 1402 is in Rainey, *Sumptuary legislation*, 65. The law of 1415 is transcribed in *Statuta*, 381–2.

147 *Consigli della Repubblica, provvisioni registri*, 164, 38r.

148 Cantini, *Legislazione*, I:320.

149 Cantini, *Legislazione*, IV:405.

150 Girolamo Tommasi, "Sommario della storia di Lucca dall'anno MIV all'anno MDCC," *Archivio storico italiano*, X, 1847, 103–4.

151 Tommasi, "Lucca," 126.

152 For Venice, see Pompeo Molmenti, *La storia di Venezia nella vita privata dalle origini alla caduta della Repubblica*, Bergamo, 1906, I:274; Diane Owen Hughes, "Representing the family: Portraits and purposes in early modern Italy," in *Art and history: Images and their meaning*, ed. Theodore K. Rabb and Robert I. Rotberg, Cambridge, 1986, 18; and Giulio Bistort, "Il magistrato alle pompe nella Repubblica di Venezia," *Miscellanea di storia veneta*, V, 1912, 107, 201–05, and 394–400.

153 Antonio Pilot, "Di alcune leggi suntuarie della Repubblica Veneta," *L'ateneo veneto*, XXVI, 1903, 453.

154 Alessandro Luzio, "La prammatica del Cardinale Ercole Gonzaga contro il lusso (1551)," in *Scritti varii di erudizione e di critica in onore di Rodolfo Renier*, Turin, 1912, 73.

155 Cantini, *Legislazione*, V:71.

156 Giovanni Ghinassi, "Sopra tre statuti suntuari inediti del secolo XVI per la città di Faenza," *Atti e memorie della regia deputazione di storia patria per le provincie di Romagna*, II, 1866, 174. In 1703 further forbidden clothing was described; see Gaetano Ballardini, "Leggi suntuarie faentine," *La Romagna*, III, 1906, 235. For further bibliography on Renaissance sumptuary laws, see Rosita Levi Pisetzky, *Storia del costume in Italia*, Milan, 1966, II:171–4, 468–73; III:280–84.

157 An account of this event is given in Bastiano Arditi, *Diario di Firenze e di altre parti della Cristianità (1574–9)*, ed. Roberto Cantagalli, Florence, 1970, 167–9. Fabulous baptisms became quite common among princely courts for centuries thereafter. See, for example, *Lettere ad un amico nella quale si da ragguaglio della funzione seguita in Napoli il giorno 6 di setembre del 1772: Per solennizzare il battesimo della reale infanta Maria Teresa Carolina primogenita del re Ferdinando IV e regino Maria Carolina arciduchessa d'Austria, e delle feste date per quest'oggetto*, Naples, 1772.

Chapter 3

1 Diane Cole Ahl, "Renaissance birth salvers and the Richmond *Judgement of Solomon*," *Studies in iconography*, VII, 1981, 158. My own examination of approximately 1380–1620 seems to indicate an even higher percentage; however, the repetition of many of the inventories throughout several volumes of the Pupilli and across many years makes it difficult to provide a definitive number.

2 This is contrary to statements made by Tancred Borenius, "Unpublished cassone panels II," *Burlington magazine*, XL, 1922, 131, Lydecker, *Domestic setting*, 254–5, and Peter Thornton, *The Italian Renaissance interior 1400–1600*, New York, 1991, 252.

3 In the past there was a tendency to categorize any small panel as a birth tray. Both damage and demand prompted unscrupulous late nineteenth- and early twentieth-century sellers to cut down larger secular panels, from wedding chests or wainscoting, to make a greater number of smaller, saleable works of art.

4 Vasari, *Vite*, ed. Milanesi, VII:20–21: "per dipignerlo in un di que tondi nei quali si porta da mangiare alle donne di parto."

5 See for example *MPAP*, 24, 207r: "unum deschum ad usum mulierum in partu."

6 *MPP*, 2664, 33r: "un tavolino da mangiare per donne di parto."

7 *MPAP*, 181, 358v.

8 *MPAP*, 160, 422r.

9 *MPAP*, 157, 175v and *MPAP*, 49, 223v. For a comment on covers for small panels, see Jill Dunkerton *et al.*, *Giotto to Dürer: Early Renaissance painting in the National Gallery*, New Haven and London, 1991, 84.

10 For information on the *camera*, see Claudio Paolini, "La camera da letto tra quattro e cinquecento: Arredi e vita privata," in *Itinerari nella casa fiorentina del Rinascimento*, ed. Elisabetta Nardinocchi, Florence, 1994, 22–45.

11 Lydecker, *Domestic setting*, 22.

12 I am grateful to Carol Sawyer and Bruce Suffield at the Virginia Museum of Fine Arts for their observations on this tray.

13 The earliest studies treated these objects as charming novelties; see U. Rossi, "I deschi da parto," *Archivio storico dell'arte*, III, 1890, 78–9, and Eugène Müntz, "Les plateaux d'accouchées et la peinture sur meubles du XIVᵉ au XVIᵉ siècle," *Fondation Eugene Piot: Monuments et memoires*, I, 1894, 203–32.

14 Various sales conducted by the American Art Association in New York attest to the popularity of Italian Renaissance furnishings on the American market in the early twentieth century; see Roberta Ferrazza, *Palazzo Davanzati e le collezioni di Elia Volpi*, Florence, 1994, 145–222. The state of the field at this period, tinged with romantic overtones, is exemplified by the description in Borenius, "Cassone panels," 131.

15 There are two monographic treatments of childbirth trays as an independent genre: Mary Eileen Fitzgerald, *Deschi da parto: Florentine birth trays of the quattrocento*, unpublished doctoral dissertation, Syracuse University, 1986; and Cecilia De Carli, *I deschi da parto e la pittura del primo rinascimento toscano*, Turin, 1997. Both, however, are largely catalogues of extant works with introductory essays. For a brief document-based treatment, see Ahl, "Birth salvers," 157–74.

16 For *tondi*, see Roberta Olson, "Lost and partially found: The tondo, a significant Florentine art form in documents of the Renaissance," *Artibus et historiae*, XIV, 1993, 31–65.

17 *MPAP*, 15, 101r: "uno descho da parto vecchio."

18 *MPAP*, 44, 257v: "I descho da parto tristo."

19 *MPAP*, 2662, 316r: "I° tondo da donne di parto dipinto cattivo."

20 Filippo Baldinucci, *Notizie de' professori del disegna da Cimabue in qua*, Florence, 1728, III:97.

21 See Guido Biagio, *Due corredi nuziali fiorentini 1320–1493 da un libro di ricordanze dei Minerbetti*, Florence, 1899, 19, and, for a similar case, *Carte strozziane*, II, 17 bis, 79r.

22 *MPAP*, 173, 201v: "Iᵃ tavoleta da dona di parto dipintta vechia" and "Iᵃ tavoleta da dona di parto dipinta nuova."

23 For such an assumption, see Martin Wackernagel, *The world of the Florentine Renaissance artist* (1938), trans. Allison Luchs, Princeton, 1981, 168.

24 *MPP*, 2657, 645r.

25 I have found relatively few references to trays with gameboards in inventories; see, for two examples, *MPAP*, 50, 97v, and Neri di Bicci, *Le ricordanze (1453–75)*, ed. Bruno Santi, Pisa, 1976, 175. However, since these boards were on the back, they would not be visible if the tray was hanging and therefore they could not be mentioned in an inventory. Gameboards were popular as autonomous objects throughout this period; in 1465 Lorenzo Morelli commissioned the woodworker Jachopo to make him one (*Archivio Gherardi Piccolomini d'Aragona*, 137, 11 left). A certain degree of upper-class assimilation is implied by a game such as chess, which was often considered a noble pursuit connected to seduction. For further information, see Patricia Simons, "(Check) mating the

grandmasters: The gendered, sexualized politics of chess in Renaissance Italy," *Oxford art journal*, XVI, 1993, 59–74.

26 Iris Origo, *The merchant of Prato: Daily life in a medieval Italian village*, London, 1992, 233–4. In my examination of the collection of various Datini inventories from around 1390–1405 which Origo consulted, I found reference to only one birth tray (Archivio di Stato, Prato, *Archivio Datini*, 236), while Origo states that there were two. There is evidence that the Datini valued this tray; an undated notation made alongside one reference stated that they brought the tray with them to Florence while they lived there temporarily.

27 For example, the estate of Giovanni di Bartolomeo Morelli included "ii forzeretti chol'arma de' Moregli, dichono essere della madre della donna di Giovanni" (*MPAP*, 168, 42v). Apparently Giovanni's wife had inherited two of her mother's chests; either her mother had married a Morelli herself (a not uncommon occurrence among families), or the heraldry was added after her own marriage.

28 *MPAP*, 1, 47v. Only two known trays can be dated to this earliest period: see Fabrizio Mancinelli, "Arte medioevale e moderna," *Bollettino dei Musei e Gallerie Pontifichie*, 1, 1977, 171–7, and Daniela Pagliali and Alessandra Uguccioni, "Un desco da parto fiorentino della fine del trecento: Temi di iconografia profana," *Notizie da Palazzo Albani*, XV, 1986, 9–18.

29 See Ellen Callmann, *A catalogue of early Italian secular art in the Yale University Art Gallery*, forthcoming. I am very grateful for Dr. Callmann's generosity in sharing her manuscript with me before publication.

30 The smallest tray is the unframed *Amorous Hunt* at the Yale University Art Gallery (48.7 cm), while the largest is the elaborately framed Medici-Tornabuoni tray at the Metropolitan Museum of Art (91.4 cm). Dimensions are problematic, however, since many trays no longer have their original moldings.

31 For example, in 1423 Andrea Mazuoli's estate included both "1° deschetto da parto" and "1° descho da parto," implying that the first tray was smaller than the second (*MPAP*, 39, 223r).

32 My thanks to conservator Norman Muller for his assistance with the technical examination of this tray, which is in The Art Museum, Princeton University, NJ.

33 In 1388 Filippo Quartucci's estate had "1 tavola tonda da parto" (*MPAP*, 4, 138r). On the relation between *tondi* and birth trays, see the discussion in Olson, "Tondo," 34.

34 For this tray, see Luciano Berti and Antonio Paolucci, *L'età di Masaccio: Il primo quattrocento a Firenze*, Milan, 1990, 102–3.

35 *MPAP*, 28, 255v. Visual evidence confirms this possibility. A drawing of *The Birth of the Virgin* by Bartolomeo Neroni, for example, includes a square tray carried by an attendant (illustrated in P. Thornton, *Interior*, 132).

36 For example, in 1404 the estate of Lorenzo Schiattini included "uno descho da parto messo ad'oro fine" (*MPAP*, 15, 184v).

37 Marriage chests were also constructed in their entirety before they were painted; see Ellen Callmann, *Apollonio di Giovanni*, Oxford, 1974, 27. This practice was, of course, adopted from monumental altarpiece production techniques; see David Bomford *et al.*, *Art in the making: Italian painting before 1400*, London, 1989.

38 Nevertheless, the functional aspect of domestic art naturally resulted in a certain degree of abrasion to the painted surfaces. Marriage chests were low on the ground and used for seating; scuff marks resulted as feet kicked back against the painted panels. Childbirth trays carried various foods and utensils that must have marred their surfaces as well.

39 The only known exception to these categories is a tray painted with an allegory of music, discussed in Callmann, *Apollonio,*

1974, 52. For an example of a mythological tray, see Eugene B. Cantelupe, "The anonymous *Triumph of Venus* in the Louvre: An early Italian example of mythological disguise," *Art bulletin*, XLIV, 1962, 238–42. On contemporary literary themes, see Paul F. Watson, *The garden of love in Tuscan art of the early Renaissance*, Philadelphia, 1979. A tray with a confinement scene is discussed in a rather romantic fashion in L. Earle Rowe, "An Italian birth salver," *Bulletin of the Rhode Island School of Design*, X, 1922, 24–6. Religious narratives are examined by Alessandra Uguccioni, *Salomone e la Regina di Saba: La pittura di cassone a Ferrara presenza nei musei americani*, Ferrara, 1988. Birth trays did not depict strictly devotional images, as Baldinucci asserted they did (*Notizie*, 97).

40 Another tray is painted with an imitation marble revetment, a decorative effect with luxurious connotations; see Fiorella Sricchia Santoro, *Da Sodoma a Marco Pino: Addenda*, Siena, 1991, 25–6. Although this design (and that of the tray illustrated in figure 48) was neither figurative nor heraldic, it was painstakingly executed and must have been meant to be seen at certain times.

41 Vasari implied as much in regard to one particularly complex tray design by Francesco Salviati; see above, pp. 70–71, and Vasari, *Vite*, ed. Milanesi, VII:21.

42 See for example the iconography of Solomon and Sheba, a popular subject for both birth trays and marriage chests, discussed in Carolyn C. Wilson, *Italian paintings XIV–XVI centuries in the Museum of Fine Arts, Houston*, Houston, 1996, 214–29, and Uguccioni, *Salomone*.

43 Nevertheless, Ellen Callmann has linked the iconography of the front and the back of a tray by Apollonio di Giovanni, to demonstrate that marriage was primarily to continue the lineage (*Beyond nobility: Art for the private citizen in the early Renaissance*, Allentown, Penn., 1980, 5–6).

44 See Cristelle L. Baskins, "Donatello's bronze *David*: Grillanda, Goliath, Groom?," *Studies in iconography*, XV, 1993, 113–34.

45 Schubring, *Cassoni*, 1915, 206.

46 Nevertheless, this has been stated by Osvald Sirén, "An Italian salver of the fifteenth century," *Burlington magazine*, XXX, 1917, 183–4, 189; Helen Comstock, "Italian birth and marriage salvers," *International studio*, LXXXV, 1926, 50; Bruce Cole, *Italian art 1250–1550: The relation of Renaissance art to life and society*, New York, 1987, 49–52; and Cristina Acidini Luchinati, ed., *Renaissance Florence: The age of Lorenzo de' Medici 1449–1492*, London, 1993, 91.

47 Frank Jewett Mather, "Three Florentine furniture panels: The Medici desco, the Stibbert Trajan, and the horse race of the Holden collection," *Art in America*, III, 1920, 148.

48 *Carte strozziane*, IV, 71, 22v.

49 For the tray attributed to Masaccio, see L. Berti, *Masaccio*, 197–201. Giovanni di Ser Giovanni's domestic oeuvre is discussed in Ahl, "Birth salvers," 160–61. Neri di Bicci listed two trays (*Ricordanze*, ed. Santi, 167–8 and 175). Pontormo executed the two low bowls catalogued in Alberto Bruschi, *Un Pontormo ritrovato: Il desco da parto Ughi-Antinori, già della collezione Elia Volpi*, Florence, 1992.

50 Vasari, *Vite*, ed. Milanesi, II:149. He also described how Ghirlandaio instructed his apprentices to paint linen baskets for women; see Vasari, *Vite*, ed. Milanesi, III:269–70.

51 For examples, see Bruce Cole, "The interior decoration of the Palazzo Datini in Prato," *Mitteilungen des kunsthistorischen Institutes in Florenz*, XIII, 1967, 61, and Sacchetti, *Trecentonovelle*, 166–72. The anonymous fifteenth-century carnival song of the Florentine sculptors also implied this practice; see Charles Singleton, ed., *Canti carnascialeschi*, Bari, 1936, 10.

52 Gino Corti, "Sul commercio dei quadri a Firenze verso la fine del secolo XIV," *Commentari*, XXII, 1971, 89.

53 Neri di Bicci, *Ricordanze*, ed. Santi, 167–8.

54 See Robert W. Scheller, *Exemplum: Model book drawings and the practice of artistic transmission in the Middle Ages (circa 900–circa 1470)*, trans. Michael Hoyle, Amsterdam, 1995, and Francis Ames-Lewis, "Modelbook drawings and the Florentine quattrocento artist," *Art history*, X, 1987, 1–11. A modelbook of Tuscan or northern Italian origin and dating from about 1370–80, in the Pierpont Morgan Library, New York, is especially relevant in this context; see Bernard Degenhardt and Annegrit Schmitt, *Corpus der italienischen Zeichnungen 1300–1450*, Berlin, 1968, I:166–72 and III:plates 132–5e. The purpose of its whimsical and often erotic drawings is not known, but many fit well with the amatory iconography of secular art from both northern Italy and France. A group of mid- to late fifteenth-century engravings called Otto prints, which often have blank *stemmi* worked into the design, have been associated with the decoration of *forzerini*, the small painted boxes given to betrothed women; see Chad Coerver, "Idealization and misogyny in Renaissance courtship imagery," forthcoming.

55 See especially Callmann, *Apollonio*, 30–35.

56 Ellen Callmann, "Apollonio di Giovanni and painting for the early Renaissance room," *Antichità viva*, XXVII, 1988, 12.

57 See also the discussion in Callmann, *Apollonio*, 36–7 and 58–9.

58 Eisenberg, *Lorenzo Monaco*, 166.

59 Vasari, *Vite*, ed. Milanesi, VII:20–21: "Avendo Francesco fatto amicizia con Piero di Marcone orefice fiorentino, e divenutogli compare, fece alla comare, dopo il parto di moglie di esso Piero, un presente d'un bellissimo disegno, per dipignerlo in un di que tondi nei quali si porta da mangiare alle donne di parto: nel quale disegno era in un partimento riquadrato, ed accomodato sotto e sopra con bellissime figure, la vita dell'uomo, cioè tutte l'età della vita umana, che posavano ciascuna sopra diversi festoni appropriati a quella età secondo il tempo; nel quale bizzarro spartimento erano accomodati in due ovati bislunghi la figura del Sole e della Luna, e nel mezzo Isais [sic], città d'Egitto, che dinanzi al tempio della Dea Pallade dimandava sapienza; quasi volendo mostrare che ai nati figliuoli si doverebbe innanzi ad ogni altra cosa pregare sapienza e bontà. Questo disegno tenne poi sempre Piero così caro come fusse stato, anzi come era, una bellissima gioia."

60 However, a drawing attributed to Salviati may be related to this; see Hermann Voss, "Über einige Gemälde und Zeichnungen von Meistern aus dem Kreise Michelangelos," *Jahrbuch der königlich preußischen Kunstsammlungen*, XXXIV, 1913, 297, figure 81. Other drawings, considered copies after Salviati, are the approximate shape of childbirth trays, but these are more likely drawings of goldsmiths' work; see Peter Ward-Jackson, *The Victoria & Albert Museum catalogues: Italian drawings, 14th–16th centuries*, London, 1979, I:140–42, and A.E. Popham and Johannes Wilde, *The Italian drawings of the XV and XVI centuries in the collection of His Majesty the King at Windsor Castle*, London, 1949, 327.

61 For example, in 1448 Antonio Vecchietti's estate included "1° bacino d'ottone choll'arme della donna" (*MPAP*, 67, 114v).

62 For a selective list of these reliefs, see Jean C. Harris, ed., *The Mount Holyoke College Art Museum: Handbook of the collection*, South Hadley, Mass., 1984, 22.

63 *Carte strozziane*, IV, 71, 22v.

64 C.M. Kauffmann, *Victoria and Albert Museum: Catalogue of foreign paintings*, London, 1973, I:13–14.

65 *MPAP*, 28, 283v.

66 *MPAP*, 61, 153r.

67 The ledger is transcribed in Callmann, *Apollonio*, 76–81. It exists today as an incomplete seventeenth-century copy of a lost document; conclusive evidence for this is provided in Callmann, "Renaissance room."

68 Callmann, *Apollonio*, 79. This tray cannot be identified with any known example.

69 For information on Benci, see de Roover, *Medici bank*, 57–8, and Francis Ames-Lewis, "Art in the service of the family: The taste and patronage of Piero di Cosimo de' Medici," in *Piero de' Medici 'il Gottoso' (1416–1469)*, ed. Andreas Beyer and Bruce Boucher, Berlin, 1993, 209. Benci may have been buying the tray for a pregnant daughter, since he had purchased a pair of marriage chests to celebrate the wedding of a daughter a year earlier; see Callmann, *Apollonio*, 79.

70 A substantial bibliography for this important tray is provided in Sotheby's (New York), *Important Old Master paintings: The property of the New-York Historical Society*, January 12, 1995, lot 69.

71 The identity of this artist has been merged with the Master of the Adimari Cassone, also known as the Master of Fucecchio; see Luciano Bellosi, Dilvio Lotti, and Anna Matteoli, *Mostra d'arte sacra della diocesi di San Miniato*, San Miniato, 1969, 56–7. His oeuvre was largely compiled by Roberto Longhi, "Fatti di Masolino e di Masaccio," *Critica d'arte*, V, 1940, 187, and Georg Pudelko, "Studien über Domenico Veneziano," *Mitteilungen des kunsthistorischen Institutes in Florenz*, IV, 1934, 163–4. For documentary references on Scheggia, see Ugo Procacci, "Le portate al catasto di Giovanni di Ser Giovanni detto lo Scheggia," *Rivista d'arte*, XXXVII, 1984, 235–57, and Margaret Haines, "Nota sulla discendenza di Giovanni di Ser Giovanni," *Rivista d'arte*, XXXVII, 1984, 257–68.

72 Aby Warburg, "Della impresa amorose nelle più antiche incisione fiorentine," *Rivista d'arte*, III, 1905, 5.

73 Spallanzani and Bertelà, *Inventario*, 27. The fact that the tray was found in Lorenzo's quarters signified his intimate connection to it, and all but excluded the possibility that the tray was made for the birth of his younger brother Giuliano in 1453.

74 For example, see *MPAP*, 168, 430v: "1° descho da parto."

75 The earliest known references to iconography are in this inventory, which cited, along with this tray, a now lost example painted with a battle scene by Masaccio, and two others specified only as painted and, in one case, round; see Spallanzani and Bertelà, *Inventario*, 80, 104, and 152.

76 Overall, most inventories ignored the particular subject matter of any work of art other than devotional images of the Madonna, and even these were described in only a cursory fashion. For example, although most marriage chests were historiated until at least around 1470, few Pupilli inventories from any date mention their subject matter. One of the two citations I encountered that explicitly referred to iconography was the reference of 1450 to two chests painted with the story of Lucrezia (see p. 7). A second citation, dated to 1502 (when painted chests were out of favor), was in the estate of Lorenzo Ghuiducci, who had "2 chasoni a sepoltura dipinti colla storia di Parisse" (*MPAP*, 184, 10r).

77 *MPP*, 2648, 525r. While many surviving trays have one or more naked boys on them, a *verso* attributed to Girolamo di Benvenuto was actually painted with a Cupid carrying a bow and arrow; see Fern Rusk Shapely, *Paintings from the Samuel H. Kress collection: Italian schools XIII–XV centuries*, London, 1966, 162.

78 *MPP*, 2647, 594v. This seems to have been an erroneous identification, however; see pp. 78–9.

79 *MPP*, 2655, 141v.

80 Cited in Christiane Klapisch-Zuber, "Les femmes dans les rituels de l'alliance et de la naissance à Florence," in *Riti e rituali nelle società medievali*, ed. Jacques Chiffoleau *et al.*, Spoleto, 1994, 17.

81 *MPAP*, 180, 161v.

82 Bec, *Livres*, 252. In 1497 Lorenzo Tornabuoni's estate included "1° libro de' Trionfi del Petrarcha" (*MPAP*, 181, 141v). Lorenzo was the son of Piero de' Medici's brother-in-law, Giovanni Tornabuoni.

83 For triumph iconography in Renaissance art, see Giovanni Carandente, *I trionfi nel primo Rinascimento*, Turin, 1963; Mario Salmi, "*I trionfi* e il *De viris illustribus* nell'arte del primo Rinascimento," *Atti dei Convegni lincei*, X, 1976, 23–47; Lutz S. Malke, "Contributo alle figurazioni dei Trionfi e del Canzoniere del Petrarca," *Commentari*, XXVIII, 1977, 236–61; and Anne Jacobson-Schutte, "Trionfi delle donne: Tematiche di rovesciamento dei ruoli nella Firenze rinascimentale," *Quaderni storici*, XLIV, 1980, 474–96. Ellen Callmann has compiled a list of Boccaccian themes in Italian painting, which includes triumph images within the larger group ("Subjects from Boccaccio in Italian painting, 1375–1525," *Studi sul Boccaccio*, XXIII, 1995, 19–78, esp. 41–6).

84 The diamond ring with feathers was also used by Cosimo de' Medici, Piero's father, but Piero added several details to the device to make it his own; this tray seems to be the earliest example of the complete device. See Francis Ames-Lewis, "Early Medicean devices," *Journal of the Warburg and Courtauld Institutes*, XLII, 1979, 122–43, and, most recently, Franco Cardini, "Le insegne Laurenziane," in *Le tems revient. 'l tempo si rinuova: Feste e spettacoli nella Firenze di Lorenzo Il Magnifico*, ed. Paola Ventrone, Florence, 1992, 55–74.

85 Piero's art patronage was first analyzed in Ernst H. Gombrich, "The early Medici as patrons of art," in *Italian Renaissance studies*, ed. Ernst F. Jacob, London, 1960, 279–311.

86 Ames-Lewis, *Piero de' Medici*, 209.

87 See, in particular, Ames-Lewis, *Piero de' Medici*, and Lorenzo Gnocchi, "Le preferenze artistiche di Piero di Cosimo de' Medici," *Artibus et historiae*, XVIII, 1988, 41–78.

88 For another case, see Ames-Lewis, *Piero de' Medici*, esp. 209–17.

89 See Gaetano Milanesi, "Lettere d'artisti italiani dei secoli XIV e XV," *Il Buonarroti*, IV, 1869, 78–9. Although Matteo does not specify exactly what medium he used, evidence points to the fact that he was illuminating a manuscript; see Francis Ames-Lewis, "Matteo de' Pasti and the use of powdered gold," *Mitteilungen des kunsthistorischen Institutes in Florenz*, XXVIII, 1984, 351–62.

90 For these panels, see Philip Hendy, *European and American paintings in the Isabella Stewart Gardner Museum*, Boston, 1974, 176–8.

91 Archivio di Stato, Siena, *Ospedale di Santa Maria della Scala*, 68, unnumbered folio. My thanks to Gino Corti for this citation.

92 Spallanzani and Bertelà, *Inventario*, 26–7.

93 There are surprisingly few contemporary references to this auction; see Luca Landucci, *Florentine diary from 1450 to 1516*, trans. Alice de Rosen Jervis, London, 1927, 91 and 93.

94 *MAP*, CXXI, 357r: "1 tondo da parto dipintovi su il Trionfo della Fama (fiorini 3.6.8)."

95 *MPP*, 2663, 336r: "1° tondo da donna di parte dipinto."

96 *MPP*, 2647, 594v: "uno tondo da donna di parto dipintovi una caccia."

97 Unfortunately, there are no known references to its whereabouts between 1579 and 1801. Presumably it remained in Florence, perhaps in the possession of further descendants of Ser Bartolomeo di Bambello. For a more detailed analysis of this tray, see Jacqueline Marie Musacchio, "The Medici-Tornabuoni *desco da parto*," *Metropolitan Museum of Art journal*, XXXIII, 1998, 137–51.

98 On intarsia generally, see Helmut Flade, *Intarsia: Europäische Einlegekunst aus sechs Jahrhunderten*, Munich, 1986. It was common enough to warrant a definition in John Florio, *Queen Ann's new world of words, or dictionarie of the Italian and English tongues, collected, and newly much augmented by John Florio, Reader of the Italian unto the Soveraigne Maiestie of Anna, Crowned Queene of England, Scotland, France and Ireland, &c. And one of the Gentlemen of hir Royall Privie Chamber. Whereunto are added certaine necessarie rules and short observations for the Italian tongue*, London, 1611, 553.

99 Antoine Wilmering, "Domenico di Niccolò, Mattia di Nanni and the development of Sienese intarsia techniques," *Burlington magazine*, CXXXIX, 1997, esp. 387.

100 Margaret Haines, *The Sacrestia delle Messe of the Florentine Cathedral*, Florence, 1983. This analysis clearly demonstrates the popularity of intarsia production in the fifteenth century.

101 Benedetto Dei, *La cronica dall'anno 1400 all'anno 1500*, ed. Roberto Barducci, Florence, 1985, 82.

102 For *spalliere* in general, see Anne B. Barriault, *Spalliera paintings of Renaissance Tuscany: Fables of poets for patrician homes*, University Park, Penn., 1994.

103 Smaller white lead *pastiglia* boxes, which survive in surprisingly large numbers, also took up similar narratives; see Patrick de Winter, "A little known creation of Renaissance decorative arts: The white lead pastiglia box," *Saggi e memorie di storia dell'arte*, XIV, 1984, 9–42.

104 Furthermore, there is virtually no discussion of this type of birth tray in the literature; for a brief mention, see P. Thornton, *Interior*, 252.

105 *MPAP*, 78, 69v.

106 *MPAP*, 181, 32r: "un tondo da parto chon tarsie al'anticha."

107 The only known exception to these dating parameters is the particularly early mention of a walnut birth tray in 1494; see *Carte strozziane*, V, 1469, 42 left.

108 For example, in 1529 Antonio Lenzi's estate had "1° deschuccio da donna di parto dal cipresso" (*MPP*, 2645, 252r).

109 *MPP*, 2653, 66v.

110 *MPAP*, 4, 46v: "descho da chucina"; *MPAP*, 177, 105v: "4 deschetti tristi da sedere a tavola"; *MPAP*, 31, 183r: "uno descho da scrivere senza piedi"; *MPAP*, 36, 129r: "1 descho da tagliari carne."

111 For example, in 1512 the estate of Chimenti Selaio included "1° tondo di Nostra Donna di terra dipinto col'arme" (*MPAP*, 182, 337r). On the definition of *tondo*, see Moritz Hauptmann, *Der Tondo: Ursprung, Bedeutung und Geschichte des italienischen Rundbildes in Relief und Malerei*, Frankfurt am Main, 1936, and Olson, "Tondo," 32–3.

112 The estate of Salvestro Neretti included "1ª tavola di Nostra Donna" in 1429 (*MPAP*, 165, 83r).

113 *MPAP*, 28, 279r.

114 Paul Hetherington, *Pietro Cavallini: A study in the art of late medieval Rome*, London, 1979, 16.

115 For Byzantine images, see in particular Jacqueline Lafontaine-Dosogne, *Iconographie de l'enfance de la Vierge dans l'Empire Byzantin et en occident*, Brussels, 1964.

116 *MPP*, 2655, 547v: "un tavolino di noce da parto con sua piedi."

117 *MPP*, 2651, 319r.

118 *MPP*, 2652, 7v and 8r.

119 *MPP*, 2652, 5r.

120 Rossi, "Deschi da parto," 79.

121 *MPP*, 2650, 174v.

122 *MPAP*, 179, 294v.

123 *MPAP*, 187, 390v.

124 See, for example, *MPP*, 2668, 654r: "una tafferia da donna di parto di legno."

125 For a comparison of these two bowls, see Bruschi, *Pontormo*, unpaginated.

126 For genealogical information, see Bruschi, *Pontormo*, unpaginated.

127 For the link between this drawing and the two *tafferie*, see Janet Cox-Rearick, *The drawings of Pontormo*, Cambridge, Mass., 1964, **I**, 273–4.

128 American Art Galleries, *Art treasures and antiquities from the famous Davanzati Palace*, New York, November 21–5 and 27–8, 1916, lot 996.

129 In addition to the three bowls discussed here, there is another, attributed to a Sienese painter, painted with a seated infant Moses testing the burning coals; see Santoro, *Addenda*, 3. This apocryphal infancy story of the Old Testament prophet, which signified his inherent innocence and honest intentions (and, perhaps, explained his alleged speech impediment), also appears on a slightly earlier birth tray attributed to another Sienese artist (Santoro, *Addenda*, 1–4). Such a reuse of earlier iconography further links this group of objects to childbirth. Stylistically the imagery has evolved, but iconographically it retains the same meanings.

130 This was a popular print with domestic artists; for a lustered maiolica plate fragment from Gubbio that also used this engraving, see Bernard Rackham, "The Ford collection of Italian maiolica," *Connoisseur*, CXLII, November 1958, 150–51. My thanks to J.V.G. Mallet and the owner of this bowl for their kind assistance.

131 *MPP*, 2665, 321r: "una tafferia dipincta con una stella ed una campanella da parto."

132 *MPP*, 2654, 575v.

133 For the Cei arms, see G.B. Crollalanza, *Dizionario storico-blasonico delle famiglie nobili e notabili italiane*, Pisa, 1886, I:274.

134 Giulio Mancini, *Considerazioni sulla pittura* (c. 1621), ed. Adriana Marucchi, Rome, 1956, I:77: "cose basse . . . tefanie da mangiar a letto per le donne di parto."

135 *MPP*, 2652, 1095v.

136 *MPP*, 2663, 50v.

137 I am grateful to both J.V.G. Mallet and James Yorke for providing information and access to this object. It was mentioned in J.V.G. Mallet, "The Painter of the Coal-Mine Dish," in *Italian Renaissance pottery: Papers written in association with a colloquium at the British Museum*, ed. Timothy Wilson, London, 1991, 62–73.

138 There is a possibility that this motif, painted in slightly different colors and with a heavy application typical of overpainting, covers an earlier coat of arms.

139 See J.V.G. Mallet and Timothy Clifford, "Battista Franco as a designer for maiolica," *Burlington magazine*, CXVIII, 1976, 387–410, and Johanna Lessmann, "Battista Franco disegnatore di maioliche," *Faenza*, LXII, 1976, 27–30.

Chapter 4

1 It is often assumed that ceramic wares entirely replaced wooden birth objects (see Giuseppe Mazzini, "Arte e maternità nella rinascenza," *Emporium*, XLVII, 1941, 82, Comstock, "Salvers," 59, and Claudia Silvia Däubler, "La tazza da parto nella collezione Pringsheim," *Ceramicantica*, VI, 1994, 28). However, it is not as simple as that. Both types of objects were used, sometimes concurrently, at least into the early seventeenth century.

2 Giuseppe M. Albarelli, *Ceramisti pesaresi nei documenti notarili dell'Archivio di Stato di Pesaro secoli XV–XVII*, ed. Paolo M. Enthler, Bologna, 1986, 515 ("una tavoletta da impagliata da tener sul letto"). My thanks to J.V.G. Mallet for bringing this book to my attention.

3 For the earliest discussion, see Eugène Müntz, "Les plateaux et les coupes d'accouchées aux xve et xvie siècles: Nouvelles recherches," *Revue de l'art ancien et moderne*, I, 1899, 426–8. Following his example, most examinations of maiolica included at least a brief and often fanciful description of birth wares; see Bernard Rackham, *The Victoria & Albert Museum: Guide to Italian maiolica*, London, 1933, 15. See also Franco Crainz, *La tazza da parto*, Rome, 1986, and Giovanna Bandini, "'Delle impagliate' ossia annotazioni intorno alle maioliche da puerpera cinquecentesche," in *Da donna a madre: Vesti e ceramiche particolari per ornamenti speciali*, Florence, 1996, 55–109. My thanks to both Dottore Crainz and Dottoressa Bandini for sending me copies of their books.

4 The Fountaine collection in England contained at least three, but perhaps as many as five, childbirth wares (Christie, Manson & Woods (London), *Catalogue of the celebrated Fountaine collection of majolica, Henri II ware, Palissy ware, Nevers ware, Limoges enamels, carvings on ivory, hone stone and rock crystal, Greek and Roman coins, ancient armour, &c., &c., removed from Narford Hall, Norfolk*, 16–19 June, 1884, lots 35, 190, 218, 336, and 401). In Germany, Alfred Pringsheim had eight (Otto von Falke, *Die Majolikasammlung Alfred Pringsheim in München*, The Hague, 1914–15, lots 201, 202, 206, 252, 386, 258, 259, and 287). The French collectors Auguste Dutuit (*Collection Auguste Dutuit: Majoliques italiennes*, Paris, 1899, lots 11 and 31) and Frédéric Spitzer (Émile Molinier, *La collection Spitzer IV: Les faïences italiennes, hispano-moresques, et orientales*, Paris, 1892, lots 85, 90, 91, and 108) had several each.

5 Each city, led by its local maiolica scholar, claimed it had the earliest surviving birth ware; see Luigi Servolini, "Il dono simbolico della città di Forlì alla Principessa di Piemonte: La 'tazza da parto' romagnola," *Illustrazione italiana*, LXVII, 10 March 1940, 304, and Giuseppe Liverani, "La tazza da impagliata," *Faenza*, XXIX, 1941, 11–16.

6 See, for example, Giuseppe Alberti, "Origine, vicende e rinascita della 'tazza da parto': Conferenza tenuta dal Dott. Alberti," *Lucina: Organo del sindacato nazionale fascista delle ostetriche*, VI, July 1939, esp. 9. This phenomenon is examined more fully below in the Conclusion.

7 *MPAP*, 181, 112r: "1° paio di schodele da partto di maiolicha." Another reference to "un descetto da parto e taglieri e schodelle" has been cited as evidence for the use of these objects in the beginning of the fifteenth century; see Däubler, "Pringsheim," 27, and Bandini, "'Delle impagliate,'" 62. However, this is an isolated reference and it seems to me that, if these *taglieri* and *schodelle* were in fact made of ceramics, they were probably utilitarian wares, associated with the *descetto da parto* only because they were found in the same place while the inventory was executed, not because they themselves were related to childbirth. No other evidence indicates the existence of specific ceramic birth wares at so early a date.

8 This very early trade has been examined by Marco Spallanzani, "Un invio di maioliche ispano-moresche a Venezia negli anni 1401–1402," *Archeologia medievale*, V, 1978, 529–41. On the export trade to Italy in general, see Timothy Wilson, *Ceramic art of the Italian Renaissance*, London, 1987, 28–32.

9 For a fifteenth-century Hispano-Moresque plate bearing the arms of the Ridolfi family of Florence, see Callmann, *Beyond nobility*, 92–3.

10 See Marco Spallanzani, "Maioliche di Valenza e di Montelupo in una casa pisana del 1480," *Faenza*, LXXII, 1986, 164–70.

11 For example, in 1476 Sienese ceramists requested that a duty be levied on all imported wares excepting "maiorica"; see Scipione Borghesi and Luciano Banchi, ed., *Nuovi documenti per la storia dell'arte senese*, Siena, 1898, 248–9.

12 See especially *MPAP*, 75, 78, 79, 94, 172–3, 175–7, 180–81,

and 186 for references to childbirth wares before the year 1500.

13 A clear analysis of available information on this development is Timothy Wilson, "The beginnings of lustreware in Renaissance Italy," *The International Ceramics Fair and Seminar*, London, 1996, 35–43.

14 Tiziani Biganti, "La produzione di ceramica a lustro a Gubbio e a Deruta tra la fine del secolo XV e l'inizio del secolo XVI: Primi risultati di una ricerca documentaria," *Faenza*, LXXIII, 1987, 215.

15 Leandro Alberti, *Descrittione di tutta Italia*, Bologna, 1550, 85 ("Sono domandati questi vasi di Magiorica, perche primieramente fu ritrovata quest'arte nell'Isola di Magiorica, & quivi portata").

16 A copy was recorded in the estate of Raffaello Santacroci in 1585; see *MPP*, 2655, 541v. Santacroci did not have an extensive library, so his ownership of this volume can be considered indicative of its popularity.

17 Cipriano Piccolpasso, *I tre libri dell'arte del vasaio* (1557), ed. Ronald Lightbown and Alan Caiger-Smith, London, 1980, II:86 and 91.

18 The available evidence leads me to discount a Ferrarese set from the late fifteenth century, which has been described as birth-related in Giovanni L. Reggi, *La ceramica graffita in Emilia Romagna dal secolo XIV al secolo XIX*, Modena, 1971, 54, and Bandini, "'Delle impagliate,'" 65–6. Their iconography suggests that these vessels were betrothal gifts. The same may be true of the bowls described in Catherine Join-Dieterle, *Musée du Petit Palais. Catalogue de céramiques I: Hispano-mauresques, majoliques italiennes, iznik, des collections Dutuit, Ocampo, et Pierre Marie*, Paris, 1984, 188–9, and Alfred Darcel and Henri Delange, *Recueil de faïences italiennes des XVe, XVIe et XVIIe siècles*, Paris, 1869, 21.

19 The link between *istoriato* wares and prints is described in Grazia Biscontini Ugolini and Jacqueline Petruzzellis-Scherer, ed., *Maiolica e incisione: Tre secoli di rapporti iconografici*, Vicenza, 1992, and the various essays in Biblioteca Apostolica Vaticana, *L'istoriato: Libri a stampa e maioliche italiane del cinquecento*, Faenza, 1993.

20 The word *istoriato* and its variations were used only rarely in Pupilli inventories. The only maiolica ware described in this manner was a plate "dipinto a storie" in the estate of Ghuglielmo Scharapucci in 1539 (*MPP*, 2647, 65v). Yet surviving objects indicate that this style was exceptionally popular for maiolica in the last three quarters of the sixteenth century.

21 For an examination of these objects see Marta Ajmar and Dora Thornton, "When is a portrait not a portrait?: *Belle donne* on maiolica and Renaissance praise of local beauties," in *The image of the individual: Portraits in the Renaissance*, ed. Nicholas Mann and Luke Syson, London, 1998, 138–53.

22 Examples are discussed in T. Wilson, *Ceramic art*, 148; Jorg Rasmussen, *Italienische Majolika*, Hamburg, 1984, 105–6; and Carmen Ravanelli Guidotti, *Faenza-faïence: "Bianchi" di Faenza*, Ferrara, 1996, 552–3.

23 A few days before Tommaso Sassetti married Caterina di Filippo da Lucingniano in 1399, he sent her "ii forzerino con cierte gioe chome s'usava in quel tempo" (*Carte strozziane*, II, 4, 113r). Conversely, the trousseau sent with the bride to her husband's home often included a number of items described as *non stimate*. These items did not count toward the father's negotiated financial obligation. But they included the most personal items for her use, such as the small ivory dolls, assorted purses, collars, and scissors found in Caterina Strozzi's *non stimate* in 1504 (*Carte strozziane*, III, 138, 129v). Maiolica spindle whorls would have been appropriate to such a list as well. And of course it is important to recall that spindles often

signified wifely duty at this time, making them even more appropriate.

24 For an examination of two maiolica inkwells, see Giuseppe Liverani, "Di un calamaio quattrocentesco al Museo di Cluny," *Faenza*, LXI, 1975, 7–12, and J.V.G. Mallet, "Un calamaio in maiolica a Boston," *Faenza*, LXII, 1976, 79–85.

25 Tuscan families often commissioned ceramists from other regions to produce maiolica for them. See, for example, the extensive *istoriato* service made for the Pucci family of Florence in Julia Triolo, "Fra Xanto Avelli's Pucci service, 1532–1533," *Faenza*, LXXIV, 1988, 32–44 and 228–84.

26 Of course, some attempts were made: the rim of one of the *tafferie da parto* by Pontormo is painted gold, but it is a dull and opaque covering, lacking the brilliant translucency of lustered maiolica.

27 See Bernard Rackham, *The Victoria & Albert Museum: Catalogue of Italian maiolica*, London, 1940, I:337–8 (no. 1006), and Mallet, "Painter of the Coal-Mine Dish," 1991, 62–73. For a sometimes problematic iconographic analysis of this plate, see Maurice L. Shapiro, "A Renaissance birth plate," *Art bulletin*, XLIV, 1967, 236–43.

28 Observed by Mallet, "Painter of the Coal-Mine Dish," 63.

29 See the compositional analysis in Rackham, *Catalogue*, I:338.

30 The inclusion of the rooster here is perhaps related to the long-standing association of poultry with pregnancy (see pp. 40–41 above). It seems unlikely that it is related to theology; nevertheless, see Shapiro, "Birth plate," 240–41.

31 This design is similar to the reverse of a contemporary but much smaller ceramic childbirth tray attributed to the same artist; see Johanna Lessmann, *Italienische majolika: Katalog der Sammlung Herzog-Anton-Ulrich Museum*, Braunschweig, 1979, 536, and Mallet, "Painter of the Coal-Mine Dish," 65.

32 *MPAP*, 172, 242v–244r.

33 In modern scholarship these wares are also described as *accouchement*. This French term, not used in Renaissance documents, has gained a sufficient amount of credence in the scholarly literature, irrespective of the original language; see, for example, the references throughout Rackham, *Catalogue*.

34 Gaetano Guasti, *Di Caffaggiolo e d'altre fabbriche de ceramiche in Italia*, Florence, 1902, 4.

35 *MPP*, 2667, 306r: "una materasso da letto ripieno di paglia con guscio cattivo."

36 Francesco Cioci, "I Della Rovere di Senigallia e alcune testimonianze ceramiche," *Faenza*, LXVIII, 1982, 256. For further support for this theory, see Paolo da Certaldo, "Libro," 35–6 (no. 154), who cautions his readers to make sure pregnant women do not get chilled.

37 Florio, *New world of words*, 237. For further etymological information, see Bandini, "'Delle impagliate,'" 59–61.

38 The references are found in *MPP*, 2664, 571v; *MPP*, 2657, 258v, 410v, and 685v.

39 But even this is not a strict rule, since the word *impagliata* was used in a Pisan sumptuary law of 1563; see Cantini, *Legislazione*, V:71.

40 Albarelli, *Ceramisti pesaresi*, 345.

41 Bandini, "'Delle impagliate,'" 59.

42 For a discussion on the difficulties of establishing unilateral terminology for Italian maiolica vessels, see A.V.B. Norman, *The Wallace Collection. Catalogue of ceramics I: Pottery, maiolica, faenza, stoneware*, London, 1976, 18–19.

43 For example, in 1390 the estate of Miniato di Piero included "iiii scodelle de maiolica" (*MPAP*, 1, 414v). For the use of the term *scodella* in a list of wares made by a ceramist from Manises, see Spallanzani, "Invio," 530.

44 Paolo Morelli noted that this Bartolomeo loaned him 600 wares, "tra taglieri e schodelle chon più altre maserizie da

chucina ci presto per fare le noze di Matteo Morelli" (*Archivio Gherardi Piccolomini d'Aragona*, 178, 71r).

45 Florio, *New world of words*, 479.

46 At times, Piccolpasso used the word *tazza* interchangeably with *schudelle*, at one point indicating that the phrase *dal impagliata* could modify either; see Piccolpasso, *Tre libri*, I:10v.

47 See, for example, the estate of Santi di Andrea in 1490, which distinguished between bowls for unspecified uses and bowls for childbirth (*MPAP*, 178, 199v).

48 Piccolpasso, *Tre libri*, I:10v: "Tra questi ve ne è di dua sorte che si fanno di dua pezzi: come le schudelle da l'impagliata, alle quai va il suo coperchio."

49 Piccolpasso, *Tre libri*, I:10v–11r: "E dunque da sapere che gli cinqui pezzi de che si compone la schudella da donna di parto, tutt'e 5 dico, fanno le sue operationi e, poste tutt'a 5 insieme, formano un vaso. Ma per essere inteso meglio veremo al dissegnio. Questi sono tutt'a 5 gli pezzi della schudella. L'ordine di farne tutto un vaso è questo: il taglieri si riversa su la schudella, cioè quel piano dov'è il numero 2 va volto sopra al concavo della schudella al n. 1, il concavo de l'ongaresca va volto sul piedi del taglieri, la saliera va posta cossì im piedi nel pie' de l'ongaresca, sopra la quale va il suo coperchio come qui si vederà. Ecovi che tutte fano un sol vaso come il presente, cosa no di poco ingegnio. Altri sono che le fanno di 9 pezzi, tenendo sempre il medsmo ordine, e queste si chiamano schudelle de' 5 pezzi o vero di 9."

50 There are a few documentary references that fall into none of these categories, although they seem to be maiolica. For example, in 1432 Filippo del Pugliese's estate included "1ᵃ misciroba da parto" (*MPAP*, 167, 47v). In 1471 a particularly confused clerk cataloguing the immense estate of Francesco Inghirammi noted "un paio di rinfreschatoi da maiolicha da donna di parto cioe novella," but then went back over the entry and indicated that the pair were actually for birth, rather than marriage (*MPAP*, 173, 267r). In 1473 Domenico Burni's household included "3 rinfreschatoi da dona di parto" (*MPAP*, 173, 317r). And in 1486 the estate of Antonio Chavalcanti recorded "1° rinfreschatoio da parto," which contextual clues identify as imported lusterware (*MPAP*, 178, 106v). A *rinfrescatoi* was usually a large basin for cooling drinks, and I know of none with iconography that can be construed as childbirth-related; on these vessels, see Johanna Lessmann, "Majoliken aus der Werkstatt der Fontana," *Faenza*, LXV, 1979, 334–5.

51 There is general confusion, however, over the actual numbers, which several sources have challenged without contemporary documentation. Some say that seven or eight was the correct number of wares in a childbirth service (Giovanbattista Passeri, *Istoria della pitture in maiolica fatte in Pesaro, e ne' luoghi circonvicini*, Pesaro, 1758, 83), while others affirm that five- or seven-piece sets were typical (Arthur Beckwith, *Majolica and fayence: Italian, Sicilian, Majorcan, Hispano-Moresque and Persian*, New York, 1877, 165), and still others suggest that three- or five-piece sets were correct (Ugolini and Petruzzellis-Scherer, *Maiolica*, 19).

52 Albarelli, *Ceramisti pesaresi*, 406 ("una scodella da impaiata di quattro pezzi").

53 Cited in Marco Spallanzani, "Maioliche di Urbino nelle collezioni di Cosimo I, del Cardinale Ferdinando e di Francesco I de' Medici," *Faenza*, LXV, 1979, 119. It is not known for whom he purchased this elaborate set; Cardinal Ferdinando became the Grand Duke of Tuscany after his brother Francesco died in 1587, but did not have children of his own until 1590.

54 Fert Sangiorgi, ed., *Documenti Urbinati: Inventari del Palazzo Ducale (1582–1631)*, Urbino, 1976, 189 ("una scodella dall'impagliata istoriata et a grotesca in pezzi n. cinquantatre, che e tutto il finimento per la tavola").

55 This bowl was last recorded in the Adda collection; see Bernard Rackham, *Islamic pottery and Italian maiolica: Illustrated catalogue of a private collection*, London, 1959, no. 427.

56 Many plates and low bowls are still catalogued according to the system of shapes devised by Rackham in 1940 (see *Catalogue*, 456–7).

57 Covers were considered part of the *scodella* and were not mentioned in inventories except, perhaps, by a particularly conscientious clerk endeavoring to enumerate every single item in an estate; see, for example, "1ᵃ iscodela chon choperchio da dona di partto," in the home of Piero Cioni in 1469 (*MPAP*, 173, 200v). The same applies to *saliere*; although a number of inventories cite salts, these seem to refer to autonomous objects, usually of metal, and none was specifically designated *da parto*. The salt for childbirth must have been entirely dependent on its accompanying vessels, making a separate listing redundant. However, a letter of 1640 described a shipment of Faenza maiolica to Florence which included "una saliera da donne di parto"; see Guasti, *Caffaggiolo*, 459.

58 *MPAP*, 172, 336r. At this date his children were fifteen and sixteen years of age.

59 *MPP*, 2645, 8v.

60 In 1429 the estate of Paolo di Ghuiglielino included "1° paio di forzieri storiati," probably indicating a matched set of chests with related narrative panels (*MPAP*, 166, 55v). Shoes were described with similar terminology: in 1528 the estate of Girolamo Freschobaldi included "uno paio di pianelle da donna" (*MPAP*, 191, 130r). For a different definition see Däubler, "Pringsheim," 27.

61 For example, in 1551 the estate of Michealangelo d'Antonio della Valle included "una scodella da parto di maiolicha" (*MPP*, 2650, 129r).

62 *MPAP*, 177, 68v.

63 *MPAP*, 177, 301r.

64 Piccolpasso, *Tre libri*, I:10v ("tutt'e 5 dico, fanno le sue operationi"). On the likelihood of individualized functions for different maiolica wares, see also J.V.G. Mallet, "Mantua and Urbino: Gonzaga patronage of maiolica," *Apollo*, CXIV, 1981, 162–4.

65 Marco Spallanzani, *Ceramiche alle corte dei Medici nel cinquecento*, Modena, 1994, 192.

66 *MPP*, 2667, 227v. For Montelupo ceramic production, see Fausto Berti, *La maiolica di Montelupo, secoli XIV–XVIII*, Milan, 1986.

67 Spallanzani, *Ceramiche dei Medici*, 192.

68 *MPP*, 2660, 54r: "una scodella da donne di parto bianca di maiolica."

69 See Ravanelli Guidotti, *Faenza-faïence*. A reference to "2 schodelle da parto di terra di Faenza dipinte di verde" in the estate of Girolamo Manzini in 1573 may have been of this type (*MPP*, 2664, 76r).

70 It generated praise even from the critical eye of the French essayist Montaigne. He noted during his travels in 1581 that these wares were "so white and clean . . . that it seems more pleasant to me for the table than the pewter of France, especially the kind you find in inns which are squalid." See Michel de Montaigne, *Montaigne's travel journal* (written 1580–81, published 1774), trans. Donald M. Frame, San Francisco, 1983, 99.

71 *MPP*, 2671, 152r: "una scodella per il parto dipinta di più colori" and "una scodella da parto con il suo coperchio nuovo."

72 But the relationship is not as direct as is implied by De Carli,

Deschi da parto, 36–9, who cites numerous maiolica wares with no link to childbirth, despite the fact that they have the same iconography as the earlier wooden trays.

73 For a discussion of the use of this motif, see Margaret Miles, "The Virgin's one bare breast: Female nudity and religious meaning in Tuscan early Renaissance culture," in *The female body in Western culture: Contemporary perspectives*, ed. Susan Rubin Suleiman, Cambridge, Mass., 1986, 193–206, and Megan Holmes, "Disrobing the Virgin: The *Madonna lactans* in fifteenth-century Florentine art," in *Picturing Women in Renaissance and Baroque Italy*, ed. Geraldine A. Johnson and Sara F. Matthews Grieco, Cambridge, 1997, 167–95.

74 An Antinori inventory of 1517 included a book of astrology (*MPAP*, 187, 341v). For information on nativities, see Helen Rodnite Lemay, "Guido Bonatti: Astrology, society and marriage in thirteenth-century Italy," *Journal of popular culture*, XVII, 1984, 83–4.

75 Biagi *et al.*, ed., *Medicina per le donne*, provides a good introduction to these texts.

76 See also the two bowls with similar scenes of women about to give birth illustrated in Bandini, "'Delle impagliate,'" 68–9.

77 See Jacqueline Petruzzellis-Scherer, "Fonti iconografiche delle opere dell'Avelli al Museo Correr di Venezia," in Comune di Rovigo, *Francesco Xanto Avelli da Rovigo*, Rovigo, 1980, 123.

78 On this set, see Carmen Ravanelli Guidotti, *Baldassare Manara faentino: Pittore di maioliche nel cinquecento*, Ferrara, 1996, 150–55, and Däubler, "Pringsheim," 26–39.

79 BNCF, *Fondo nazionale*, II, II, 357, 59r: "uno paio di schodele di maiolicha da parto per la Nanina."

80 It has been said that these wares were sold in apothecary shops, which is interesting given that Tribaldo himself was an apothecary. But there is no known evidence for this; see Edgcumbe Staley, *The guilds of Florence*, London, 1906, 254.

Chapter 5

1 I use the term "sympathetic magic" as it was defined by James George Frazer, *The golden bough: A study in magic and religion* (12 vols., 1890–1915), New York, 1990, 1:52–4. The type of magic most common to Renaissance childbirth involved Frazer's homeopathic, or imitative, magic, in which "like produces like." A version of this chapter was published as "Imaginative conceptions in Renaissance Italy," in *Picturing women in Renaissance and Baroque Italy*, ed. Geraldine A. Johnson and Sara F. Matthews Grieco, Cambridge, 1997, 42–60.

2 This kind of sexual division of control is analyzed in Guido Ruggiero, *Binding passions: Tales of magic, marriage, and power at the end of the Renaissance*, New York, 1993.

3 David Freedberg, *The power of images: Studies in the history and theory of response*, Chicago, 1989.

4 One of the few works to discuss these statuettes is John Pope-Hennessy, *Catalogue of Italian sculpture in the Victoria & Albert Museum*, London, 1964, 1:406–9.

5 *MPAP*, 181, 148r: "2 banbini dorati abracciati insieme."

6 See also Freedberg, *Images*, 2–4.

7 Saint Augustine, *Against Julian* (c. 410), trans. Matthew A. Schumacher, New York, 1957, 291–3. For a similar story, see also Tommaso Campanella, *The city of the sun* (1623), trans. Daniel J. Donno, Berkeley, 1981, 85.

8 Cited in Clarissa W. Atkinson, *The oldest vocation: Christian motherhood in the Middle Ages*, Ithaca, NY, 1991, 208.

9 Biagi *et al.*, *Medicina per le donne*, 92–5.

10 Marsilio Ficino, *The book of life* (1489), trans. Charles Boer, Irving, 1980, 143.

11 This is discussed in Michael Camille, *The Gothic idol*, Cambridge, 1989, 23.

12 T.H. White, ed., *The bestiary: A book of beasts, being a translation from a Latin bestiary of the twelfth century* (1952), New York, 1960, 89–90.

13 Benedetto Varchi, *Opere di Benedetto Varchi ora per la prima volta raccolte*, Trieste, 1859, II:669.

14 Ambroise Paré, *On monsters and marvels* (1573), trans. Janis L. Pallister, Chicago, 1982, 38–9. Monsters and deformities were always a matter of some concern; see the discussion of these occurrences in Katharine Park and Lorraine Daston, *Wonders and the order of nature, 1150–1750*, New York, 1998.

15 This theory carried much weight long past the period under discussion here. See, for example, Paul-Gabriel Boucé, "Imagination, pregnant women, and monsters in eighteenth-century England and France," in *Sexual underworlds of the Enlightenment*, ed. G.S. Rousseau and Roy Porter, Chapel Hill, 1988, 86–100.

16 L.B. Alberti, *Art of building*, 1988, 299.

17 Kanter *et al.*, *Painting and illumination*, 311 ("Faccia Iddio sana ogni donna chffiglia epadri loro . . . ro . . . ernato sia sanza noia orichdia isono unbanbolin chesuli[sol?] a dimoro fo lapiscia dariento edoro"). The ellipses signify large gaps in the inscription. It has been suggested that the arms are those of the Montauri family of Siena, who were goldsmiths, thus making the inscription personal to them (see Kanter *et al.*, 312). However, this naked and urinating boy seems to be a *topos* related to fertility, so the connection to the Montauri may be only coincidental.

18 Ser Lapo Mazzei, *Lettere di un notaro a un mercante del secolo XIV*, ed. Cesare Guasti, Florence, 1880, 1:xlvi.

19 Keith Christiansen, "Lorenzo Lotto and the tradition of epithalamic paintings," *Apollo*, CXXIV, 1986, 166–73.

20 *Carte strozziane*, IV, 71, 27v: "A spese di Charlo mio figliuolo, lire una soldi x e per lui a Martino dello Scharfa e compagnia per 90 coralli per fargli un vezzo." Further analysis of the use of coral is found in Danièle Alexandre-Bidon, "La dent et le corail, ou la parure prophylactique de l'enfance à la fin du Moyen Age," *Razo*, VII, 1987, 5–33, and Gabriele Borghini *et al.*, ed., *Una farmacia preindustriale in Valdelsa: La spezieria e lo spedale di Santa Fina nella città di San Gimignano secc. XIV–XVIII*, San Gimignano, 1981, 169–71. I am grateful to Richard Goldthwaite for the last reference.

21 On this, see Jacqueline Marie Musacchio, "The rape of the Sabine women on quattrocento marriage panels," in *Marriage in Renaissance Italy*, ed. Trevor Dean and Kate J.P. Lowe, Cambridge, 1998, 66–82.

22 First suggested by Ernst H. Gombrich, "Apollonio di Giovanni: A Florentine cassone workshop seen through the eyes of a humanist poet," *Journal of the Warburg and Courtauld Institutes*, XVIII, 1955, 21.

23 The subject of this scene, long thought to represent the story of Lionora de' Bardi and Filippo Buondelmonte, has now been identified as the Justice of Trajan; see Christiane Klapisch-Zuber, "Les noces feintes: Sur quelques lectures de deux thèmes iconographiques dans les *cassoni* florentines," *I Tatti studies*, VI, 1995, 11–30. If this is the case, the analysis still stands. The widow could be transporting her belongings in her old marriage chests, which were kept in the home long after marriage for practical purposes.

24 These chest lids are among the few Renaissance representations of almost naked men, in the service of neither religion nor mythology. Naked women, however, were more popular. For example, see the estate inventory of Andrea Tolomei in 1586: "quadretto piccolo drentovi una donna nuda dipinta" (*MPP*, 2666, 642v).

25 Mancini, *Considerazione*, 1:143.

26 On contemporary perceptions of procreation, see Danielle

Jacquart and Claude Thomasset, *Sexuality and medicine in the Middle Ages* (1985), trans. Matthew Adamson, Cambridge, 1988, and Thomas Walter Laqueur, *Making sex: Body and gender from the Greeks to Freud*, Cambridge, 1990.

27 Mancini, *Considerazione*, I:143.

28 For a facsimile copy see Virgilius, *Opera, Bucolica, Georgica, Aeneis: Manoscritto 492 della Biblioteca Riccardiana*, Florence, 1969.

29 See, for example, White, *Beasts*, 91–3, and Krystyna Moczulska, "The most graceful Gallerini and the most exquisite ΓΑΛΕΗ in the portrait of Leonardo da Vinci," *Folia historiae artium*, I, 1995, 77–86.

30 John Hunt, "Jewelled neck furs and 'Flohpelze,'" *Pantheon*, XXI, 1963, 150–57, and Guenther Schiedlansky, "Zum sogenannten Flohpelze," *Pantheon*, XXX, 1972, 469–80.

31 Giuseppe Bernoni, *Credenze popolari veneziane*, Venice, 1874, 14–15 and Angelo de Gubernatis, *Storia comparata degli usi natalizi in Italia e presso gli altri popoli Indo-Europei*, Milan, 1878, 40–41. During the nineteenth century, a bride was presented with a small candy doll to guarantee that she would produce an equally lovely child; see Bernoni, *Credenze*, 15. The continuing belief in the felicitous effects of the maternal imagination is also exhibited by the contemporary practice of painting or hanging an angel over the bride's bed, in the hope that she would engender a child like the one she saw when she woke; see Molmenti, *Storia di Venezia*, II:556–7.

32 See the discussion in Klapisch-Zuber, *Women, family, and ritual*, 319. In 1384 Paolo Sassetti allocated 15 *soldi*, "per dare al fanciullo posto in collo" (*Carte strozziane*, II, 4, 70r). A sumptuary law enacted in 1388 forbade tipping the servant who carried this child more than a florin; see Dominici, *Regola*, 233.

33 BNCF, *Fondo nazionale*, II, II, 357, 56v: "2 tovagliolini da parto."

34 *Acquisti e doni*, 302, insert 1, loose folio: "iii brievi da banbini con oro et perle."

35 For an examination of this unique painting, see Chiara d'Afflitto, "La 'Madonna della Pergola': Eccentricità e bizzarria in un dipinto pistoiese del cinquecento," *Paragone*, XLV, 1994, 47–59. Further information on charms can be found in Borghini *et al.*, *Farmacia*, 167–8.

36 Several examples are cited in Klapisch-Zuber, *Women, family, and ritual*, 311–13. A possibly similar item, described as "1° banbino di terra o si Dio d'amore," was listed in the estate of Raffaello di Lorenzo in 1544 (*MPP*, 2648, 837v).

37 *Carte strozziane*, V, 41, 170 left: "uno Messere Domenedio con vesta di brochato e corona d'oro e perle."

38 Paul Barolsky, *Infinite jest: Wit and humor in Italian Renaissance art*, Columbia, Miss., and London, 1978, 24.

39 Lynne Lawner, ed., *I modi. The sixteen pleasures* (1527), Evanston, 1988.

40 Richard C. Trexler, "Florentine religious experience: The sacred image," *Studies in the Renaissance*, XIX, 1972, 7–41.

41 *Carte strozziane*, IV, 418, 6r.

42 *MPAP*, 182, 335v.

43 ASP, *Archivio Datini*, 1089, 7 September 1393: "uno inpiastro ch'elle si ponghono in sul corpo . . . ma . . . pute molto forte, diche ci à di que'mariti che ll'anno gittato via."

44 *MPAP*, 152, 199v. On the other hand, a couple in fourteenth-century Montaillou used an unidentified herb wrapped in linen and placed on a cord around a woman's neck as a contraceptive; see Le Roy Ladurie, *Montaillou*, 172–3.

45 *MAP*, XLVI, 258: "Questa per avisarvi chome questo dì a ore dieci, mediante la grazia di Dio e della vostra ricetta, i'ò auto un bello fanciullo maschio." For this reference and the one in the following note, my thanks to Gino Corti.

46 *MAP*, VI, 585: "Io ve . . . mando [una ricepta da ingravidare], prego Dio che ve sia giovevole. Questa è cosa che non ve può nocere, et a quelle che l'aveano provate, a ttutte è giovate, cioè a quilli che non'anno facto più figli . . . Credo che magiormente giovarà a voi, perchè havete el corpo acto a cciò."

47 *MPAP*, 167, 41r: "1° libraccio grande di ricietțe di medicine."

48 BNCF, *Magliabecchiano*, cl. XV, cod. CXV, unpaginated.

49 See, for example, Alberto Magnus, *De le virtu de le herbe, & animali, & pietre preciose, & di molte maravogliose cose del mondo e secreti delle donne e degli huomini dal medesimo authore composti*, Venice, 1537, unpaginated.

50 Arturo Castiglioni, *Incantesimo e magica*, Milan, 1934, 107–8, and Borghini *et al.*, *Farmacia*, 163–4.

51 Niccolò Machiavelli, "The Mandragola," in *Five Italian Renaissance Comedies*, ed. and trans. Bruce Penman, London, 1978, 27. The same plant was considered an aphrodisiac for elephants; see White, *Beasts*, 25–6.

52 ASP, *Archivio Datini*, 1089, loose folio (16 September 1393): "il quale inpiastro fa la donna di Nofri di Messer Lapo Arnolfi, e chom'io l'avea parlato, e dicieva si faciela dopo Ognisanti."

53 *Ricettario fiorentino* (1499), unpaginated.

54 Loren MacKinney, *Medical illustrations in medieval manuscripts*, London, 1965, 94.

55 *MPAP*, 191, 130v.

56 Biagi *et al.*, ed., *Medicina per le donne*, 62–3.

57 Biagi *et al.*, ed., *Medicina per le donne*, 62.

58 Antoine Schnapper, *Le géant, la licorne, et la tulipe: Collections et collectionneurs dans la France du XVIIᵉ siècle*, Paris, 1988, 1:26–7. See also C.N. Bromehead, "Aetites or the eagle-stone," *Antiquity*, XXI, 1947, 16–22, and A.A. Barb, "Birds and medical magic," *Journal of the Warburg and Courtauld Institutes*, XIII, 1950, 316–18. This has been described as a German tradition, still popular in the nineteenth century; see Clemente Rossi, *Superstizioni e pregiudizi ossia veglie contadinesche esposte in forma dialogica per il popolo*, Milan, 1877, 416–18.

59 Ruberto di Guido Bernardi, *Una curiosa raccolta di segreti e di pratiche superstiziose fatta da un popolano fiorentino del secolo XIV* (1364), ed. Giovanni Giannini, Città di Castello, 1898, 71.

60 Luzio and Renier, *Mantova e Urbino*, 70.

61 Ficino, *Book of life*, 123.

62 *MPP*, 2668, 531v: "una pietra da donna di parto legata in oro." For contemporary examples of birth charms, see Ronald W. Lightbown, *Mediaeval European jewellery, with a catalogue of the collection in the Victoria & Albert Museum*, London, 1992, 23–32, and Richard Kieckhefer, *Magic in the Middle Ages*, Cambridge, 1989, 102.

63 For a general discussion of the use of precious stones and gems as amulets and talismans, see Lightbown, *Jewellery*, 96–100.

64 *MPAP*, 177, 77r: "1ᵃ rossa di gierusaleme da done di parto."

65 Schnapper, *Géant, licorne, tulipe*, VI:36–7. I am grateful to Katy Park for indicating this possibility to me.

66 *MPAP*, 4, 8r: "1 pietra di Santa Margherita legata in ariento."

67 For Margaret's life and martyrdom, see Jacobus de Voragine, *The Golden Legend*, trans. Granger Ryan and Helmut Ripperger, New York, 1941, 351–4.

68 *MPP*, 2650, 88r.

69 *MPAP*, 157, 61v.

70 BNCF, *Fondo nazionale*, II, II, 357, 115v.

71 Cited in Helen Lemay, "Women and the literature of obstetrics and gynecology," in *Medieval women and the sources of medieval history*, ed. Joel T. Rosenthal, Athens, Ga., 1990, 197.

72 Peter Burke, *The historical anthropology of early modern Italy*, Cambridge, 1987, 122.

73 Walter J. Dilling, "Girdles: Their origin and development, particularly with regard to their use as charms in medicine,

marriage and midwifery," *Caledonian medical journal*, IX, 1912–14, 337–57, 403–25. Lucille B. Pinto discussed a twelfth-century scroll with medical information regarding women and childbirth in "The folk practice of gynecology and obstetrics in the Middle Ages," *Bulletin of the history of medicine*, XLVII, 1973, 513–23. For an English example of around 1500, see S.A.J. Moorat, *Catalogue of Western manuscripts on medicine and science in the Wellcome Historical Medical Library*, London, 1962, I:491–3. Medieval Hungary had a similar custom; see Gábor Klaniczay, "Le culte des saints dans la Hongrie médievale (problèmes de recherche)," *Acta historia academiae scientiarum hungaricae*, XXIX, 1983, 69–70 (I am grateful to Scott Montgomery for this reference).

74 ASP, *Archivio Datini*, 1103, 23 April 1395: "Io Niccholo mi credo che le farebbe più d'utile e più bene a quello a ch'ella la vole adoperare che lla desse manggiare a 3 poveri 3 venerdì, e non andare dietro a parole che dichono le femine." Bianca Cappello is said to have employed a wide variety of similar devices; see Saltini, *Cappello*, 187, 291–2.

75 My thanks to Timothy Wilson for drawing this bowl to my attention. This term does not seem to have been particularly common; for another use of the word, in reference to a pregnant pig, see Lotto, *Libro*, 214.

76 William Warren Vernon, *Readings on the Paradiso of Dante, chiefly based on the commentary of Benvenuto da Imola*, New York, 1909, II:208.

77 Sacchetti, *Trecentonovelle*, 514–16.

78 MPP, 2653, 353r: "una schatolina drentovi più breve et cose da donne di parto." There was also "1 schatolino di legnio entrovi 1 breve da donne di parto et cordone s'adoperano a donne di parto" in the estate of Giovanbattista Marchetti (MPP, 2650, 420r).

79 *Acquisti e doni*, 21, 16r. In 1598 the estate of Messer Raffaello from Volterra included "un cassettino d'avorio con otto brevi da bambini" (MPP, 2668, 90v).

80 Biblioteca Riccardiana, Florence, MS 1258, 39r: "Queste sono le messe che si vogliono dire quando è entrata ne'nove mesi del partorire." My thanks to Gino Corti for this reference.

81 CRSGF, 102, appendix 16, 36v: "Da Giovanni Tornabuoni a dì 8 detto lire cinque sono per l'ufficio di monna Francesca sua donna facto a dì 26 di settembre."

82 Godefridus Henschenius and Daniel van Papenbroeck, ed., *Acta Sanctorum. Maji.*, Venice, 1737, I:348–9. Antonino also aided infertile women; see I:332–3.

83 Lemay, *Medieval women*, 197. In England, churches assembled collections of certain relics expressly to loan out for the assistance of pregnant women; see Keith Thomas, *Religion and the decline of magic*, New York, 1971, 28.

84 MPAP, 173, 266v: "uno schatolino dipinto entrovi uno tondo di cristallo e una anpollina di relique e uno chordiglia biancho e uno nastro di seta biancho chon orelique a picchato da porre a dosso a donna di parto."

85 Brendan Cassidy, "A relic, some pictures and the mothers of Florence in the late fourteenth century," *Gesta*, XXX, 1991, 91–9. In France, assistance was sought from replicas and badges of the Virgin's tunic from Chartres; see A. Lecocq, "Recherches sur les enseignes de pèlerinages et les chemisettes de Notre-Dame-de-Chartres," *Mémoires de la Société archéologique d'Eure-et-Loir*, VI, 1876, 194–224.

86 BNCF, *Fondo nazionale*, II, II, 357, 59v. Nanina vowed also to dress her son like a Franciscan monk for a year; see BNCF, *Fondo nazionale*, II, II, 357, 59v.

87 *Acquisti e doni*, 293, loose folio.

88 *Acquisti e doni*, 301, insert 1, loose folio.

89 *Archivio Gherardi Piccolomini d'Aragona*, 713, 116v.

90 Of the vast literature on ex-votos, see Angelo Turchini, *Ex-voto: Per una lettura dell'ex-voto dipinto*, Milan, 1992, and Giulio Busti *et al.*, *Gli ex-voto in maiolica della chiesa della Madonna dei Bagni a Casaline presso Deruta*, Florence, 1983.

91 On the importance of verisimilitude in these offerings, see Freedberg, *Images*, 225–9.

92 CRSGF, 119 (53), 124v: "una inmagine di argento, il quale era il suo primogenito, di grandezza di un braccio, che era un bambino facciato di peso di libre dodici d'argento per gratia ricevuta di una infirmita."

93 See, for example, CRSGF, 119 (107), 3v–13v, and CRSGF, 119 (50), 18r–19r.

94 See Gino Masi, "La ceroplastica in Firenze nei secoli XV–XVI e la famiglia Benintendi," *Rivista d'arte*, IX, 1916, 124–42.

95 *Carte strozziane*, IV, 71, 75v: "A spese di [my son] Charlo lire una soldi tredici e per loro a Orsino ceraiuolo per la immagine sua offerse [my wife] la Francesca nella Nuziata."

96 *Archivio Gherardi Piccolomini d'Aragona*, 139, 165r.

97 Arnout von Buchell, "Iter Italicum," *Archivio delle reale società romana di storia patria*, XXV, 1902, 129–30.

Conclusion

1 Arnold van Gennep, *The rites of passage* (1908), trans. Monika B. Vizedom and Gabrielle L. Caffee, London, 1960, esp. 41–9. Van Gennep's rites of separation, transition, and reincorporation can be compared with practices in seventeenth-century English childbirth; see Wilson, *Women as mothers*, 68–107.

2 Jeffrey Spier, "Medieval Byzantine magical amulets and their tradition," *Journal of the Warburg and Courtauld Institutes*, LVI, 1993, 25–62.

3 Anke A. van Wagenberg-Ter Hoeven, "Het schuitje naar de Volewijk: Een interpretatie van een nachtelijk tafereel op een achttiende-eeuws drinkglas," *Antiek*, XXVI, 1991, 22–30.

4 For information on this and other Dutch birthing customs, see T. H. Lunsingh Scheurleer, "Enkele oude Nederlandse kraamgebruiken," *Antiek*, VI, 1971–2, 297–332.

5 Isolde Thyret, "'Blessed is the tsaritsa's womb': The myth of miraculous birth and royal motherhood in Muscovite Russia," *Russian review*, LIII, 1994, 479–96.

6 On the female identity see especially Christiane Klapisch-Zuber, "Images without memory: Women's identity and family consciousness in Renaissance Florence," *Fenway Court*, 1990–91, 37–43.

7 For one analysis of these many objects and their meanings, see Christiane Klapisch-Zuber, "Le 'zane' della sposa: La donna fiorentina e il suo corredo nel rinascimento," *Memorie*, XI–XII, 1984, 12–23.

8 For example, in 1559, the estate of Lione Castellani included three lightweight head towels and six lightweight caps, both specified as for widows (MPP, 2651, 379v). In 1576 the estate of a certain widowed Madonna Lessandra included a black overcoat and a black veil, both designated as for widows (MPP, 2665, 322r).

9 Archivio Guicciardini, *Albizzi fondo*, Ricordanze 289, 31r.

10 On the importance of costume in relation to a woman's identity, see Elizabeth Wayland Barber, "On the antiquity of East European bridal clothing," *Dress*, XXI, 1994, 17–29.

11 CRSGF, 90 (84), 18v: "dette saliere [d'ariento] mandai a Monna Allexandra, donna di Lorenzo di Messer Palla mio cognato, che avea partorito un figlolo maschio a Padova."

12 *Carte strozziane*, II, 15, 45r: "5 holtellini tutti d'arientto da dona."

13 In my examination of the Pupilli, the only metalwork described in this manner was a silver bowl (MPP, 2649, 604r: "una scodella d'argento da parto con li manichi quale pesa

once tredici") and a brass basin (*MPP*, 2658, 143r: "un bacino d'ottone liscio da parto").

14 See, for example, excerpted inventories of a furrier, a mason, various merchant men, and Lorenzo de' Medici in *L'oreficeria nella Firenze del quattrocento*, Florence, 1977, 268–72.

15 Klapisch-Zuber, *Women, family, and ritual*, 237–9.

16 Gift-giving dictated much of a woman's life during this time: she was given in marriage; she was given a dowry by her father; either her father or her future husband gave her the chests to carry the material portion of this dowry to her new home; and she was given various objects to celebrate marriage and childbirth. For an anthropological assessment of gifts and the importance of reciprocity, see Marcel Mauss, *The gift: The form and reason for exchange in archaic societies* (1925), trans. Ian Cunnison, Glencoe, Ill., 1954, and more recently Annette B. Weiner, *Inalienable possessions: The paradox of keeping-while-giving*, Berkeley, 1992.

17 As early as the fourteenth century, ceramics described as *porcellana* appeared in Tuscan inventories. On the variable meanings of this term, see Marco Spallanzani, *Ceramiche orientale a Firenze nel Rinascimento*, Florence, 1978, 36–9.

18 *MPP*, 2671, 1262r: "una scudella da parto con piatto di porcellana fine."

19 Spallanzani, *Ceramiche dei Medici*, 41.

20 For Medici porcelain, see Galeazzo Cora and Angiolo Fanfani, *La porcellana Medicea*, Milan, 1985.

21 Giuseppe Liverani, "Maiolica e porcellana in un quadro di Alessandro Allori," *Faenza*, XXVIII, 1940, 51–5.

22 See Lia Chinosi, ed., *Nascere a Venezia dalla serenissima alla prima guerra mondiale*, Turin, n.d., 80–83.

Bibliography

Manuscript Sources

Archivio di Stato, Florence
  Acquisti e doni
  Archivio Bartolomei
  Archivio Gherardi Piccolomini d'Aragona
  Archivio di Urbino
  Carte Gondi
  Carte strozziane
  Consigli della Repubblica, provisioni registri
  Corporazione religiose soppresse dal governo francese
  Guardaroba
  Magistrato dei Pupilli avanti il Principato
  Magistrato dei Pupilli del Principato
  Manoscritti
  Mediceo avanti il Principato
  Mediceo del Principato
  Notarile antecosimiano
  Panciatichi
  Prestanze
  Ufficiali della Grascia

Archivio Guicciardini, Florence
  Albizzi fondo

Biblioteca Laurenziana, Florence
  Archivio Capitolare di San Lorenzo

Biblioteca Nazionale Centrale, Florence
  Fondo nazionale
  Magliabechiano
  Manoscritti
  Panciatichi

Biblioteca Riccardiana, Florence
  MS

Archivio di Stato, Prato
  Archivio Datini
  Ceppi

Printed Sources

Cristina Acidini Luchinati, ed., *Renaissance Florence: The age of Lorenzo de' Medici 1449–1492*, London, 1993.

Chiara d'Afflitto, "La 'Madonna della Pergola': Eccentricità e bizzarria in un dipinto pistoiese del cinquecento," *Paragone*, XLV, 1994, 47–59.

Diane Cole Ahl, "Renaissance birth salvers and the Richmond *Judgement of Solomon*," *Studies in iconography*, VII, 1981, 157–74.

Marta Ajmar and Dora Thornton, "When is a portrait not a portrait?: *Belle donne* on maiolica and Renaissance praise of local beauties," in *The image of the individual: Portraits in the Renaissance*, ed. Nicholas Mann and Luke Syson, London, 1998, 138–53.

Giuseppe M. Albarelli, *Ceramisti pesaresi nei documenti notarili dell'Archivio di Stato di Pesaro secoli XV–XVII*, ed. Paolo M. Enthler, Bologna, 1986.

Giuseppe Alberti, "Origine, vicende e rinascita della 'tazza da parto': Conferenza tenuta dal Dott. Alberti," *Lucina: Organo del sindacato nazionale fascista delle ostetriche*, VI, July 1939, 7–9.

Leon Battista Alberti, *The Albertis of Florence: Leon Battista Alberti's Della famiglia (1430s)*, ed. Guido A. Guarino, Lewisburg, 1971.

Leon Battista Alberti, *De re aedificatoria* (completed 1452, published 1485), trans. Joseph Rykwert *et al.* as *On the art of building in ten books*, Cambridge, Mass., and London, 1988.

Leandro Alberti, *Descrittione di tutta Italia*, Bologna, 1550.

Alberto Magnus, *De le virtu de le herbe, & animali, & pietre preciose, & di molte maravogliose cose del mondo e secreti delle donne e degli huomini dal medesimo authore composti*, Venice, 1537.

Danièle Alexandre-Bidon, "La dent et le corail, ou la parure prophylactique de l'enfance à la fin du Moyen Age," *Razo*, VII, 1987, 5–33.

Danièle Alexandre-Bidon and Pierre Riché, *L'enfance au moyen age*, Paris, 1994.

Maria Luisa Altieri Biagi *et al.*, ed., *Medicina per le donne nel cinquecento: Testi di Giovanni Marinello e di Girolamo Mercurio*, Turin, 1992.

American Art Galleries, *Art treasures and antiquities from the famous Davanzati Palace*, New York, November 21–5 and 27–8, 1916.

Francis Ames-Lewis, "Early Medicean devices," *Journal of the Warburg and Courtauld Institutes*, XLII, 1979, 122–43.

Francis Ames-Lewis, "Matteo de' Pasti and the use of powdered gold," *Mitteilungen des kunsthistorischen Institutes in Florenz*, XXVIII, 1984, 351–62.

Francis Ames-Lewis, "Modelbook drawings and the Florentine quattrocento artist," *Art history*, X, 1987, 1–11.

Francis Ames-Lewis, "Art in the service of the family: The taste and patronage of Piero di Cosimo de' Medici," in *Piero de' Medici "il Gottoso" (1416–1469)*, ed. Andreas Beyer and Bruce Boucher, Berlin, 1993.

Gian Mario Anselmi *et al.*, *La 'memoria' dei mercatores: Tendenze ideologiche, ricordanze, artigianato in versi nella Firenze del quattrocento*, Bologna, 1980.

Saint Antoninus, *Confessionale volgare intitolato spechio di coscienze*, Florence, 1490.

Bastiano Arditi, *Diario di Firenze e di altre parti della Cristianità (1574–79)*, ed. Roberto Cantagalli, Florence, 1970.

Philippe Ariès, *Centuries of childhood: A social history of family life* (1960), trans. Robert Baldick, New York, 1962.

Kirsten Aschengreen Piacenti and Caterina Chiarelli, *Moda alla corte dei Medici: Gli abiti restaurati di Cosimo, Eleonora, e Don Garzia*, Florence, 1993.

Clarissa W. Atkinson, *The oldest vocation: Christian motherhood in the Middle Ages*, Ithaca, NY, 1991.

Saint Augustine, *Against Julian* (c. 410), trans. Matthew A. Schumacher, New York, 1957.

Lorrayne Y. Baird, "Priapus gallinaceus: The role of the cock in fertility and eroticism in classical antiquity and the Middle Ages," *Studies in iconography*, VII–VIII, 1981–2, 81–111.

Filippo Baldinucci, *Notizie de' professori del disegna da Cimabue in qua*, 6 vols., Florence, 1681–1728.

Gaetano Ballardini, "Leggi suntuarie faentine," *La Romagna*, III, 1906, 225–40.

Giovanna Bandini, "'Delle impagliate' ossia annotazioni intorno alle maioliche da puerpera cinquentesche," in *Da donna a madre: Vesti e ceramiche particolari per ornamenti speciali*, Florence, 1996, 55–109.

A.A. Barb, "Birds and medical magic," *Journal of the Warburg and Courtauld Institutes*, XIII, 1950, 316–18.

Elizabeth Wayland Barber, "On the antiquity of East European bridal clothing," *Dress*, XXI, 1994, 17–29.

Paul Barolsky, *Infinite jest: Wit and humor in Italian Renaissance art*, Columbia, Miss., and London, 1978.

Hans Baron, *The crisis of the early Italian Renaissance*, Princeton, 1966.

Anne B. Barriault, *Spalliera paintings of Renaissance Tuscany: Fables of poets for patrician homes*, University Park, Penn., 1994.

Cristelle L. Baskins, "Griselda, or the Renaissance bride stripped bare by her bachelor in Tuscan *cassone* painting," *Stanford Italian review*, X, 1991, 153–75.

Cristelle L. Baskins, "Donatello's bronze *David*: Grillanda, Goliath, Groom?", *Studies in iconography*, XV, 1993, 113–34.

Cristelle L. Baskins, "Corporeal authority in the speaking pictures: The representation of Lucretia in Tuscan domestic painting," in *Gender rhetorics: Postures of dominance and submission in history*, ed. Richard C. Trexler, Binghamton, 1994, 187–200.

Michael Baxandall, *Painting and experience in fifteenth-century Italy*, Oxford and New York, 1972, 2/1988, repr. 1989.

Christian Bec, *Les livres des fiorentins (1413–1608)*, Florence, 1984.

James Beck, *Jacopo della Quercia*, 2 vols., New York, 1991.

Arthur Beckwith, *Majolica and fayence: Italian, Sicilian, Majorcan, Hispano-Moresque and Persian*, New York, 1877.

Luciano Bellosi, Dilvio Lotti, and Anna Matteoli, *Mostra d'arte sacra della diocesi di San Miniato*, San Miniato, 1969.

John F. Benton, *Trotula, women's problems, and the professionalization of medicine in the Middle Ages*, Pasadena, 1984.

Bernardino da Siena, *Le prediche volgari di San Bernardino da Siena dette nella Piazza del Campo l'anno MCCCCXXVII*, ed. Luciano Banchi, 3 vols., Siena, 1880–88.

Ruberto di Guido Bernardi, *Una curiosa raccolta di segreti e di pratiche superstiziose fatta da un popolano fiorentino del secolo XIV* (1364), ed. Giovanni Giannini, Città di Castello, 1898.

Giuseppe Bernoni, *Credenze popolari veneziane*, Venice, 1874.

Fausto Berti, *La maiolica di Montelupo, secoli XI–XVIII*, Milan, 1986.

Luciano Berti, *Masaccio*, Florence, 1988.

Luciano Berti and Antonio Paolucci, *L'età di Masaccio: Il primo quattrocento a Firenze*, Milan, 1990.

Guido Biagio, *Due corredi nuziali fiorentini 1320–1493 da un libro di ricordanze dei Minerbetti*, Florence, 1899.

Biblioteca Apostolica Vaticana, *L'istoriato: Libri a stampa e maioliche italiane del cinquecento*, Faenza, 1993.

Tiziani Biganti, "La produzione di ceramica a lustro a Gubbio e a Deruta tra la fine del secolo XV e l'inizio del secolo XVI Primi risultati di una ricerca documentaria," *Faenza*, LXXIII, 1987, 209–20.

Paul Binski, *Medieval death: Ritual and representation*, London, 1996.

Jean-Noël Biraben, *Les hommes et la peste en France et dans les pays européens et méditerranées*, 2 vols., Paris, 1975–6.

Giulio Bistort, "Il magistrato alle pompe nella Repubblica di Venezia," *Miscellanea di storia veneta*, V, 1912, 107, 201–5, 394–400.

Renate Blumenfeld-Kosinski, *Not of woman born: Representations of Caesarian birth in medieval and Renaissance culture*, Ithaca, NY, 1990.

Giovanni Boccaccio, *The Decameron* (c. 1350), trans. Guido Waldman, Oxford, 1993.

Francesco Bocchi, *Le bellezze della città de Firenze*, Florence, 1591.

David Bomford *et al.*, *Art in the making: Italian painting before 1400*, London, 1989.

Edmond Bonnaffè, *Voyages et voyageurs de la Renaissance*, Paris, 1895.

Tancred Borenius, "Unpublished cassone panels II," *Burlington magazine*, XL, 1922, 131–2.

Scipione Borghesi and Luciano Banchi, ed., *Nuovi documenti per la storia dell'arte senese*, Siena, 1898.

Gabriele Borghini *et al.*, ed., *Una farmacia preindustriale in Valdelsa: La spezieria e lo spedale di Santa Fina nella città di San Gimignano secc. XIV–XVIII*, San Gimignano, 1981.

Eve Borsook and Johannes Offerhaus, *Francesco Sassetti and Domenico Ghirlandaio at Santa Trinità, Florence: History and legend in a Renaissance chapel*, Doornspijk, 1981.

Paul-Gabriel Boucé, "Imagination, pregnant women, and monsters in eighteenth-century England and France," in *Sexual underworlds of the Enlightenment*, ed. G.S. Rousseau and Roy Porter, Chapel Hill, 1988, 86–100.

William Boulting, *Women in Italy, from the introduction of the chivalrous service of love to the appearance of the professional actress*, New York, 1910.

C.N. Bromehead, "Aetites or the eagle-stone," *Antiquity*, XXI, 1947, 16–22.

Judith C. Brown, *Immodest acts: The life of a lesbian nun in Renaissance Italy*, New York, 1986.

Gene Brucker, ed., *Two memoirs of Renaissance Florence*, trans. Julia Martines, New York, 1967.

Gene Brucker, ed., *The society of Renaissance Florence: A documentary study*, New York, 1971.

Gene Brucker, *Giovanni and Lusanna: Love and marriage in Renaissance Florence*, Berkeley, 1986.

Alberto Bruschi, *Un Pontormo ritrovato: Il desco da parto Ughi-Antinori, già della collezione Elia Volpi*, Florence, 1992.

Arnout von Buchell, "Iter Italicum," *Archivio delle reale società romana di storia patria*, XXV, 1902, 103–35.

Peter Burke, *The historical anthropology of early modern Italy*, Cambridge, 1987.

Giulio Busti *et al.*, *Gli ex-voto in maiolica della chiesa della Madonna dei Bagni a Casaline presso Deruta*, Florence, 1983.

Romolo Caggese, ed., *Statuti della Repubblica fiorentina*, 2 vols., Florence, 1910–21.

Piero Calamandrei, "Il totocalcio demografico di Benvenuto Cellini," in *Scritti inediti celliniani*, ed. Carlo Cordié, Florence, 1971, 149–64.

Ellen Callmann, *Apollonio di Giovanni*, Oxford, 1974.

Ellen Callmann, "The growing threat to marital bliss as seen in fifteenth-century Florentine paintings," *Studies in iconography*, V, 1979, 73–92.

Ellen Callmann, *Beyond nobility: Art for the private citizen in the early Renaissance*, Allentown, Penn., 1980.

Ellen Callmann, "Apollonio di Giovanni and painting for the early Renaissance room," *Antichità viva*, XXVII, 1988, 5–18.

Ellen Callmann, "Subjects from Boccaccio in Italian painting, 1375–1525," *Studi sul Boccaccio*, XXIII, 1995, 19–78.

Ellen Callmann, *A catalogue of early Italian secular art in the Yale University Art Gallery*, forthcoming.

Michael Camille, *The Gothic idol*, Cambridge, 1989.

Tommaso Campanella, *The city of the sun (1623)*, trans. Daniel J. Donno, Berkeley, 1981.

Roberto Cantagalli, "Bianca Cappello e una leggenda da sfatare: La questione del figlio supposto," *Nuova rivista storica*, XLIX, 1965, 636–52.

Eugene B. Cantelupe, "The anonymous *Triumph of Venus* in the Louvre: An early Italian example of mythological disguise," *Art bulletin*, XLIV, 1962, 238–42.

Lorenzo Cantini, ed., *Legislazione toscana*, 32 vols., Florence, 1800–08.

Gino Capponi, *Storia della repubblica di Firenze*, 3 vols., Florence, 1876.

Giovanni Carandente, *I trionfi nel primo Rinascimento*, Turin, 1963.

Girolamo Cardano, *Della mia vita*, ed. Alfonso Ingegno, Milan, 1982.

Franco Cardini, "Le insegne Laurenziane," in *Le tems revient. 'l tempo si rinuova: Feste e spettacoli nella Firenze di Lorenzo il Magnifico*, ed. Paola Ventrone, Florence, 1992, 55–74.

Cecilia De Carli, *I deschi da parto e la pittura del primo rinascimento toscano*, Turin, 1997.

Ann G. Carmichael, *Plague and the poor in Renaissance Florence*, Cambridge, 1986.

Julia Cartwright, *Beatrice d'Este, Duchess of Milan 1475–1497: A study of the Renaissance*, New York, 1903.

Brendan Cassidy, "A relic, some pictures and the mothers of Florence in the late fourteenth century," *Gesta*, XXX, 1991, 91–9.

Arturo Castiglioni, *Incantesimo e magica*, Milan, 1934.

Cherubino da Siena [*sic*], *Regole della vita matrimoniale*, ed. Francesco Zambrini and Carlo Negroni, Bologna, 1888.

Alberto Chiappelli, "Di un singolare procedimento medico-legale in Pistoia nell'anno 1375 per supposizione d'infante," *Rivista di storia delle scienze mediche e naturali*, X, 1919, 129–35.

Lia Chinosi, ed., *Nascere a Venezia dalla serenissima alla prima guerra mondiale*, Turin, n.d.

Stanley Chojnacki, "Dowries and kinsmen in early Renaissance Venice," *Journal of interdisciplinary history*, V, 1975, 571–600.

Stanley Chojnacki, "The power of love: Wives and husbands in late medieval Venice," in *Women and power in the Middle Ages*, ed. Mary Erler and Maryanne Kowaleski, Athens, Georgia, 1988, 126–48.

Christie, Manson & Woods (London), *Catalogue of the celebrated Fountaine collection of majolica, Henri II ware, Palissy ware, Nevers ware, Limoges enamels, carvings on ivory, hone stone and rock crystal, Greek and Roman coins, ancient armour, &c., &c., removed from Narford Hall, Norfolk*, June 16–19, 1884.

Keith Christiansen, "Lorenzo Lotto and the tradition of epithalamic paintings," *Apollo*, CXXIV, 1986, 166–73.

Christine de Pisan, *A medieval woman's mirror of honor: The treasury of the city of the ladies (1405)*, trans. Charity Cannon Willard, New York, 1989.

Raffaele Ciasca, *L'arte dei medici e speziali nella storia e nel commercio fiorentino dal secolo XII al XV*, Florence, 1927.

Francesco Cioci, "I Della Rovere di Senigallia e alcune testimonianze ceramiche," *Faenza*, LXVIII, 1982, 251–8.

Chad Coerver, "Idealization and misogyny in Renaissance courtship imagery," forthcoming.

Samuel K. Cohn Jr., *The cult of remembrance and the Black Death: Six Renaissance cities in central Italy*, Baltimore, 1992.

Samuel K. Cohn Jr., *Women in the streets: Essays on sex and power in Renaissance Italy*, Baltimore, 1996.

Bruce Cole, "The interior decoration of the Palazzo Datini in Prato," *Mitteilungen des kunsthistorischen Institutes in Florenz*, XIII, 1967, 61–82.

Bruce Cole, "Some thoughts on Orcagna and the Black Death style," *Antichità viva*, XXII, 1983, 27–37.

Bruce Cole, *Italian art 1250–1550: The relation of Renaissance art to life and society*, New York, 1987.

Helen Comstock, "Italian birth and marriage salvers," *International studio*, LXXXV, 1926, 50–59.

Comune di Venezia, *Venezia e la peste, 1348–1797*, Venice, 1980.

Galeazzo Cora and Angiolo Fanfani, *La porcellana Medicea*, Milan, 1985.

Andrea Corsini, *Malattie e morte di Lorenzo de' Medici, Duca d'Urbino*, Florence, 1913.

Gino Corti, "Sul commercio dei quadri a Firenze verso la fine del secolo XIV," *Commentari*, XXII, 1971, 84–91.

Janet Cox-Rearick, *The drawings of Pontormo*, 2 vols., Cambridge, Mass., 1964.

Franco Crainz, *La tazza da parto*, Rome, 1986.

Raymond Crawfurd, *Plague and pestilence in literature and art*, Oxford, 1914.

G.B. Crollalanza, *Dizionario storico-blasonico delle famiglie nobili e notabile italiane*, 3 vols., Pisa, 1886–90.

Monika Dachs, "Zur ornamentalen Freskendekoration des florentiner Wohnhauses im späten 14. Jahrhundert," *Mitteilungen des kunsthistorischen Institutes in Florenz*, XXXVII, 1993, 71–129.

Alfred Darcel and Henri Delange, *Recueil de faïences italiennes des XVe, XVIe et XVIIe siècles*, Paris, 1869.

Claudia Silvia Däubler, "La tazza da parto nella collezione Pringsheim," *Ceramicantica*, VI, 1994, 26–39.

Bernard Degenhardt and Annegrit Schmitt, *Corpus der italienischen Zeichnungen 1300–1450*, 8 vols., Berlin, 1968.

Benedetto Dei, *La cronica dall'anno 1400 all'anno 1500*, ed. Roberto Barducci, Florence, 1985.

Walter J. Dilling, "Girdles: Their origin and development, particularly with regard to their use as charms in medicine, marriage and midwifery," *Caledonian medical journal*, IX, 1912–14, 337–57, 403–25.

Giovanni Dominici, *Regola del governo di cura familiare* (1403), ed. Donato Salvi, Florence, 1860.

Jill Dunkerton *et al.*, *Giotto to Dürer: Early Renaissance painting in the National Gallery*, New Haven and London, 1991.

Collection Auguste Dutuit: Majoliques italiennes, Paris, 1899.

Hermann Egger, *Francesca Tornabuoni und ihre Grabstätte in Santa Maria sopra Minerva*, Vienna, 1934.

Marvin Eisenberg, *Lorenzo Monaco*, Princeton, 1989.

Robert Etienne, "Ancient medical conscience and children," *Journal of psychohistory*, IV, 1976, 144–50.

Otto von Falke, *Die Majolikasammlung Alfred Pringsheim in München*, The Hague, 1914–15.

Roberta Ferrazza, *Palazzo Davanzati e le collezioni di Elia Volpi*, Florence, 1994.

Rosario Ferreri, "Rito battesimale e comparatico nelle novelle senesi della VII giornata," *Studi sul Boccaccio*, XVI, 1987, 307–14.

Marsilio Ficino, *The book of life* (1489), trans. Charles Boer, Irving, 1980.

Nadia Maria Filippini, "The church, the state, and childbirth: The midwife in Italy during the eighteenth century," in *The art of midwifery: Early modern midwives in Europe*, ed. Hilary Marland, London, 1993, 152–75.

Aurora Fiorentini Capitani and Stefania Ricci, ed., *Il costume al tempo di Lorenzo il Magnifico: Prato e il suo territorio*, Milan, 1992.

Mary Eileen Fitzgerald, *Deschi da parto: Florentine birth trays of the quattrocento*, unpublished doctoral dissertation, Syracuse University, NY, 1986.

Helmut Flade, *Intarsia: Europaische Einlegekunst aus sechs Jahrhunderten*, Munich, 1986.

John Florio, *Queen Ann's new world of words, or dictionarie of the Italian and English tongues, collected, and newly much augmented by John Florio, Reader of the Italian unto the Soveraigne Maiestie of Anna, Crowned Queene of England, Scotland, France and Ireland, &c. And one of the Gentlemen of hir Royall Privie Chamber. Whereunto are added certaine necessarie rules and short observations for the Italian tongue*, London, 1611.

James George Frazer, *The golden bough: A study in magic and religion* (12 vols., 1890–1915), 9 vols., New York, 1990.

David Freedberg, *The power of images: Studies in the history and theory of response*, Chicago, 1989.

Arnold van Gennep, *The rites of passage* (1908), trans. Monika B. Vizedom and Gabrielle L. Caffee, London, 1960.

Giovanni Ghinassi, "Sopra tre statuti suntuari inediti del secolo XVI per la città di Faenza," *Atti e memorie della regia deputazione di storia patria per le provincie di Romagna*, II, 1866, 167–77.

Carlo Ginzburg, *The cheese and the worms* (1976), trans. John and Anne Tedeschi, Baltimore, 1980.

Lorenzo Gnocchi, "Le preferenze artistiche di Piero di Cosimo de' Medici," *Artibus et historiae*, XVIII, 1988, 41–78.

Richard A. Goldthwaite, *The building of Renaissance Florence: An economic and social history*, Baltimore, 1980.

Richard A. Goldthwaite, "The empire of things: Consumer demand in Renaissance Italy," in *Patronage, art, and society in Renaissance Italy*, ed. F.W. Kent and Patricia Simons, Canberra, 1987, 153–75.

Richard A. Goldthwaite, *Wealth and the demand for art in Italy 1300–1600*, Baltimore, 1993.

Ernst H. Gombrich, "Apollonio di Giovanni: A Florentine cassone workshop seen through the eyes of a humanist poet," *Journal of the Warburg and Courtauld Institutes*, XVIII, 1955, 16–34.

Ernst H. Gombrich, "The early Medici as patrons of art," in *Italian Renaissance studies*, ed. Ernst F. Jacob, London, 1960, 279–311.

Robert S. Gottfried, *The Black Death: Natural and human disaster in medieval Europe*, London, 1983.

Monica Helen Green, *The transmission of ancient theories of female physiology and disease through the early Middle Ages*, unpublished doctoral dissertation, Princeton University, 1985.

Monica H. Green, "Documenting medieval women's medical practice," in *Practical medicine from Salerno to the Black Death*, ed. Luis Garcia-Ballester *et al.*, Cambridge, 1994, 322–52.

Heather Gregory, "Daughters, dowries and family in fifteenth-century Florence," *Rinascimento*, XXVII, 1987, 215–37.

Gaetano Guasti, *Di Caffaggiolo e d'altre fabbriche de ceramiche in Italia*, Florence, 1902.

Angelo de Gubernatis, *Storia comparata degli usi natalizi in Italia e presso gli altri popoli Indo-Europei*, Milan, 1878.

Louis Haas, "*Il mio buono compare*: Choosing godparents and the uses of baptismal kinship in Renaissance Florence," *Journal of social history*, XXIX, 1995, 341–56.

Margaret Haines, *The Sacrestia delle Messe of the Florentine Cathedral*, Florence, 1983.

Margaret Haines, "Nota sulla discendenza di Giovanni di Ser Giovanni," *Rivista d'arte*, XXXVII, 1984, 257–68.

Jean C. Harris, ed., *The Mount Holyoke College Art Museum: Handbook of the collection*, South Hadley, Mass., 1984.

Moritz Hauptmann, *Der Tondo: Ursprung, Bedeutung und Geschichte des italienischen Rundbildes in Relief und Malerei*, Frankfurt am Main, 1936.

Paul Heitz, *Pestblätter des XV. Jahrhunderts*, Strassburg, 1901.

Philip Hendy, *European and American paintings in the Isabella Stewart Gardner Museum*, Boston, 1974.

Godefridus Henschenius and Daniel van Papenbroeck, ed., *Acta Sanctorum. Maji.*, Venice, 1737.

Jacqueline Herald, *Renaissance dress in Italy 1400–1500*, London, 1981.

David Herlihy, "Population, plague, and social change in rural Pistoia," *Economic history review*, XVIII, 1965, 225–44.

David Herlihy, *The family in Renaissance Italy*, St. Charles, Miss., 1974.

David Herlihy, *The Black Death and the transformation of the West*, ed. Samuel K. Cohn Jr., Cambridge, Mass., 1997.

David Herlihy and Christiane Klapisch-Zuber, *Tuscans and their families: A study of the Florentine catasto of 1427*, New Haven and London, 1985.

Paul Hetherington, *Pietro Cavallini: A study in the art of late medieval Rome*, London, 1979.

Megan Holmes, "Disrobing the Virgin: The *Madonna lactans* in fifteenth-century Florentine art," in *Picturing women in Renaissance and Baroque Italy*, ed. Geraldine A. Johnson and Sara F. Matthews Grieco, Cambridge, 1997, 167–95.

Herbert P. Horne, *Alessandro Filipepi, commonly called Sandro Botticelli*, London, 1908.

Diane Owen Hughes, "Sumptuary law and social relations in Renaissance Italy," in *Disputes and settlements: Law and human relations in the West*, ed. John Bossy, Cambridge, 1983, 69–99.

Diane Owen Hughes, "Representing the family: Portraits and purposes in early modern Italy," in *Art and history: Images and their meaning*, ed. Theodore K. Rabb and Robert I. Rotberg, Cambridge, 1986, 7–38.

Alan Hunt, *Governance of the consuming passions: A history of sumptuary law*, New York, 1996.

John Hunt, "Jewelled neck furs and 'Flohpelze,'" *Pantheon*, XXI, 1963, 150–57.

Judith W. Hurtig, "Death in childbirth: Seventeenth-century English tombs and their place in contemporary thought," *Art bulletin*, LXV, 1983, 603–15.

Anne Jacobson-Schutte, "Trionfi delle donne: Tematiche di rovesciamento dei ruoli nella Firenze rinascimentale," *Quaderni storici*, XLIV, 1980, 474–96.

Jacobus de Voragine, *The Golden Legend*, trans. Granger Ryan and Helmut Ripperger, New York, 1941.

Danielle Jacquart and Claude Thomasset, *Sexuality and medicine in the Middle Ages* (1985), trans. Matthew Adamson, Cambridge, 1988.

Lisa Jardine, "Isotta Nogarola: Women humanists – education for what?," *History of education*, XII, 1983, 231–44.

Lisa Jardine, *Worldly goods*, London, 1996.

Catherine Join-Dieterle, *Musée du Petit Palais. Catalogue de céramiques I: Hispano-mauresques, majoliques italiennes, iznik, des collections Dutuit, Ocampo, et Pierre Marie*, Paris, 1984.

Laurence B. Kanter *et al.*, *Painting and illumination in early Renaissance Florence 1300–1450*, New York, 1994.

C.M. Kauffmann, *Victoria and Albert Museum: Catalogue of foreign paintings*, 2 vols., London, 1973.

Joan Kelly-Gadol, "Did women have a Renaissance?," in *Becoming visible: Women in European history*, ed. Renate Bridenthal and Claudia Koonz, Boston, 1977, 137–64.

Richard Kieckhefer, *Magic in the Middle Ages*, Cambridge, 1989.

Margaret King and Albert Rabil Jr., ed., *Her immaculate hand: Selected works by and about the women humanists of quattrocento Italy*, Binghamton, 1983.

Margaret L. King, *The death of the child Valerio Marcello*, Chicago, 1994.

Julius Kirshner and Anthony Molho, "The dowry fund and the marriage market in early quattrocento Florence," *Journal of modern history*, L, 1978, 403–38.

Gábor Klaniczay, "Le culte des saints dans la Hongrie médievale (problèmes de recherche)," *Acta historia academiae scientiarum hungaricae*, XXIX, 1983, 57–78.

Christiane Klapisch-Zuber, "Le 'zane' della sposa: La donna fiorentina e il suo corredo nel rinascimento," *Memorie*, XI–XII, 1984, 12–23.

Christiane Klapisch-Zuber, *Women, family, and ritual in Renaissance Florence*, trans. Lydia G. Cochrane, Chicago, 1985.

Christiane Klapisch-Zuber, "Images without memory: Women's identity and family consciousness in Renaissance Florence," *Fenway Court*, 1990–91, 37–43.

Christiane Klapisch-Zuber, "Les femmes dans les rituels de l'alliance et de la naissance à Florence," in *Riti e rituali nelle società medievali*, ed. Jacques Chiffoleau *et al.*, Spoleto, 1994, 1–23.

Christiane Klapisch-Zuber, "Les noces feintes: Sur quelques lectures de deux thèmes iconographiques dans les *cassoni* florentines," *I Tatti studies*, VI, 1995, 11–30.

Benjamin G. Kohl and Ronald G. Witt with Elizabeth B. Welles, *The earthly republic: Italian humanists on government and society*, Philadelphia, 1978.

Catherine Kovesi Killerby, "Practical problems in the enforcement of Italian sumptuary law, 1200–1500," in *Crime, society and the law in Renaissance Italy*, ed. Trevor Dean and Kate J.P. Lowe, Cambridge, 1994, 99–120.

Paul Oskar Kristeller, "Learned women of early modern Italy: Humanists and university scholars," in his *Studies in Renaissance thought and letters*, Rome, 1985, II:189–205.

Thomas Kuehn, *Law, family, and women: Toward a legal anthropology of Renaissance Italy*, Chicago, 1991.

Jacqueline Lafontaine-Dosogne, *Iconographie de l'enfance de la Vierge dans l'Empire Byzantin et en occident*, Brussels, 1964.

Andrea Lancia, "Ordinamenti contro alle soperchie ornamenti delle donne e soperchie spese de' mogliazzi e de' morti," *Etruria*, I, 1851, 370–82 and 429–42.

Luca Landucci, *Florentine diary from 1450 to 1516*, trans. Alice de Rosen Jervis, London, 1927.

Thomas Walter Laqueur, *Making sex: Body and gender from the Greeks to Freud*, Cambridge, 1990.

Lynn Laufenberg, *The legal status of women in trecento Florence*, unpublished doctoral dissertation, Cornell University, 1999.

Lynne Lawner, ed., *I modi: The sixteen pleasures* (1527), Evanston, 1988.

A. Lecocq, "Recherches sur les enseignes de pèlerinages et les chemisettes de Notre-Dame-de-Chartres," *Mémoires de la Société archéologique d'Eure-et-Loir*, VI, 1876, 194–224.

Volker Lehmann, *Die Geburt in der Kunst*, Braunschweig, 1978.

Helen Rodnite Lemay, "Guido Bonatti: Astrology, society, and marriage in thirteenth-century Italy," *Journal of popular culture*, XVII, 1984, 79–90.

Helen Lemay, "Women and the literature of obstetrics and gynecology," in *Medieval women and the sources of medieval history*, ed. Joel T. Rosenthal, Athens, Ga., 1990, 189–209.

Emmanuel Le Roy Ladurie, *Montaillou: Cathars and Catholics in a French village* (1975), trans. Barbara Bray, London, 1978.

Johanna Lessmann, "Battista Franco disegnatore di maioliche," *Faenza*, LXII, 1976, 27–30.

Johanna Lessmann, *Italienische Majolika: Katalog der Sammlung Herzog-Anton-Ulrich Museum*, Braunschweig, 1979.

Johanna Lessmann, "Majoliken aus der Werkstatt der Fontana," *Faenza*, LXV, 1979, 333–49.

Lettere ad un amico nella quale si da ragguaglio della funzione seguita in Napoli il giorno 6 di setembre del 1772: Per solennizzare il battesimo della reale infanta Maria Teresa Carolina primogenita del re Ferdinando IV e regino Maria Carolina arciduchessa d'Austria, e delle feste date per quest'oggetto, Naples, 1772.

Rosita Levi Pisetzky, *Storia del costume in Italia*, 5 vols., Milan, 1964–6.

Ronald W. Lightbown, *Mediaeval European jewellery, with a catalogue of the collection in the Victoria & Albert Museum*, London, 1992.

Giuseppe Liverani, "Maiolica e porcellana in un quadro di Alessandro Allori," *Faenza*, XXVIII, 1940, 51–5.

Giuseppe Liverani, "La tazza da impagliata," *Faenza*, XXIX, 1941, 11–16.

Giuseppe Liverani, "Di un calamaio quattrocentesco al Museo di Cluny," *Faenza*, LXI, 1975, 7–12.

Roberto Longhi, "Fatti di Masolino e di Masaccio," *Critica d'arte*, V, 1940, 145–91.

Lorenzo Lotto, *Il 'libro di spese diverse' con aggiunta di lettere e d'altri documenti* (1538–56), ed. Pietro Zampetti, Venice, 1969.

Alessandro Luzio, "La prammatica del Cardinale Ercole Gonzaga contro il lusso (1551)," in *Scritti varii di erudizione e di critica in onore di Rodolfo Renier*, Turin, 1912, 65–78.

Alessandro Luzio and Rodolfo Renier, *Mantova e Urbino: Isabella d'Este ed Elisabetta Gonzaga nelle relazioni famigliari e nelle vicende politiche*, Turin, 1893.

John Kent Lydecker, *The domestic setting of the arts in Renais-sance Florence*, unpublished doctoral dissertation, Johns Hopkins University, Baltimore, 1987.

Joseph H. Lynch, *Godparents and kinship in early medieval Europe*, Princeton, 1986.

Niccolò Machiavelli, "The Mandragola," in *Five Italian Renaissance Comedies*, ed. and trans. Bruce Penman, London, 1978, 11–58.

Loren MacKinney, *Medical illustrations in medieval manuscripts*, London, 1965, 94.

Lutz S. Malke, "Contributo alle figurazioni dei Trionfi e del Canzoniere del Petrarca," *Commentari*, XXVIII, 1977, 236–61.

J.V.G. Mallet, "Un calamaio in maiolica a Boston," *Faenza*, LXII, 1976, 79–85.

J.V.G. Mallet, "Mantua and Urbino: Gonzaga patronage of maiolica," *Apollo*, CXIV, 1981, 162–4.

J.V.G. Mallet, "The Painter of the Coal-Mine Dish," in *Italian Renaissance pottery: Papers written in association with a colloquium at the British Museum*, ed. Timothy Wilson, London, 1991, 62–73.

J.V.G. Mallet and Timothy Clifford, "Battista Franco as a designer for maiolica," *Burlington magazine*, CXVIII, 1976, 387–410.

Fabrizio Mancinelli, "Arte medioevale e moderna," *Bollettino dei Musei e gallerie pontifichie*, I, 1977, 171–7.

Giulio Mancini, *Considerazioni sulla pittura* (c. 1621), ed. Adriana Marucchi, 2 vols., Rome, 1956.

Maria Luisa Mariotti Masi, *Bianca Cappello: Una veneziana alla corte dei Medici*, Milan, 1986.

Louise Marshall, "Manipulating the sacred: Image and plague in Renaissance Italy," *Renaissance quarterly*, XLVII, 1994, 485–532.

Gino Masi, "La ceroplastica in Firenze nei secoli XV–XVI e la famiglia Benintendi," *Rivista d'arte*, IX, 1916, 124–42.

Frank Jewett Mather, "Three Florentine furniture panels: The Medici desco, the Stibbert Trajan, and the Horse Race of the Holden collection," *Art in America*, III, 1920, 148–59.

Marcel Mauss, *The gift: The form and reason for exchange in archaic societies* (1925), trans. Ian Cunnison, Glencoe, Ill., 1954.

Ser Lapo Mazzei, *Lettere di un notaro a un mercante del secolo XIV*, ed. Cesare Guasti, 2 vols., Florence, 1880.

Giuseppe Mazzini, "Arte e maternità nella rinascenza," *Emporium*, XLVII, 1941, 82–7.

Millard Meiss, *Painting in Florence and Siena after the Black Death*, Princeton, 1951.

Silvia Meloni Trkulja, "Due opere di misericordia rettamente interpretate," *Paragone*, 479–81, 1990, 110–14.

Edith Patterson Meyer, *First lady of the Renaissance: A biography of Isabella d'Este*, Boston, 1970.

Gaetano Milanesi, "Lettere d'artisti italiani dei secoli XIV e XV," *Il Buonarrotti*, IV, 1869, 78–9.

Margaret Miles, "The Virgin's one bare breast: Female nudity and religious meaning in Tuscan early Renaissance culture," in *The female body in Western culture: Contemporary perspectives*, ed. Susan Rubin Suleiman, Cambridge, Mass., 1986, 193–206.

Jerzy Miziolek, *Soggetti classici sui cassoni fiorentini alla vigilia del Rinascimento*, Warsaw, 1996.

Krystyna Moczulska, "The most graceful Gallerini and the most exquisite ΓΑΛΈΗ in the portrait of Leonardo da Vinci," *Folia historiae artium*, I, 1995, 77–86.

Anthony Molho, *Marriage alliance in late medieval Florence*, Cambridge, 1994.

Émile Molinier, *La collection Spitzer IV: Les faïences italiennes, hispano-moresques, et orientales*, Paris, 1892.

Pompeo Molmenti, *La storia di Venezia nella vita privata dalle origini alla caduta della Repubblica*, 3 vols., Bergamo, 1905–8.

Michel de Montaigne, *Montaigne's travel journal* (written 1580–81, published 1774), trans. Donald M. Frame, San Francisco, 1983.

S.A.J. Moorat, *Catalogue of Western manuscripts on medicine and science in the Wellcome Historical Medical Library*, 2 vols., London, 1962.

Francesca Morandini, "Statuti e ordinamenti dell'Ufficio dei Pupilli et Adulti nel periodo della Repubblica Fiorentina (1388–1534)," *Archivio storico italiano*, CXIII, 1955, 522–51; CXIV, 1956, 92–117; CXV, 1957, 87–104.

Giovanni di Pagolo Morelli, *Ricordi* (1393–1421), ed. Vittore Branca, Florence, 1956.

Edward Muir, "Images of power: Art and pageantry in Renaissance Venice," *American historical review*, LXXXIV, 1979, 16–52.

Robert Müllerheim, *Die Wochenstube in der Kunst*, Stuttgart, 1904.

Eugène Müntz, "Les plateaux d'accouchées et la peinture sur meubles du XIVe au XVIe siècle," *Fondation Eugene Piot: Monuments et memoires*, I, 1894, 203–32.

Eugène Müntz, "Les plateaux et les coupes d'accouchées aux XVe e XVIe siècles: Nouvelles recherches," *Revue de l'art ancien et moderne*, I, 1899, 426–8.

Jacqueline Marie Musacchio, "Imaginative conceptions in Renaissance Italy," *Picturing women in Renaissance and Baroque Italy*, ed. Geraldine A. Johnson and Sara F. Matthews Grieco, Cambridge, 1997, 42–60.

Jacqueline Marie Musacchio, "Pregnancy and poultry in Renaissance Italy," *Source*, XVI, 1997, 3–9.

Jacqueline Marie Musacchio, "The rape of the Sabine women on quattrocento marriage panels," in *Marriage in Renaissance Italy*, ed. Trevor Dean and Kate J.P. Lowe, Cambridge, 1998, 66–82.

Jacqueline Marie Musacchio, "The Medici-Tornabuoni *desco da parto*," *Metropolitan Museum of Art journal*, XXXIII, 1998, 137–51.

Neri di Bicci, *Le ricordanze* (1453–75), ed. Bruno Santi, Pisa, 1976.

Mary Newett, *Canon Pietro Casola's pilgrimage to Jerusalem*, London, 1907.

A.V.B. Norman, *The Wallace Collection. Catalogue of ceramics I: Pottery, maiolica, faenza, stoneware*, London, 1976.

Christina Olsen, "Gross expenditure: Botticelli's Nastagio degli Onesti panels," *Art history*, XV, 1992, 146–70.

Roberta Olson, "Lost and partially found: The tondo, a significant Florentine art form in documents of the Renaissance," *Artibus et historiae*, XIV, 1993, 31–65.

L'oreficeria nella Firenze del quattrocento, Florence, 1977.

Iris Origo, *The world of San Bernardino*, London, 1964.

Iris Origo, *The merchant of Prato: Daily life in a medieval Italian village*, London, 1992.

Henk van Os, "The Black Death and Sienese painting: A problem of interpretation," *Art history*, IV, 1981, 237–49.

Daniela Pagliali and Alessandra Uguccioni, "Un desco da parto fiorentino della fine del trecento: Temi di iconografia profana," *Notizie da Palazzo Albani*, XV, 1986, 9–18.

Claudio Paolini, "La camera da letto tra quattro e cinquecento: Arredi e vita privata," in *Itinerari nella casa fiorentina del Rinascimento*, ed. Elisabetta Nardinocchi, Florence, 1994, 22–45.

Paolo da Certaldo, "Libro di buoni costumi" (1370), in *Mercanti scrittori*, ed. Vittore Branca, Milan, 1986, 3–99.

Ambroise Paré, *On monsters and marvels* (1573), trans. Janis L. Pallister, Chicago, 1982.

Katharine Park, "The criminal and saintly body: Autopsy and dissection in Renaissance Italy," *Renaissance quarterly*, XLVII, 1994, 1–33.

Katharine Park and Lorraine Daston, *Wonders and the order of nature, 1150–1750*, New York, 1998.

Giovanbattista Passeri, *Istoria della pitture in maiolica fatte in Pesaro, e ne' luoghi circonvicini*, Pesaro, 1758.

Susan M. Pearce, *Museum studies in material culture*, London, 1989.

Alessandro Perosa, ed., *Giovanni Rucellai e il suo zibaldone I: Il zibaldone quaresimale*, London, 1960.

Jacqueline Petruzzellis-Scherer, "Fonti iconografiche delle opere dell'Avelli al Museo Correr di Venezia," in Comune di Rovigo, *Francesco Xanto Avelli da Rovigo*, Rovigo, 1980, 121–51.

Mark Phillips, *The memoir of Marco Parenti: A life in Medici Florence*, Princeton, 1987.

Sara Piccolo Paci, "Le vesti della madre: Considerazioni socio-antropologiche dalla preistoria al XX secolo D.C.," in *Da donna a madre: Vesti e ceramiche particolari per momenti speciali*, Florence, 1996, 7–54.

Cipriano Piccolpasso, *I tre libri dell'arte del vasaio* (1557), ed. Ronald Lightbown and Alan Caiger-Smith, 2 vols., London, 1980.

Gaetano Pieraccini, *La stirpe de' Medici di Cafaggiolo*, 3 vols., Florence, 1925.

Antonio Pilot, "Di alcune leggi suntuarie della Repubblica Veneta," *L'ateneo veneto*, XXVI, 1903, 449–67.

Lucille B. Pinto, "The folk practice of gynecology and obstetrics in the Middle Ages," *Bulletin of the history of medicine*, XLVII, 1973, 513–23.

E. Polidori Calamandrei, *Le vesti delle donne fiorentine nel quattrocento*, Florence, 1924.

Agnolo Ambrogini Poliziano, *Prose volgari inedite e poesie Latine e Greche edite e inedite*, ed. Isidoro del Lungo, Florence, 1867.

John Pope-Hennessy, *Catalogue of Italian sculpture in the Victoria & Albert Museum*, 3 vols., London, 1964.

A.E. Popham and Johannes Wilde, *The Italian drawings of the XV and XVI centuries in the collection of His Majesty the King at Windsor Castle*, London, 1949.

Ugo Procacci, "Le portate al catasto di Giovanni di Ser Giovanni detto lo Scheggia," *Rivista d'arte*, XXXVII, 1984, 235–57.

Georg Pudelko, "Studien über Domenico Veneziano," *Mitteilungen des kunsthistorischen Institutes in Florenz*, IV, 1934, 145–200.

Bernard Rackham, *The Victoria & Albert Museum: Guide to Italian maiolica*, London, 1933.

Bernard Rackham, *The Victoria & Albert Museum: Catalogue of Italian maiolica*, 2 vols., London, 1940.

Bernard Rackham, "The Ford collection of Italian maiolica," *Connoisseur*, CXLII, November 1958, 148–51.

Bernard Rackham, *Islamic pottery and Italian maiolica: Illustrated catalogue of a private collection*, London, 1959.

Ronald E. Rainey, *Sumptuary legislation in Renaissance Florence*, unpublished doctoral dissertation, Columbia University, 1985.

Jorg Rasmussen, *Italienische Majolika*, Hamburg, 1984.

Carmen Ravanelli Guidotti, *Donazione Paolo Mereghi*, Bologna, 1987.

Carmen Ravanelli Guidotti, *Faenza-faïence: "Bianchi" di Faenza*, Ferrara, 1996.

Carmen Ravanelli Guidotti, *Baldassare Manara faentino: Pittore di maioliche nel cinquecento*, Ferrara, 1996.

Giovanni L. Reggi, *La ceramica graffita in Emilia Romagna dal secolo XIV al secolo XIX*, Modena, 1971.

Ricettario fiorentino (1499), ed. Luigi Crocetti, Florence, 1968.

Tommaso Rinuccini, *Le usanze fiorentine del secolo XVII*, Florence, 1863.

Raymond de Roover, *The rise and decline of the Medici bank 1397–1494*, Cambridge, 1963.

James Bruce Ross, "The middle-class child in urban Italy, fourteenth to early sixteenth centuries," in *The history of childhood*, ed. Lloyd de Mause, New York, 1974, 183–228.

Sheila McClure Ross, *The redecoration of Santa Maria Novella's Capella Maggiore*, unpublished doctoral dissertation, University of California, Berkeley, 1983.

Tommaso Rosselli Sassatelli del Turco, "La chiesetta di San Martino dei Buonomini di Firenze," *Dedalo*, VIII, 1928, 610–32.

Clemente Rossi, *Superstizioni e pregiudizi ossia veglie contadinesche esposte in forma dialogica per il popolo*, Milan, 1877.

U. Rossi, "I deschi da parto," *Archivio storico dell'arte*, III, 1890, 78–9.

L. Earle Rowe, "An Italian birth salver," *Bulletin of the Rhode Island School of Design*, X, 1922, 24–6.

Guido Ruggiero, *Binding passions: Tales of magic, marriage, and power at the end of the Renaissance*, New York, 1993.

Roberto Rusconi, "San Bernardino of Siena, the wife, and possessions," in *Women and religion in medieval and Renaissance Italy*, ed. Daniel Bornstein and Roberto Rusconi, Chicago, 1996, 182–96.

Franco Sacchetti, *Il trecentonovelle* (c. 1392–6/7), ed. Antonio Lanza, Milan, 1993.

Mario Salmi, "*I trionfi* e il *De viris illustribus* nell'arte del primo Rinascimento," *Atti dei Convegni lincei*, X, 1976, 23–47.

Guglielmo Enrico Saltini, *Bianca Cappello e Francesco I de' Medici*, Florence, 1898.

Luigi Samoggia, "Lodovico Bonaccioli medico ostetrico di Lucrezia Borgia in Ferrara," *Atti della Accademia dei fisiocritici in Siena*, XIII, 1964, 513–31.

Fert Sangiorgi, ed., *Documenti Urbinati: Inventari del Palazzo Ducale (1582–1631)*, Urbino, 1976.

Francesco Sansovino, *Venetia: Città nobilissima et singolare*, Venice, 1581.

Michele Savonarola, *Il trattato ginecologico-pediatrico in volgare: Ad mulieres ferrarienses de regimine pregnantium et noviter natorum usque ad septennium* (c. 1460), ed. Luigi Belloni, Milan, 1952.

Scott Schaefer, "*Io Guido Reni Bologna*, man and artist," in *Guido Reni 1575–1642*, ed. Susan L. Caroselli, Los Angeles, 1988, 1–16.

Robert W. Scheller, *Exemplum: Model book drawings and the practice of artistic transmission in the Middle Ages (circa 900–circa 1470)*, trans. Michael Hoyle, Amsterdam, 1995.

T. H. Lunsingh Scheurleer, "Enkele oude Nederlandse kraamgebruiken," *Antiek*, VI, 1971–2, 297–332.

Attilio Schiaparelli, *La casa fiorentina e i suoi arredi nei secoli XIV e XV*, ed. Maria Sframeli and Laura Pagnotta, 2 vols., Florence, 1983.

Guenther Schiedlansky, "Zum sogenannten Flohpelze," *Pantheon*, XXX, 1972, 469–80.

Antoine Schnapper, *Le géant, la licorne, et la tulipe: Collections et collectionneurs dans la France du XVIIe siècle*, 2 vols., Paris, 1988.

Frida Schottmüller, "Zwei Grabmäler der Renaissance und ihre antiken Vorbilder," *Repertorium für Kunstwissenschaft*, XXV, 1902, 401–8.

Paul Schubring, *Cassoni: Truhen und Truhenbilder der italienischen Fruhrenaissance*, 3 vols., Leipzig, 1915 and 1923.

Luigi Servolini, "Il dono simbolico della città di Forlì alla Principessa di Piemonte: La 'tazza da parto' romagnola," *Illustrazione italiana*, LXVII, March 10, 1940, 304.

Fern Rusk Shapely, *Paintings from the Samuel H. Kress collection: Italian schools XIII–XV centuries*, London, 1966.

Maurice L. Shapiro, "A Renaissance birth plate," *Art bulletin*, XLIV, 1967, 236–43.

Patricia Simons, *Portraiture and patronage in quattrocento Florence with special reference to the Tornaquinci and their chapel in Santa Maria Novella*, unpublished doctoral dissertation, University of Melbourne, 1985.

Patricia Simons, "(Check) mating the grandmasters: The gendered, sexualized politics of chess in Renaissance Italy," *Oxford art journal*, XVI, 1993, 59–74.

Charles Singleton, ed., *Canti carnascialeschi*, Bari, 1936.

Osvald Sirén, "An Italian salver of the fifteenth century," *Burlington magazine*, XXX, 1917, 183–9.

Sotheby's (New York), *Important Old Master paintings: The property of the New-York Historical Society*, January 12, 1995.

Marco Spallanzani, *Ceramiche orientale a Firenze nel Rinascimento*, Florence, 1978.

Marco Spallanzani, "Un invio di maioliche ispano-moresche a Venezia negli anni 1401–1402," *Archeologia medievale*, V, 1978, 529–41.

Marco Spallanzani, "Maioliche di Urbino nelle collezioni di

Cosimo I, del Cardinale Ferdinando e di Francesco I de' Medici," *Faenza*, LXV, 1979, 111–26.

Marco Spallanzani, "Maioliche di Valenza e di Montelupo in una casa Pisana del 1480," *Faenza*, LXXII, 1986, 164–70.

Marco Spallanzani, *Ceramiche alle corte dei Medici nel cinquecento*, Modena, 1994.

Marco Spallanzani and Giovanna Gaeta Bertelà, ed., *Libro d'inventario dei beni di Lorenzo il Magnifico*, Florence, 1992.

Jeffrey Spier, "Medieval Byzantine magical amulets and their tradition," *Journal of the Warburg and Courtauld Institutes*, LVI, 1993, 25–62.

Paula Lois Spilner, *Ut civitas amplietur: Studies in Florentine urban development 1282–1400*, unpublished doctoral dissertation, Columbia University, 1987.

Fiorella Sricchia Santoro, *Da Sodoma a Marco Pino: Addenda*, Siena, 1991.

Edgcumbe Staley, *The guilds of Florence*, London, 1906.

Statuta popoli et communis Florentiae: Publica auctoritate, collecta, castigata, et praeposita anno salutis MCCCCXV, 3 vols., Friburgi [*sic*], 1778.

Lawrence Stone, "The return of narrative," *Past and present*, LXXXV, 1979, 3–24.

Sharon T. Strocchia, *Death and ritual in Renaissance Florence*, Baltimore, 1992.

Alessandra Macinghi Strozzi, *Lettere di una gentildonna fiorentina del secolo XV al figliuoli esuli*, ed. Cesare Guasti, Florence, 1877.

Roberta Sulli, "Il monumento funebre a Pereyra-Camponeschi: Contributo allo studio della cultura antiquariale a L'Aquila nel secondo quattrocento," *Bullettino della Deputazione abruzzese di storia patria*, LXXVII, 1987, 207–28.

Michael D. Taylor, "Gentile da Fabriano, Saint Nicholas, and an iconography of shame," *Journal of family history*, VII, 1982, 321–32.

Keith Thomas, *Religion and the decline of magic*, New York, 1971.

Dora Thornton, *The scholar in his study: Ownership and experience in Renaissance Italy*, New Haven and London, 1997.

Peter Thornton, *The Italian Renaissance interior 1400–1600*, New York, 1991.

Isolde Thyret, " 'Blessed is the tsaritsa's womb': The myth of miraculous birth and royal motherhood in Muscovite Russia," *Russian review*, LIII, 1994, 479–96.

Girolamo Tommasi, "Sommario della storia di Lucca dall'anno MIV all'anno MDCC," *Archivio storico italiano*, X, 1847, 1–250.

Lucrezia Tornabuoni, *Lucrezia Tornabuoni: Lettere*, ed. Patrizia Salvadori, Florence, 1993.

Richard C. Trexler, "Florentine religious experience: The sacred image," *Studies in the Renaissance*, XIX, 1972, 7–41.

Richard C. Trexler, "The foundlings of Florence, 1395–1455," *History of childhood quarterly*, I, 1973, 259–84.

Richard C. Trexler, *Public life in Renaissance Florence*, New York, 1980.

Richard C. Trexler, *Dependence in context in Renaissance Florence*, Binghamton, 1994.

Julia Triolo, "Fra Xanto Avelli's Pucci service, 1532–1533," *Faenza*, LXXIV, 1988, 32–44 and 228–84.

Trotula, *Sulle malattie delle donne* (1547), ed. Pina Cavallo Boggi, Turin, 1979.

Trotula, *Medieval woman's guide to health*, ed. Beryl Rowland, London, 1981.

Angelo Turchini, *Ex-voto: Per una lettura dell'ex-voto dipinto*, Milan, 1992.

Graham Twigg, *The Black Death: A biological reappraisal*, London, 1984.

Grazia Biscontini Ugolini and Jacqueline Petruzzellis-Scherer, ed., *Maiolica e incisione: Tre secoli di rapporti iconografici*, Vicenza, 1992.

Alessandra Uguccioni, *Salomone e la Regina di Saba: La pittura di cassone a Ferrara presenza nei musei americani*, Ferrara, 1988.

Laurel Thatcher Ulrich, *A midwife's tale: The life of Martha Ballard, based on her diary, 1785–1812*, New York, 1990.

Benedetto Varchi, *Opere di Benedetto Varchi ora per la prima volta raccolte*, 2 vols., Trieste, 1859.

Giorgio Vasari, *Le vite de' più eccellenti pittori, scultori ed architettori* (1550, 2/1568), ed. Gaetano Milanesi, 9 vols., Florence, 1878–85.

A.F. Verde, "Libri tra le parete domestiche: Una necessaria appendice a lo studio fiorentino 1473–1503," *Memorie domenicane*, XVIII, 1987.

William Warren Vernon, *Readings on the Paradiso of Dante, chiefly based on the commentary of Benvenuto da Imola*, 2 vols., New York, 1909.

Matteo Villani, *Cronica* (1348–63), ed. Francesco Gherardi Dragomanni, 3 vols., Florence, 1846.

Virgilius, *Opera, Bucolica, Georgica, Aeneis: Manoscritto 492 della Biblioteca Riccardiana*, Florence, 1969.

Hermann Voss, "Über einige Gemälde und Zeichnungen von Meistern aus dem Kreise Michelangelos," *Jahrbuch der königlich preuszischen Kunstsammlungen*, XXXIV, 1913, 297–320.

Martin Wackernagel, *The world of the Florentine Renaissance artist* (1938), trans. Allison Luchs, Princeton, 1981.

Anke A. van Wagenberg-Ter Hoeven, "Het schuitje naar de Volewijk: Een interpretatie van een nachtelijk tafereel op een achttiende-eeuws drinkglas," *Antiek*, XXVI, 1991, 22–30.

Aby Warburg, "Della impresa amorose nelle più antiche incisione fiorentine," *Rivista d'arte*, III, 1905, 1–14.

Aby Warburg, *Gesammelte Schriften*, 2 vols., Leipzig, 1932.

Peter Ward-Jackson, *The Victoria & Albert Museum catalogues: Italian drawings, 14th–16th centuries*, 2 vols., London, 1979.

Paul F. Watson, *Virtù and voluptas in cassone painting*, unpublished doctoral dissertation, Yale University, 1970.

Paul F. Watson, *The garden of love in Tuscan art of the early Renaissance*, Philadelphia, 1979.

Annette B. Weiner, *Inalienable possessions: The paradox of keeping-while-giving*, Berkeley, 1992.

T.H. White, ed., *The bestiary: A book of beasts, being a translation from a Latin bestiary of the twelfth century* (1952), New York, 1962.

Merry E. Wiesner, "Early modern midwifery: A case study," in *Women and work in preindustrial Europe*, ed. Barbara Hanawalt, Bloomington, 1986, 94–113.

Antoine Wilmering, "Domenico di Niccolò, Mattia di Nanni and the development of Sienese intarsia techniques," *Burlington magazine*, CXXXIX, 1997, 387–97.

Adrian Wilson, "The infancy of the history of childhood: An appraisal of Philippe Ariès," *History & theory*, XIX, 1980, 132–53.

Adrian Wilson, "The ceremony of childbirth and its interpretation," in *Women as mothers in pre-industrial England: Essays in memory of Dorothy McLaren*, ed. Valerie Fildes, London, 1990, 68–107.

Carolyn C. Wilson, *Italian paintings XIV–XVI centuries in the Museum of Fine Arts, Houston*, Houston, 1996.

Timothy Wilson, *Ceramic art of the Italian Renaissance*, London, 1987.

Timothy Wilson, "The beginnings of lustreware in Renaissance Italy," *The International Ceramics Fair and Seminar*, London, 1996, 35–43.

Patrick de Winter, "A little known creation of Renaissance decorative arts: The white lead pastiglia box," *Saggi e memorie di storia dell'arte*, XIV, 1984, 9–42.

Shelley Elizabeth Zuraw, *The sculpture of Mino da Fiesole (1429–1484)*, unpublished doctoral dissertation, New York University, 1993.

Index

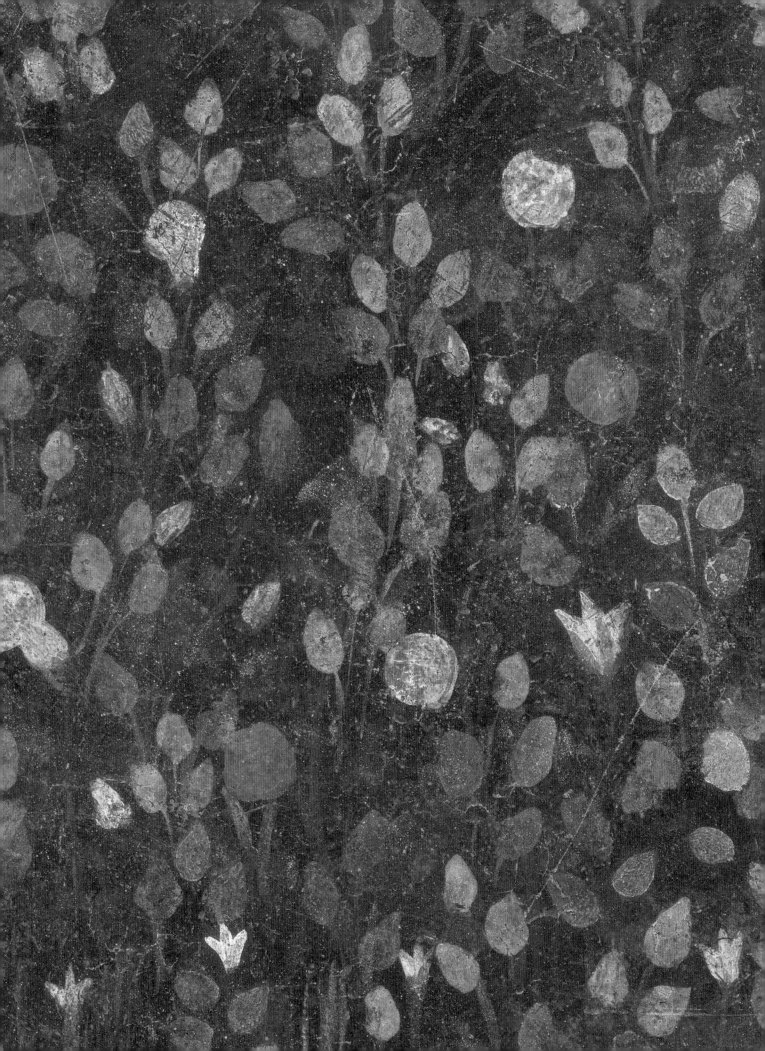